WORLD JR. HOCKEY
CHAMPIONSHIP
IIHF
26·12·90 – 4·1·91
SASKATCHEWAN, CANADA

XII ЧЕМПИОНАТ МИРА
МОСКВА
ХОККЕЙ 1986

IIHF
2008
WORLD U20
CHAMPIONSHIP
CZECH REPUBLIC
Pardubice
Liberec

2009
IIHF
WORLD JUNIOR
CHAMPIONSHIP
CANADA
Ottawa

2007
IIHF
WORLD U20
CHAMPIONSHIP
SWEDEN
Leksand · Mora

THIRTY YEARS OF THE GAME AT ITS BEST

THIRTY YEARS OF THE GAME AT ITS BEST
EDITED BY GARE JOYCE

VIKING
CANADA

VIKING CANADA

Published by the Penguin Group

Penguin Group (Canada), 90 Eglinton Avenue East, Suite 700, Toronto, Ontario, Canada M4P 2Y3
(a division of Pearson Canada Inc.)

Penguin Group (USA) Inc., 375 Hudson Street, New York, New York 10014, U.S.A.
Penguin Books Ltd, 80 Strand, London WC2R 0RL, England
Penguin Ireland, 25 St Stephen's Green, Dublin 2, Ireland (a division of Penguin Books Ltd)
Penguin Group (Australia), 250 Camberwell Road, Camberwell, Victoria 3124, Australia
(a division of Pearson Australia Group Pty Ltd)
Penguin Books India Pvt Ltd, 11 Community Centre, Panchsheel Park,
New Delhi – 110 017, India
Penguin Group (NZ), 67 Apollo Drive, Rosedale, Auckland 0632, New Zealand
(a division of Pearson New Zealand Ltd)
Penguin Books (South Africa) (Pty) Ltd, 24 Sturdee Avenue, Rosebank,
Johannesburg 2196, South Africa

Penguin Books Ltd, Registered Offices: 80 Strand, London WC2R 0RL, England

First published 2011

1 2 3 4 5 6 7 8 9 10

Copyright © Canadian Hockey Association, 2011

The credits on page 248 constitute an extension of this copyright page.

Manufactured in the U.S.A.

LIBRARY AND ARCHIVES CANADA CATALOGUING IN PUBLICATION

Thirty years of the game at its best / edited by Gare Joyce.

ISBN 978-0-670-06594-3

1. World Junior Championships (Hockey)—History.
2. Hockey—Tournaments—Canada—History. I. Joyce, Gare, 1956-

GV847.7.T48 2011   796.962'620971   C2011-905129-X

Visit the Penguin Group (Canada) website at **www.penguin.ca**

Special and corporate bulk purchase rates available;
please see **www.penguin.ca/corporatesales** or call 1-800-810-3104, ext. 2477 or 2474

CONTENTS

INTRODUCTION

MURRAY COSTELLO,
FORMER PRESIDENT,
HOCKEY CANADA

Getting the Program of Excellence off the ground wasn't easy. We had to sell the program before we built it.

In the late 1970s and early '80s, the Canadian Amateur Hockey Association sent the defending Memorial Cup champions to the International Ice Hockey Federation's world under-20 tournament over the holiday season. You might think that would have given Canada a fairly representative team in the tournament. It didn't play out that way, however.

Major junior teams are built to win one season, and often they'll load up on older players to make that run. The following season, though, many if not most of their top players have graduated and the best have gone on to the pros—an experienced team one season is often a rebuilding one the next. You have a 16-year-old skating in place of a 19-year-old elite player, a very tough place to put a young man in.

The Memorial Cup champions sometimes picked up a few top players from other teams in their league, but that still wasn't enough to be competitive. I think this point was driven home when the Cornwall Royals went to Füssen in 1981. They were a great team when they won the Cup, but they struggled the next year. They had Dale Hawerchuk, who would be a Hall of Famer, but he was only 17 at the time. What we had in place wasn't fairly representing the Canadian game, and it wasn't fair to the players either. I remember Canada losing to West Germany 7–6, and we just said that it's no longer acceptable.

In the spring of 1981, we went to the Canadian major junior hockey leagues with a proposal for a national junior program. The first part of our plan was to bring together the best tournament-eligible players at a training camp during the summer. The second part of our plan was going to require the major junior teams to loan us their best players for the duration of the world junior tournament. We also proposed instituting a feeder system: an under-17 program. As we laid it out, major junior leagues would send their best young players to play regional teams in a tournament that would give the CAHA an opportunity to identify talent for world junior tournaments down the line. It would also give young players an opportunity to test themselves against the best in their class and a chance to get acquainted with our program.

In other words, we went to the leagues with a proposal that three decades later remains the foundation of the Program of Excellence.

If you were to look at our best moments—the gold medals, the great games and players—over the course of those years, you might think that it was an easy sell. It wasn't, and we knew it wouldn't be.

The initial resistance was understandable, really. Major junior teams were going to be reluctant to give up their best players if they were contending for playoff spots, especially over the holidays when teams would draw some of their biggest crowds of the season. And then there was the risk of injury. We had to use all our powers of persuasion to make our case. Over several meetings, we were able to convince the WHL, OHL, and QMJHL that the tournament would benefit their teams and players. Pretty quickly they came to understand that club teams raised their profiles and focused attention on junior hockey when their top players represented Canada internationally. At the start some teams and players were reluctant, but it has been a long time since a team or a player looked at an invitation to the world junior camp as anything less than the chance of a lifetime.

The three major junior leagues each have a seat on the Program of Excellence's policy committee, and Hockey Canada has a fourth vote. In a short time, those on the committee developed a solid working partnership.

We had a vision of what we could do and how we wanted to do it, and key to that was attention to detail at every level and in every aspect of the program. For instance, we wanted coaches to dedicate 100 percent of their attention to getting the team ready. Often, coaches at all levels of hockey have to handle logistics—whether it's travel, accommodations, or meals. From the start we had to have staff to clear the table for the coaches who came in. There would be no worries about schedules, buses, travel—we'd look after all of that. We also wanted the coaches to have the last word on the selection of the team with no input or veto from the CAHA on the final roster. In the management of any team or program, you don't want to give a coach a chance to pin a loss on a decision that wasn't his or her own.

The attention to detail had to carry over to the players, of course. We had to reinforce the idea to players that we were doing everything we could to give them the best chance to win. We also had to get them to understand it's a different game that's played internationally on Olympic ice. They were going to see different calls. They had to understand that pick plays called for interference penalties in the WJC were just part of the international game, or that good clean checks by our standards would get penalties in Europe. We wanted the players to know all this going in, and be able to adapt instead of finding out the hard way.

One of the worst images of Canada in international hockey came back in the Summit Series in 1972, when J.P. Parisé skated up to a referee in Moscow and threatened him with his stick, swinging it like he was going to take the ref's head off. I joke with J.P. every time I see him that for 30 years we've been able to use his stunt as an example of what not to do. Part of understanding that it's a different game is accepting that there are going to be frustrations and that you just have to check your emotions and move on. That attitude and emotional control are keys to winning internationally. To be frank, when we were starting up the program I wasn't sure that we would be able to get that message across. But in '82, the first year for the Program of Excellence, we had two big defencemen, Gord Kluzak and Gary Nylund, who were as tough and mean as anybody in major junior hockey. When I saw that they couldn't be goaded into retaliation penalties, I knew that players—the best players—are fast learners and capable of adapting.

I'm not going to say that it was only our planning that has put the Program of Excellence where it is today. We've evolved and grown over the years, but still the core values have stayed in place. And we've been lucky.

Because of the players we've had the pleasure of working with, the program has enjoyed good fortune. Those players always looked to measure themselves against the most talented players in the country. We've been lucky because the best coaches in junior hockey have come to view the Program of Excellence as an opportunity for their development, too. And we've been fortunate to be able to maintain a great working partnership with the major junior leagues.

On the ice, we were lucky to have immediate success, coming away with gold in Minnesota in 1982. That gave the program instant credibility and momentum. We were able to get off to a flying start. There's no overestimating how important that gold medal was 30 years ago.

We were also lucky that the world juniors became a huge television event. In the first years, CBC would broadcast only one tournament game—and the network was obliged to do that only if Canada was contending for a gold medal. Later, we found a great partner in The Sports Network and Réseau des sports—basically, the Program of Excellence, TSN, and RDS grew together.

And I consider myself lucky to have had a chance to work with some of the best and brightest people in the sport. Going back to those first years, that list would include Dennis McDonald, our technical director; Dave Draper, our scout in the launch years; and Dave King, who was coaching at the University of Saskatchewan when he helmed the 1982 team.

When we went to the major junior leagues with our plan in '82, we were aiming to improve our performance at the under-20 tournament. We also thought that the Program of Excellence would help our organization send better-prepared players to international hockey events, including the Olympics. I think we've been successful on that count, given that so many of the players on two Olympic championship teams had ties with the program.

We never imagined that the world junior tournament would grow like it has and become so significant in the sport. That's just a happy by-product of the success. The Program of Excellence was tough to get off the ground, but once we were able to do that, over the years it took flight thanks to the top-notch players, coaches, and officials I've had the honour of working with behind the scenes.

1982

ROCHESTER
THE OFF-KEY ANTHEM

DAVE MORRISON

The Program of Excellence's team-building strategies paid immediate dividends in Minnesota.

I was in a unique position. I experienced the world juniors before the Program of Excellence, and then again with the program in place.

I played my junior hockey for the Peterborough Petes and we went to the 1980 tournament in Finland as the Memorial Cup champions. I say "we" but the fact is I didn't play. I was just 17 and the team picked up a few top players in the OHL. We took the top line from the Ottawa 67's, Shawn Simpson, Jim Fox, and Yvan Joly, and we brought in Dino Ciccarelli from London, among others. The younger guys on the Petes went on the trip and practised with the team but didn't dress for games. We went for the experience and it wasn't pretty. We lost our first two games to the Finns and the Soviets and ended up in fifth place. It wasn't that we didn't have the personnel. We had a lot of talent. And it wasn't that we didn't have the coaching. Mike Keenan was our coach and he was one of the best coaches at any level of the game. Mike did everything he could to prepare the team for the tournament but we weren't positioned to win. We had a lot of things working against us. Too much, as it turned out. Just when the team started to come together, the tournament was over.

It was a completely different experience two years later. A lot of what you see in the Program of Excellence today was there in '82, including the summer camp and

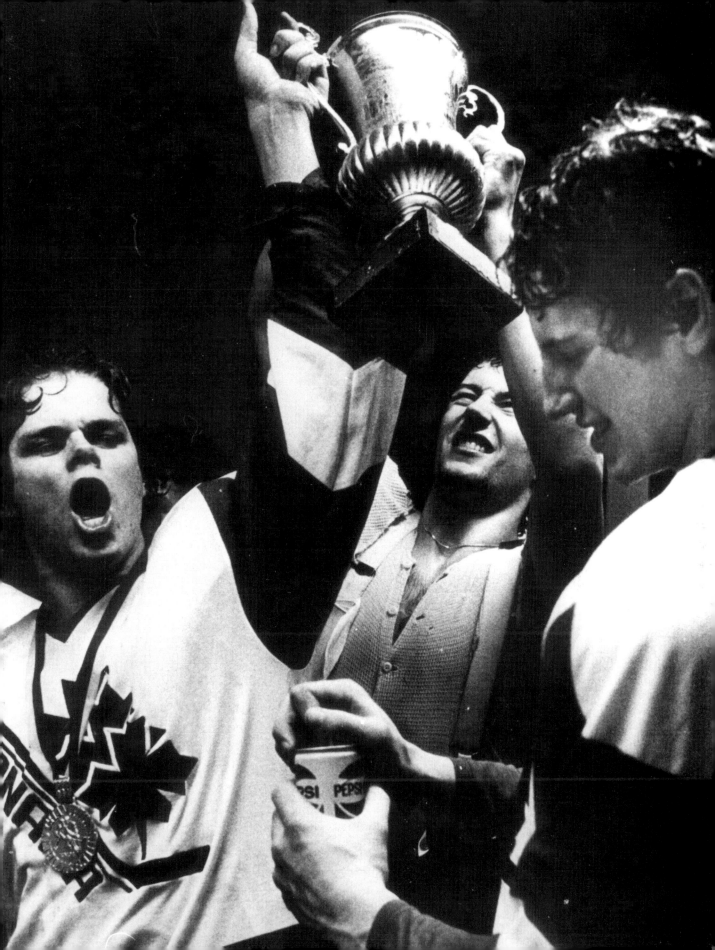

Coach Dave King delivered what would be an enduring message to Canadian players: disciplined play is the key to victory.

the tryout camp in December. When we had gone to the 1980 tournament, it was like we had a standing start, but in '82 we weren't starting at square one. Our coach, Dave King, let us know just what to expect in the tournament. He let us know that staying out of the penalty box was key—if we just played our usual game, we'd get penalty calls going against us and the European teams' power plays could hurt us.

We weren't the most talented team that ever represented Canada in the world juniors but we were a good fit to our roles. I don't think that would have been possible if we didn't have the opportunity to play together in the summer and get to know each other. Having to play your way onto the team in December raised the stakes—you couldn't possibly take a shift off or you could lose your chance to play for your country. The competitiveness of our selection camp carried over to the tournament.

That year the WJC was being played in Manitoba and Minnesota. The Soviet Union had been the dominant team in the tournament's history—I remember in 1980 Vladimir Krutov had two or three goals against us and it seemed like there was nothing you could do to stop him. It was a different story in '82, though. We beat

Troy Murray, here flying through the air, and his teammates played in a packed arena in Winnipeg, but a near-empty rink in Minnesota.

the Soviets 7–0 in Winnipeg in front of a crowd that was just going crazy. It was an amazing atmosphere. I can't say the same about the scene when we went to Rochester, Minnesota, for our game against Czechoslovakia, the last game in the round robin. We were playing in this little arena that sat about 3,000 and probably wasn't half-filled. In Winnipeg, on home ice, it felt like we were involved in something historic. It really wasn't like that in Rochester.

In that final game we needed only a tie against Czechoslovakia to win the gold. Before the game the coaches somehow got hold of a gold medal and brought it into the dressing room and everyone in the room touched it. I don't know that we could have been any more motivated than we were before that, but it got our attention.

We were down 2–1 to the Czechoslovaks after two periods, and the score could have been a lot worse. Our goaltender Mike Moffat kept us in the game for 40 minutes. We poured it on in the third—we had 19 shots in the last 20 minutes. Marc Habscheid and Mike Moller scored to give us the lead but then the Czechoslovaks came back to tie it up. I just remember how tense the last few minutes were—we were just hanging on. It was a tough time, but we had come together and understood our roles well enough that we could handle it.

Mike Moller (left) and his teammates stayed out of the penalty box but didn't totally sacrifice physical play en route to the gold medal.

People who have followed the world junior program over the years might not know the name of a single player on that team, or might never have seen a video of the action from that game, but a lot of them know what happened afterwards. The hosts didn't have the Canadian national anthem—or it wouldn't play, we never really heard the definitive story on that. So we stood on the blue line and sang "O Canada." It was really just a spontaneous thing but it's the first thing people think about when they think about that '82 team, our signature moment. And 30 years later it's become one of the great stories in the history of the Program of Excellence. At the time, though, we had no idea that it would have so much staying power. In fact, it wasn't until my hockey career was over that it really hit home.

I finished my career playing a few seasons in Europe, and over that time the world junior tournament really took off. When I retired and our family was spending our first holiday at home, my wife and I bumped into our daughter's teacher at the supermarket and we asked her what she was planning to do at Christmas. She said that her family did the same thing every year—about 30 of them gathered for a party and to watch the world junior tournament. My wife and I just looked at each other—we couldn't believe the tournament had taken on a life of its own.

Dave Morrison (third from the left) didn't realize the impact of his team's victory until after his retirement years later.

1983

LENINGRAD
THE TOUGHEST ROAD GAME

MIKE SANDS

Canadian junior players about to go on to NHL stardom struggled in the pivotal game against the Soviets in Leningrad. Here, Dave Andreychuk is run into the boards by defenceman Ilya Byakin as Mario Lemieux looks on.

There are tough road games, and then there are *tough* road games.

A tough game on the road might be your third game in three nights and you're up against one of the league's best teams. Those types of road games are tough. I had seen enough of them as a goalie with Sudbury in the Ontario Hockey League.

Being in another country and playing a game you're not used to—that makes your life tougher. If you ask anyone involved in the Program of Excellence who ever played or coached in a tournament held in Europe, they'll tell you that it's a challenge.

To be a Canadian team playing in Russia? That's *tough*. And it was even tougher back in the days of the former Soviet Union. If you were a bunch of teenagers—well, let's say that, no matter how good and experienced you were in major junior, you had never been in a situation quite like it.

We went to Leningrad as the defending world junior champions, taking a really talented team there, a lot more talented than we actually realized at the time. We didn't know that Mario Lemieux was someday going to be in the conversation when people talked about the most talented players ever. We didn't know that Steve Yzerman would be the captain of three Stanley Cup winners. That Dave Andreychuk, our leading scorer, would end up with 640 goals in his NHL career.

The Canadian juniors had no answers for the Soviets' speed and skill. Here, Vladimir Turikov slips by Mike Eagles.

That Gary Leeman was going to have a 50-goal NHL season down the line. Or that James Patrick, who was back from the '82 gold-medal winners, would play in the NHL until he was 42. No, we didn't lack for talent. We had enough that a future Hockey Hall of Famer, Doug Gilmour, was one of the last cuts.

We were just teenagers—a few amazingly talented; the rest very good juniors. But teenagers.

We were just old enough to remember Team Canada going to play in Moscow in 1972—we would have been in elementary school at the time. We all had heard about the teams from the Soviet Union when we were growing up—we had seen the USSR's best beat our best NHL players. We knew enough about hockey to understand that these guys could really *play*.

The Soviets were good. And they were at home.

I think it's different now. I think kids are more worldly than we were. Most of us had never been to Europe. None of us had been to Eastern Europe. And what we knew about the Soviet Union we learned from the movies: spies lurking around the corners, soldiers in the streets, people living in fear of the gulag. Were we scared when we took on the Soviets in Leningrad in '83? On the ice, I'd say no. Were we comfortable? Not even close.

We'd won our first three games at the tournament, beating West Germany, the United States, and Finland pretty comfortably, and went into our round-robin game against the Soviets looking at it as the contest that would decide the gold medal.

Even before we hit the ice, we knew it was going to be a different game completely. In our first three tournament games, the arena was practically empty and almost silent. When I was standing in the crease in those games, I could hear guys talking on the bench. But for our game against the Soviets, we could hear the crowd while we were sitting in the dressing room.

Then there were the head games. We got the call to go out and we got our game face on—but when we were just about to step on the ice, the officials sent us back to the dressing room. It seems like a small thing but it wouldn't happen anywhere else. It wasn't a big thing; it was just *another* thing. We had been through the long stare-down with customs officers, dirty looks from soldiers, sneers from people working around the arena, and other stuff. We were warned that the food was bad but we couldn't have imagined just how bad it was—I thought they might have been trying to poison us. All that wouldn't rattle you if you were a professional, but we were teenagers. For sure, it unsettled us.

Dave King returned to the head coaching post for a shot at a second gold. The Canadians stayed with their game plan from the year before, and it came up just a bit short.

Sylvain Turgeon celebrates after putting the puck by goaltender John Vanbiesbrouck in Canada's 4–2 victory over the United States. The win left Canada undefeated after the first two games in Leningrad.

So did the whistling.

As soon as we stepped on the ice, the whistling started—the European equivalent of booing. And whenever we touched the puck, the whistling got even louder. It was just ear-splitting. We'd gone from playing in a silent rink to one where you couldn't hear yourself think.

It was a whistle that really threw us off. We thought it was a referee's whistle. We were sure it was. Maybe it was just the ringing in our ears.

We were on a power play in the first period. The Soviets had scored a couple of goals against us on consecutive shifts at about the 10-minute mark and I was doing my best to keep us in the game. The power play was going to be our chance to get back in it. A goal at that point would have given us a huge boost. James Patrick, who was playing the point on our power play, had the puck at the Soviet blue line when he heard a whistle and figured it was an offside call. He came to a dead stop and so did everyone else. It was a whistle from the crowd—at least that's the story we were told. Before anyone could react and get back in the play, a Soviet player picked up the loose puck, skated the length of the ice, and beat me. It was a backbreaker. I guess it's like boxing—you have to defend yourself at all times, even after the bell.

Dave King was our returning coach and, even though we had guys who would score hundreds of goals in the NHL, he had really set us up to be a defensive team. Mike Eagles probably had a bigger role than a lot of the better known players on

our team. We didn't play a run-and-gun style of game, but instead were going to win our games with a few goals and tight checking. Mounting a comeback from that 3–0 hole would be tough anytime. In Leningrad, in 1983, we didn't get close to pulling it off. I'll shoulder my share of the blame. I wasn't good enough. I gave up six goals in 40 minutes and I was pulled in favour of Mike Vernon.

The final score was 7–3.

We were rattled. The next game, we tied Czechoslovakia 7–7, and then lost to Sweden 5–2. We were still thinking about the Soviet game. It was like the whistles were still ringing in our ears.

Canada ended up with the bronze medal. It could have been a silver pretty easily with a better effort against the Czechs or the Swedes.

I played for Canada's national team for a stretch a few years later. I've worked as a scout in the NHL for more than a decade. When I've seen a Canadian team perform well and win in Europe, I know all about the challenges those players and coaches have overcome. The Program of Excellence does a great job to prepare Canada's best juniors to play in the toughest road games. And those who win on an opponent's turf are prepared to handle things way out of their control—like a fan in the crowd blowing a referee's whistle.

Pat Flatley has his legs taken out from under him in Canada's disappointing 5–2 loss to Sweden.

1984

NYKÖPING
THE FIRST CHANCE
TO PLAY FOR CANADA

DEAN EVASON

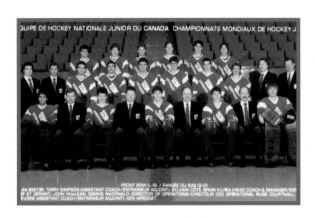

ÉQUIPE DE HOCKEY NATIONALE JUNIOR DU CANADA CHAMPIONNATS MONDIAUX DE HOCKEY J

FRONT ROW (L-R) / RANGÉE DU BAS (G-D):
AN BESTER, TERRY SIMPSON (ASSISTANT COACH/ENTRAÎNEUR ADJOINT), SYLVAIN CÔTE, BRIAN KILREA (HEAD COACH & MANAGER/ENT
EF ET GÉRANT), JOHN MacLEAN, DENNIS McDONALD (DIRECTOR OF OPERATIONS/DIRECTEUR DES OPÉRATIONS), RUSS COURTNALL,
RIVIÈRE (ASSISTANT COACH/ENTRAÎNEUR ADJOINT), KEN WREGGET

J. J. Daigneault, flanked by linemate Lyndon Byers, crashes the net in Canada's 6–0 trouncing of West Germany. Canada's third straight victory put them in a strong position for a medal.

I was lucky enough to play for Canada in the world junior championships. I was even luckier to get a chance to pull on a red and white sweater and play for our country years after. A fair number of players from the world junior program do go on to play in the Olympics and world championships. I don't think that anyone, though, has had quite the experiences I've had. "Unusual" would be one word to describe them. "Unforgettable" would be another.

It's hard for me to express how much just getting an invitation to try out for the WJC team meant to me when I was 19. I was playing on a very good team in Kamloops and I was having a pretty solid season, but I never considered myself more than a good junior player. I was honoured to get the invitation, but I went to the camp without a lot of expectations. I didn't even really give a lot of thought to my chances of making the team and going to the WJC. Everything just happened so fast.

I was one of the last players selected to the team and a lot of things had to fall into place for me to make the cut. Some things were beyond my control. A big one was Mario Lemieux deciding not to play in the tournament even though he had been on the WJC team the year before. Even with Mario out I figured I was on the bubble. I had a couple of goals in the last exhibition game before the final cut and

that probably sewed up a spot for me. I ended up on right wing beside two pretty talented offensive players, Russ Courtnall and Dave Gagner. My role was to look after the defensive end and allow Russ and Dave to use their skills.

Our coach was Brian Kilrea—who, as everybody knows, is the only major junior coach in the Hockey Hall of Fame. Brian was the ultimate old-school hockey man. He wasn't so worried about systems and strategy—he just demanded that we play hard and encouraged us to have fun. I loved playing for him. I was used to the "hardcore" coach—I played for Bill Laforge in Kamloops and he had the same approach to the game.

So much of the WJC in the round-robin format rode on a good start. We didn't get one and ultimately that's what really hurt us. We lost our first game 4–2 to the Finns, who ended up with the silver medal. Four straight wins came after that, though, against the United States, Switzerland, Germany, and Sweden. We felt we were really coming together as a team and had a shot at winning the tournament when we went into a showdown with the Soviet Union.

The Soviets were the defending champions and we had a lot of respect for their talent. We thought they were the best team in the tournament, but we were confident we could stick with them. There was a bit of a scene before the game. We knew that they played head games in the warmup—at the end of their skate, they'd go up to centre ice and stare down the opposition, like you'd see a boxer do as the ref is giving him instructions before a bout. Brian Kilrea told us to give it right back to them. So when the Soviets stood at centre ice and were giving us dirty looks, we stared right back and held our sticks at head level. We let them know that we weren't going to be intimidated.

I remember it being a great game. We gave as good as we got and managed to take the Soviets off their game. Gary Leeman and John MacLean gave us a 2–0 lead in the first period. The Soviets tied it up in the second period—the second goal was by Nikolai Borschevsky, who ended up playing for the Toronto Maple Leafs years later. Kirk Muller gave us another lead but we couldn't hold on. We outshot them 37–30 and that's a fair representation of the game. We outplayed them but they got away with a 3–3 tie.

We took the result hard. We didn't have a shot at the gold and the best we could do was a bronze going into our final game against Czechoslovakia. Our attitude was gold or nothing, and after playing our best game against the Soviets we played our worst against the Czechs, losing 6–4 after taking a lead into the third period. The Czechs went away with the bronze and we came home empty-handed. Kilrea and his assistant Terry Simpson pushed us as hard as they could, but we weren't motivated. It was strictly our fault.

Russ Courtnall ended up being our leading scorer: seven goals and six assists in seven games. John MacLean picked up seven goals as well. I had six goals and three assists and probably was playing better then than I ever had before. Playing in the WJC was a real turning point in my hockey career. It gave me confidence going forward and took me places I never imagined.

I ended up playing 13 years in the NHL, over 800 career games, and I'm proud of my career. Still, I wasn't a threat to play on a Canada Cup team. I was a professional but not an all-star. I had to fight to make my spot on the roster every season. Years when my team didn't make the playoffs, I didn't get invited to play for Canada at the world championships. I made my peace with the idea that I'd just have that one shot to wear the maple leaf. By the summer of '96 it looked like my NHL career was winding down—Calgary had bought out my contract and all I had was a couple of tryout offers, nothing concrete. I had a chance to make some money playing pro in Europe. And that's when I got a call from Andy Murray, who was coaching the national team for Hockey Canada that season.

I knew Andy from growing up and playing in Manitoba as a teenager. He told me that he had a very young team and asked me if I'd be interested in being a player–assistant coach, a veteran who could help him out. He couldn't offer a lot of money—I think it was about $15,000 for the season—but at least I had a chance to play and maybe an NHL team would notice so that I might get another shot. I'd had such a good time playing in the Program of Excellence, even with the fourth-place finish at the WJC, and I took that into consideration.

I took the job with Andy and it was a great experience to play wearing the maple leaf—but then midway through the season I got an offer to play for an American Hockey League team and maybe get a final shot at the NHL. When I told Andy, he told me that he needed my help. If I stuck it out the rest of the way, he promised me a spot on the team that would play in the world championships at the end of the season—that I'd be playing alongside all the NHLers who'd join the team that spring. It was another chance not just to wear the maple leaf but to do it with a world title on the line, a chance to get the gold that got away 13 years before.

On that Canadian roster at the 1997 worlds there were a bunch of future Hall of Famers, including Mark Recchi, Rob Blake, Chris Pronger, and Jarome Iginla—all guys who had won gold at the world juniors. There was only one player who wasn't on an NHL roster. Me. It was an honour when they named me captain and a thrill when we won the gold. If it hadn't been for the experience I'd had in the Program of Excellence, I might have made a different decision when Andy offered me the player–assistant coach job. And I would have missed out on the greatest hockey experience of my life.

I played only one more season after that, a winter in Europe. I feel like my career started and ended wearing the maple leaf.

1985

HELSINKI
THE ONLY SHIFT ON THE WING

STEVE MILTON

With a gold medal
on the line against
Czechoslovakia,
Bob Bassen couldn't
completely duck under
a head shot in open
ice to make a play.

Jeff Jackson had never been so happy to be stuck on the bench.

Late in the afternoon of New Year's Day 1985, Jackson, who had just killed a penalty and was, admittedly, "really sucking wind," was told by Team Canada head coach Terry Simpson to take a breather while his regular linemates Brian Bradley and Adam Creighton were joined for a shift by a relatively unknown Saskatoon Blade named Wendel Clark.

"It kind of worked out," Jackson recalled with a laugh.

Indeed. It worked out to the point that Canadian international hockey history was made and permanently altered.

It was the last day of the 1985 world junior championships at the Helsingin Jäähalli (Helsinki Ice Hall), and Canada was trailing favoured Czechoslovakia 2–1 with less than seven minutes remaining in their final game. There were no playoffs in those days, so the round robin among the eight nations would determine the winner of the tournament—which Canada had won only once before, and had never won in Europe.

Going into the game, Czechoslovakia and Canada were undefeated, each with five wins, and a tie against Finland. Canada possessed a solid edge in goal differential so required only a tie to become the first Canadian team of any kind in 24 years to win a world championship in Europe.

Czechoslovakia had arrived in Helsinki as tournament co-favourites along with Finland and Russia. Canada was rated no higher than fourth, partly because that's where they'd finished the two previous years with much more high-profile rosters. Canadian hockey fans might not have heard of any of the Canadian kids before they went to Helsinki, but they knew all about them by the end of the first day of 1985.

Clark and John Miner of the Regina Pats were the two swing players on the team, defencemen who would play forward when the situation dictated. Simpson felt Clark's heavy shot might come in handy with a faceoff in the Czech zone to the right of the goalie who'd been stoning the Canadians, Dominik Hasek.

Simpson had Clark and Bradley flip-flop wings, with Clark and his left-hand shot playing to the right of centre Adam Creighton and closer to Hasek. Off the draw, Creighton pushed the puck ahead and Bradley moved forward to gain control.

"I hadn't played forward much, except in minor hockey, so I wasn't always sure where to go, and that was my first shift of the game on the wing," Clark recalls. "I saw Adam push the puck behind their centre, and headed right to the net. Then I pulled back from their defence to give myself a bit of space, and Brian fed me from the side. And I one-timed it."

Right into the history books.

The quick shot beat Hasek, triggering a furious final six minutes and 13 seconds during which Czechoslovakia blitzed Canadian goalie Craig Billington, looking

for the winning goal that separated them from their first-ever gold medal. It never came.

"Hasek was really good," Creighton said. "But Billington absolutely stood on his head."

After the Canadians survived a faceoff and frenzied attack over the final 20 seconds of the game, they knew they had won the gold medal, and celebrated accordingly—but it wasn't absolutely official. There was still a night game between the Soviet Union and Finland, and if the Finns won by eight or more goals they could finish first.

"And we knew those teams were too good for that," Clark recalled. "But we still had to stay and watch, just to make sure. It was really rare in international hockey then for Canada to be up on goal differential, but that was Craig Billington's goaltending. We took a lot of penalties, as we always do over in Europe, but Billy saved us. We allowed only one power-play goal all tournament, and that was the goal differential right there."

Unfathomably, Billington didn't make the tournament all-star team, but he did win the IIHF Directorate Award as best goaltender.

Billington, of the Belleville Bulls, and his backup from Michigan State, Norm Foster, had been the centre of a mild, but public, controversy during the pre-Christmas selection camp when they made the team and Patrick Roy was cut.

Dan Hodgson, here on a breakaway against West Germany, chipped in with five goals and two assists in seven tournament games.

"They left a lot of guys off the team who became Hall of Fame type of players, like Patrick and Gary Roberts, and some NHL players like Mario [Lemieux] and [Kirk] Muller weren't sent back," said Creighton, who was loaned to the juniors by the Buffalo Sabres, as was Bobby Dollas by the Winnipeg Jets. "That may be why we weren't considered very highly. We weren't expected to win by anybody, but on the team we expected to win."

Clark pointed out that in the fall of 1984 there weren't the advanced, and electronic, scouting techniques there are today. There was no under-18 national team and no summer training camp, and the Canadian Amateur Hockey Association had relied heavily upon Simpson, head coach of the Prince Albert Raiders, to know the western players, assistant Ron Lapointe of Shawinigan to be familiar with the Quebec players, and general manager Sherry Bassin of the Oshawa Generals to keep tabs on the Ontario players.

"And they went with their gut feeling," Clark said. "We were a kind of no-name team but there were a lot of guys who eventually made the NHL. Out of 20, I'll bet 16 played in the NHL for more than a cup of coffee."

His guesstimate is bang on: Every player on the 1985 team spent time in the big leagues, accumulating a collective total of 209 seasons, and 10 players had NHL careers that lasted 13 years or longer.

"The reason we were able to do so well was that no one on that team had an ego about ice time or being the star," Jackson recalled. "Wendel was going to be a high first-round draft pick, maybe even first, but he told the coaches that he'd do anything to make the team."

And the coaches told him that "anything" meant playing both defence and forward. It also meant cutting his shaggy hair. He agreed immediately to both conditions.

After a team-building training camp and exhibition games in Scandinavia, the Canadians arrived in Helsinki still unsure about their chances. The Czechs had the tournament's best player in Michal Pivonka. "I thought for sure Pivonka would be the next one to score 100 points for 10 seasons in the NHL," Clark said. They also had the best goaltender in Hasek. The Finns were led by the two Esas: Esa Tikkanen, who had played some junior hockey in Regina, and Esa Keskinen, who would set a tournament record for assists over the next 12 days. And the Soviets had history on their side as winners of the previous two tournaments, and six of the first eight.

"When you're going into the tournament now, you know a lot about the other teams, but we really didn't know anything," Clark said. "The teams from behind the Iron Curtain, the Russians and the Czechs, you'd watch them practice and the way they moved the puck … and you weren't sure how you'd do against them. The European and North American systems hadn't melded yet, and it was a completely different style of play with all that puck movement, difficult to get used to, especially on the big ice.

"But it's the way we play, our style of game, which won us that tournament."

Canada had plenty of role players, striking the template for future national teams, and what they may have lacked in marquee power they made up for in physicality. Whenever they needed the big hit, they got it.

Simpson set a calm but determined atmosphere, Lapointe was more fiery and an instigator—before the Finn game he told Tikkanen, "We're coming to get you Esa, we're coming to get you"—and general manager Bassin, choosing his moments carefully, lit the emotional fire.

And the players, having trouble adjusting to Finnish food, "were living on Coke and chocolate bars," Creighton said with a laugh.

Their diet might have been sketchy, but their play certainly wasn't.

After beating Sweden with surprising ease 8–2 to open the tournament, Canada clobbered Poland 12–1 on Christmas Day, and dispensed with West Germany 6–2 on Boxing Day. Then, in their first stern test, against a U.S. team that included Mike Richter, Eric Weinrich, Craig Janney, and Brian Leetch, Canada was forechecked mercilessly and fell behind 4–3 after two periods. But in the third period Simpson switched to a two-man-deep forecheck, and 28 seconds in Clark tied the

Claude Lemieux, left, and Dan Hodgson, right, celebrate a goal in their 8–2 rout of Sweden in the tournament's opening game.

Wendel Clark, seen here skating toward his celebrating teammates, scored what turned out to be the gold-medal-winning goal. Months later, he would be the first overall pick in the NHL draft.

score. Nearing the middle of the third period Creighton scored twice and Stéphane Richer once within a span of 3:18, and Canada won 7–4, going away.

That created a four-way tie for first, with the USSR, Czechoslovakia, Finland, and Canada all at four wins. Their games against each other would determine the medals, and the championship.

Canada's fifth game was against the two-time defending champion Soviet Union, "and we were very psyched up for sure," Clark recalls. Sherry Bassin did a lot of the psyching, during a rollicking pre-game speech in which he called on his players' patriotism and evoked images of his own family history of persecution in Stalinist Russia.

"He's probably one of the best motivational types I've ever heard," Clark said, still in awe. "For that age group, especially."

"I think Sherry even went into the Russia room and reamed them out, too," Jackson said. "I remember him starting on the plane on the way over, and keeping it up all tournament, the motivation, telling us that this was our chance, showing us his ring from '82.

"And it was just us. There was no entourage like there is today. No TV cameras, and just one reporter from Canada who was there for the whole tournament. One reporter. Kids today wouldn't believe that."

The CBC's Fred Walker called the games on radio, but only two were on TV. Yet as they continued to win, momentum and interest was building back in Canada—unbeknownst to the players in an era long before cellphones, the internet, and twenty-four-hour international sports TV networks.

One of those televised games was against the USSR. To counter the puck-savvy Soviets, Simpson put together a line of Clark and Bob Bassin plus Jim Sandlak—who had originally been cut, but was summoned to Europe when Dave Goertz was injured before the tournament.

"We were all very physical and we hit them," Clark said, "all over the rink."

The bang-'em-up principle worked perfectly, in large part because of Billington and the short-handed units. The Soviets were knocked off their game by big hits and fell behind 2–0. Then Canada managed to kill six straight penalties and finish fast, scoring three times in less than two minutes in the third period to win 5–0. Finland and the Czechs tied, leaving Canada as the only team with a perfect record.

Finland was next, and Tikkanen, never a shrinking violet, predicted a home side victory on New Year's Eve, especially since Canada's towering defenceman Jeff Beukeboom had been hurt against the Americans and would miss the game. But it ended 4–4, setting the stage for Canada vs. Czechoslovakia the next day.

"It was before the Iron Curtain fell, so they had both the Czech Republic and Slovakia to draw players from," said Creighton. "They were very skilled, and they had Hasek. We didn't know much about him. But he was very good."

Craig Billington matched Dominic Hasek save for save in the biggest game of his career.

And so was Billington, as the Canadians had to kill five penalties and Czechoslovakia only two. The Czechs opened the scoring in the second period, but Sandlak tied it with five minutes to go in the frame. Pivonka, the dominant forward in the tournament, scored at 12:23 of the third period and a confident Czechoslovakia began thinking gold.

But just over a minute later, Simpson had his brainstorm, and sent Clark out for his only shift of the game at left wing.

"When I first saw Wendel I couldn't believe how tough he was for a young guy and how hard he could shoot that puck," Creighton marvelled.

The last shot Creighton saw Clark take that week gave him and his 19 teammates the gold medal.

"We had no idea how excited everybody was back in Canada," said Clark, who was the NHL's No. 1 overall draft choice six months later, and played only forward in the league, partly because of that goal. The die was cast when scouts had seen him play up front with such impact in Helsinki.

"There were huge crowds to greet us at the airports when we got home. But when I got back to Saskatoon I went straight from the airport to the team bus, for that hard three-game swing through Alberta with my junior team."

Putting his goal and those 12 days in historical perspective, Clark said, "It was one of the most pivotal world junior tournaments ever because TV was just getting into carrying the games and Canadians saw us beat Russia and tie the Czechs. Canada became the best just when the tournament was coming back to Canada the next year. So the country had a lot of pride in that. And they sold a lot of tickets in Hamilton because of it."

1986

HAMILTON
THE LUCKIEST BREAK FOR LUC
STÉPHANE LEROUX

Playing for Canada at the WJC was a big step up for ninth-round draft pick Luc Robitaille, but it set him on course for scoring records, awards, a world championship, and a Stanley Cup down the line.

During his Hall of Fame career they called him Lucky Luc. You could make a case that the luckiest break Luc Robitaille ever got was a chance to play for the Canadian team at the 1986 WJC.

Unlike most players who end up on the Canadian roster at the tournament, Luc Robitaille wasn't a high draft pick. The Los Angeles Kings selected him 171st overall in 1984. Those who have been first-rounders arrive with high expectations and often a lot of publicity. For Robitaille, he came in through the back door.

When his name wasn't among the 44 players originally invited to the national team's 1985 summer camp, Robitaille was disappointed. Then Luc got lucky. As it so often turns out, one man's misfortune spells another man's big break.

"Pat Burns, my coach with the Hull Olympiques, contacted me in the middle of July, a few days before the start of the camp, and asked me if I was in shape," Robitaille says. "I told him yes, of course. He then went on to tell me that that was a good thing because I was to likely replace Stéphane Richer at the national junior team's camp."

Richer had injured himself during the summer and that injury gave Robitaille a chance to show what he was capable of in front of Terry Simpson, who was back as head coach of the national team for a second year in a row after winning gold in the previous season in Finland.

So Robitaille showed up at camp with a knife between his teeth, determined to impress the team's management staff. His play was a revelation to the Canadian team's staff.

"I was the best scorer during the intra-squad games at the summer camp and gave them no other choice but to invite me back to the final camp in December."

Robitaille's play was also a revelation to the team that had drafted him. At the Canadian team's camp, Robitaille outperformed Los Angeles first-round draft pick Dan Gratton, who was selected by the Kings 10th overall in 1984. Luc was lucky to get an invitation, but outperforming Gratton was no fluke. Robitaille would end up scoring 668 goals in his 20-year NHL career and Gratton only seven in his cup-of-coffee stint.

Robitaille's play in the QMJHL merited his selection to the team: he had regis-tered 36 goals and 63 assists in only 33 games when he made the trip to the Canadian team's camp. Still, his big break almost came undone on the eve of the WJC. Just before the Canadian team's camp was set to start, he suffered an ankle injury during a regular-season game in the QMJHL. Robitaille did his best to hush up the fact that he was less than 100 percent. "I wanted to be part of that experience so badly that I wasn't going to let a minor injury force me to abandon it all."

Robitaille was among the 20 players selected by Terry Simpson. His selection over Tony Hrkac, a member of the Olympic team coached by Dave King, caused quite a stir at the time, especially since Hrkac had played well with the national team

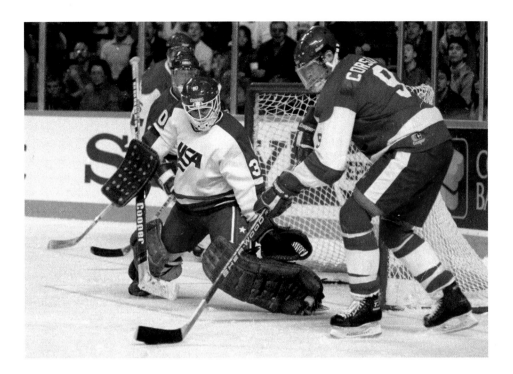

that was preparing for the 1988 Olympic Games. It also turned out that Robitaille was the only Quebec league player on the team. Two other Quebeckers, Alain and Sylvain Côté, were also on the WJC roster, on loan from their respective National Hockey League teams.

The WJC was a bigger stage than any Robitaille had played on to that point in his junior hockey career. Adding to the excitement was the fact that the tournament was being held on Canadian soil for the first time since 1978. A huge crowd at Hamilton's Copps Coliseum cheered for the Canadian teenagers, who started the tournament with a 12–1 pounding of Switzerland. The one-sided nature of the game didn't take anything away from Robitaille's excitement.

"I had never experienced anything like it at the time," Robitaille said. "It was a great experience for me to play for my country even though I wasn't on the ice often, being part of the fourth line. Playing for Canada at age 19 was incredible," he said.

The Canadian team went on to win its next four games. On January 2, Canada and the Soviet Union, tied for first place with identical records of 5-0-0, were to play for the gold medal because there was no medal round at the time. The sixth game was going to be the ultimate confrontation. The Soviets had a decided edge over Canada in WJC experience, with 10 players back from the bronze-medal winners the previous year.

"In 1986, playing against the USSR was a big deal," Robitaille said. "We didn't really know the Soviet players and there was without a doubt a lot of nervousness

Shayne Corson brought muscle up front for Canada and led the team in goal scoring with seven tallies in seven games.

Craig Billington emerged as the starting goaltender and carried the team to five straight wins en route to the pivotal game against the Soviet Union.

and a great atmosphere in the locker room. We had big, physical players like Shayne Corson, Jim Sandlak, Terry Carkner, and that was part of our game plan to use this to our advantage and intimidate the opponent."

Corson, the best Canadian scorer in 1986, sent the Copps Coliseum crowd to its feet in Hamilton when he beat Evgeny Belosheikin, the Soviet goaltender, at the seven-minute mark of the first period, but it was to be the only such moment for the crowd: the USSR won the game 4–1. "We played a very physical game, but we had a lot of penalties and that just cut our legs from underneath us," said Robitaille. When he harkens back to that game against the Soviets, he says the disappointment feels as fresh as if it happened yesterday.

Robitaille and his teammates had to settle for silver. Still, the experience was a catalyst to a breakthrough in his play.

"When I returned to play with the Hull Olympiques, everything seemed easier," he says. "I had just spent a month with the best junior players in the world and my confidence had been given an incredible boost even though we didn't win the gold medal. I had the impression of being so much faster than my opponent."

Robitaille won the QMJHL scoring title in 1985–86, the Guy Lafleur Trophy as the playoff MVP, and the President's Cup with the Olympiques before losing the Memorial Cup final to the Guelph Platers. Lucky Luc, who was inducted into the Hockey Hall of Fame in 2009, was also chosen as the CHL player of the year after his breakout season in 1986.

Robitaille went on to represent Canada on two other occasions, at the 1991 Canada Cup and at the 1994 world hockey championship. "I always loved to represent my country. For me, it was not about representing the QMJHL or Quebec—I played for Canada and I was extremely proud of it."

The Los Angeles Kings had closely followed the 1986 WJC and realized they had lucked into a born scorer. "The impression I made at the WJC helped me so much when I arrived at the Kings' camp the following season," Robitaille said. "I felt that I had a chance to make the team even if I was only 20 years old."

Robitaille did a lot more than make the team at age 20. That season he scored 45 goals with the Kings and won the Calder Trophy as the NHL's rookie of the year.

The 1986 tournament gave the hockey world a glimpse of another future 50-goal scorer and Hall of Famer, Joe Nieuwendyk.

Luc Robitaille won a gold medal with the Canadian team at the world championship in '94, and he'd end up hoisting the Stanley Cup with the Detroit Red Wings eight years after that. Yes, he's disappointed that it was "only" a silver at the WJC in Hamilton. But when he's asked how he went from a ninth-round pick to the Hockey Hall of Fame, he points to the WJC as a turning point. He couldn't have anticipated that someday he'd make the Hockey Hall of Fame, but he came away from Hamilton with a medal and the confidence that he was going to make the NHL with more talent than luck.

1987

PIESTANY
THE 33-MINUTE GAME

GARE JOYCE

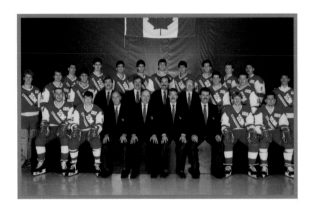

Goalie Shawn Simpson gave away at least 60 pounds to the Soviets' backup netminder Vadim Privalov during the infamous bench-clearing brawl at the 1987 WJC, but he didn't shy away.

I wasn't in the arena when Canada played the Soviet Union with a gold medal on the line in the final game of the 1987 world junior championship in Piestany, Czechoslovakia. I experienced that game like most people familiar with it: I watched it live on television and in replays for years after. Two decades after the fact I wrote a book about the game and ended up talking to almost all who played on the Canadian team and many who played on the Russian side. I talked to many others, including the widow of the Canadian coach and the assistant coach on the Canadian team, Pat Burns. I talked to those who broadcast the game for CBC, Don Wittman, Sherry Bassin, and Fred Walker. And I talked to a linesman who saw trouble coming and a novice referee whose failure to take charge led to the disqualification of both teams from the tournament.

It was indisputably the worst moment in the history of the Program of Excellence, and one of the most important. I was at some level obsessed by the game and it drove me to write a book about it. I guess I was trying to figure out how, as the late Don Wittman put it in introducing the broadcast, Canadians were "guaranteed a medal even with a loss," and yet they skated off empty-handed even though they scored two more goals than the Soviets. The game became the source of endless debate and editorials. Some argued that the Canadian teenagers had disgraced the country.

Pierre Turgeon, Theoren Fleury, and Everett Sanipass went to Czechoslovakia with hopes of bringing home a gold medal—they still were favourites to win the championship midway through their final game in the round robin.

Some argued that the Canadian teenagers had been put in an impossible position and hung out to dry. Maybe both were true, and maybe neither fully explains how and why it happened. Or didn't happen, I suppose. If you went by the International Ice Hockey Federation history of the tournament, it was never played. When I went to the IIHF for the game sheet in the archives, they told me it hadn't been saved.

The linesman, a Finn named Peter Pomoell, had worked in many world championships and recognized that the situation was a recipe for disaster: take a bunch of hot-blooded Canadian teenagers, mix with a Soviet team that was already eliminated from the medals, and toss in a referee, Hans Rønning of Norway, who had never refereed a major international game. "I asked him, 'Do you want my help on calls—majors, misconducts?'" Pomoell recalled. "Rønning said, 'No, I'll call my own game.' Canada vs. the Soviets … those two teams produced the best hockey

Virtually every Canadian and Soviet player was caught up in the brawl. Even before the benches emptied, the game was hot-tempered and rife with cheap shots.

but they were also the toughest games to work. I knew this; maybe Rønning didn't. If Rønning had spoken to the captains and coaches before the game or during the game … maybe it could have been avoided."

That was exactly what Canadian Amateur Hockey Association executive Dennis McDonald asked IIHF officials to do: Instruct the referee to speak with the teams before the opening faceoff. "The first thing I thought about was the tournament in Hamilton the year before," McDonald said. "He worked a few smaller games in Hamilton and he was the lowest-rated official there. He was out of his league—just not ready or qualified to work a game like that."

The game was a riveting one for as long as it lasted—which was exactly 33 minutes and 53 seconds of playing time. The score at that point was Canada 4, Soviet Union 2, with a pair of goals by the diminutive Theoren Fleury and single markers by Dave Latta and Steve Nemeth. With the possible exception of Fleury, Canada's best player was Jimmy Waite, a young goaltender thrust into service when the projected starter

Shawn Simpson went down with an injury earlier in the tournament. The game was wide open. It was also mostly untamed. Instead of trying to establish control of the game early with penalty calls, Rønning ignored slashes, cross-checks, elbows, charges, and face-washes from the very first shift. With the line of Fleury, Everett Sanipass, and Mike Keane on the ice with seven minutes to go in the second period, a line brawl broke out.

If you go to YouTube you can find footage of the game's end, an old-fashioned bench-clearing brawl. The 15 minutes of mayhem look like they were lifted from a barroom scene in the last reel of an old western. You can't see who left the bench first, though those in attendance told me that it was a Soviet player, likely Evgeni Davydov. You can see Rønning, with a dozen scraps going on in front of him, stuffing his whistle in his pocket like a sheriff putting an empty gun back in his holster. And you can see him ducking into the corner to watch frontier justice play out and then helplessly skating off the ice to get out of Dodge. At one point

Theoren Fleury (under Pavel Kostichkin) was on the ice with line-mates Mike Keane and Everett Sanipass when the fight broke out.

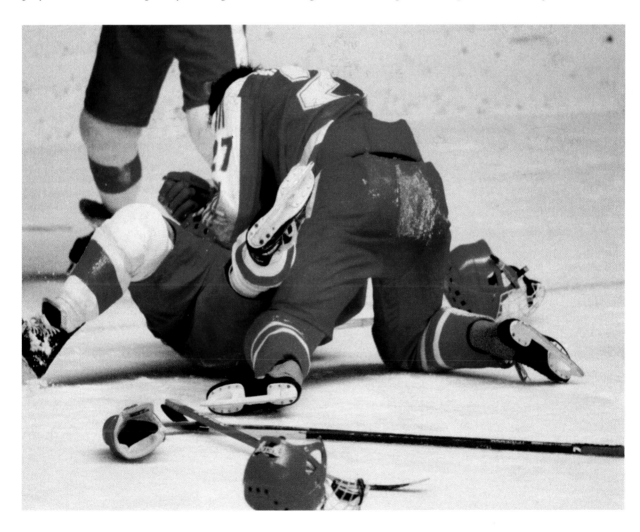

Polish linesman Julian Gorski tries to break up a fight between Everett Sanipass (left) and Sergei Shesterikov. Eventually, referee Hans Rønning led his linesmen off the ice and watched the brawl from the sidelines.

officials in the arena ordered that the lights be turned out, and Czechoslovakian soldiers waited for the two teams to punch themselves into exhaustion or unconsciousness.

Dennis McDonald held out hope that, even if the game was ruled a forfeit, the Canadian teenagers would be allowed to hold on to third place in the standings and bronze medals. Instead, it was the rawest of deals. The IIHF decided to throw Canada and the Soviet Union out of the tournament and void their previous results.

Even with this perfect storm of circumstances, a blood rivalry and an overmatched referee, it shouldn't have turned out the way it did. Many people absolved the Canadians of any responsibility because they weren't the first over the boards. Those who defended the Canadian team said it was a simple matter of self-preservation. Still, it did go well past the point of self-defence. "It was a tough tournament for me and I didn't have any chance to contribute," said Shawn Simpson, who, at 150 pounds, took on and pinned the Soviets' 225-pound backup goaltender at centre ice in what wasn't the most violent fight but the most comical one. "Maybe I was just getting out my frustrations in the fight."

Like Simpson, at least a few players from the Canadian team seemed to enjoy themselves once the chaos started. It would have turned out differently if many Canadian teams from different years were in the same position. The Canadian team that went to the 1987 world juniors was a younger team than those previous. They didn't lack for talent. Brendan Shanahan would go on to an NHL career that will land him in the Hockey Hall of Fame. Pierre Turgeon and Glen Wesley would go on to play well over 1,000 games. But they were 18 and had yet to be drafted. Theoren Fleury was a year older but had been so little thought of that he hadn't been drafted the previous June. It was the only team in the history of the Program of Excellence to hit the ice without a single returning player. In retrospect, a few experienced returnees in the lineup might have steadied a rocky ride. Might it have changed things and allowed Canada to skate away with a medal? Possibly.

In the aftermath, blame was laid at the feet of Bert Templeton, a veteran major junior coach. To put it kindly, he was a tough-love type of guy, so much so that Pat Burns, feared by his players wherever he coached, was good cop to Templeton's bad cop. After the forfeiture and disqualification from the tournament, Templeton was criticized for losing control of his players. But at least some of the players were on a program of their own. "We became sort of a rebel team," Shawn Simpson said. "We broke curfew and a bunch of us got trashed. We were the Bad News Bears and that's how we played and acted the whole tournament. [We were] a bunch of knuckleheads."

In fact, before the Soviet game, Bert Templeton was receiving praise from the media. Thanks to Templeton's coaching, the young Canadian team had improved with each game and, arguably, overachieved in being in a position to win a gold medal. The Canadians stumbled at the start of the tournament, tying Finland 6–6 in a sloppy effort and then falling to the host Czechoslovakians 5–1. A sound 6–2 win over the United States was a turning point and set the stage for a dramatic 4–3 win over the Swedes, most credit due to a breakout performance by Jimmy Waite.

All the good work went for naught, and in that way it was awful for the players. It tarnished the image of the Program of Excellence. The team had strayed a long way from the discipline that Murray Costello and Dennis McDonald saw as a foundation of the program. And yet, Canada versus the Soviet Union in Piestany was a hugely important game in the Program of Excellence's history. It showed exactly what was at risk when that discipline was lost or abandoned. It wasn't a coincidence that the most undisciplined and infamous moment would be followed a year later by a glorious win with a team that played smart and poised hockey in even more hostile circumstances. The team that went to Moscow a year later understood the risks of any lapse in discipline, as have all the teams that have represented Canada in the tournament since.

1988

MOSCOW
THE SWEETEST PAYBACK

FRANK ORR

Goaltender Jimmy Waite, one of four returning players from the Canadian team disqualified in Piestany, exacted a measure of revenge in Moscow. Waite's inspired performance sealed both the win over the Soviets and the gold medal.

I was a young sportswriter six months into my first newspaper job in Cornwall, Ontario, back in November 1957. I bought my own train ticket and paid my way into Maple Leaf Gardens for an exhibition game between the Soviet Union's national team and the Whitby Dunlops. It was the Soviets' first tour of North America and the Dunlops, one of the best amateur teams ever assembled, gave up two early goals but roared back for a 7–2 victory.

I didn't miss too many instalments of the game's fiercest rivalry over the next generation or two. In 1966, again at Maple Leaf Gardens, I covered a game between the Soviet nationals and the Toronto Marlboros, a strong junior team further forti-fied by a teenager from the Oshawa Generals, Bobby Orr. The Marlboros lost the game 4–3 but Orr was brilliant, rushing through the Russians repeatedly and giving a portent of a great NHL career. In 1972, I was in the arenas for the first four games of the historic Summit Series. The 1975 New Year's Eve game between the Red Army and the Montreal Canadiens, the 1976 Canada Cup, all manner of tourna-ments and exhibitions: Canada versus the Soviet Union was a recurring theme in my career. If you're writing about hockey, it's hard to lose with us versus them.

It wasn't until late 1987, however, that I made my first trip to the USSR. And it wasn't a case of being parachuted in for a game or two. It was a five-week jaunt

to cover, first, the pre-Christmas Izvestia Tournament involving the top teams for the 1988 Olympic Games in Calgary—Canada, Russia, Finland, Sweden, and Czechoslovakia. In a surprise, the Canadians won the gold medal with a narrow win over the Russians in the concluding game. As he had done with the Canadian junior team back in 1982, coach Dave King had his team at the Izvestia well-prepared for the countless attempts by the Europeans, notably the Czechoslovaks and Russians, to incite them into retaliation penalties with assorted stealthy fouls.

That provided the perfect lead-in for the junior championship in Moscow. In the wake of Piestany, the Canadian team was selected carefully for of course skill, but almost as important, for the discipline to ignore the irritating attempts by opponents to draw penalties.

Undoubtedly, their best move was bringing back one player who covered himself in glory until chaos reigned in Piestany: goaltender Jimmy Waite of the Quebec Major Junior League's Chicoutimi Saguenéens. In Moscow Waite played in all seven games and surrendered a meagre 16 goals. Waite was outstanding in all games but absolutely brilliant in Canada's 3–2 win over the Russians in the pivotal game of the tournament. The Russians held a 40–16 margin in shots on goal, 17–4 in each of the second and third periods.

"In my entire hockey career, I never saw goaltending as good as Jimmy [Waite] was in Moscow, especially in that game against the Russians," said Theoren Fleury, captain of the '88 team. After being part of the Piestany debacle, Fleury went to Moscow a year later looking for redemption and got it.

That Canadian team had three other players back from Piestany—two defencemen, Greg Hawgood and Chris Joseph, and goaltender Waite. The Russians had four returnees, including their exceptional stars, forwards Alexander Mogilny and Sergei Fedorov, both of whom became all-stars in the National Hockey League.

"The Russians had a high skill level led by the offensive excellence and exceptional speed of Mogilny and Fedorov with Valeri Zelepukin not far behind," said Canadian head coach Dave Chambers. "Our scoring was not as explosive but more balanced and our defencemen, especially Greg Hawgood (Canada's leading tournament scorer with a goal and eight assists), were intelligent offensively.

"Our advantage was that all our forwards, even the high scorers, could play both ways. We used four lines through much of the tournament with no fall-off in quality or production."

Reflecting years later, Chambers felt the game against Czechoslovakia was important in Canada's gold-medal journey. As they often did against Canadian teams, the Czechs played a sneakily aggressive game with countless little spears, jabs, hooks, and elbows, and then staged elaborate dives when the Canucks retaliated with muscle. The Canadian teenagers spent much of that game shorthanded and, as he was throughout the tournament, Waite proved to be their best penalty killer in a 4–2 win.

"We learned the hard way that in international hockey it's almost always the retaliator, not the instigator, who gets the penalty," Chambers said. "We had a lengthy meeting after that game, one of the few we had, and you could feel the entire team vow to take all the baloney they threw at us and skate away from it. The players did for the rest of the games."

Against Russia, Canada opened with a strong first period and a 2–0 lead on goals by Fleury and Trevor Linden, a poised 17-year-old who finished off a dazzling rush by Hawgood.

In a familiar pattern for Canuck junior teams in international play, they didn't press the advantage in the second period. Instead, they concentrated on defensive play, which gave the Russian speedsters the chance to get their high-speed, quick-transition game into high gear. A goal by Harije Vitolinish at 6:55 gave the Russians a big lift and it seemed the Canadian lead would not last.

Defenceman Marc Laniel, a staunch defensive presence throughout the event, restored the two-goal margin with a slapshot from the point at 11:45. But the lift to

Theoren Fleury (wearing the captain's C) had been in the eye of the storm in Piestany, but he emerged as a leader on the disciplined 1988 championship team.

the Canadians didn't even last a shift. Less than half a minute later Zelepukin got the goal back and again put the Russians on the attack.

With almost half the game to play, the fans at Luzhniki Arena anticipated a batch of goals from their star shooters. But Waite showed the main quality of all great goalies: the ability to be unbeatable at a crucial point in an important game.

"It was as if Jimmy [Waite] decided there was absolutely no way he was going to allow the Russians to tie that game," Canadian assistant coach Ken Hitchcock said. "The Russians threw everything but the Kremlin at him and he never cracked."

While Waite did make several difficult stops against Mogilny and Fedorov, the Canadian forwards did strong defensive work against the Russian aces. Little centre Rob DiMaio led the man-to-man shadowing, a defensive job that was his specialty in an NHL career that would last 17 seasons.

In the third period, the Canadians were effective in keeping the Russians on the outside in their zone, away from the high-percentage shot area. But Waite made

seven difficult stops, five in the last 10 minutes, one a breathtaking split-pad save on Stanislav Ranfilenkov.

But in the last six minutes of the game, Canada actually carried the play to the Russians.

"We had an idea by then that Jimmy wasn't going to allow them to score another goal," winger Warren Babe said. "It was a big lift and we took it to them a little but carefully. That eased things a bit."

"We didn't want our guys to hang back quite as much as they did but when the Russians got momentum, their great passing made forechecking risky because of their breakout plays," Chambers said. "That forced us into a bit of a defensive shell to guard against odd-man rushes. Overall, we did a good job against them, a smart, straightforward approach. But, in the end, the kid in goal made the difference."

Waite somewhat reluctantly acknowledged that he had faced difficult shots.

"Some saves were quite tough to make," he said. "But my confidence was good

Canadian players in Piestany poured over the boards to join the ugly brawl, but a year later they hit ice to celebrate Canada's first major triumph in Moscow since the 1972 Summit Series.

and I was pleased with the way I played. When we got ahead, I figured that if I played good, we could win."

Through the tournament, Waite's laid-back approach was both a source of wonderment and encouragement to his teammates. "The rest of us would be all wound up tight, ready to head for the rink at noon for a night game, and Jimmy would go to his room, stretch out and have a snooze," said centre Joe Sakic. "I asked him if he ever worried about anything and his reply was that he didn't because worrying never did any good."

While the victory over the Russians had every trapping of the tournament championship match, Canada had two games to play against West Germany and Poland, which they won easily to claim the world title.

Fleury, the 5-foot-5, 150-pound captain, had played the tournament—in fact, the entire season as Western Junior League scoring champ—with a burning desire, inspired by the Piestany incident. His lead-by-example intensity inspired his mates to duplicate it. He and Rob Brown tied for the team goal-scoring lead with six.

"For a whole year, including many sleepless nights, I thought only about how the Russians took away something very special that belonged to me—a world championship gold medal," Fleury said. "Now that we have it, a big load is off my back. It has bugged me for a year—really badly, too, sometimes."

The victory was a career milestone for all 20 players on the roster, boosted by a strong team feeling that developed quickly at the selection camp before the trip to Moscow. "It was all for one because that's how it had to be for a shot at the gold," Sakic said. "The camaraderie was terrific and there were no little groups going their own way. That's why it was really sad when we got back to Canada and went our own ways."

Centre Mark Recchi was an important two-way player in the tournament. "I remember very well the empty feeling when the team got to old Mirabel Airport in Montreal and the guys all went to their own teams," Recchi said. "We had met a really big challenge and we would never have the chance to do it again. But what happened in Moscow will never be forgotten by any of us. All through my NHL career, I'd be, say, lining up for faceoff, look up and see a Theo Fleury, Joe Sakic, Trevor Linden, or Adam Graves, any of the Moscow guys, looking at me. We both would give a little nod or smile that said, 'Hey, you old dog! You and me did something really special one time.'"

The Canadian roster was built on the evaluation of CAHA director of scouting Dave Draper. He started the construction process at the '87 midsummer four-nation (Russia, Czechoslovakia, Sweden, Finland) junior tournament in Estonia.

"We knew then the type of teams four top contenders were building and the style of team we had to send to be competitive," Draper said. "Maturity in all areas was a prime necessity after Piestany and, with the tournament in Moscow, culture shock was a big factor with different living accommodations and food. We brought a solid, mature group of young men who also could play some hockey. They did Canada and themselves proud."

Head coach Chambers, who had much international coaching experience, was on sabbatical from his job as director of athletics at Toronto's York University.

The low-key Chambers made restraint his theme and Hitchcock, a hard-driver from the Kamloops Blazers, and easygoing Jean Begin, from the Drummondville Voltigeurs, were the ideal "bad cop–good cop" duo as assistant coaches.

Given the many NHL successes of the alumni from '88, you could make an argument that this was the best-ever Canadian junior team. Of the 20 players on the roster, 18 played at least a few games in the NHL. Six (Fleury, Sakic, Recchi, Graves, Linden, and Eric Desjardins) played more than 1,000 games. Five played on Stanley Cup winners.

Since '88, several members of the team expressed their surprise that two key parts of the Moscow effort—goalie Waite and defenceman Laniel—did not have distinguished big-league careers. Waite played 191 NHL games in 10 different stints over 11 seasons plus good minor pro stretches, but never relocated the brilliance of Russia. Laniel never played an NHL game in a six-year pro career.

"Over the years I've met guys from the Moscow team and we shake our heads when they think how good Jimmy was in that tournament and how he struggled in the NHL," Recchi said. "Marc Laniel? How could a guy who was so solid in his own zone, such a smart player with size and skill, not do in the pros what he did so beautifully in Moscow?"

There is no easy answer for the question, like so many others in the game. Nonetheless, the Canadian juniors that year had an answer to a powerful Soviet team: Jimmy Waite. In the toughest road game in the sport, he played as well as any goaltender I had ever seen. I would have paid my own way and bought my ticket to see it.

1989

ANCHORAGE
THE RUNAWAY TRAIN

TOM WEBSTER

Rob Cimetta and his teammates went to Alaska as defending champions, but faced the greatest team the Soviets ever sent to the world juniors.

My chance to coach the Canadian junior team came two years after I had to miss out on the tournament. I was named as an assistant coach on the team that went to Piestany, but after I had worked with the team at the summer camp the New York Rangers called me and offered me the head coach's job. I was coaching the Windsor Spitfires a couple of years later when I got the call from Team Canada to work with the team that was going to Anchorage as defending champion.

I thought our team played well and I'm proud of the job our players did. We went in wanting to put the team in a position to win a gold medal or any other medal. We were in that position down to the wire—we had four wins, a loss to Sweden, and a tie with Czechoslovakia going into our last game of the round robin. But we ran into a runaway train: the Soviets.

That Soviet team is probably one of the best that ever played in the world juniors and I'd say that there's never been a better line than Pavel Bure, Sergei Fedorov, and Alexander Mogilny in that tournament. Mogilny had an injury and wasn't even supposed to play in that game but he turned it on against us. We had managed to hang around in the first period, but in the second there were a couple of marginal penalty calls and Mogilny picked up a hat trick. That line was tough to hold off at even strength and impossible when you're playing short-handed.

Sheldon Kennedy, crashing the net against Sweden, was named Canada's captain and was one of two players returning from the team that won gold in Moscow.

We ended up losing 7–2. That left us with a 4-2-1 record in the round robin, tied with the Czechoslovakians, but they got the bronze by virtue of a better goal differential.

It was a tough way to miss out on a medal and a tough stretch for the program.

NHL teams were starting to change their approach with their young players. The kids that they drafted in June would go directly into NHL lineups the following October. In years past a few had made the jump—the exceptional prospects like Mario Lemieux, the top couple of 18-year-olds. But by the late '80s a lot of players were rushed into the pros. There were at least a dozen guys who would have been eligible for our team but weren't released back to us by their NHL clubs—Joe Sakic, Trevor Linden, Brendan Shanahan, and Pierre Turgeon, just to name a few. We weren't surprised by that and truthfully we didn't hold out much hope for getting those guys. It was just the way things were at the time.

I was lucky that my friend Pat Burns, whom I'd worked with in the summer camp a couple of years before, released Eric Desjardins back to us for the tournament. Eric, who was one of the real leaders for us, and Sheldon Kennedy were the only returning players from the gold-medal winners the year before. We might have had some benefit from a few more players who brought some more world junior experience to the team, but really it wasn't inexperience that cost us in

the end. We happened to run into one of the best teams that ever played in this tournament.

Going into the tournament we knew we didn't have a lot of high-end skill like the Soviets. We were going to have to look at rolling all four lines, taking a scoring-by-committee approach and having our players going in the dirty areas. I thought that our scout, Dave Draper, did a great job going out to find talent when a lot of the top young players we might have hoped to be available were sticking in the NHL. We all tried to bring something to the table in terms of the knowledge of players we'd invite to the selection camp. For coaches in our position, you want to keep tabs on the best players and try to get to know them in advance of the camps. Alain Vigneault was my assistant and he knew the players in the Quebec Major Junior Hockey League from coaching the Hull Olympiques. I knew those in the Ontario Hockey League and I went up to Michigan State to watch Rod Brind'Amour a few times—Rod was one player who really improved from the summer camp through to December. Dave Draper went across the country and we all shared our knowledge when we were putting together our invitation lists and tournament roster.

Because we were going to have trouble scoring, we had to play smart and avoid unnecessary penalties. It was a time when there was an eye-for-an-eye attitude

Mike Ricci, here backchecking against the Swedes, was luckier than most of his teammates. He was young enough to return to the WJC the following year for another shot at gold.

Goaltenders Gus Morschauser (pictured) and Stéphane Fiset gave a Canadian team depleted by the absence of tournament-eligible stars on NHL rosters a chance at a medal going into the final game.

among junior players, even really good ones. We had to separate them from that. The team excelled at that the year before in Moscow, and our players did a good job buying into an idea that some others might have had trouble with.

Wayne Halliwell, our team psychologist, did a really good job in helping get the message across to the team. He met with the players as a group and individually. We went through team-building exercises. He really helped get the players focused and aware that each and every shift is important in a short tournament like the world juniors. And, really, when you get the best junior players in Canada

Dan Lambert takes a spill in a loss to the Swedes that was a blow to Canada's medal hopes.

Reggie Savage, here with the puck behind the Swedish net, picked up four goals and five assists in seven games for a Canadian team that had to rely on scoring by committee.

together, almost all of them are going to respond to that type of direction and coaching.

It's a small world and it seems even smaller in hockey. After the tournament I went back from Anchorage to Windsor with Darrin Shannon, one of the leaders on that Canadian team and one of my players with the Spitfires. Later I was working in the Philadelphia organization when Rod Brind'Amour and Eric Desjardins were playing there and it made for a special relationship—you've shared an experience and gone to war with a young man in what was the biggest moment of his life to that point. Whenever I'd see players from the world junior team we'd always talk and have a laugh. I feel like I made a lot of friends through that opportunity to coach in the Program of Excellence.

I haven't coached for a few years now, but I've stayed active in hockey as a scout and I've seen the impact that Hockey Canada and the Program of Excellence have had on the game. The Program of Excellence has made tremendous strides over the years—we didn't always have the under-17 and under-18 programs to identify and work with the best young players, priming them for success at the world juniors. And the quality of hockey has just shot up. When you see players on Canadian teams at the world championships, at the World Cup, and at the Olympics, you're seeing players who have been put into a position to succeed because they've been made familiar with the challenges they are facing.

No matter who is on the roster, every Canadian team goes into international play expecting to win. Every loss stings, but to miss out on a medal because of goal differential was especially bitter for the 1989 team.

1990

TURKU
THE OUT-OF-TOWN SCORE

BOB McKENZIE

The 1990 edition of the Canadian team knew going into the tournament that it would have to rely on scoring by committee, and the players came through. Here, Stu Barnes celebrates a goal against Sweden.

It wasn't as if it was a moral dilemma, but I was a little confused on how to handle the information I'd just been given.

This wasn't anything that had been covered in my three years of journalism school and, to be honest, there hadn't been anything in my 11 years in the newspaper business that left me with a high degree of confidence on the "right" or "proper" thing to do. Besides, this was really my first foray into the world of broadcasting a live sports event, so who knew the protocol?

I certainly didn't.

There I was on January 4, 1990, in a frigid arena in Turku, Finland, wearing my royal blue CBC blazer as a member of the broadcast team for the 1990 world junior championship. The late Don Wittman was doing play-by-play up in the booth with legendary coach Scotty Bowman as the colour commentator, and Brian Williams was the host. I was a broadcast novice serving as the intermission analyst and self-appointed rinkside reporter once the game had started.

I had taken up a position at ice level right alongside the Team Canada bench, which is to say nobody booted me out of there. Today, they would fashionably call it "Between the Benches," but this was 1990 after all, and if I had decided to sit on the

Wes Walz slides the puck by the sprawling Soviet netminder in a 6–4 victory that kept the Canadians undefeated after their stiffest challenge. Even though they beat their old rivals, Canada would need a lot of help to capture gold.

end of the long and open bench area, I'm not sure anyone other than Team Canada head coach Guy Charron would have said anything.

Canada was playing its final game of the 1990 tournament, facing a talent-laden Czechoslovakian team led by junior scoring machine Robert Reichel, flanked on either side by man-child Bobby Holik and a big, baby-faced kid with flowing locks, Jaromir Jagr. When they dropped the puck to start that game in Turku, it was thought to be nothing more than the final match of the tournament to decide who would get the silver and bronze medals.

The Canadian team had wasted a big win over the favoured Soviet Union by losing to Sweden and tying Finland and was sitting with nine points, needing a victory over Czechoslovakia to get silver. The Czechoslovaks, meanwhile, had only one blemish on their record, a loss to the Soviets, and, with 10 points, a tie or a win against Canada would guarantee them silver. The Soviets, meanwhile, were in full control. Like the Czechs, they had 10 points, but they were playing Sweden in Helsinki at the same time as Canada-Czechoslovakia. No one thought it possible for Sweden to pull off an upset. If the Czechoslovaks beat Canada and the Soviets beat Sweden they would both finish with 12 points, but the Soviets owned the tiebreaker

with the head-to-head win over Czechoslovakia. And, with the initial reports out of Helsinki putting the Soviets out in front of Sweden, this Canada vs. Czechoslovakia tilt had the look and feel of a consolation game.

Maybe that was to be expected. The pundits had been concerned from the outset about Team Canada's defence, a not-exactly-star-studded unit of Patrice Brisebois, Kevin Haller, Dan Ratushny, Adrien Plavsic, Jason Herter, and Stewart Malgunas. And, sure enough, if not for an out-of-this-world netminding performance from Stéphane Fiset, Canada may not have been playing for a medal at all. It was a young team—half of the players, including 16-year-old Eric Lindros, who had scored four goals in the tourney, were eligible to play in the next year's 1991 WJC in Saskatoon. So a silver or bronze medal would not have been a surprise, or even necessarily a disappointment.

Nevertheless, Charron's players played hard that day. It was a terrific, up-and-down game. The Czechoslovaks jumped out to a 1–0 lead late in the first period on a Reichel goal, assisted by Jagr. But Canada came back strong in the second period. Mike Craig tied the game, and nine minutes later Newfoundlander Dwayne Norris put Canada ahead 2–1. Things got dicey in the third period when Canada took three

Finland gave Stéphane Fiset and his teammates all kinds of problems in their 3–3 round-robin tie. Although the Finns didn't win a medal in 1990—they wound up in fourth place—their strong play against Canada helped to sustain the tournament's drama right up until its final minutes.

straight minor penalties in a six-minute span, but Fiset stood tall with more of the tournament-long excellence that, even today, is considered one of Canada's most dominant goaltending efforts at the WJC.

Occasionally, over the course of the game, there were dispatches from Helsinki—and always the Soviets were comfortably ahead of the Swedes. The most recent had the Soviets up 5–3 in the third period. So Canada-Czechoslovakia remained a battle for silver.

But with about five minutes left in the game in Turku, I received word through my earpiece connecting me to the CBC production truck that Sweden had mounted a late-third-period comeback and, unbelievably, scored two goals, including a buzzer-beater at 19:59 of the third period. Final score: Soviet Union 5, Sweden 5.

The scene in the rink in Helsinki was said to be frenzied. The Soviet players were up on the dasher, ready to vault over the boards and celebrate their gold-medal win, when Swedish forward Patric Englund, set up by Nicklas Lidstrom, tied the game just as the buzzer sounded. Instead of swarming their goaltender, the Soviet players smashed their sticks on the dasher, cursed, and protested that the goal had been scored after time had expired. But the goal was ruled good.

Armed with that information, I could hardly contain myself. But I quickly, in my mind, did the math to be 100 percent. The Soviets finished the tournament 5-1-1, with 11 points. If the Canadians held on to their 2–1 lead against the Czechoslovaks, they would also finish at 5-1-1 with 11 points, but by virtue of beating the Soviets in the head-to-head matchup would get the gold medal.

Suddenly, right out of the blue, this silver-medal contest had become a gold-medal game with only five minutes to play.

And that's when I asked myself, How exactly do I handle this?

I was close enough to the Canadian bench to be able to tap one of the players on the shoulder and just tell him, "You better protect that lead because you'll win the gold medal if you do." But it struck me that a media member maybe shouldn't be interacting with players in the middle of a game and, had I done that, I'm pretty sure it would have resulted in some hysteria on the Canadian bench. I didn't want to be responsible for that.

But I'm not going to lie; I was fairly bursting to tell someone. This was huge news. It was exciting. I mean, I think that's why anyone in the media ever goes into the business in the first place—because they like to find out news first, before anyone else, and be "that guy" to tell everyone something they don't know.

There was a stoppage in play and I caught Team Canada head coach Guy Charron's attention and discreetly waved him over. He came down to the end of the bench, bent over, and I whispered in his ear, "The Swedes just tied the Soviets. The game is over. If you hold on to win this game, you win the gold medal. I don't know

Left: An unheralded blue line looked like one of the question marks hanging over the team when it left for Finland, but by the end Canada had allowed only 18 goals in seven games, half as many as they had scored. Here, defenceman Adrien Plavsic congratulates Eric Lindros on one of his four goals of the tournament.

if you want to tell your players or not. I won't say anything to them, but I thought you should know."

Charron's eyes lit up. If I recall correctly, he just said, "Really?" I nodded and he scooted back down the bench and immediately conferred with assistant coach Dick Todd.

More than 20 years later, Charron still marvels at how it all went down.

"I remember it being brought to our attention that the Swedes had tied the Soviets. I always thought it was Mats Sundin who scored the tying goal," Charron said. "It was you who told me? I didn't remember that part. I just knew we found out but the kids didn't know at that point and I talked to Dick [Todd] and [other assistant coach] Perry [Pearn] and we decided not to tell the players. They were playing the game. We didn't want to drop all that emotion on them—this is now a gold-medal game—and throw them all out of whack."

So the seconds ticked away and the magnitude of the little secret known by so few seemed to grow with every brilliant save Fiset made. It was high tension, to be sure, though at that point the players were oblivious to the stakes having been increased so dramatically.

But with about 90 seconds left in the game, during a stoppage in play, there was a public address announcement that the Soviets and Swedes had played to a 5–5 tie.

The players on both benches—Canada's and Czechoslovakia's—erupted. The Canadian players were celebrating their opportunity, all standing up, hooting and hollering and bouncing off each other with kinetic energy that you can't even imagine. That image is burned into my memory.

"What I recall is how garbled the P.A. was," said Team Canada winger Kent Manderville. "It was really hard to hear, but someone picked out that the Soviets and Swedes tied and it spread like wildfire all up and down the bench. It was crazy. We started the game thinking the best we could do was get a silver and now there's a very sudden realization ... we can win gold!"

The Czechoslovaks also rose up on their bench, more with grim determination and steely resolve than outright excitement, knowing a win over Canada would give them the gold and even a tie would create a three-way logjam with them, the Soviets, and Canadians that would require the calculators to come out.

Everything about the game had suddenly changed. It was the highest of high drama. All Charron was trying to do was maintain order, finish the job.

"It was crazy," Charron said. "When that announcement was made, the players went nuts on the bench. We had to try to stay focused."

Manderville said the striking memory of the final 90 seconds was that Reichel, Holik, and Jagr never came off the ice, and just how dominant they were.

"Those three guys were all-world in that tournament and Reichel was scary good,

Right: The Canadians protested this goal in their game against Finland, but it would later be the Soviets crying foul in their pivotal game against Sweden.

Stéphane Fiset, named the outstanding goaltender of the 1990 WJC, preserved a fragile one-goal lead against the surging Czechs in the tournament's final game.

so dangerous," Manderville said. "I was on the bench the whole time, but they just kept coming at us. It was electric, but it was scary, too. The time couldn't come off the clock fast enough."

Charron says he won't ever forget those final moments, how Fiset made some terrific saves. But for him, two things stand out.

"They had the puck in our end in the final minute but they never pulled their goalie," Charron said. "European teams and coaches didn't pull the goalie like we do. I thank heaven for that because this was a situation where you would want the goalie out for the extra skater. But they didn't do it. I was happy for that.

"Then there was a faceoff in our end late, I don't recall exactly how many seconds were left but it was to the right of Fiset. I had to decide who should take the faceoff. I had been using Stu Barnes for those faceoffs because he's a right-hand shot and I was using Kris Draper for the faceoffs to the left of Fiset because he's a left shot. Kris asked me if he could take the faceoff; he told me he could win it. I had Kris when I was coaching the Olympic team and I had a lot of confidence in him. So I had him take the faceoff—I know Stu Barnes was really disappointed it wasn't him—and Kris won it. We killed the clock. We won. I'll never forget it."

There was some talk in the immediate aftermath of the game that the Soviets were officially protesting the tie with Sweden—that the Patric Englund goal had been scored after time expired and they had video to prove it. But as Russian star Pavel Bure said many years later, "It was very close. Maybe it was 19:59, maybe it was 20:00, but there wasn't the technology then like now. The bottom line is the goal counted. We lost the gold medal."

"It's funny," said Charron from his Kamloops Blazers office, where he's been the head coach since the fall of 2009. "I'm not sure I realized then what a big deal the world juniors were. We wanted to win of course—Canada always wants to win—but I had been in the Olympics and I went into the junior tournament thinking it would be a good experience. I suppose now that the world juniors have grown to what they are, I know how important it is and how much it means to be a world junior champion in Canada.

"I have two pictures up in my [Kamloops] office. One is when I won the Memorial Cup with the 1969 Montreal Junior Canadiens and the other is from that 1990 world junior. I like to think those are things the kids who play junior hockey now can relate to. They are special."

Special, indeed. But for me, what I'll always remember—aside from figuring out whom to tell once I found out the Soviets and Swedes had tied and Canada was in a gold-medal game—is that some years a team wins a gold medal at the world juniors when it seemingly has no business winning one, and other years it loses when by all rights it should have won.

And it didn't take very long for history to repeat itself, right down to a Newfoundlander scoring the game-winning goal in a most improbable gold-medal victory.

1991

SASKATOON
THE SECOND LIFE

BOB McKENZIE

Goaltender Trevor Kidd came up with an impressive performance in Canada's 3–2 victory over the Soviets in the final game of the 1991 WJC.

The world junior championship has evolved from an annual tournament into a hockey phenomenon, especially in Canada. Though there have been many stages in that evolution, the 1991 tournament in Saskatoon, Saskatchewan, was a crucial catalyst.

It was the perfect storm in every way.

It was the first time Canada won the WJC on home ice. Hockey fans from Regina to Saskatoon—and all points in between, all over hockey's heartland—braved 10 days of –40°C temperatures to fill the rinks.

It was the first time TSN had televised the tournament—CBC previously held the broadcasting rights—and the first time all seven Canadian round-robin games were broadcast nationally. The tournament immediately became TSN's signature event, with a ratings bonanza of more than 1 million for what turned out to be the gold-medal game between Eric Lindros and Team Canada and Pavel Bure and the Soviet Union. It was unquestionably the launching pad that rocketed the WJC into the Canadian sporting stratosphere, making it what it has become now—the most highly anticipated and most-watched annual sporting event in Canada.

The images from January 4, 1991, remain strong to this day: The giant Canadian flag being unfurled at one end of a sold-out SaskPlace; Newfoundlander John

Slaney's unforgettable game-winning goal on the seeing-eye shot from the point in the final minutes to give Canada a 3–2 win.

For many, that goal and that tourney are synonymous with—or emblematic of—the WJC itself.

Fair enough—it really was something special. But those of us who were there and covering the entire tournament share a knowing smile at the remarkable set of circumstances that even allowed the Canada-Soviet game to become a gold-medal, winner-take-all showdown.

By rights, it never should have happened.

I was part of the TSN broadcast team that year. Jim Hughson and Gary Green did play-by-play and colour commentary, respectively. I provided pre-game and intermission analysis with Paul Romanuk hosting.

The 1991 tournament attracted more public attention than any previous WJC, and that can be attributed to one player: Eric Lindros. It was the Big E's NHL draft year, and by the holiday season he was at the centre of a full-blown media circus. At 18, he was possibly the most-discussed name in the game.

Peterborough Petes coach Dick Todd was the behind-the-bench boss that year, and he had a group that was considered a strong team but by no means an overwhelming favourite. Lindros was obviously the marquee talent, but he was one of seven returnees from the 1990 team that won gold in Helsinki. Still, there were question marks. Some wondered if Trevor Kidd and Félix Potvin were up to the challenge in net. And, as was the case in 1990, the somewhat generic defence: Patrice Brisebois, Jason Marshall, Chris Snell, Karl Dykhuis, Dave Harlock, a draft-eligible Scott Niedermayer (who played only three games), and Slaney. The blue line was scrutinized and, by some, doubted.

Making the odds of a repeat even longer was the strong competition Canada was facing. Bure was the electrifying phenom leading a strong Soviet team. Doug Weight led a talented U.S. entry and Martin Rucinsky, Ziggy Palffy, and Jiri Slegr led an impressive squad from Czechoslovakia.

Canada blanked Switzerland to start the tournament, hit a speed bump in a 4–4 tie with the U.S., but then reeled off comfortable wins over Norway, Sweden, and Finland to go 4-0-1 in their first five games. The Soviets, though, were perfect after five contests, having beaten the U.S., Norway, Sweden, Switzerland, and Czechoslovakia. With two games remaining for each of Canada and the Soviets, the arch-rivals looked to be on a collision course in the final game of the tournament.

But on January 2 in Saskatoon, Czechoslovakia beat Team Canada 6–5. Canada was trailing 4–2 in the second period but the dynamic Oshawa Generals duo of Lindros and Mike Craig went to work with three straight goals. Craig scored two goals and one assist, and Lindros one goal and two assists to give Canada a 5–4 lead midway through the third period. But the Czechs scored a power-play goal with less than five minutes to go and Rucinsky scored the game-winner with less than three minutes left.

That outcome was a disaster for Canada, because the next night in Regina the mighty Soviets were taking on a non-contender, Finland. A Soviet win seemed preordained—and if it materialized, the Soviets would clinch gold without having even played Canada.

"I think it's fair to say we thought we were done after that loss to the Czechs," head coach Dick Todd said 20 years after the fact from his retirement home in Florida. "That whole tournament was a struggle in many respects. Nothing came easy, and when we lost to the Czechs it was tough. There were a lot of things happening behind the scenes, some people who fell off the bandwagon. The atmosphere (after the loss to Czechoslovakia) wasn't very good."

Any time Team Canada fails to win, it doesn't take long for the sharks to circle, questioning everything from the selection of certain players to myriad coaching decisions and tactics. This was no exception.

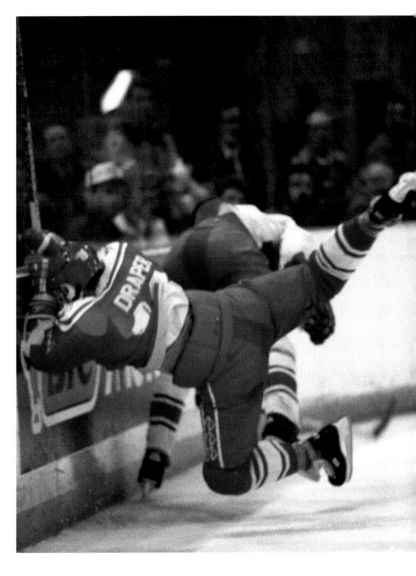

Kris Draper went into the boards face first here, but he was face to face with Soviet star Pavel Bure in Canada's victory over the Soviet Union.

There could not have been any more doom and gloom in the Team Canada ranks than there was on January 3, leading up to that night's game between the Soviets and Finns at the Agridome, home of the WHL's Regina Pats. No one was giving Finland any chance at all.

TSN wasn't able to broadcast the Soviet-Finland game because it had other programming commitments that night, but the network, recognizing the significance of the game, dispatched Paul Romanuk and me to Regina to provide live updates over the course of the night into TSN programming.

It was wickedly cold that night in Regina. Team Canada sent advance scout Dave Draper to Regina for the game, but the rest of the team, including head coach Todd,

Canadian captain Steven Rice and his teammates had to wait for the results of the Soviet Union-Finland game to see if they would still have a shot at a gold medal.

stayed back in their Saskatoon hotel, hoping for a miracle from the Finns.

Team Canada winger Kent Manderville, a returnee from the 1990 gold-medal team that got an improbable gift from the Soviets a year earlier, recalls that January night like it was yesterday.

"We had the whole floor of the hotel to ourselves and everyone's doors were open and we were all just wandering around from room to room and through the hall," Manderville said. "It was like being a kid in a minor hockey tournament again, there with all your teammates, but we were waiting for the [Soviet-Finland] game to start. We were obviously down after losing to the Czechs but we hoped Finland might be able to pull off the upset. We were all gathered around the TVs, just watching TSN [for the updates]."

It turned out to be a night of theatre of the absurd.

Less than 14 minutes into the second period in Regina, the spunky Finns jumped out to a 4–0 lead on the Soviets, including two goals from Jere Lehtinen.

"We couldn't believe it," Manderville said. "We were going crazy but we also knew the lead wasn't safe, not with all the firepower [the Soviets] had, especially Bure."

There wasn't a huge crowd in the Agridome that night, but those who were there couldn't believe their eyes. I can recall the excitement building with each Finnish goal and the breathless TSN updates with Paul Romanuk, suggesting that maybe, just maybe, Canada was going to have an opportunity at redemption.

But the euphoria was relatively short-lived.

Less than two minutes after the Finns made it 4–0, the Soviets answered. Then, at 17:52 of the second, Bure scored to make it 4–2—and the sense of foreboding returned in a big way.

Less than five minutes into the third period, Bure scored again to close the Soviet deficit to one goal. He was literally taking over the game. He wasn't finished, and neither were the Soviets. Oleg Petrov scored at 11:08 to tie the game, and, 1:21 later, Bure got the hat trick and the Soviets were back in front 5–4. It was a tour de force by one of the game's most exciting players, as dynamic a 15-minute stretch of game action by one player as I've ever witnessed.

"It was like a roller-coaster ride," Manderville said. "We were so high when the Finns were up 4–0, out running up and down the halls between rooms celebrating, and we were so low when Bure scored his third goal. We figured that was it; it was over for us."

It certainly seemed that way. The Soviet defence included future NHLers Dmitry Yushkevich, Darius Kasparaitis, Sandis Ozolinsh, Boris Mironov, and Alexei Zhitnik. Up front, they had Bure, Slava Kozlov, Sergei Berezin, and Sergei Zholtok, among others. Now, after having been in a four-goal hole, it was unimaginable to think the Soviets would surrender their lead.

What happened next, though, truly qualifies as "you had to be there."

At 17:57, the Soviets took a too-many-men-on-the-ice penalty. The Finns pulled their goalie, playing six on four. The Soviets had changed goaltenders, from Sergei Zvyagin to Sergei Tkachenko, and the Finns were having a tough time mustering any real good scoring chances on their final power play.

But with less than 20 seconds to go, Finnish forward Jarkko Varvio backhanded a harmless looking bloop shot from the hash marks at the boards, to the right of Tkachenko—and the puck skittered between his legs and into the net.

If I hadn't been there to see it myself, I'm not sure I would have believed it. The Varvio power-play goal was scored at 19:45 of the third. Final score: Finland 5, Soviet Union 5. As was the case a year earlier at the 1990 WJC, the Soviets found a truly bizarro way to let Canada back into the gold-medal hunt.

"It was bedlam in the hotel," Manderville said.

"Just crazy," Todd added. "We were back in it. We had a chance."

"What I remember about all of that," Manderville said, "was the picture on TV of the Russian goalie, just sitting on the ice, all by himself, looking totally depleted."

What I remember is Pavel Bure, standing despondently during the post-game presentations on the blue line, his chin resting atop his gloves, which were on top of his stick—in sort of a forlorn Ken Dryden pose, staring off into space.

"I could not believe it," Bure said. "Honestly, I don't remember a lot of the details, it was so long ago, but I am sure I was thinking, how did this happen? That was two years in a row we did not do what we had to. We gave [gold] to Canada twice."

John Slaney's winning goal ultimately overshadowed the unlikely events that led up to the title game. Victory was made sweeter by the fact that the Canadian juniors thought gold was likely out of reach just 24 hours earlier.

The despondent Soviets had to bus back north to Saskatoon after the game, with the now-gold-medal game the next night, while the Team Canada coaching staff strategized a game plan at the hotel in Saskatoon. The Canadian players, meanwhile, tried to calm themselves after the roller-coaster night of emotions, counting their blessings and trying to sleep.

Todd's game plan involved matching stalwart defensive forward Kris Draper against Bure. Draper brought a game and experience to the role, having been Guy Charron's go-to faceoff man in the final minute of the gold-medal game in the 1990 tournament.

As Bure recalled it, he didn't get much room in the final game against Canada.

"Was it Draper who was checking me?" Bure asked. "I didn't realize then that it was him. I do remember I didn't get as much room and as many chances in the Canadian game."

With Draper blunting the key piece of the Russians' offence, the game was a tense, tight-checking affair. With the score tied two-all and just over five minutes left in the third period, Slaney provided the magic moment that would become one of the most replayed goals in the history of the event. It was the second year in a row a Newfoundlander scored the game-winning goal for gold after a Soviet miscue opened the door for the big prize.

It's funny, though, what different people remember most about that 1991 tournament and that Slaney goal.

"What a lot of people don't realize is that the Soviet winger had flown their zone and was way out in the neutral zone looking for the breakaway," Todd said. "I saw the puck coming up the boards and I was screaming for Slaney to pull out and go back to get the guy in the neutral zone, but he didn't. I thought they were going to get a breakaway but John knocked the puck down, shot, and scored. It was a great play by him but I had been terrified he was taking a risk that was going to cost us. Funny how that goes."

Unquestionably, the 1991 WJC will forever be known as John Slaney's moment—but at the very least there should be a footnote for Jarkko Varvio and yet another improbable scenario paving the way for Canada to win gold when all had seemed so lost.

1992

FÜSSEN
THE FAILED CHEMISTRY
EXPERIMENT

SHELDON FERGUSON

In a break from its usual approach to team building, Hockey Canada added Eric Lindros to the roster of the 1992 WJC squad at the eleventh hour. He led the team in scoring, but anything short of a gold medal would have been deemed a failure for the most celebrated junior player in Canadian history.

It really came down to one play, one call. There were less than 10 seconds left in our game against Sweden and we were in front 2–1. I could see the players on the bench, standing up, getting ready to celebrate. We were just a deep breath from a third straight victory to start the tournament. That breath turned out to be in the cheeks of the ref who blew a whistle on an icing call that brought the puck back into our end for a faceoff and a last chance for the Swedes. It was a real close call, too. I had seen a lot like it not get called.

The Swedes pulled their goaltender. It was Eric Lindros against Peter Forsberg on the faceoff. Forsberg won the draw and next thing you know the puck is in the net, past our goalie Trevor Kidd, who had been very solid for us. It wasn't his fault. You couldn't blame him. You couldn't blame Eric for losing the draw—he was out there against a heck of a player in Forsberg. It just happened.

It was a tie that felt like a loss. When I looked at the bench, I saw that all the energy that had been there just 10 seconds before was gone. When I watched the players after they came off the ice, I saw a team that was deflated. It was a turning point. I knew that it was going to be tough to rebound, especially in the format of

Paul Kariya went to Füssen as an under-age player. He would have to wait until the following January for gold in the WJC.

the tournament back then. There were no do-overs and a tie was just about as bad as a loss for your chances at getting the gold.

The team was hurting after that game and hurting worse after the game the next day: a 2–2 tie with the Finns. If we had a day off, maybe the team would have had a chance to refocus. As it was, that second tie took us out of contention for the gold medal and in those days it was the mentality that prevailed with Canadian players—we were there for the gold, not second or third place. I think the Program of Excellence has made real strides in getting the players away from the all-or-nothing thinking in a challenging situation in the years since, but that's how it was for our players in 1992. It was going to be all or nothing and, unfortunately, it turned out to be the latter.

If you look at our lineup and not the final standings, you'd think it was a very strong team, maybe even a powerhouse. We had a player who's going into the Hockey Hall of Fame, Scott Niedermayer, back from the previous year's team to lead our blue line, as well as a couple of other defencemen, Karl Dykhuis and John Slaney, who had played for the team that beat the Soviets for gold in Saskatoon. Trevor Kidd had played for that team. Eric Lindros was back—as an underage player he had been great for the team in Saskatoon and everyone expected him to be that much better in Germany. Martin Lapointe was another key player returning for a shot at a second gold. It looked like that experience would serve us well in '92.

We had a lot of talent beyond that. Paul Kariya was such a dynamic player. We had a couple of defencemen, Richard Matvichuk and Darryl Sydor, who would be the foundation of Dallas's blue line when the Stars won the Stanley Cup. We had tremendous size, too, averaging 6-foot-2 across our blue line plus Eric, Martin, and Turner Stevenson up front who would make other teams pay a physical price on our forecheck. The team had a lot going for it. There were such high expectations. And it went downhill so fast that it seemed like we didn't know what hit us until it was over. We ended the tournament with a couple of bad losses to Czechoslovakia and the former Soviet Union and finished sixth.

It's hard to pinpoint exactly what went wrong.

After the tournament some people wanted to pin it on Eric Lindros, but that's not fair or deserved. One player doesn't win a tournament for you unless it's a goaltender. He played well for us under the circumstances and he did that with so much pressure and publicity and hype surrounding him—far more than, say, Mario Lemieux or Wayne Gretzky had as teenagers. He was also fighting the flu when he joined the team. That's not uncommon for a player or two in your lineup at that time of year, but I don't think we'd ever had one of our frontline players hurting so badly during a tournament. It's one thing to have someone in a minor role play through it—a few shifts here and there. I think, though, that given his style of play and how

Having won gold playing alongside elite NHLers at the Canada Cup, Eric Lindros went to Füssen with unmatched and unrealistic expectations that he would singlehandedly carry his team to victory.

much we asked of him, it really dragged Eric down. He simply wasn't himself. And it wasn't just illness that weighed on Eric. He was in a very difficult position, too, that was part of a decision we made. Previously, the Program of Excellence had required all players to attend the summer development camp and the entire evaluation camp in December. Eric couldn't come to the summer camp—he was committed to the Canada Cup team, playing with the best pros even though he hadn't played an NHL game. And that winter, because he hadn't signed an NHL contract yet, he had joined the Olympic program. We brought him in late, only three days before we headed off to Europe. We named him captain, which only put more pressure on him. To an extent, we looked at him and his teammates looked at him, thinking, "Okay, Eric's here and he'll take over." We didn't put him in the best possible position to succeed, and we hurt our team chemistry by bringing in Eric, forward Kimbi Daniels, and Trevor Kidd so late in the process. In retrospect, would we have gotten a better read on Eric's illness and on his fit with the other teammates had he been with us all along? There's no way to know for sure—but we might have.

Some said that our coach, Rick Cornacchia, was guilty of favouritism in the way he dealt with Eric because he had been his coach with the Oshawa Generals. It just wasn't true. It was nothing that his assistant coaches Tom Renney and Gary Agnew would have sat still for. It's nothing that Hockey Canada would have tolerated.

Some years we benefited from some good breaks when we won gold. In Germany, we didn't really get a single one. But we couldn't pin it on bad luck. You have to give the other teams credit, too—it's a hard tournament to win and all those teams had very good players. That said, our team underachieved.

It was a bad tournament, but I think you can make a case that it was an important one for the Program of Excellence, maybe even a necessary one.

After the WJC, we analyzed what had happened in Füssen and came up with one major conclusion.

We did have an issue with team chemistry in Füssen. That really showed through when the team first faced adversity and never recovered. It was decided that we had to take what had been that team's flaw and make it a strength in our program going forward. We determined that we had to put a real emphasis on team building—Perry Pearn, who had been both an assistant and head coach of our world junior teams and a major contributor to the Program of Excellence, was a key guy in developing the team-building strategies.

I don't doubt for a second that we had the right players and the right coaches in Füssen. I believe, though, that we didn't do them any favours before the WJC. I'd love to take that same team back to the tournament and have another try. If we had everyone pulling together—everyone at the summer camp, everyone there for the evaluations in December, everyone through the team-building programs—I'd like our chances for gold in that field. I'd like our chances even more if the players had been through the under-17 and under-18 teams in the years before the world juniors.

It was my first year scouting for the Program of Excellence—I had worked as a scout for the Quebec Nordiques and as general manager of the Seattle Thunderbirds. The '92 world juniors was a tough introduction. That said, I think that Füssen taught us a lot about what it was going to take to win the world juniors. And it's no coincidence that after our poorest showing to that point, Canadian teams would bring home the gold the next five years.

1993

GÄVLE
THE BULLETIN BOARD

TIM WHARNSBY

Defenceman Joël Bouchard coolly controls the puck in Canada's 9–1 rout of the Russians. The Canadian defence faced a tougher test against a high-flying Swedish team featuring Peter Forsberg.

The turning point in the 1993 world junior tournament in Gävle, Sweden, wasn't a goal, a save, or a hit. It was a bold prediction made by Sweden's star forward Peter Forsberg, who told reporters that his team had nothing to fear in playing Canada the next day.

The Canadian juniors were underdogs because of their youth and because the Swedish roster featured plenty of returnees from the team that lost 4–3 to Russia in the gold-medal-deciding game a year before. Forsberg centred wings Markus Näslund and Niklas Sundstrom on the most productive line in tournament history. The three would combine for 30 goals and 69 points in 1993 on a Swedish team that scored a remarkable 53 goals in the seven-game tournament.

A much less experienced Canadian team featured the top teenage prospects in Alexandre Daigle, Chris Pronger, Chris Gratton, Paul Kariya, and Rob Niedermayer. They would wind up filling the first five slots at the NHL entry draft six months later.

The young Canadians hadn't exactly instilled fear into the Swedes when they dropped an 8–5 decision to the host country in an exhibition game days before the tournament. It was an undisciplined effort that saw Sweden check in with seven power-play goals—impressive firepower considering that Forsberg sat out the game because of the flu. A few days later there was Forsberg rinkside, watching

the first period of Canada's tournament opener against the United States. The Canucks prevailed against their North American rival with a 3–0 win, but Forsberg wasn't impressed.

"They are not so good," he said. "We are going to beat them. We are a much better team. We are better skaters. They play tough, but it's a bigger ice surface and they're going to have problems with that. They may be good, but they are not so tough."

Forsberg underestimated the roly-poly figure that guarded the Canadian goal. His name was Manny Legace, and he turned in one of the most memorable netminding performances from a Canadian junior in the program's long list of stellar goalies.

Legace gave Forsberg and other tournament observers a hint of what was to come with his wonderful 31-save effort against the United States. His shutout was preserved with 35 seconds left when forward Brian Rolston rang a shot off the post on Legace's blocker side.

Winger Martin Lapointe was one of three players returning from the 1992 team that had fallen flat in Füssen.

"I remember kissing the post afterwards," recalled Legace. "My ears were ringing from that shot. He beat me. But that game was not only a big confidence booster for me and for the whole team. We couldn't have asked for a better result going into the big game against Sweden."

With Forsberg's remarks about what he believed to be an inferior Canadian team taped to the wall of the Canadian dressing room, hard-nosed centre Tyler Wright stood up and addressed his teammates before the Sweden game. Along with Kariya and Martin Lapointe, Wright was one of three returning players from the junior team that endured the debacle in Füssen.

Part of Wright's message was about how it all started to unravel for Canada in Germany after Forsberg beat Eric Lindros on a faceoff in Canada's end late in the game, which led to a tying goal in the dying seconds. Wright also had insight into what made Forsberg tick. The two had the same agent, Winnipeg-based Don Baizley, and they had become friends at the 1991 draft. Wright had trained with Forsberg the previous summer and Forsberg had also visited Wright at his home in Kamsack, Saskatchewan.

Wright's speech didn't have the impact he hoped for. Canada was badly outplayed, but because of Legace's determination the Canadian juniors were down only 1–0 after 20 minutes. Canadian head coach Perry Pearn blasted his teenagers in the first intermission. The harsh words did the trick. It was 3–2 for Canada after two periods and the kids hung on for a 5–4 victory.

It wasn't Wright's speech or Pearn's tirade that did the trick. It was Forsberg's braggadocio. "What [Forsberg] said definitely gave us a boost," Canadian defenceman Brent Tully said.

The usually circumspect Pearn took a not-so-subtle shot at Forsberg afterwards. "I would like to know what Peter Forsberg thinks about our team now."

Even in defeat, though, Forsberg didn't concede anything. "I thought we were a better team," he said. "But obviously they were the better team. We lost. Sure, I regret saying it now. But we are still going to win [the tournament] anyway. I hope I don't regret saying that. But I think Canada will lose at least one more game."

The Canadians did lose to Czechoslovakia in their final game in the round-robin tournament, but they had already locked up the gold medal by then. They had rolled over Russia 9–1 in a game that pitted Daigle against Viktor Kozlov, who was touted as a possible first-overall selection, two days after the sweet victory over Sweden. Then they escaped with a 3–2 win over Finland.

Defenceman Scott Niedermayer and four of his teammates on the Canadian roster would be the first five picks in the NHL draft months after the victory in Gävle.

In the win over Finland, Pearn and Legace again played key roles. Pearn, who went on to the NHL as a long-time, valuable assistant coach in Winnipeg, Ottawa, New York, and Montreal, is a master tactician but was not known at the time for his motivational skills. In fact, he wasn't even first choice to coach the Canadian junior team that year. Alain Vigneault was originally named to head the coaching staff but had to resign in the summer when he accepted a position as an assistant coach with the Ottawa Senators.

In came Pearn, who had been an assistant coach to Guy Charron in 1990 and Dick Todd a year later. Both tournaments saw Canada win gold.

With Canada holding on to a slim 2–1 lead over Finland after 40 minutes, Pearn walked into the dressing room and cleared off the trainer's table. He then took off the 1990 world junior championship ring that he won in Finland and placed it on the table. Pearn didn't utter a word and left the room. He returned later to say: "This is what we came here to win, so let's go out there and do it."

He knew that with only Germany, Japan, and Czechoslovakia remaining on the docket, a win over Finland would lock up gold. When the final buzzer sounded, Canada improved to 4-0 with a 3–2 win. The shot clock indicated that Finland outshot Canada 60–38. The Hockey Canada staff kept its own stats and its tabulation was 45–23.

"I don't think I faced 60 shots," Legace said. "All I know is I was getting pretty tired."

Underneath his equipment Legace wore the threadbare t-shirt that he had pulled over his shoulders since his peewee days with the Don Mills Flyers, but he might as well have been wearing a Superman shirt.

"I don't think I was Superman," he said. "I just went there to do a job for my team and my country. I was just trying to do my best."

When 32 hopefuls gathered in Kitchener for the selection camp in early December, Legace was considered a long shot to crack the roster. His competition included Jocelyn Thibault, Norm Maracle, and Philippe DeRouville. At that time only DeRouville had been drafted, the previous June in the fifth round by the Pittsburgh Penguins. Thibault and Maracle were considered two of the top goalie prospects for the 1993 draft.

None of the four distinguished themselves at the selection camp, but Pearn and chief scout Sheldon Ferguson were first impressed by Legace in the summer at the evaluation camp. They liked how hard Legace competed and they had a hunch he would be the guy they could depend on.

"I just thought Manny was a big-game goalie," said Pearn, who went to grade school with Ferguson in Stettler, Alberta. "[Legace] is the type you want in there when you need a win. He is an extremely quick goaltender, who moves from side to side well. When you do that well in the international game, you will be successful."

Legace, a month shy of his 20th birthday at the time, was too good to be true on the ice and as humble as they come off the ice. He was so honoured to play for Canada that he stood ramrod straight as the national anthem played after each victory.

While Thibault went 10th overall to the Quebec Nordiques in the 1993 draft and Maracle was taken by the Detroit Red Wings five rounds later, Legace had to wait until the eighth round before the Hartford Whalers called his name. The native of Alliston, Ontario, spent a season with the national team and then toiled away in the minors for almost five years before he made his NHL debut with the Los Angeles Kings. He wound up winning a Stanley Cup with the 2001–02 Red Wings as Dominik Hasek's backup.

Before he could claim his WJC gold, Legace wound up beating Germany 5–2 to set up an anticlimactic gold-medal-clinching 8–1 win over Japan before a small crowd of 625 in Hudiksvall, a fishing village 130 kilometres north of Gävle. The Hudiksvall rink was a beautiful wooden structure built in 1989 and provided a

church-like setting for Canada's subdued celebration.

The Canadian juniors still had one more game to play against the former Czechoslovakia, which broke up into the Czech Republic and Slovakia at midnight on New Year's Eve. Legace gave way to DeRouville in the tournament finale that turned out to be a 7–4 loss for Canada.

But Legace already had locked up a spot on the tournament all-star team and top goaltender honours with his sparkling 6-0 record, 1.67 goals-against average, and .955 save percentage.

"Manny was by far the best goalie, and maybe the best player overall in the tournament," Wright said. "He did more than anybody on our team."

Many consider Manny Legace's performance in the 1993 tournament as the greatest ever by a Canadian goaltender in the WJC. His numbers (6-0 record, 1.67 goals-against average, .955 save percentage) have not been matched to date.

1994

OSTRAVA
THE PLUCKY UNDERDOGS

TIM WHARNSBY

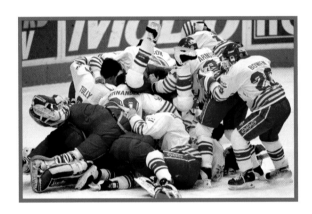

A narrow win over the Swedes in the final game of the round robin set off a wild celebration. Here, captain Brent Tully leaps into the arms of his teammates.

The depth of the Canadian junior program had never been tested like it was in 1994, when 10 junior-aged players had fixed themselves with addresses in the NHL or were trying to earn a spot on the Canadian Olympic team roster.

The total almost had been 11, but Olympic team head coach Tom Renney released Martin Gendron to the Canadian juniors. This was a welcome development, because Gendron, the Washington Capitals' 1992 third-round pick from Valleyfield, Quebec, was a prolific scorer who had checked in with five goals in seven games in the 1993 world junior tournament and would score six times for Canada in 1994.

The Winter Games in Lillehammer were a mere eight weeks away when Canadian junior head coach Joe Canale and his assistants Mike Johnston and Danny Flynn assembled in Kitchener for the selection camp. After the debacle in Füssen two years prior, the Canadian junior program had adopted a policy requiring all possible candidates to participate in the selection camp. This policy was intended to help team cohesion—on and off the ice—during the selection camp.

That made juniors Paul Kariya, Todd Warriner, and Brett Lindros unavailable because they were slated to play for the Olympic team hopefuls in the Izvestia Tournament in Moscow before Christmas, and they also were expected to see action on a six-game exhibition tour in Russia and the Czech Republic over the holidays.

The younger Lindros didn't end up accompanying Kariya and Warriner to Lillehammer because he didn't make the final cut, but in the end, whether or not Lindros suited up for Canada at the WJC did not matter. The seven junior-aged Canadians in the NHL were Alexandre Daigle, Chris Pronger, Chris Gratton, Rob Niedermayer, Jason Arnott, Mike Rathje, and goalie Jocelyn Thibault.

"We knew a lot would be said about who was not here, those 10 juniors playing in the NHL or with the Canadian Olympic team," said Canadian junior captain Brent Tully, who along with Gendron and defenceman Joël Bouchard were the only returnees from 1993. "In a way not having those guys was a good thing for us. It took pressure off us. The 22 players we had were excellent players, very capable of winning a gold medal. If we were looked upon as underdogs, then great. It was all that more sweet when we won."

This edition of the Canadian junior team had the perfect coach in Canale to lead the way. He overcame an episode of extreme adversity earlier in his life when his junior coaching career was just beginning, but he patiently persevered.

Back on February 20, 1978, Canale was a few months into his first major junior coaching job with the Shawinigan Dynamos when he was awakened by RCMP officers and arrested at his home on charges of trafficking narcotics in a Montreal coffee house that he had invested in.

Though Canale was later pardoned, his coaching career had taken a hit. A dozen years passed before brave Chicoutimi Saguenéens owner Jeannot Harvey took a risk and hired Canale, who rewarded that faith by steering the Saguenéens to their first QMJHL title and a trip to the 1991 Memorial Cup tournament in Quebec City.

"Joe was one of the best coaches I've had," said former Toronto Maple Leafs netminder Félix Potvin, who starred for Chicoutimi during that championship season. "He cared about us as people. But he also knew the right time to lean on us and push us."

Canale, who assisted Perry Pearn at the previous world junior tournament, continued to push the right buttons in Ostrava, Czech Republic, in 1994, and he left an impression.

"I was lucky enough to have Joe Canale as a coach for two gold medals," Tully said. "As far I was concerned Canada should have had him coaching every year. But the way this one finished, it was definitely sweeter. You couldn't ask for a better finish."

Canadian defenceman Chris Armstrong dumps Finnish centre Juha Lind in a victory that was likely the team's best game in Ostrava.

Not only did Canale have Johnston and Flynn by his side, but Pearn was in Ostrava, too. He was coaching in Switzerland for Ambri-Piotta and was on a break. Pearn was there to help in any way he could. But despite the absence of some of Canada's best junior-aged talent, Canale had his team's title defence headed in the right direction after opening victories against Switzerland and Germany by a combined score of 10–3.

The third game of the tournament against Russia, however, was a different story. The Canadian juniors blew a 3–0 lead in the third period and starting goalie Jamie Storr was ineffective. So Canale made the move to backup Manny Fernandez for the next three games and the change had an immediate impact. Canada put forth its best all-around performance of the tournament in a 6–3 win over Finland.

"We definitely proved with this win we are one of the top teams in this tournament," said Canadian winger Anson Carter, who came to the forefront with a goal and an assist. "I'll admit we were down on ourselves after blowing a 3–0 lead to Russia. We doubted ourselves after that game. But now we have nothing but confidence. We're going to finish off these final three games with our best hockey yet and get that gold."

Canada beat the United States 8–3 and the Czech Republic 6–4 to set up a gold-medal-deciding game against Sweden on the final day of the round-robin tournament. All of a sudden the underdog Canadians were a win away from another championship.

When the Canadians arrived at Ostrava a couple days before the tournament began, they found themselves in a hardscrabble setting. Ostrava was a steel town and the arena was on its outskirts. If the streetcar across the street went left, you wound up downtown. If it turned right, a few blocks later you were right in the middle of a steel mill.

There were security concerns. Ostrava is near the Polish border. Pickpockets and thieves had their run of the city's streets. Players were warned of the dangers and were kept under close watch. Storr's father Jim had a jacket lifted in a downtown restaurant. Flynn woke up one night in his hotel room to find an intruder that he scared away with a shout before any damage was done.

Because of these circumstances the Canadians were confined to one floor of the hotel that was right beside the rink. This turned out to be a good thing, because these teenagers quickly built cohesion, a togetherness.

Jason Botterill, here fighting through a check, would end up with the shiniest medal collection of any player to come through the Program of Excellence. He won the first of his three gold medals in Ostrava.

"As a coaching staff we didn't focus on who could be on the team, but simply who wanted to be there," Johnston said. "When we met for the summer camp and again for our training camp in Switzerland just prior to the tournament, our number one priority was to build this group into a real team. We tried to drive home the message that even though we had no NHL experience and no stars, we could come together and be a team."

The Swedish team was staying at the same hotel as the Canadians. The young Canadians saw up close and personal just how confident the Swedes were. The Swedes strutted around, believing nobody could touch them. They had finished second in the previous two tournaments, and their lineup boasted high-end talent like Kenny Jonsson, Mattias Öhlund, Mats Lindgren, Niklas Sundstrom, Jesper Mattsson, and Anders Eriksson.

They looked at the Canadians like they were a bunch of no-names. Canale and his staff played the underdog card to motivate their team.

"We weren't even picked to win a medal," defenceman Bryan McCabe said. "Everyone had written us off because guys like Pronger and Kariya weren't made available to us. But I thought the coaching staff did a tremendous job in using it as a rallying point. We just used it as motivation and ran with it."

The Canadians, 5-0-1, had what they wanted—a shot at gold. A loss or tie did them no good against the Swedes, who had six wins in six games. Canada needed a win. In the off-day before the showdown, there was a noticeable change around the hotel. All of a sudden the confident Swedes didn't appear as sure about the outcome. They could see a determination in the Canadians.

"We had nothing to lose," Harvey said. "The pressure was on them because we weren't even supposed to win a medal."

The only decision left for Canale was his starter in goal. Fernandez wasn't sharp against the Czechs, so he went back with Storr. The move turned out to be golden. The Canadians jumped out to leads of 2–0 and 5–2 on goals from Aaron Gavey, Yanick Dubé, Jason Allison, and Gendron with a pair. But the Canadians didn't make it easy on themselves. The Swedes beat Storr twice in the third period to set up a frantic final minute.

Rick Girard embodied the breakneck commitment of the 1994 Canadian juniors. Here, he crashes the crease, literally, going headfirst over American Kevyn Adams and into the net.

Canada was short-handed and the Swedes pulled their goalie for a 6-on-4 advantage. Gavey made a sensational play when he intercepted a pass that would easily have been converted for the final goal. Then Rick Girard stripped Jonsson of the puck and scored into an empty net with six seconds remaining.

Every one of the Canadian players jumped off the bench to celebrate. Luckily, the on-ice officials decided against a delay-of-game penalty for the exuberant bunch. Instead, the final seconds were ticked off the clock and real celebrations began.

Harvey played with a painful hip injury, but exhibited tremendous grit. Girard persevered through a bothersome shoulder ailment. Tully underwent an emergency appendectomy in late October and had to play himself back into condition during the tournament.

"Being called a bunch of no-names hit a lot of us in the heart," Gavey said. "We wanted to prove we were good enough to win. We are proud of where we come from. We all worked hard to get here."

1995

RED DEER
THE DREAM TEAM

TIM WHARNSBY

Head coach Don Hay brought in forward Darcy Tucker (right) and defenceman Nolan Baumgartner from his Kamloops Blazers, the defending Memorial Cup champions. After adding a WJC gold, Hay, Tucker, and Baumgartner would lead the Blazers to a second consecutive Memorial Cup.

All eyes were on head coach Don Hay when he blew his whistle to begin the 34-player Canadian junior selection camp in Edmonton in mid-December 1994. The country was three months into the NHL lockout and the 1995 world junior championship in Red Deer could not have come at a better time.

Fans were starving for something to sink their teeth into. So there was Alexandre Daigle, Ed Jovanovski, Ryan Smyth, and Co. ready for the intense spotlight. The NHL was on hiatus and the tournament was being contested on home soil, where it matters the most.

The media dubbed the Canadians the "Dream Team." Theirs was a powerhouse squad even though out-of-work junior-aged NHLers Chris Gratton and Brendan Witt decided not to report to their junior teams in Kingston and Seattle and thus weren't eligible to play for Canada in Red Deer.

Either way, Hay detested hyperbole. He was a fireman and preached teamwork. He preached chemistry. He wanted players to buy into the team concept, not believe the hyperbole.

"I didn't like this Dream Team image," Hay said. "I don't think it was fair to the kids. Putting that label on it hurt them. We just kept stressing that there were a lot of good teams out there and they hadn't won anything yet."

The Dream Team idea was hard to ignore, however. Seven players already were under contract to NHL teams. Daigle was the first selection in the 1993 NHL entry draft and Jovanovski went first overall in 1994. Wade Redden was expected to be among the first two choices in 1995. In total, 17 of the 34 juniors invited to the camp were first-round NHL picks. Two more, in Redden and Brad Church (who didn't make the team), were drafted in the first round six months later.

On the final day of the evaluation camp, Hay made two controversial cuts: Jocelyn Thibault and Brett Lindros. Thibault had made 29 appearances for the Quebec Nordiques in 1993–94, but had seen limited action prior to the camp because of a shoulder ailment. The Lindros decision was a surprising development that the player didn't take well.

Asked if he was bitter, the younger brother of NHL superstar Eric snapped, "big time."

"I thought I played well enough to make this team—evidently not," Lindros said. "Donnie just said, 'Hey, you're more suited to the pro style.' There's no arguing with that. I'm pretty disappointed. He said he wanted a checker, and I checked. Now he wants more finesse out of me. I just don't know."

Hay remarked at the time that Lindros's skating held him back. "He has good assets, but we were probably looking for somebody that could skate a little better," Hay said. "More speed. In international games, speed is so important."

Once the roster was finalized, Hay had to keep his players from being distracted by the spotlight. This wasn't the only powerhouse team that Hay had coached. The previous spring he had won the Memorial Cup as the Kamloops head coach, but even more instructive were lessons he learned working as an assistant to Ken Hitchcock with the same club a few seasons before. That earlier edition of the Blazers had won the WHL championship to advance to the 1991 Memorial Cup, and though they were loaded with talent, they were the first team eliminated from the tournament. When they were asked for opinions afterwards as to what went wrong in Hamilton, the players remarked they weren't given much downtime and spent too much time sequestered in their hotel.

Hay made sure that wasn't going to be an issue in Red Deer. There were volleyball matches organized, walks in the park, and even an outdoor game of shinny was played prior to the tournament. Hay also had plenty of inspirational sayings plastered on the walls of the dressing room. One of the coach's favourites: "You can't count the days, you've got to make the days count."

"You have to pay attention to the player's mental state just as much as his physical

Defenceman Bryan McCabe contributed a big goal in a come-from-behind victory over the Czechs, the only stiff challenge the Dream Team faced throughout play in Red Deer.

skills," Hay said. "The mental part of the game is just as important. The motivation part also is key in a tournament like this where you have to refocus very quickly. In 1990 we went to the Memorial Cup and we had a pretty good hockey team, but it was like we were in jail all week and we didn't play very good."

Hay's Canadian junior team was very good in 1995. They opened the eight-team round-robin tournament with three lopsided victories, 7–1 over Ukraine, 9–1 against Germany, and 8–3 over the rival United States. But the games were about to become more difficult.

The Canadians travelled south to Calgary to take on the Czechs and escaped with a hard-fought 7–5 victory. Canada trailed 3–1 after the first period, but tied it up at 4–4 in the second period on goals from Bryan McCabe, Marty Murray, and Todd Harvey, only to see the Czechs go ahead 5–4 before the second intermission. Redden drew Canada even with four minutes remaining, then blueliner Jamie Rivers put Canada ahead for good with 2 minutes, 24 seconds left.

McCabe crashes the net in Canada's 8–3 rout of the United States. In their first three games, the Canadians lived up to the Dream Team hype, outscoring opponents 24–5.

"The Czechs always gave us trouble and we were playing before a crazy crowd that night," Harvey recalled. "I remember the coaching staff told us to tighten up defensively and that there was to be no pinching from the defencemen. So Jamie Rivers pinches in all the way into the corner, picks up the puck, and scores."

The Canadian juniors went to Edmonton for a New Year's Day tilt against Finland and prevailed 6–4 to secure a medal. They returned to Red Deer for a game against Russia, which they won 8–5, though they didn't clinch the gold until 40 minutes after the final horn, thanks to Finland's late-game comeback to tie Sweden 3–3.

"To be honest, I thought the Finland-Sweden game was supposed to start in a few hours," said forward Jason Allison, who won a world junior gold medal for the second time. "Then I was undressing and somebody yelled it was 3–1 Sweden. I came out of the shower and some of the guys were yelling it was 3–3. It's great to win a second, but it would have been better winning it out on the ice against Sweden."

Jere Karalahti provided the heroics for Finland with his game-tying goal with 2:51 remaining. It was just another bizarre chapter in his life. Earlier in the tournament, he'd gone AWOL from the Finnish team after he met some new friends in a local bar and went off with them to party for a few days.

Winger Eric Daze was unheralded before the tournament but emerged as one of Canada's best players and a WJC all-star.

"Find out where Jere is staying, we have to send him something," Harvey yelled after the goal.

With the gold medal locked up, Canada went off to a country bar to celebrate. They had a day off before the tournament finale against Sweden. At stake not only was Canada's first perfect 7-0 record at a world junior tournament, but also the fact that if they could beat Sweden, Canada would do a favour for their new-found Finnish friends. A Sweden loss and a Finland win over Russia on the final day of the tournament would give Finland the silver medal.

Finland, however, was beaten 6–2 by Russia. Canada enjoyed a 4–3 win after Sweden made it close with goals 18 seconds apart with two minutes remaining in the third period.

For all the attention given to heralded pro prospects, two of the least-known players might have been the best during the tournament: Marty Murray and Eric Daze. Both were taken in the fourth round of the 1994 NHL entry draft. The Chicago Blackhawks chose Daze six spots before the Calgary Flames took Murray. Murray, a cousin of former Los Angeles Kings and St. Louis Blues coach Andy Murray, checked in with six goals and 15 points for Canada, while Daze scored eight times in seven games. His big outing came when he scored a hat trick against Russia.

"I just wanted to make the team," he said. "I would have never dreamed of scoring three against Russia."

The guy Daze beat out to make the Canadian roster was Brett Lindros.

"Going into the Edmonton camp [Daze] was probably fifth or sixth on the depth chart," Hay said. "He kept getting better and better. I thought he was one of the best players in camp. He put some right wingers out of a job. He had great hands for a big guy and he skated really well for a guy his size."

Daze was raised in Laval, Quebec, and played his minor hockey with Daigle. He mostly played with Daigle in the tournament, and off the ice Daze also enjoyed the company of the outgoing Daigle, who was thrilled about his linemate's success. "Everybody was focusing on me, but right now he's the centre point and he's got to enjoy it, too," Daigle said after the Russia game.

"I'm a shy guy and I don't talk a lot," Daze said. "[Daigle] talked to me a lot and brought me along with the rest of the guys."

Unfortunately, Daze's career with the Blackhawks was limited to 226 goals in 601 games because he was forced to retire after chronic back woes. While Daze was the biggest player on the Canadian roster at 6-foot-5, 205 pounds, the 5-foot-9, 168-pound Murray was the smallest.

But Murray, who grew up on a crop and cattle farm near Lyleton in southern Manitoba, not far from the U.S. border, had a tremendous amount of character. His passion for hockey ran deep. He would play for two teams some seasons in his youth—both his rural team and the nearby city team.

Murray ran up against the old not-big-enough stigma. But he was big enough and skilled enough to play 14 pro seasons on both sides of the pond, including 261 NHL games for the Flames, Kings, Flyers, and Hurricanes, and win a Calder Cup championship with the 2000–01 Saint John Flames.

"He has excelled at every level," Hay said after the perfect 7-0 run. "He's probably the smartest player I've ever coached and just has tremendous feel for the game."

That's one of the most remarkable achievements of the Program of Excellence. It's not just that Team Canada draws on the immense talent this country produces or showcases future stars on their way to professional stardom. It's that every year there will be a guy who may never be a household name or a millionaire, who nevertheless shines among those future stars on the brightest stage any of these young men have ever encountered.

Centre Jason Allison (right) was just one of a crowd of Canadian players who would jump directly to the NHL the following fall.

1996

BOSTON
THE BREAKTHROUGH FOR JAROME

GARE JOYCE

Jarome Iginla, who would go on to lead Canada to two Olympic gold medals, first burst onto the scene at the WJC in Boston. Just days before the start of the tournament, the Dallas Stars traded Iginla's NHL rights to the Calgary Flames.

The 1996 tournament will be remembered for many things but it won't be remembered by many hockey fans in Boston. The stands were virtually empty for most games, including the medal-round games. It wasn't entirely a lack of interest in hockey. *The Boston Globe* put citizens on alert for the storm of the century not once, not twice, but three times over the course of 10 days. The streets of the city seemed to be deserted, though someone might have been buried under a drift. "Find a Way" was adopted as the Canadian team's motto during its training camp, but for many on hand, finding a way to the arena was a challenge.

Those who were there or watched the tournament back in Canada remember the 1996 WJC as the coming-out party for Jarome Iginla. The Edmonton-born right winger put in arguably the best-ever performance by a Canadian forward in any under-20 championship and one that has been matched only a couple of times by individual players regardless of position or nationality. He led the tournament in scoring with five goals and seven assists in six games—but those numbers only hint at his impact. Whenever Canada needed a big play, Iginla was on the scene.

Today it's hard to think of Iginla arriving. It seems like he has always been there. There's a generation of hockey fans who can't remember a time when Iginla wasn't a fixture in the Canadian lineup. He was a leader in 2002, scoring two goals against

Jarome Iginla was a member of the Memorial Cup champion Kamloops Blazers when he was added to the Canadian roster. He led the team in scoring with five goals and seven assists in 12 games and was picked as the tournament's top forward.

the U.S. in the final in Salt Lake City when the Canadian men's team won its first Olympic gold in hockey in 50 years. Eight years later he dug the puck out of the corner and hit Sidney Crosby with the pass that set up Sid the Kid for the golden goal in the overtime victory over the Americans at the Vancouver Olympics.

In 1996 Iginla was making his debut on a major international stage, but NHL scouts knew all about him, having watched him with the two-time Memorial Cup champion Kamloops Blazers. He had been the 11th-overall pick of the Dallas Stars the previous June. Fans in Calgary would have recognized his name—the week before the tournament, the Stars traded him to the Flames for two-time 50-goal scorer and fan favourite Joe Nieuwendyk. Many of those fans were at first critical of the trade, but in Boston Iginla gave them reason to suspect he'd someday be the Flames' captain.

The Canadian Hockey Association had Iginla on its radar early. He'd played for Team Pacific, the bronze medallists from the 1994 world under-17 challenge in Amos, Quebec. Later that year he'd played in the national under-18 program,

leading the Canadian team in scoring in summer-tournament play in the Czech Republic.

He was known to the coach of the 1996 Canadian junior team. Marcel Comeau had coached his Kelowna Rockets against Iginla and the Kamloops Blazers. In fact, three of Iginla's Blazers teammates would also make the Canadian team's roster: two blueliners, team captain Nolan Baumgartner and Jason Holland, and left winger Hnat Domenichelli. Domenichelli had played across from Iginla for two seasons and, though they meshed seamlessly, they couldn't have been more different. Iginla, at 6-foot-1 and 190 pounds, was a power forward who rolled over and went through defenders, while Domenichelli relied on speed to slip in and out of traffic.

When players reported to the evaluation camp in Campbellton, New Brunswick, Comeau and Team Canada's management had a clear idea of the talent they were going to be working with. "We will have to be a disciplined two-way team and we will have to be opportunistic offensively," the coach said on the eve of the tournament. "We will not blow anybody out of the water. I think we have enough

Hnat Domenichelli, here on a scoring chance against Sweden in the final, played on Canada's top line with Iginla, his Kamloops teammate, and centre Daymond Langkow.

offence to get us there." Comeau had projected Iginla as a first-liner, the most likely source of that offence. Iginla was, Comeau said, "a real handful down low, too much of a handful for most anyone in the Western Hockey League." Playing with Domenichelli and gritty centre Daymond Langkow, he lived up to those expectations and far exceeded them.

Comeau did have his team pegged. The Canadian roster featured only a couple of forwards over 6 feet and more than 200 pounds. Iginla, Langkow, and Alyn McCauley were the only players up front who would end up playing any significant time in the NHL. After Iginla, the next forward who was slotted as a pure scorer was Jason Podollan, a 40-goal shooter with the Spokane Chiefs that season. Podollan didn't score until the semifinal, and he would wind up registering just one NHL goal in 41 career games. The team had to lean on Iginla for offence.

Iginla's numbers were impressive, but the idea that he was something special crystallized when Canada faced its stiffest challenge. In fact, after four fairly routine wins in the preliminary round, the semifinal against Russia was the first real challenge the Canadian teens had to stare down. These rivals ranked as the two best teams in the tournament—the best by far, really. That they met in the semis rather than the final might be misleading. The Russians lost their first game in Boston to the Czechs but gave every indication that they weren't showing all their cards early. They moved their phenom Sergei Samsonov from the fourth line only just before their quarter-final win over the Finns, a 6–2 rout. The Russians looked like a different team from the one that had lost to the Czechs, and Alexei Morozov raised his game to the point where he was challenging Iginla for the tournament's top forward honours. More than a few folks at the tournament figured the Russians were sandbagging and hoping to catch Canada by surprise.

Iginla's moment came in the third period against the Russians. Canada was clinging to a 3–2 lead despite being outshot almost two-to-one—the final shot numbers were 49 for Russia and 28 for Canada, and the defending champions were only in the game thanks to an impressive performance by goaltender José Théodore. The pivotal play came on a Russian power play. Though Iginla was the Canadian team's best offensive threat, he was also the first choice for the penalty kill, and he showed the opportunism that Comeau had ranked as necessary to gold-medal hopes. Morozov circled back into the Russian end to retrieve a loose puck. Iginla gave chase but Morozov had a couple of steps on him. It looked like Iginla was just putting token pressure on the Russian forward but would peel back into the neutral zone once Morozov took possession. When Iginla kept coming, Morozov thought he had a chance to slip by Iginla and leave him in his wake going back up the ice. Rather than making a safe play, clearing the puck and regrouping, Morozov decided to get cute—too cute, as it turned out.

Right: Defenceman Chris Phillips led a Canadian blue line that improved going into the medal round. The key game was a tense contest with the Russians in the semifinal.

Iginla had a good idea that Morozov was going to try to do something along those lines. Scouting the Russians' earlier games in Boston, the Canadian staff had spotted their tendency to make high-risk plays in their own end during power plays. Iginla and the Canadian penalty killers had read the scouting report and were put on high alert. "We wanted to pressure their power play, because we knew they liked to dipsy-doodle around a little in the centre ice area," Iginla said after the game. "We were looking for it."

When Morozov tried to flip the puck by Iginla, the Canadian forward snared it—blocking the puck in his mid-section, letting it drop to the ice, and then taking it in flight on the Russian goal. Morozov was caught leaning the wrong way and couldn't get back into the play. He could only watch as Iginla went in on Russian goaltender Alexei Egorov and beat him cleanly to make it 4–2.

Often, a goal coming against play—especially a short-handed one—might have been a soul-crusher, but the Russians continued to surge and Morozov scored a few minutes later to pull the Russians back within a goal. In fact, with 10 seconds left in the game, he almost fully atoned for his gaffe, setting up Ruslan Shafikov alone in front of the Canadian goal with Théodore out of position and helpless. Shafikov, however, fanned on the shot and before he could take a second stab at it Iginla arrived at the edge of the crease to lock him up.

With his 46 saves, José Théodore's performance would have been the big story in almost any other circumstances. This, however, was Iginla's night. It wasn't, however, the end of his heroics in Boston. Canada still had to beat Sweden in the final for the gold.

Since the WJC went to a playoff format, the '96 final stands among the most anticlimactic of gold-medal games. The Swedes had a few talented players, but they gave you the feeling they were just happy to have made it as far as the final. On the eve of the final, club teams in the Swedish elite league called back two of the three best defencemen on the juniors' roster. It would have been hard for anyone to like the Swedes' chances, including the Swedes.

The Canadian juniors weren't in their top form in the final. They had spent a lot of emotion in the semifinal and for 20 minutes allowed the Swedes to hang around. With the score tied one-all, Iginla again made a defining play that led to the winning goal. He didn't score it, but he created it with a smart read of the play and brute force. In a battle for the puck along the boards, Iginla knocked Swedish defenceman David Halvardsson reeling in the corner and then made a pass from behind the net to his centre Daymond Langkow. It wound up being one of Iginla's three assists in a 4–1 win. What's more, it sent messages. To his teammates, the message was that physical intensity was going to deliver them gold. To the Swedes, it was that you get in Jarome Iginla's way at your peril.

Iginla's wasn't the biggest hit in the game—honours for that would go to defenceman Denis Gauthier, who put an open-ice charge into a Swedish forward who had his head down. On impact, you could hear him grunt and groan even if you were halfway up the empty stands. Thereafter, the Swedes moved farther and farther out on the perimeter and almost out of the Boston area code—and by game's end, though trailing, they just rolled back into the neutral zone and were trying to keep the score relatively close.

Celebrating in the dressing room—and with his gold medal still hanging around his neck—Iginla said he hoped to be in the NHL at the start of the 1996–97 season. If he was going to be back in junior, he said, he wanted to help Canada go for a fifth consecutive gold at the WJC. "Having that maple leaf on our chests gives us more energy at times, being part of Canada's hockey tradition. When the going gets tough, it gives us a little extra, because when we were young we would watch Canada play and we always prevailed."

CHA executives weren't counting on his availability for Geneva. The Program of Excellence is a learning program, and Jarome Iginla's education, at least this part of it, was complete. They knew that they had seen a young man already primed for bigger things. If they had any illusions about that, Iginla's performance on his return to Kamloops obliterated them—he would end up scoring 79 goals in 79 WHL regular-season and playoff games and leading Kamloops to a third consecutive Memorial Cup championship. But it turned out he'd get a chance to wear the maple leaf on his chest sooner than he might have expected. In the spring of '97, after his rookie year with the Flames, Iginla was the youngest player selected to join Canada's team at the world championships—picking up a couple of goals, three assists, and another gold medal.

For Iginla, it has come full circle 15 years later. In that dressing room in Boston, after a game played in a vacant arena, Jarome Iginla talked about watching Canada play and prevail when he was young. He couldn't have imagined the influence he'd have down the line or his place in the program's tradition. The play Iginla made in the gold-medal game in Boston looked an awful lot like that pass to Sidney Crosby as he poured in on the American net in overtime in Vancouver. And when Jarome Iginla emerged as a star in Boston, Sidney Crosby was eight years old.

1997

GENEVA
THE RESILIENT OVERACHIEVERS

MIKE BABCOCK

Centre Alyn McCauley won his second WJC gold in Geneva. He was a key penalty killer and also set up linemate Boyd Devereaux's game-winning goal in the semifinal versus Russia.

Our team in Geneva wasn't the most talented team that Canada ever sent to the world juniors. We weren't especially talented at all. More talented Canadian teams have played in the tournament—and played well—and not won. I remember a reporter who had covered a lot of the tournaments coming up to me on Christmas Day and telling me that we weren't going to finish higher than sixth. I didn't think so, but I don't think that anyone looked at the team as a favourite for the championship or even a safe bet to win a medal. There was incredible pressure on the players after the program had won four straight championships. I know I felt it.

I wouldn't claim that my coaching "won" the tournament. What we had, though, were a bunch of young men who weren't the best pro prospects but knew how to play the game. We did have Joe Thornton, but that was before he was drafted first overall—he was the youngest player on our roster and he had limited ice time. We were lucky to have a few players who played their best hockey in the most important games of their career. We had players who were smart enough to figure out a way to win and had the nerve to step up when things got really tough.

I wouldn't claim that the coaches brought the team together. The leaders in our room brought us together. The one I'd point to first was our captain, Brad Larsen. He wasn't the most skilled guy but he worked hard and took charge in the room.

Goaltender Marc Denis started every game for the Canadian team and capped the tournament with a shutout victory over the United States in the gold-medal final.

He made sure that everyone was involved, that everyone parked his ego at the door. A player in the room, not a coach, has to deliver the message that team success is the only goal and individual accomplishments don't mean anything. Brad was the perfect one to deliver that message. He was comfortable standing up and talking to his teammates. He was in the centre of everything—he could put himself there but it was natural, not forced. If it was setting up a card game, he was dealing. If it seemed like some of the boys were down or maybe feeling left out, he was bringing them in. The role he took wasn't something you could ask someone to do or try to show him how to fill. When I came into the room, Brad was the one I looked to when I wanted to get a read of the team's energy and emotion. Brad wasn't a great pro prospect but he was maybe the most important player on that team.

Our road to the medal round wasn't easy. There were times when we didn't get calls that we were sure we deserved and other times we ended up on the wrong end with the referees—it was a quick education for our players that it's a different game when you're playing in Europe.

Then we had a couple of tough games in the opening round. We had been down 4–3 to the United States with about four minutes left and Peter Schaefer came through for us and tied the game. And then in our final game in the opening round, we had a one-goal lead in the last minute against the Czechs. We were on the power

play and had a chance to dump the puck into their end to ice the game. Instead, we turned the puck over, trying to force an unnecessary play.

The Czechs took the puck the other way and they beat our goalie Marc Denis with 10 seconds left.

We didn't get a bye into the medal round and those ties put us in against the Russians, a strong team, in the semis. But those two ties were good for us in the long run. They were good for building the team and getting us ready for the semis and then the final. Adversity made that team.

In the semis we were down 2–1 to the Russians after two periods, which would have been a tough spot but it was made a heck of a lot tougher when the ref gave Jason Doig a five-minute major for slashing. We lost Jason, our second-best defenceman behind Chris Phillips, and had a five-minute penalty kill. The funny thing was that the players weren't down in any way. They were sure that they were going to kill the penalty and get back into the game. I didn't need to try to pick them up or reassure them. They were really ready for this moment—all the time they had spent together in the weeks leading up to that point were going to pay off.

It really was an amazing thing. The Russians didn't get a shot during those five minutes. I was joking when I told the reporters after the game that the Russians killed off the major themselves—but, fact was, they weren't ready to deal with the

Christian Dubé, here celebrating with Brad Isbister looking on, was an important piece of the puzzle in his second trip to the world juniors.

advantage and we were ready to handle the adversity. Boyd Devereaux, who really hadn't played a lot early in the tournament, scored a couple of shifts into the penalty kill to tie the game. Boyd and Alyn McCauley were just great on that penalty kill and all through that game. Alyn set Boyd up with the winning goal midway through the period. It's a credit to the players on that team that, when things looked really tough for them, they had composure—even confidence that they were going to find a way to win.

Our kids had to come up with a clutch performance to tie the U.S. in the opening round, but in the final against the Americans they were a different team. They really had learned what they needed to do to win. Each player knew his individual responsibilities and everyone was confident that his teammates were going to do their jobs. Boyd and Alyn ended up being our two most important forwards in the medal round

and Boyd scored the winning goal when we won the final 2–0. Still, it wasn't any one player's show or one line's show. Everyone had a reason to feel his job was important, and that was how the team ended up being more than the sum of its parts.

A player who really represented the character of that team was Trent Whitfield, a winger who played for me at the time in Spokane. He wasn't invited to the national junior camp the previous summer. He has managed to play professionally for a long time and he had some injury problems that held his career back, but back in '97 he was a great junior. I didn't select him because I coached him in Spokane—in fact, in the team selection I recused myself when his name came up. On that team, though, he was a perfect utility forward. I felt like I could send Trent out—like Alyn, like Boyd—in the important situations. If the other team sent one of the top scorers out, I could send Trent to stick with him. If Trent was out on the wing and his centre was thrown out of the faceoff circle, he would come in and win the draw. He was like other players on that team—you could count on him to do all the little things right. If we had taken the 22 most talented players in major junior or the 22 best pro prospects he wouldn't have been on the team. But the Program of Excellence focuses on team building, finding players to fill roles, and Trent, as much as anybody on that team, filled his role perfectly.

Coaching that team was a tremendous opportunity for me. I'll admit that, at the time, I wasn't thinking about the opportunity as much as the pressure to win. I felt that, and everybody on the roster and involved in the program had to feel it. But in the years after, that tournament has had a huge impact on my career, like it has for other coaches who have taken Canadian teams to the WJC. My involvement with the under-20 program and the Olympic team has allowed me to meet and talk with and work with those coaches, and all of them have been generous to share what they've learned through their experiences.

For me, Geneva in '97 was an opportunity for personal and professional growth, and I know that others who have worked with these teams over the years feel the same way. I'm sure that it was an important educational experience for the players, too. I've stayed in touch with Brad Larsen—he's a coach now and he's going to be a great one. He might have picked up a thing or two from me, but I'm sure he picked up a whole lot more from his role as captain of a championship team. He learned about what it takes to win from his experience with a team that won the hard way.

Left: Cameron Mann, Jason Doig (plate aloft), and Daniel Brière (in flag cape) celebrate Canada's victory over the United States in the gold-medal game. The team's chances of getting to the final looked dim when Doig was assessed a major penalty at the end of the second period in the semifinal against Russia.

1998

HÄMEENLINNA
THE HUMBLING GAME

JESSE WALLIN

Forward Josh Holden holds up a Russian opponent in Canada's 2–1 quarter-final overtime loss. After that game, Holden, the team's leading goal scorer, was suspended along with defenceman Brad Ference and forward Brian Willsie for team discipline violations.

The Program of Excellence has given me great memories from victories and awful ones from the most humiliating defeat you can imagine. I learned a lot about the game from both.

I was named captain of the '98 team in Finland. Cory Sarich and I were the two returning players from the Geneva team. We had a great experience in '97 and we saw how the Program of Excellence could and should work. We had outstanding leadership in '97—from Mike Babcock, from our captain, Brad Larsen, and from other players in the room. Everyone bought in and had faith. Everyone took a lot of pride, and anyone who had to play a different role didn't hesitate—Alyn McCauley was one of the best junior players in Canada, maybe the best, and Mike asked him to play the third line. It wasn't a problem. He took it as a challenge and so did everyone else who was asked to do something different from what he was used to with his junior team. We all understood how hard it was going to be to win that tournament.

In '98 we had the talent to win gold again but things felt different, even before the tournament started. It just felt different. It's hard to put a finger on exactly why. It wasn't just one thing. We had an inexperienced group, but that wouldn't be enough to explain how things fell apart. We might have been the favourites in '98, and a lot of players on the team were more talented than players on the '97 squad. But in '98 there were cliques

Forward Matt Cooke sticks with a Russian winger in the quarterfinal. Cooke would be knocked out of the tournament with a concussion.

on the team, just a different attitude overall. A lot of the players were focused on the wrong things. They were worried about themselves first and foremost, taking an I'm-on-my-own-page attitude. What happened on the ice was a by-product of that attitude and a loss of discipline off the ice as well.

When we left for Europe after the training camp I thought things would get straightened out, but I knew we were in trouble after the first period of our first game in the tournament. We were playing the Finns in Helsinki on Christmas Day, a real challenge. When we went back to the dressing room in the first intermission, I felt like we were still in a good position to win—the game was scoreless and we were as good as the Finns. But I was shocked by what I saw in the room—one of our players slammed his stick and helmet down and started complaining about not being on the power play. That just wouldn't have happened in '97.

We showed that we had a pretty talented team in that game. We jumped out to a 1–0 lead and Alex Tanguay scored to tie the game two-all in the third period after Finland had fought back. But the Finns scored a goal with less than four minutes to go and won 3–2. We almost tied the game again right at the end. Maybe things would have turned out differently if we had, but there's no way to know. The Finns ended up winning the tournament and we barely lost to them, even though they had twice as many power plays as we did and we were still supposed to be coming together as a team—supposed to be.

But we started to fall apart at that point. We lost to the Swedes the next game 4–0 and we didn't compete. At that point we started to take undisciplined penalties, retaliatory penalties. We spent a full period of that game shorthanded—a few minors would have been okay but we had unsportsmanlike penalties and roughing calls, penalties that really hurt us. We were taking retaliatory penalties right at the time when we needed to suck it up, take one for the team, and be disciplined. We had a couple of guys who were benched after taking completely unnecessary penalties. It was embarrassing.

It looked like we might get it together in our next two games to advance to the quarter-finals. First we beat the Czechs 5–0; then we beat Germany 4–1. My time

Centre Vincent Lecavalier, a 17-year-old scoring sensation with Rimouski in the QMJHL, was expected to be an offensive catalyst but registered only one goal and one assist in seven games.

It seemed that it couldn't get worse for Canada after losses to Finland, Sweden, Russia, and the United States. But the loss to Kazakhstan in the seventh-place game added insult to injury. It was Canada's worst finish in the history of the WJC.

on the ice ended in the German game. I broke a bone blocking a shot and I was in a cast and crutches the rest of the tournament. I learned the hardest way possible that you can't lead a team from the sidelines.

I wanted to win a gold medal in '98 even more than I did in '97. Winning it once made me want it more the next time. I had come back from a broken arm that I had suffered that fall in a car accident and I probably came back too soon, but that's how much I wanted to play in the world juniors again. It was agonizing not to be able to play. What I saw the rest of the way was a lack of commitment and there was nothing I could do about it.

In the quarter-finals we played the Russians in Hämeenlinna. It started out strangely. Our team had to wear the sweaters of the Hämeenlinna club team in the first period because we thought we were scheduled for red sweaters, not our whites. So we were the first and so far only Canadian team not to wear the maple leaf. Our white sweaters didn't arrive until the intermission. That was typical of the game and the tournament—everything just felt a little bit off. We still had a great chance to go ahead to the medal round. It was one-all at the end of regulation and Eric Brewer hit the post with a shot from the point in overtime. But with 30 seconds left in the first overtime period, there were a bunch of mistakes, a shift that was too long, a safe play that could have been made and wasn't, a pinch at the wrong time, and the Russians took the puck the other way and scored.

I thought that it could never get worse in hockey than that loss. Not even close. In the consolation rounds, we played the United States first—a game that we should have been able to get up for, no matter what had happened against the Russians. But our team was really falling apart.

Two other guys were knocked out because of injuries and three more were benched for discipline reasons, showing up late and missing meetings. With a short bench, we lost to the U.S. and it never felt like we were in the game. It was humbling watching the Americans celebrate.

Again I thought that it could never get worse than that loss. Again I was wrong.

We didn't even show up for the seventh-place game against Kazakhstan. We should have been able to dominate that game, even with the injuries and a short bench. The Kazakhs even started their backup goaltender. I remember going into the dressing room and yelling at the guys between periods. I don't remember what I said, but it wouldn't matter now because it didn't make a difference then. It was a complete collapse. We lost 6–3 to a team that had half a dozen sticks in the rack by their bench and skates that didn't match.

I believe you learn something, as a player and later as a coach, from every experience you have with a team. I learned what was possible with the right attitude and discipline with the Canadian team in '97; I learned the risks of having the wrong attitude and a lack of discipline with the team in '98. I think things are different in a lot of ways today. The under-18 teams deliver players to the world junior teams who have a lot more international experience than back in the '90s. I was an example of that—I had none when I went to Geneva and there were players on our team in Finland in the same situation.

One thing that I learned as a coach in the Program of Excellence is that "discipline" doesn't mean rules and no fun. I worked as an assistant to Pat Quinn with the Canadian team that won the world under-18s in Russia in 2009. It was an amazing thing to see how Pat was able to get his message across and to instill in a team discipline without being draconian about it—it's not all bad medicine if you just make it a habit. A team with good habits doesn't even feel like it's working with a tough system of discipline. It's something I strive for with my junior teams in Red Deer these days. I wish it was something that we'd had in Finland in '98.

1999

WINNIPEG
THE COLDEST NIGHTS

DAMIEN COX

1999 CANADIAN NATIONAL JUNIOR HOCKEY TEAM

Goaltender Roberto Luongo was Canada's best player in Winnipeg. It turned out that great wasn't good enough to win the host team a gold medal against Russia in the final.

The indelible signature to the 1999 tournament was supplied by goaltender Roberto Luongo. Even in defeat, Luongo's remarkable efforts in nearly single-handedly capturing gold for Team Canada on a frigid January evening at the Winnipeg Arena set a standard only a handful of Canadian junior goalies have been able to match over the long history of the event.

With arch-rival Russia as the opponent it didn't turn out to be Canada's night, despite the relentless, screaming support of the sea of white, but it surely was Luongo's night. If not for Luongo, if it had been a goaltender who was only very good, the Russians would have run Canada out of the old barn under the giant portrait of Queen Elizabeth II that night, and ruined the sense that the home country had bounced back after the eighth-place finish at the world juniors the previous year in Finland.

"Roberto was our best player throughout the tournament," defenceman Robyn Regehr recalled. "But I thought he saved his best performance for that game."

That, of course, was exactly what Luongo was supposed to do. At the time, he was the highest drafted goaltender in the history of the NHL, with the New York Islanders selecting him fourth overall in 1997. He had been part of the Canadian junior squad that had suffered a shocking defeat to Kazakhstan in 1998. Luongo,

Fans gave the Canadian juniors the full "sea of white" support at Winnipeg Arena. The atmosphere in the building after the semifinal rout of favoured Sweden was in sharp contrast to the silence that followed Artem Chubarov's overtime goal in the final.

one of five returnees from the '98 team, was the focus of attention from the start. "I've heard all these things about him," said head coach Tom Renney. "Now I look forward to seeing them."

Every member of the 22-man Canadian team would eventually play in the NHL, but it wasn't a powerhouse, particularly offensively. That meant it was clear that if Canada were to rebound—"This Is for Pride" was the team's slogan for the competition—Luongo would have to lead the way.

Canada had won three of the four previous times the event was held on its soil, including four years earlier with a dominant performance in Red Deer, Alberta. But this was a bigger stage at a turning point in the history of the world juniors, when the event was looking to bigger cities and bigger arenas, and greater exposure around the world. The 10-team event was to include games in Brandon, Selkirk, Portage La Prairie, Morden, and Teulon, spreading the wealth of the international junior game around a province starved for big-time hockey. Still, the games and atmosphere in Winnipeg are what the players remember most.

"The fans in Winnipeg were fantastic," Regehr recalled. "I remember they were truly excited. They had the sea of white going, and it had been a few years since they'd lost the Jets so they were really excited to see hockey again in that way."

Renney, a CHA vice-president at the time, searched for chemistry as he formed his team, cutting five NHL first-rounders before settling on his roster. Mike Van Ryn was the captain, Daniel Tkachuk of the OHL's Barrie Colts was to be the top centre, and Brad Stuart of Rocky Mountain House, Alberta, had turned down an NHL contract from San Jose for one more year of junior hockey and a chance to fight for a world title. The roster featured skill possessed by the likes of Simon Gagné and defenceman Brian Campbell, but the team was defined by the grit of those who skated in front of Luongo—grinders like Tyler Bouck, Kent McDonell, Brenden Morrow, and Adam Mair.

A 5–3 pre-tournament victory over Russia in Kenora, Ontario, seemed to suggest that Renney had chosen well, but the opening game of the tournament told a different story. Slovakian hockey officials declined to invite their top two tournament-eligible players, Marian Hossa and Robert Dome, but those who did play against the host nation made it tough. Canada couldn't score a single goal on Jan Lasak in the Slovakia goal, stunning the fans at the Keystone Centre in Brandon. But Luongo wouldn't be beaten either, stopping 36 shots and leaving the impression that while Canada had certainly not shone, it had an ironclad insurance policy between the pipes.

"The whole tournament was that way for me," said Luongo, who had been traded from Val-d'Or to Acadie-Bathurst two days before leaving to join the national team. "I just remember being in a zone the whole time."

Canada's next game, against Finland, was expected to be a classic goaltending matchup, pitting Luongo against Mika Noronen, who had been brilliant the year before in helping the Finns win gold in Helsinki. Instead, it was a shootout. The Canadian offence burst to life, producing a 6–4 triumph. Tkachuk scored twice, his linemates Kyle Calder and Rico Fata each scored once, and Gagné found an empty net to put the game away. Luongo posted his second shutout two days later, 2–0 over the Czech Republic, to keep Canada unbeaten.

But after being beaten 5–2 on New Year's Eve by the previously winless Americans (led by Brian Gionta and David Legwand), Canada was forced into a quarter-final game and it seemed possible that for a second straight year, the national program might not produce a medal. The opponent was, once again, Kazakhstan, featuring Toronto first-round pick Nikolai Antropov, who had been part of the squad that had

Defencemen Andrew Ference and Mike Van Ryn (wearing the captain's C) were part of a solid blue-line corps that, along with Luongo's brilliance, helped push the final into overtime.

Russia's speed in transition forced the Canadian team to scramble back on defence in the gold-medal game. Here, Van Ryn tries to close the gap on a Russian forward.

upset mighty Canada 12 months earlier. This time, however, there would be no such upset. Gagné scored four times, Canada led 8–0 after two periods, and the final 12–2 score set up a clash with the Swedes in the semifinals.

Sweden—managed by two former New York Islanders, Stefan Persson and Mats Hallin—came in featuring the much-discussed Sedin twins, Henrik and Daniel, and a new attitude. "The days of the chicken Swede are long gone," said Hallin, the coach of the team. "We ain't backing down." Armed with that belligerent new attitude, the unbeaten and untied Swedes were heavy favourites. Canada hadn't beaten a team with a winning record, while Tre Kronor had scored 25 goals in four games and received 21 points from its top line of the Sedins alongside Christian Berglund.

Before a sellout crowd of 14,000, the game was emotional and physical from the start. Each team had a player ejected in the first period. Canada's Brad Ference was tossed for a heavy check on Gabriel Karlsson that saw Karlsson carried off on a stretcher, while Berglund was mistakenly given a game misconduct for high-sticking Tyler Bouck (as replays showed, it was actually Berglund's skate that had accidently clipped the Canadian forward). Even the coaches, Renney and Hallin, got into it, shouting at each other across the benches.

Sweden scored first, but then McDonell tied it in the second, Gagné scored short-handed, and Tkachuk put the third Canadian goal past nervous Swedish netminder Andreas Andersson. The rout was on. By the end, it was 6–1 for Canada, a spectacular result for a national squad that had looked flat for so much of the tournament but had come to life when challenged by the Swedes.

On the other side of the draw was Russia, a team with talented forwards like Maxim Afinogenov, Artem Chubarov, Roman Lyashenko, and Maxim Balmochnykh, and a CHL netminder in Alexei Volkov, who played for the Halifax Mooseheads. The Russians had lost the gold-medal game to the Finns in overtime the year before, and, while strong defensively, they didn't seem to have an overwhelming array of offensive weapons to throw at Canada. What they did have, however, was an emotionally spent opponent—spent from the intense battle against Sweden the night before.

"I felt the tank was empty by the six-minute mark of the first period," Renney said.

From the start, the Russians dominated the contest as they searched for their first world junior title in seven years. Luongo was all the Canadians really had in response, as their attack managed just nine shots over the first two periods. But the Russians could build only a 2–1 lead by late in the third thanks to Luongo's heroics. When defenceman Bryan Allen's knuckler skipped past Volkov with six minutes left, an overtime classic was at hand.

Again Luongo bared his teeth at the Russian attack, and by the five-minute mark of the extra session had stopped 37 of 39 shots. Moments later, Chubarov, who had scored in the first, grabbed a loose puck along the boards in the Canadian zone, cut to the middle of the ice, and let a shot go.

"He kind of fanned on it," Luongo said. "It was a bit of a knuckler, and I kind of whiffed on it. Then it hit the post and went in."

Disbelief immediately set in. This wasn't the fairy-tale ending the Winnipeg crowd had anticipated. Just as the Jets had packed up and left, Team Canada had arrived and come up with silver, but not gold. And yet Luongo defined the gold-medal game and the tournament. His heroic efforts in the final gave his exhausted team a chance to win.

Brenden Morrow and other Canadian forwards rocked Sweden with a punishing forecheck to get to the gold-medal game. By the final, however, the host team had run out of gas and faded, despite Luongo's heroics.

"It was 12 years ago, and so much has happened since then for me," said Luongo, recalling the '99 junior tournament. "The Olympics, world championships, I've had international experiences, and they've kind of taken over from that. Maybe it would be different if we had won."

Different, perhaps. More memorable, probably not. Anyone who was there will always remember that game, that performance, that cold night in Winnipeg when a hot goalie was nearly enough.

2000

SKELLEFTEÅ
THE WEIRD TIMES

DAMIEN COX

One of the players to win a surprise spot in the lineup was Michael Ryder, who played for Canadian coach Claude Julien's Hull Olympiques.

Distant and remote. A land without light. Foreboding. Hardly the place most teenage boys want to spend New Year's Eve.

Yet perfect for an unexpected shot in the dark. Or a save.

Going overseas to challenge for the world junior hockey championship, of course, had always required a special effort for Canadian national teams. Problems from simple homesickness to illness to bad food to poor behaviour had, on occasion, tripped up the junior nats, often making the job of winning gold more difficult.

And then there was the 2000 WJC in northern Sweden.

Shared between the cities of Skellefteå and Umea, it was a trip for 22 Canadian hockey players to one of the least exotic parts of Sweden at a time of year when simple daylight is at a premium. Sometimes the sun shines for only a few hours a day just south of the Arctic Circle, producing a gloomy holiday season for the unprepared.

"We basically had three hours of light per day," recalled Claude Julien, the head coach of that Canadian team. "We told the guys to leave the lights on in the hotel room, because that's where you got your energy from. Whenever it was light outside we'd go for a walk and really tried to utilize the light as best we could."

An assistant to Tom Renney with the 1999 team, Claude Julien came back the next year as head coach and faced an entirely different set of challenges in Skellefteå.

Far from home, in the dark and without big-time reinforcements from NHL teams, Team Canada needed no more obstacles, particularly with the defending gold-medal-winning Russians having brought another strong team, and with the Swedes featuring the Sedin twins, Daniel and Henrik, for their third straight attempt at winning a world junior medal.

But there was one more obstacle, at least a psychological one. As the end of 1999 approached, the world was engulfed with concern—mass hysteria, really—over the so-called Y2K problem, or the Millennium Bug, as it was popularly known. Whether it was a global hoax, as some claimed, or an international problem ameliorated by hundreds of billions of dollars of pre-emptive planning remains a debate. But before the clock struck 12 on December 31, 1999, there was at the very least great uncertainty across the world. Would nuclear plants be tripped up by the problem of computers having used two digits to designate years for so long rather than four digits? How would the world banking industry be affected? Would the lights go out in Skellefteå, already one of the darkest places most of the Canadian hockey players had ever visited?

"It was New Year's, 2000, and it was a big sacrifice for our guys to be there," said Julien. "That was something unique. Everybody was waiting for all the computers in the world to shut down, thought the world was going to end." As it turned out, it was more like the Comet Kohoutek than catastrophe, and the world experienced only a

few minor problems. In gloomy Skellefteå, 2000 was brought in with champagne, "Auld Lang Syne," a spectacular fireworks show—and nothing out of the ordinary.

For Julien that was helpful, since he was already dealing with anything but an ordinary Canadian team.

For starters, it was a squad that featured 16-year-old defenceman Jay Bouwmeester, the youngest player to ever skate for a Canadian national junior team. And the next youngest? That was Jason Spezza of the Mississauga IceDogs, who was on the roster as well. These were two magnificently talented kids, to be sure, but their presence was very much the result of an absence of returning players and the reluctance of most NHL teams to lend their eligible players to Canada for the event.

So, no Vincent Lecavalier, Mike Fisher, Jonathan Girard, Simon Gagné, Robyn Regehr, or Rico Fata, some of whom had been available the year before when the Canadians weren't quite good enough to beat Russia at the '99 world juniors in Winnipeg.

Oddly enough, the New York Rangers were willing to make Manny Malhotra available after declining to release him for the Winnipeg tourney. Malhotra had played for the junior nats two years earlier at the disaster in Finland, an eighth-place finish, so his experience was very useful. Montreal made available slick centre Mike Ribeiro, and the New York Islanders sent big Mathieu Biron, a godsend for Julien given that not a single member of the '99 defence corps was back.

Julien departed from convention with his selection of two 16-year-old phenoms, defenceman Jay Bouwmeester and centre Jason Spezza, to that point the two youngest players ever in the Canadian juniors' lineup.

Only backup goalie Brian Finley and forward Tyler Bouck were back from the defending silver medallists, with a third returnee, Blair Betts, unavailable due to injury.

The back end featured future NHLers like Bouwmeester and Barret Jackman, but also players like Matt Kinch, Joe Rullier, and Kyle Rossiter who would not go on to significant NHL careers. This, Julien understood from the outset, was not going to be one of the strongest, most talented teams Canada had ever sent to the world juniors. The team wasn't even particularly big, which meant the heavy-hitting style of the previous year's squad would not be repeated.

"We had to really dig deep without the talent Team Canada is used to having," said Julien. "But we had a lot of hard-working guys." Julien had been an assistant coach under Tom Renney on that 1999 team and previously a Memorial Cup champion, and perhaps he was also a fellow shaped by destiny to be a head coach. After all, 16 years earlier he and Gord Donnelly had been traded by the St. Louis Blues to the Quebec Nordiques for the rights to coach Jacques Demers.

Having been traded for a coach, perhaps it made sense Julien would in turn trade his holidays for a chance at coaching for gold. The team would have been even smaller had the diminutive Mike Comrie not been the last cut. Up the middle there

Maxime Ouellet had the bulk of the work in net but in the bronze-medal game, Julien opted for his backup Brian Finley.

was Brad Richards, Brandon Reid, and Ribeiro, while Malhotra would centre a checking line. In goal, Finley made the team, but was challenged from the outset by Maxime Ouellet.

If there was a player expected to be a star, it was University of Wisconsin sniper Dany Heatley. On a team filled with players already drafted, or too young for the NHL draft, Heatley was already being watched very closely by NHL talent scouts as a potential top pick in the 2000 draft.

After being crushed by the Swedes in a pre-tournament game, the Canadians started the round robin with Ouellet in goal and beat the Finns 3–2. Stuck in the toughest of the two pools, it was clear Canada couldn't afford to struggle in the early going or the team would risk finishing out of the medals. Ouellet then delivered a 34-save performance against the Czechs, pushing Canada to 1-0-1 after two games.

Spezza, meanwhile, was a big story, and not for his play—it was Julien's decision to hardly use him at all that became a daily source of speculation and rumour. The IceDogs centre had been shifted to right wing behind Michael Ryder, Chris Nielsen, Jamie Lundmark, and Mark Bell, had played only two shifts against Finland, and then didn't play at all against the Czech Republic.

Even Switzerland's stick work couldn't hold up Brandon Reid or his teammates, and Canada cruised to an 8–3 victory.

A 1–1 tie with the Czechs set Canada on course for second place in Pool A and a semifinal meeting with the Russians.

Bouwmeester played a little more, but it was clear the two 16-year-olds were not going to be featured pieces on this Canadian junior team, one that had scored five goals in four games (two pre-tourney, two round robin).

"Sure, it's hard to sit on the bench when we're only scoring one goal," said Spezza, who had tallied 38 points in 28 games with Mississauga to that point in the OHL season. "I don't know why [Julien] won't play me."

The fact that the crowds for most of the games ranged from small to pitiful, an enormous contrast to the enthusiastic sellout throngs the previous year in Manitoba, added to the sense that this was not going to be a year to remember at the world juniors, for Canada or any other country.

After getting some offence going against Slovakia in a 4–1 win, the Canadians finished the round robin with a 1–1 tie against the United States, stoned by Philippe Sauvé in the American net and once again shown to be a team without a great deal of firepower. Eric Chouinard was the only Canadian to beat Sauvé as the Canadians headed for a quarter-final game against the Swiss.

That turned out to be not much of a challenge for Canada, and the big news came in the other quarter, with the United States ousting the Sedins and the Swedes by an embarrassing 5–1 score on their native soil. In three world junior events, the Sedins had come away with no medals, and in big games against Russia and the U.S. in the 2000 event, the twins had been held pointless.

Against Russia in the semifinals, Heatley scored, as did Matt Pettinger. But the Russians led the whole way despite being outshot 25–20, including 14–6 in the third, and Canada was forced to play for bronze. It was not a predicament Canada was used to being in, and when it had happened in previous years, teams hadn't fared well—not surprising given the national mantra that only gold mattered.

Still, the players argued that this was different. "We've travelled a quarter of the way around the world and we don't want to go home with nothing," said Malhotra, who already knew the empty feeling of playing in the world juniors and not winning a medal.

It would be a North American clash in the bronze-medal game between the U.S. and Canada, a precursor to the major junior battles that lay ahead between the two countries in future tournaments. Ouellet had started all the games, but Julien turned to Finley for the bronze game, hoping he might deliver something special.

The 4-1-2 Canadians fell behind 2–0 after a period, and still trailed by a goal going into the third before fighting back and forcing overtime, then a shootout. Two years earlier in Nagano, of course, a Canadian Olympic team led by Wayne Gretzky had lost to the Czechs in a shootout, and since then the term, let alone the actual exercise, had been looked down on by many Canadians as a gimmick, something not quite hockey.

Yet here it was staring Julien in the face, and without a particularly skilled offensive team at his disposal. But what he had came through. First, U.S. winger Andy Hilbert missed, and then Lundmark scored. Pat Aufiero scored on Finley, but Reid put another one into the U.S. net past Sauvé. Big American winger Jeff Taffe missed, but Heatley found twine, putting the Americans in a do-or-die position with Boston University winger Daniel Cavanaugh lined up at centre.

"I tried to make them all deke," said Finley afterwards.

Cavanaugh deked, to his backhand. Finley stuck out his right pad and Canada had bronze—bronze that, given the team, the conditions, and the darkness, seemed to gleam like gold.

"The one thing we wanted was to at least get a medal, and we did that," said Julien. "The States was a big rivalry, and we wanted to make sure we came up with a medal on that day." A bronze medal for Canada.

And the world didn't end.

The 2000 WJC gave hockey fans their first chance to see high-scoring University of Wisconsin winger Dany Heatley, who would be the second pick overall in the 2000 NHL entry draft.

2001

MOSCOW
THE THIRTEENTH FORWARD

TERRY KOSHAN

Winger Raffi Torres brought his hard-hitting game to the WJC in Moscow. His one-timer won the bronze-medal game in overtime against the Swedes.

Often, veterans of the Program of Excellence will drop by and speak to young players in the formative stages of their careers with Hockey Canada—not only about the demands that come with the crest on the front of the sweater, but also about the accompanying privilege and the organization's rich history.

Those guys over in the corner? Well, they might be a former coach talking to the current one, offering salient pieces of advice.

Stan Butler took everything in when he spoke with Mike Babcock, who had coached Canada to a gold medal at the 1997 world junior championship in Geneva. In major junior and NHL play, those who would be the 13th forward or 7th defenceman on the depth chart would be sitting up in the press box on game nights. But with expanded rosters in international hockey, a 13th forward and a 7th defenceman aren't castaways. They're on the bench and on call, ready to jump the boards on a second's notice.

"I told Stan you have to trust those guys, and if you trust those guys, in big moments they can be good for you," Babcock said. "And if those players happen to be the guys you know really well, that is a benefit. I just knew that when I coached that team, it was an important part of the process.

Maxime Ouellet played well for Canada through to the semifinal, but he struggled in the loss to the Finns that sent the team to the bronze-medal game.

"You know if they don't play one shift, everything is rosy and they are with you."

Babcock's extras who became integral in 1997 were centre Trent Whitfield and defenceman Hugh Hamilton, two players he coached in Spokane in the Western Hockey League. Both Whitfield and Hamilton ended up playing bigger roles than even they might have imagined.

Butler was mindful of Babcock's advice when he assembled the roster for the team that would go to Moscow for the 2001 world juniors. For his 7th defenceman Butler took Jay Harrison, whom he coached on the Brampton Battalion in the Ontario Hockey League. For his 13th forward he took Mike Zigomanis, the captain of the Kingston Frontenacs. Butler had never coached Zigomanis, but he had coached against him. He knew that Zigomanis was carrying a full load of courses at Queen's University and had been nominated for the league's academic excellence award. Butler and Zigomanis shared hockey roots, both coming out of the Wexford minor hockey association.

"I had known Michael for a long time," Butler said. "I had always admired him as a player."

It's true that in the world juniors, players are experiencing things they never have before. For some, they're hearing for the first time in their career that they're not going to be getting a regular shift. Zigomanis was winding down an excellent junior career with the Frontenacs when Butler chose him for the squad that was going to Moscow. The 19-year-old had put up 94 points in 1999–2000 with Kingston and was a second-round pick of the Buffalo Sabres. In other words, if hockey was going to be a living, Zigomanis had a long hockey career ahead of him.

He could not help but bristle a bit when Butler told him he wouldn't be starting among the 12 forwards.

But the feeling didn't take long to dissipate.

"I was playing a lot in Kingston and to go into that extra-player role was a change," Zigomanis said. "You are one of the 22 players going over there, and that is an accomplishment."

Of course, Zigomanis had no idea at the time how his career would unfold. He also could not say what would happen in the next couple of weeks.

But he had not been designated as the extra forward just because he had the fortune of knowing the head coach. "When you're talking about Ziggy, you're talking about a team player," said Barry Trapp, who was the head scout for the program at the time and as such spent months travelling the country, watching more hockey games than most people do in 10 years.

"If there was a choice between taking a highly skilled player who had no character and one who might not have been as skilled but had lots of character, I would take the second guy. I would always have room on my team for a Zigomanis."

As the tournament started, Zigomanis had sporadic shifts—today, he says that if he had enough time to think about it, he could recall each one.

Canada won two games, tied one, and lost one in the preliminary round. A 5–2 loss to Finland in the semifinal meant Canada's medal hopes rested on a bronze, not a gold, or even a silver.

The Canadians had been dealing with various illnesses over the course of the

Canada's leading scorer in the 2000 tournament, Val-d'Or forward Brandon Reid, was back for a second shot at the gold in Moscow.

Jay Bouwmeester clears U.S. forward Kris Vernarsky from the front of the Canadian net.

Sweden blunted the Canadian offence though 60 minutes of the bronze-medal game. Here, Brandon Reid gets muscled off the puck.

tournament, but even those who stayed healthy had to feel a bit off. This was before Hockey Canada sent a chef to the championship to feed an eager bunch of teenagers. The food in Russia, Butler said, fell well short of what his players were accustomed to in Canada.

Though the players had no desire to travel back to Canada without a medal, their final game—versus Sweden, and with the bronze medal to be awarded at the end—did not start with much intensity. It was clear that Butler's team needed energy, and quickly.

Zigomanis, despite his lack of ice time, had produced a goal and an assist to that point. "You don't think about [getting few shifts] at the time," Zigomanis said. "It was one of those things where you just have to live in the now. I still try to do that in every game. You build off your past shifts. But you can't reminisce about your shifts and what you did wrong and what you did right. You are only as good as your last shift, and you have to give it everything you have on your new one. That is how I took that tournament—do everything you can when you are on the ice."

Butler recalled what he told Zigomanis, and would give the same message to Jay McClement a year later. "You are one injury away from getting more ice time, or you are one play away from a coach getting fed up with a player and putting you in a spot," Butler said. "At least you are on the bench. You can't get on the ice if you

Another player returning to the Canadian lineup, Mike Cammalleri would get going against the Swedes to claim his second bronze medal.

Stan Butler was faced with what has proven to be the most unenviable task for a Canadian coach in international competition: rallying the troops for a bronze-medal game.

are not on the bench, and one thing I always tried to tell guys in those roles, that you are dressed and on the bench, which means there is a chance you will play."

Not long after the game started, Butler sensed that the trio of Jason Spezza, Raffi Torres, and Brad Boyes required a change. Off came Boyes and in came Zigomanis. Zigomanis and Torres had played minor hockey together, so there was another connection that made the transition a fairly simple one. Butler's switch worked. Zigomanis, after only a couple of shifts, tied the game in the second period.

The line was effective through regulation, but so was Swedish goalie Henrik Lundqvist.

Overtime, however, did not last long. Butler's new-found strong line was on the ice for a faceoff in Sweden's end barely a half-minute after the sudden-death period began.

"I remember Spezza was struggling in the circle all game, and I went to him and said, 'Are you going to win the draw or not?'" Zigomanis said. "'Because if I take it, I am going to win it.' And he looked at me, and he had a little fire in his eyes, and he said he was going to win it. He won the draw and put it right on Raffi's tape. I went to the net and screened, and we went home with some hardware."

Torres's one-timer rocketed into the top corner of the net and Canada had a 2–1 victory at the 37-second mark. If Lundqvist saw it, he had no time to react.

"Every player wants to play and they want a regular shift in the tournament and they want to make a difference," Zigomanis said. "For me, it was better late than never. I was just happy to be out there."

In the end, the trust that Butler had in Zigomanis, the trust that Babcock had said was essential in that 13th forward, was paid back. In a big moment, Zigomanis was good for Butler.

Zigomanis was one of two Canadian players—Brandon Reid was the other—who was not on the ice for any goals against in Canada's seven games. Zigomanis's mark of plus-5 was tops on the team. And though he played on the wing, when Zigomanis was summoned to the faceoff circle, he won 10 of the 13 draws he took.

"He adapted," Butler said. "There never was a thought that he was a bad player, but you have to decide who will be that 13th forward. It was him, and there were a lot of kids released from that team who would have liked to have had that opportunity."

Fortitude wasn't the only factor in Zigomanis's positive handling of the initially limited role. In teammates such as Boyes, Torres, Mike Cammalleri, and roommate Mark Popovic, Zigomanis had people close by to whom he could talk about his role.

"I had known him for a while, and he was just thrilled to be there," Brad Boyes said. "Whatever he was given, he took advantage of it. He played well in that tournament."

"It was a tournament I had watched growing up," said Zigomanis. "I used to get up with my dad on those early mornings and turn the TV on. To actually be there, to win a medal—it felt like a gold medal to me—was a great experience. It was better to win the bronze than the silver, because you go out winning."

The pockets of ice time that Zigomanis had in Russia were to

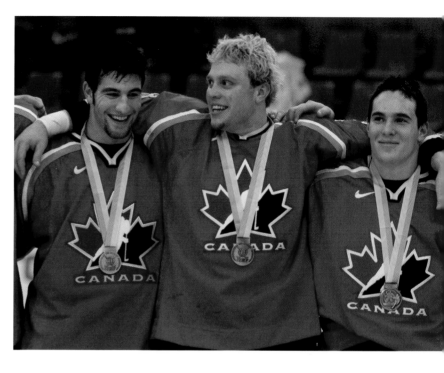

be reflected when he became an NHL player. Zigomanis spent the majority of the 2010–11 season with the Toronto Marlies of the American Hockey League, but previously he had stints with five NHL teams.

"I think it helped me out in the long run," Zigomanis said of his world junior experience. "I learned to play with limited ice, and most of my 200 games in the NHL have been between five and eight minutes. It was a good test for me and it was something I was able to apply to my game [in the professional ranks]." At his home, Zigomanis has a collection of his personal hockey memorabilia. In one frame are the bronze medal, his sweater, a program, and a puck.

Upon the players' return to Canada, pictures of Zigomanis with his medal appeared in the *Toronto Sun* and the *Toronto Star*. Before he rejoined his teammates in Kingston, people on the streets of Toronto recognized him.

Not bad for a kid who began the tournament as the 13th forward.

"I had a lot of adrenaline in that tournament, a lot of energy and the crowds in Moscow were great," Zigomanis said. "I can tell you it is something I will remember forever. I was there."

After playing sparingly as the thirteenth forward, Mike Zigomanis (left) finally got to contribute on the bronze-medal-winning overtime goal by Raffi Torres (centre). Mike Cammalleri is at right.

2002

PARDUBICE
THE TEST OF DISCIPLINE

TERRY KOSHAN

The youngest member of the Canadian team in Pardubice, high-flying Rick Nash had his first of many opportunities to play for Canada in major international tournaments.

Brian Sutherby couldn't count the times he had been jostled after a whistle over his junior career. A shove, maybe a stealthy elbow or slash—they were all part of the game. A few times after a whistle he had dropped his gloves to defend himself or send a message or both.

But only once, during the 2002 world junior championship in the Czech Republic, was Sutherby spit on.

"The first thing that came to me was shock," Sutherby said. "I couldn't believe it happened."

The Canada-Russia hockey rivalry has had dozens of intense chapters. Sutherby lived one. More than nine years after Russian forward Alexander Svitov spat in Sutherby's face during a round-robin game at the 2002 WJC, there's no hesitation when Sutherby recalls the incident.

"We were up 5–2 late in the game, and there was under a minute left," Sutherby said. "There was not really a hit or a slash or anything, but we came together after the whistle. He spit on me, and it landed just above my upper lip. I turned away, and when I looked back, he was long gone. I think I said something to the referees and looked over at their bench, but nothing happened."

Flanked by Mike Cammalleri (left) and Jay Bouwmeester (centre), Brian Sutherby faced the ultimate test of discipline in two games against Russia.

Sutherby was livid. He struggled to keep his composure after the game when fielding questions from reporters. Not retaliating, he said, was "probably the toughest thing I ever had to do in my life." Sutherby was so visibly shaken that assistant coach Marc Habscheid had to corral the 19-year-old in the dressing room and try to settle him down.

For Sutherby, there was no option other than to pretend Svitov hadn't just crossed one of those imaginary hockey lines that have been in place for decades.

From the initial moment that Hockey Canada takes teenaged players under its wing— whether it's in preparation for the world junior or much earlier, when players are gearing up for the under-17 championship, or at any other point—the importance of properly representing the country is emphasized. So too do the players have to accept that retaliation or acting out is selfish. If one isn't willing to check his personal agenda at the dressing-room door, chances are he won't make it out of a selection camp and he won't be missed by the coaches or those who do make the team.

"Everyone talks about the pride, but they often look past the sacrifices that go into what it takes to put that sweater on," said Jay Harrison, another member of the 2002 world junior team. "This tournament is the pinnacle of your junior career. The discipline has to be dead on. And what Brian did, to not retaliate, was a prime example. There was something a lot bigger going on there."

It's not just the coaches who drive home that defining message in the Program of Excellence. It's a theme delivered early and often by Hockey Canada. Harrison recalled that prior to an under-18 tournament, former Canadian juniors Mike Van Ryn and Manny Malhotra spoke to the team, and what they emphasized was playing for the crest on the front of the sweater.

The learning process for Sutherby involved a couple of incidents during the exhibition games in the days prior to the 2002 tournament. Sutherby had made the team; he was a strapping forward who had earned a spot on the Washington Capitals' roster coming out of training camp, but was returned to Moose Jaw of the Western Hockey League after playing in seven games for the Capitals.

In short, Team Canada was counting on Sutherby and he wasn't going anywhere, no matter what transpired in Canada's exhibitions.

On two occasions, though, Stan Butler, Canada's head coach, had to summon Sutherby for one-on-one meetings.

"I had elbowed a kid from Finland and I think I punched a guy in a game against the Czech Republic in the exhibition games," Sutherby said. "Butler had to pull me aside and [emphasize] what was at stake."

In Butler's mind, it was crucial that Sutherby know the entire landscape of the world junior tournament

"Brian was going to play a big role on our team," Butler said. "He was on a line with Steve Ott and Jarret Stoll, and they were going to play against the best line of the other team. When you play against the top line, one of the things you can't do is take penalties.

"Not so much for Stoll, but for Sutherby and Ott, we had to change their game for international hockey, and make sure they understood that the game would be called a little bit different. They were key players and we needed them on the ice."

When Sutherby later did not respond to Svitov, it was hard proof that the message had been ingrained.

"I was as angry as I have ever been, but I was not going to put myself above anybody else," Sutherby said. "It was a difficult situation for me because I don't back down. I mean, it was a gob of spit on my face. I wanted to react in a much different way."

Though Sutherby had never been spat on before, and it has not happened to him in a professional career that has stretched over 10 seasons and included more than 460 NHL games, it's not entirely surprising that Svitov let fly. During the 2001 world junior, he was ejected twice from games and led all players with 58 penalty minutes. In 2002, Svitov still was playing off the same page. He again led all players in penalty minutes, this time with 43, and one game after spitting at Sutherby and getting away without a penalty, he jumped a Swiss player and was suspended for two games.

After Sutherby told the media about the spitting incident, reporters went to Svitov to get his version of the story. The Russian tuned out their questions, but he didn't try to deny that he did it.

Scottie Upshall, here giving a Swedish opponent a rough ride into the boards, was just one of the Canadian players who understood that you can play with an edge but also with discipline.

Sutherby would love to relate that everything turned out well in the end. Yet that's not quite what happened.

After the Canadians beat the Russians in the round robin on December 29, 2001, both teams advanced to the gold-medal game. Canada led 2–1 after the first period but allowed three goals in the second and wound up losing 5–4. Sutherby had to watch a gold medal be placed around Svitov's neck, knowing that he'd lost the chance to exact revenge—not that he would have anyway.

"I had zero intention of doing anything stupid in that game, no matter what the score might have been," Sutherby said. "It was not on my mind at that point. What he had done was sickening and it ate me up inside, but my focus entirely was on winning.

"And then to lose to them ... I didn't shake his hand. I couldn't."

The hockey gods wanted to play around with Sutherby one more time. As the Canadians gathered in their hotel lobby the next morning to make the long trek home, the Russians straggled past, still wearing their gold medals after a night of celebration.

Goaltender Pascal Leclaire registered a sparkling .937 save percentage in five games, but Canada failed to protect a two-goal lead against the Russians in the gold-medal game.

"You could tell by the look in his eyes that Brian was still angry," Butler said. "I just had to remind him that the way he handled the thing was classy. Something could have got pretty ugly."

As it was, Sutherby figured he and Svitov would meet again one day in the National Hockey League. And they did. But this story, for Sutherby, doesn't have a happy ending where he was able to make it clear to Svitov he had not forgotten.

Svitov was the third pick overall by the Tampa Bay Lightning in the 2001 entry draft, but soon provided evidence that high-end picks don't always become top-notch NHLers, let alone have lengthy careers. Svitov didn't have discipline on the international stage as a teenager, and though he had skills in abundance, he played just 179 games in three seasons with the Lightning and Columbus Blue Jackets.

Sutherby and Svitov squared off against each other just once in the NHL, during the 2002–03 rookie season for both.

"There was one game where I went after him and it looked like something was going to happen, but Chris Dingman jumped me from behind and that was it," Sutherby said. "I figured I would have lots of opportunities to get him back. You know, I still think about it a lot, especially at Christmas.

"It's something I will never forget. If I ever play him again, I will let him know that. But I don't think it's going to happen."

At the time, Svitov said through a translator that he did not worry whether Sutherby would respond one day in the NHL "because first we both have to make it." Almost a decade on, Svitov has become a veteran of the Kontinental Hockey League, not having skated in the NHL since 2007.

In Butler's mind, when Sutherby turned away from Svitov and did not physically attack the Russian in 2002, there was no greater example for future teenagers who have earned the privilege of wearing Canada's colours. What's true, though, is that many would have applauded had Sutherby not turned away.

"What happened there was a disgusting act, and was something that should never be tolerated in hockey," Butler said. "Brian took away his personal feelings to do what was best for the team and for the country.

"I think what you have to understand is that when you put a Team Canada jersey on, the standards are higher for you to begin with, even to get a chance to try out for that team.

"That's what separates the type of people who wear the Hockey Canada jersey. They do whatever it takes to be successful, but if that means putting aside anything personal, they do it time and time again."

Brad Boyes was one of the offensive leaders for a Canadian team that beat the Russians handily in the preliminary round but couldn't seal the deal in the final.

2003

HALIFAX
THE QUIET ROOM

BRENDAN BELL

Defenceman Brendan Bell (here skating against the Czechs in the opening round) said Canada had a relatively easy route to the final in Halifax but knew that the Russians were going to be a stiff challenge.

We were leading Russia 2–1 at the end of the second period in the final and we were playing in front of a crowd that was 100 percent behind us. We hadn't lost a game. We weren't ever in too much trouble during our run to the gold-medal game. And our goaltender Marc-André Fleury had been lights-out all tournament long. People in the stands in Halifax and those who were watching that game on television would have thought that things were going our way when Scottie Upshall scored a power-play goal in the second period to give us the lead. They would have been confident of a win and a gold medal for Canada, the first one that the program would have won at home in eight years.

But when we went back to the dressing room after the second period, hardly anyone was talking. It hadn't been that way for other games. We always talked a lot, had a lot of fun, and kept things loose. Not this time. We had a lead but we also knew that this was anybody's game. Ours was a good team that played better as the tournament went along, but we also knew that the Russians were a really strong team and they were coming on. We could tell that they had a surge left and we had to be ready for it. We also knew that this was the last time all of us were going to play together. We had 20 minutes to bring everything to a close and we knew that

we didn't have anything locked up at that point. We'd been hanging on at the end of the second period.

Looking back at the 1983 WJC, we didn't have the high-end skill that a lot of other Canadian world junior teams have had over the years. We had thought that Jason Spezza was going to be on the team, but he was in the NHL when Team Canada sent out the invitations to the evaluation camp. Derek Roy was probably our best scoring threat. We weren't going to run up scores against teams in this tournament. We knew that in order to win, we had to play a tight, grinding game with guys like Jordin Tootoo making teams pay the price on our forecheck. We beat the U.S. 3–2 in our semifinal and knew we were going to have to win a close game like that in the gold-medal finale. And we had a goaltender who could win those types of games. In the summer, we thought that goalie was going to be Dan Blackburn, but the New York Rangers decided to keep him on their roster that season. No one thought it was going to be Marc-André Fleury back in the summer, but he turned out to be not just our youngest player but more importantly our best one.

We couldn't have been better prepared than we were before the final. For all of our games, our coaches—Marc Habscheid and his assistants Mike Kelly and Mario

Centre Kyle Wellwood, in an opening-round game, scores one of the most spectacular goals in the history of the tournament, sliding on his right hip through the slot and firing the puck by the Czech goaltender.

Durocher—were giving us detailed scouting reports on the opposition. Everything was broken down and we all knew our roles and what we had to do to be successful. The coaches and scouts would be working opponents' games; at practice we'd watch video. Everything that matters was covered—it was a football mentality, and we dissected opponents as much as possible. It was my first experience with that kind of NHL-quality advance work and I'm sure it was for a lot of the others on our roster. I thought it was great. We were working with an amazing amount of support. And Marc, Mike, and Mario knew everyone on the roster really well. During the summer and in the tryout camp, they were watching us and talking to us all the time, on and off the ice.

It was a funny thing—we knew how strong the Russians were, but fans probably didn't. The Russian group played their round-robin games in Cape Breton and there weren't even highlights of the games on television. They didn't play in Halifax until their semifinal game against the Finns. But we had seen them on video and we knew what they were capable of.

The media had focused on Alexander Ovechkin during the tournament and before the final, and that was understandable because everyone had projected him as the first pick in the 2004 NHL

Winger Pierre-Alexandre Parenteau scored 12 minutes into the first period of the final to give Canada a 1–0 lead against the Russians.

draft. But as good as he was, Ovechkin skated on the Russians' third line. They had a lot of big and talented guys up front. And with the scouting reports, we knew what we were up against.

The Russians just came with so much in the third period. I was playing beside Steve Eminger on the blue line and we had worked together all through the training camp and the tournament. We were on the ice when the Russians scored the tying goal about four minutes into the third period. Their top line, Igor Grigorenko, Andrei Taratukhin, and Alexander Perezhogin, came down on us on a three-on-two and a pass squirted through to Grigorenko, who put it past Fleury. Yuri Trubachev scored what turned out to be the tournament-winning goal with nine minutes left in regulation. Over those last minutes we struggled to get anything going. We just couldn't mount any offence at all and ended up with only four shots on goal in the third period. That wasn't going to get it done. Our best wasn't good enough—that's all there was to it. It ended up being 3–2, but, really, it didn't feel like a one-goal game in the third period.

It was hard to watch the Russians celebrating on the ice after the game and we were hugely disappointed. That said, I still think of the world juniors in Halifax as my best experience in the game. The support we got from the fans there was amazing. I've played in front of bigger crowds in the NHL, but none louder or more enthusiastic. Even away from the arena we had a sense of the energy and excitement in the city, and I think our team fed off that. It really didn't begin and end in Halifax. Everyone talks about how this team comes together over a few weeks for the tournament, but that's not the whole story. I had played with Steve Eminger, Derek Roy, and others with the Ontario under-17 team back in 2000. I had played with a bunch of guys who were on our roster at the summer under-18 tournament. And there was the summer development camp. You get to know the other players pretty well over the course of that time, and even those players who come up from other parts of the country work within the same sort of system. You don't start preparing for

Pierre-Marc Bouchard (left) celebrates after setting up Parenteau with the opening goal in the gold-medal game.

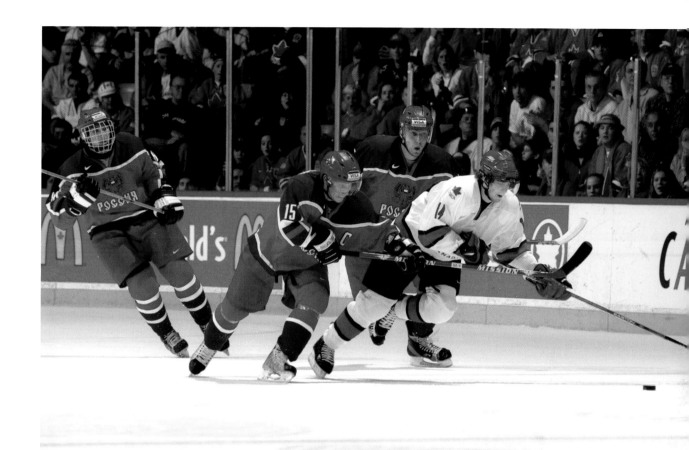

this tournament in the tryout camp. The process begins when you get the call for the under-17s. And it doesn't end at the tournament either. I've stayed in touch with a lot of the players on that team—any time we've played against each other in the pros we've met up in the hallways of the arena after the game. It's a different feeling than you might get with teammates from the pros. With those teammates you may never have been part of something big. But in the Program of Excellence, all of us who played shared something very special. We played for our country, and had the added bonus of playing *in* our country. It's maybe a little like being war veterans—at the risk of sounding overdramatic: we went to war. Everyone in that room before the third period of the final knew that we would be tested like never before. We went through something many people can only imagine. Words on a page can't express the tension we were feeling at that moment or the disappointment of watching the Russians come away with their gold medals. I've been lucky enough to play for the Canadian team that's gone to the Spengler Cup the last couple of years. Any time Hockey Canada calls, I'll answer.

Matt Stajan and other Canadian forwards struggled to skate through the stronger Russians. Even though the Canadians carried a one-goal lead into the third period, they knew the Russians were surging.

2004

HELSINKI
THE UNLUCKIEST BOUNCE

STÉPHANE LEROUX

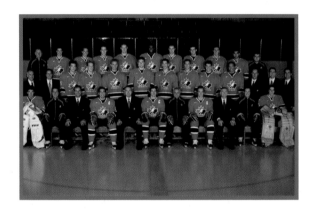

January 5, 2004, is a day that Marc-André Fleury would like to forget. That's the day Canada's star goalie went between the pipes in the WJC gold-medal game against the United States. More than that day or that game, there was a moment, a play in the third period—something that seemed routine, even inconsequential in the lead-up; something that was over in a split second. That moment is what the goaltender wishes he could erase from his bank of memories. Many Canadian hockey fans feel that way, too. So do all of Fleury's teammates who were on the ice, or on the bench, in Helsinki at that moment. But it haunts Fleury like no one else.

The funny thing is, people seem to have forgotten everything leading up to the play. Let me refresh your memory and throw that awful moment into context.

At the beginning of the third period, the Canadian team, under the guidance of head coach Mario Durocher, was ahead 3–1 over the United States in the final game thanks to two goals by Nigel Dawes and one by Anthony Stewart. Canada seemed to be in complete control of the situation and on its way to winning its first WJC gold medal since 1997. Nothing should have been taken for granted—Canada had seen third-period leads evaporate during the final games of the previous two tournaments.

Still, neither of those teams had looked as dominant as this one. No team they had played in the tournament had come within three goals of Team Canada, and

they were coming off a 7–1 thrashing of the Czechs in the semi-finals. Though the Americans had been medal favourites heading into the tournament, in Mike Richards, Jeff Carter, Dion Phaneuf, Brent Seabrook, Ryan Getzlaf, and of course Sidney Crosby, the Canadian team was loaded with guys who could step right into the NHL. If there was one thing these players should have had after two periods, it was confidence.

With a 3–1 lead going into the third period of the championship game against the United States, it looked like Fleury and his teammates were going to bring gold medals back to Canada for the first time since 1997.

"I remember that the mood was calm in the locker room in the second intermission," said Durocher, who had been an assistant coach under Marc Habscheid at the 2003 championship in Halifax 12 months earlier. "The only thing that we reminded the players, especially our defencemen, was to be on the lookout for the stretch pass beyond the red line, a rule with which our players weren't familiar at the time compared to the American university players."

No one expected what happened next to the Canadian squad, especially to the 19-year-old Fleury. The Pittsburgh Penguins had drafted him with the first overall pick largely based on his impressive performance as an underager in Halifax the year before. The Penguins then tried to rush Fleury onto the NHL roster, where the youngster sometimes struggled, in the fall of '03. As the promising young star

started to fade in the big league, the Penguins ended up loaning him to the WJC team in the hope of getting him work and boosting his confidence.

And it seemed to be working. Playing against the best junior-aged players in the world, Team Canada had allowed only five goals in the five games heading into the final against the Americans. And after two periods, the much-touted Americans had managed only one.

In the Americans' dressing room before the third period, coach Mike Eaves was trying to rally his squad, and looking for offence. He decided to shuffle his lines in the last frame, putting Ryan Kesler with Zach Parise and Steve Werner on his top line. Eaves's second line would feature his son, Patrick, along with Drew Stafford and Patrick O'Sullivan.

The changes paid immediate dividends.

Less than five minutes into the third, O'Sullivan scored on Fleury, and reduced the lead to one goal.

A little more than two minutes later, Ryan Kesler finished off a play started by defenceman Dan Richmond—one of the long stretch passes the Canadian coaches had warned their players about in the intermission.

Panic then set into the Canadians' play with the score suddenly tied at three.

"Marc-André became extremely nervous, much like every member of our defensive squad," Durocher said. "I thought of taking a time out after the third American goal in order to calm things down, but a commercial break was imminent and I thought that we would be able to regain our composure then. I wanted to keep my time out for the end of the game in case we needed it."

If he had a chance to do it over again, Durocher would almost certainly have done it differently.

The United States continued to pressure the Canadian defence, and then—with 5:12 to go in the third period—came the play, the one that haunts the coach and his players. And no one more than Marc-André Fleury.

With the puck lying near the crease, and open ice in front of him, Fleury made what looked like the safe play—he leaned into a shot to fire the puck out of the Canadian end. But instead of clearing the zone, the puck hit defenceman Braydon Coburn in the chest.

Then, with Fleury out of position at the top of the crease, and his defencemen too far away, the team could only watch helplessly as the puck somehow bounced into the net.

Hockey is a game of bounces, and this one cost Canada a gold medal.

Patrick O'Sullivan was credited with the goal and suddenly the Americans were leading 4–3, their first lead of the game. O'Sullivan would never score a bigger goal with less effort.

Two photos from the shocking sequence on the Americans' winning goal in the gold-medal game: Marc-André Fleury came out his crease and tried to clear the puck, but it bounced off defenceman Braydon Coburn. Despite his best efforts, the goaltender could only helplessly watch the puck roll across the goal line.

"Marc-André and I were confused as to who should play the puck," said Coburn after the game. "I thought that he wanted to play the puck but he only wanted to clear it away from the front on the net."

Over the last five minutes of regulation, the Canadians tried desperately to find a tying goal but time wound down. For the first time in WJC history, the United States had won gold.

After the game, Marc-André Fleury was inconsolable. He felt that he had let the entire team down after it had played brilliantly throughout the tournament. In the seven years since, Fleury has won a Stanley Cup and an Olympic gold, yet the memory of Helsinki is still clearly painful. And that's perfectly understandable: This had been the biggest game of his life up to that point, a chance to make good after carrying a team that was just 20 minutes away from gold the year before. "That play is now part of hockey history," Fleury said. "Every time a similar situation arises, TSN brings out the footage as part of a montage of the worst blunders. I have no choice but to live with it for the rest of my career."

The hard times for the teenager from Sorel, Quebec, didn't start or end there. After the WJC tournament, Fleury returned to the Penguins. Later that month, after 12 losses in his last 13 NHL games, Fleury was reassigned to the Cape Breton

Through two periods, Fleury and his teammates were almost unchallenged, thoroughly outplaying a U.S. team that featured Ryan Kesler. The only time the Canadians trailed in Helsinki was during the last 5:02 of the gold-medal game.

Jeff Tambellini (number 19) and captain Daniel Paille create havoc in front of American goaltender Al Montoya.

Screaming Eagles. Upon his return to the junior ranks, Fleury had a good run, going 8-1-2. "I always believed in Marc-André Fleury," said Pascal Vincent, his coach at the time. "He was so good and he had done so much for us since the age of 16 that I knew he would bounce back."

However, during the playoffs, Fleury faltered—and, after three straight losses to Chicoutimi, Vincent had to give the No. 1 job to Martin Houle. So a goaltender who had been Canada's No. 1 for the last two WJCs ended his junior career sitting at the end of the bench at the Centre 200 in Sydney, Nova Scotia. The Screaming Eagles, who had finished second overall with 103 points, lost in five games to the Saguenéens, who had ended the season 28 points behind them in the standings.

It should have been the end of the torment for Fleury, but it didn't even stop there. Pittsburgh assigned Fleury to the Wilkes-Barre/Scranton Penguins in the American Hockey League, but coach Michel Therrien had him start only one game in the playoffs, a game that he lost.

If 2004 had been the ruin of Marc-André Fleury, it would have seemed cruel, if not tragic. Eventually, though, Fleury got his game back on the rails and more. Not only would he go on to win a Stanley Cup with the Penguins, but it was his incredible, acrobatic save on Detroit's Nicklas Lidstrom in the dwindling moments of Game 7 that preserved Pittsburgh's one-goal lead and won them the Cup. It was the kind of heroic save goalies dream of making, at the biggest moment of his career and the perfect time for his team.

If anything could erase the memory of that botched clearing attempt in 2004, it was that save. Mario Durocher thought Fleury took too much blame back in Helsinki. "Sidney Crosby and Ryan Getzlaf both missed great opportunities to put the game out of reach of the Americans at the beginning of the third period," he said. "When the score was 3–1, those goals would have broken the Americans' back."

There were so many good things that came out of the 2004 WJC. Jeff Carter and Dion Phaneuf were named to the tournament's all-star team and Nigel Dawes ended up the top scorer with six goals and five assists. In six games in Helsinki, Canada scored 35 goals and allowed only nine. During those six games, Mario Durocher's team trailed during only eight minutes and 42 seconds. All that is easy to forget.

What people remember is what still weighs most heavily on the mind of the goaltender who watched helplessly when his clearing attempt ended up in the back of his own net. You needn't shed a tear for Fleury, though. There had been many remarkable performances by goaltenders en route to the world junior championships—by Jimmy Waite, Manny Fernandez, Marc Denis, and José Théodore, among others. In the narrowest of victories they managed to avoid the unlucky bounce that burned Fleury. In his two world championship tournaments Fleury had come away with silver, steeping himself in glory but for that awful moment. The other goaltenders with whom he'll be compared do have gold medals, but he alone has a Stanley Cup ring.

2005

FARGO
THE POWERHOUSE

ED WILLES

Corey Perry had doubts about winning a place on the Canadian roster. He ended up playing on the wing beside the two best-known players in the lineup: Sidney Crosby and Patrice Bergeron.

It wasn't exactly a secret at the time, but Corey Perry knew the makings of something special were there with Team Canada at the 2005 WJC.

He just didn't know if he'd be a part of it.

Starting with the late-summer camp in Calgary, Perry, along with the other invitees, all fought for a spot on the deepest, most talented Canadian team in the history of the world junior championship. That team was stocked with the players from the impossibly rich 2003 draft, many of whom had played for Canada in the '04 tournament in Helsinki. The NHL lockout that year ensured half a dozen players who'd normally be playing in The Show—centre Patrice Bergeron had already played a full season with the Boston Bruins, for pity's sake—would be made available to Team Canada.

True, Perry had some credentials of his own. He was coming off a 113-point season with the London Knights, he'd been a first-rounder in that '03 draft, and he'd been a late cut of the '04 team. But all that résumé earned him was an invitation to the selection camp in Winnipeg—which is why, when the phone rang on cut-down day, Perry's first thought was, "This can't be happening again."

Turned out it wasn't. Turned out Perry would play a role on the best-ever team in the history of the WJC.

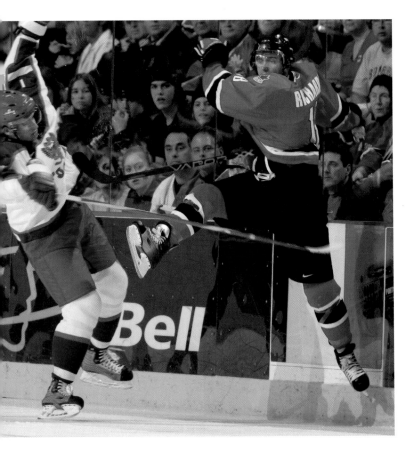

But there was a price to pay.

"I thought I was getting cut again," says Perry. "Then [head coach Brent Sutter] called and said, 'Do you want to be the 13th forward? If you do, you have to cut your hair.'

"That was a sacrifice I was willing to make."

It wouldn't be the last time someone took one for that team.

The kids from Grand Forks have since morphed into a collection of the game's greatest stars—and, less than a decade after their starring turn in North Dakota, their accomplishments continue to stagger. Six players from Sutter's team would win a gold medal with Team Canada at the 2010 Winter Olympics. The graduates included Sidney Crosby, generally regarded as the game's greatest all-around player; Perry and Ryan Getzlaf, who'd win the Stanley Cup in Anaheim as 22-year-olds; and

Centre Mike Richards played with a physical edge that keyed Canada's dominance of the field leading up to the medal round.

Mike Richards and Jeff Carter, who'd help form the nucleus of the Philadelphia Flyers that made the Stanley Cup final in 2010. The blue line featured Shea Weber, Dion Phaneuf, Brent Seabrook, and Braydon Coburn. Six of the players on that roster went on to become captains of their NHL teams. As a group, they were talented. They were mature. They were focused. And, for all that, their greatest achievement was not in meeting the great expectations which had been placed on them.

It was in exceeding them.

"The biggest thing is we started in August with a highly competitive camp," said Sutter. "There was one goal and one goal only and that was to be a totally dominant team. We wanted to make sure the players understood the coaches were very serious about the way we wanted them to play. They got the message and it just carried on from there."

And everyone connected with that team shared the feeling.

"We were kids but you kind of realized what we had," said Perry. "That was a stacked team.

"We had that feeling going into every game. Brent had a game plan for us in every game and we didn't take anyone lightly. We didn't want to be scored on. That

was our whole mindset. Grind things out. Then guys started scoring. We were just running teams out. That was the kind of team we were."

Perry, as things transpired, had an interesting time of it all the way around with that team. That year, Team Canada featured 12 veterans from the '04 team that lost the gold medal in Helsinki to the United States on Marc-André Fleury's infamous clearing gaffe late in the third period. Canada had also gone seven years without a gold medal, and that drought, coupled with the returnees, ensured motivation wouldn't be a problem.

Then again, this group didn't need a lot of help in that department. At the August camp in Calgary, Sutter divided the players into two teams, then watched as Phaneuf and Colin Fraser, who were teammates with the Red Deer Rebels, dropped their gloves in one of the first scrimmages.

"That's the kind of team it was," the coach said.

By the time the December selection camp rolled around in Winnipeg, the competition was even more fierce and Perry found himself battling a handful of players, including Eric Fehr of the Brandon Wheat Kings, for the final forward spot. In that final inter-squad game Perry scored three goals, which punched his ticket for Grand

The Canadian blue-liners didn't just shut down opposing forwards—they punished other teams for simply trespassing. Here, Dion Phaneuf decks a Swedish forward in the opening round.

Forks. In the pre-tournament schedule, he then received a battlefield promotion when Jeremy Colliton, a rugged, two-way winger with the Prince Albert Raiders, suffered a knee injury. Colliton would come back and play one game for the maple leaf in Grand Forks before he was scratched from the tournament. Perry would move up and take his place.

His linemates? Crosby and Bergeron.

"You couldn't ask for much more than that," he says.

"Through that process there were a couple of players who were right there," said Sutter. "It came down to Corey and a couple of others in the last exhibition and Corey just took it to another level."

Which also pretty much describes what happened with the team.

Following the selection camp, the group repaired to the Manitoba resort town of Gimli, where they celebrated Christmas at the home of former NHLer Ted Irvine. Irvine, as it turned out, is the father of professional wrestler Chris Jericho, and Jericho and some of his wrestling colleagues made a video wishing the junior team good luck.

Thus fortified, the team travelled to Grand Forks and, in their four round-robin games, they beat, in order, Slovakia, Sweden, Germany, and Finland by a combined score of 32–5. Perry, Bergeron, and Crosby would form the nominal No. 1 line, but

Patrice Bergeron was in an unprecedented position in Fargo: He made his debut in the WJC after having played a full season with the Boston Bruins and having won a gold medal at the senior men's world championships in 2004.

the dropoff from their unit to the rest of the lineup was imperceptible. Getzlaf centred a line with Carter and Andrew Ladd. Richards played with Anthony Stewart and a bit with Nigel Dawes. The fourth line, such as it was, consisted of Stephen Dixon, Clarke MacArthur, and Fraser and they played a huge role throughout the tournament.

"I never looked at who was our 13th forward or our first line," said Sutter. "I looked at it as we had a unique group and they were going to determine who was going to play and how much they were going to play.

"They just kept getting better and better. It was exciting to watch. We didn't match lines too much. On that team, we didn't have to."

Still, the Perry-Bergeron-Crosby line led the way, offensively at least. Bergeron topped the team in scoring, Crosby was second in goals with six, and Perry recorded seven points in the six games. Bergeron and Crosby remain close friends from that experience.

"Good players don't always play well together," said Perry. "But we just clicked and it happened pretty quickly."

Following the round robin, Canada would get its biggest scare of the tournament, relatively speaking, in the semifinal game with a 3–1 win over the Czech Republic. But even that score was a tad misleading. Czech goalie Marek Schwarz, the tournament's all-star 'keeper, stopped 39 of the 42 shots sent his way while his teammates mustered a puny 11 shots at Canadian goalie Jeff Glass. (It became a running joke in Grand Forks when Hockey Canada officials brought Glass out for post-game media scrums. By the end of each night he'd faced more hard questions than he had testing shots.) The win over the Czechs set up the gold-medal game against the Russians. Again, motivation wouldn't be an issue.

The Russians were led by Alexander Ovechkin and Evgeni Malkin, who had been taken first and second respectively in the 2004 draft. They had also dismantled a strong American team—Ryan Suter, Drew Stafford, Phil Kessel, Ryan Callahan— 7–2 in their semifinal game.

Before the gold-medal game, Ovechkin, who was playing in his third WJC, heard his name mentioned as he walked by a TV monitor.

"What are they saying?" he asked a media type.

"They're saying Canada is going to play the Bergeron line against you with Phaneuf and Weber," Ovechkin was told.

"Good luck," he sneered.

Luck, however, was the last thing the Canadians needed. Luck was something Ovechkin was going to run out of before the first intermission

By the time the final rolled around, Grand Forks had almost become an unofficial Canadian city. Hockey-mad fans from Winnipeg and environs had made the three-hour trek down the highway for the entire tournament, making each Canadian contest

Corey Perry, here skating against Germany, says head coach Brent Sutter kept the team "on an even keel and made sure everyone checked their ego at the door." Ego might have been the only thing that could have stopped the 2005 team.

a virtual home game. The final would be played in front of another rabid, red-clad sellout crowd of just under 11,000 at the magnificent Ralph Engelstad Arena.

They got their money's worth. In the first period, Ovechkin was hit by, in order, Crosby, Phaneuf, Richards, and Bergeron. He then came out for one shift in the second period before he excused himself for the evening.

Getzlaf, meanwhile, scored 51 seconds in and the Canadians drove Russian starter Anton Khudobin from the game early in the second period. The Canadians, in fact, were leading 6–1 midway through the second when they finally took their foot off the gas.

That suited the Russians, who were playing like they wanted the night to end as quickly as possible. When they'd won gold in Halifax two years earlier, the Russians trash-talked the host team during and after the final. Ovechkin and his teammates would go out quietly and peacefully this time.

"We went out and dominated physically," said Perry. "Guys knew what they wanted and we didn't stop. We just kept going and going."

Then the final horn went. Then it all started to sink in.

The Canadians had done to the tournament field what Genghis Khan did to Asia Minor. Over the six games of the tournament they outscored their opposition 41–7, allowing an average of 17 shots on goal per game in the process. They took apart the mighty Russians, holding Ovechkin and Malkin off the scoresheet while allowing just 11 shots on goal over the first two periods. They were never seriously challenged in the gold-medal game or the tournament. They set out on a mission. The mission was accomplished to the fullest extent possible.

"The kids were focused and they were prepared," said Sutter. "They just wanted to get better and it was great to watch them come to the rink every day. They knew what they wanted."

OK, this team didn't exactly need a master coaching job, but Sutter laid out a plan for them four months before the tournament and received the maximum buy-in from every player on the roster.

"He kept on us," said Perry. "He didn't want our heads to get too big. He kept us on an even keel and made sure everyone checked their ego at the door and played for their country, not for themselves. He's a tough guy to play for but he gets the best out of players."

And there was a lot to get out of that group. Bergeron, who led Canada and the tournament in scoring with 13 points, was named the tournament MVP but it could have gone to Carter, who had seven goals, or Getzlaf, who had 12 points and played a huge two-way game. Phaneuf, Carter, and Bergeron were named to the tournament all-star game. Crosby could have been named. Weber didn't record a point but played with Phaneuf on the fearsome shutdown pairing. And, for all that, the most impressive thing about this team was the whole was still greater than the sum of those considerable parts.

The real measure of the team, moreover, is still being counted. The next season, 12 of Sutter's players would step into the NHL. And no one imagines that the legacy of this team ended in Vancouver, when Olympic golds were draped around the necks of Crosby, Bergeron, Richards, Weber, Seabrook, and Perry. No other team so fully lived up to the Program of Excellence's central objectives: in the short run, to win the world junior championships, and in the long run, to prepare the country's best players to compete in major international tournaments, the Olympics foremost among them.

"It's crazy when you look at the guys on that team and what they've been able to do at a young age," said Perry.

Crazy? Maybe. But what that team accomplished in Grand Forks was real enough.

2006

VANCOUVER
THE BEST FRIENDS

ED WILLES

Luc Bourdon (pictured at the 2008 tournament) heard cheers at Vancouver's GM Place, the arena where he had hoped to play for the Canucks.

As is often the case with close friends, the pair was a study in contrasts.

Kris Letang was a city kid from Montreal. Luc Bourdon was from the tiny fishing community of Shippagan on New Brunswick's northeast coast. Letang was a little more worldly; a little more certain of himself and his place. Bourdon, for his part, was just taking his first steps into the bigger world and learning about the possibilities that awaited.

On the ice it was a similar story. Letang was an undersized defenceman who compensated for his lack of mass with skill and an outsized hockey sense. Bourdon was a thoroughbred, a size-and-speed blueliner who played on instinct and impulse.

"When he hit guys, he'd just destroy them," says Letang.

So, superficially at least, they didn't have a lot in common. But it was a funny thing. From the moment they met at a summer camp in 2004, before they joined the Val-d'Or Foreurs, Letang and Bourdon discovered something about each other that made all their differences seem irrelevant.

"We were great friends from the first time we met and it grew," says Letang. "We used to hang out after every practice. We had races. We shot pucks. We tried to push each other. That's the way I remember Luc: how passionate he was; how much he loved the game and I was the same way."

But Letang has another memory of his friend; a memory so pure and powerful that it gives him comfort when he thinks about Bourdon, who died in a motorcycle accident near his hometown on May 29, 2008. At the 2006 world junior championship in Vancouver, they were part of a Team Canada that put together one of the most improbable runs in this country's history at the WJC. A year after a super team had demolished the field in Grand Forks on the way to a gold, head coach Brent Sutter would mould a far-less-celebrated group of players into a team that didn't have the star power of the '05 squad but was just as efficient.

Canada would win all six tournament games, blasting Russia and Evgeni Malkin 5–0 in the final to capture gold before a sellout crowd of 18,000-plus at GM Place.

Letang and Bourdon played every game in that tournament on the same defensive pairing. They were also on the ice together when the final horn sounded in the gold-medal game; friends and teammates forever. It's not an aspect of the Program of Excellence that draws cheers or shows up in newspapers or on sportscasts, but it's something that looms large for players in every lineup: when a team is brought together, the seeds of friendship are planted. The players share a special experience—living and playing together for a couple weeks in the summer, then gathering again in December for the most important games of their career to that point.

"It was just unbelievable," says Letang. "Everything. The crowd, the emotion. And I was able to share it with my friend."

"He had this charisma about him," Sutter says of Bourdon. "He was intense but he was also loose and guys were drawn to that. It was a terrible, terrible thing that happened. He had such a tremendous life ahead of him."

———————

If ever a team was a reflection of its coach, it was the Canadian entry at the '06 WJC. The year before Sutter had won with a group that included, among others, Sidney Crosby, Ryan Getzlaf, Corey Perry, Jeff Carter, Mike Richards, Shea Weber, Dion Phaneuf, and Brent Seabrook. That team simply required a coach who could open the door to the players' bench.

The '06 team was different.

For starters, there was just one returning player—defenceman Cam Barker, who'd missed the latter stages of the Grand Forks tournament with mononucleosis. Many on the team were unproven and unheralded. There was no go-to star, no elite first line. There were no big scorers, no big reputations. There was, however, balance and quality throughout the lineup, and if Sutter didn't have a team that would overwhelm with firepower, he did have one that could wear down the opposition through its diligence and determination.

In the end, it was the perfect Sutter team—a "wolf pack" that was committed to the greater good and the coach's vision.

"They didn't have as much talent but our work ethic and leadership was just as strong [as the '05 team]," Sutter says. "It was exactly the same game plan. The guys were on a mission. They wanted to be as good as the team in '05. They wanted to be as dominant."

And if they didn't earn any style points along the way, they met their goal. The Canadians would surrender just six goals in the tournament, shutting out Finland in the semifinal and the Russians in the gold-medal game. Goalie Justin Pogge, who was something of a surprise selection over Carey Price before the tournament, was the team's MVP for the tournament, but the larger story was the totality of Canada's team game and the work of the head coach.

"A lot of coaches could have won [with the '05 team]," Hockey Canada president Bob Nicholson said after the win over the Russians. "There aren't a lot of coaches who could have won with this team."

If there was a player who epitomized Sutter's grand plan it was forward Steve Downie, a fireplug who'd been a late invite to the Team Canada summer camp and who carried some baggage on to the squad. The season before, Downie had been involved in a much-publicized fight with Windsor Spitfires teammate Akim Aliu over a hazing incident. That summer he'd also been a first-round selection of the Philadelphia Flyers, and when Downie arrived at the camp, Sutter explained the way things would be on his team.

"Obviously there was so much going on with Steve," says Sutter. "Basically it was just getting him into a situation where he was really focused. I never had an issue with his emotional level. I just wanted him disciplined. We spent time with him on a daily basis and he was huge for us."

Downie would be named to the tournament all-star team, but this doesn't begin to tell the story of his contribution. Playing with Dustin Boyd and Blake Comeau in what passed for Sutter's first line, Downie was everywhere throughout the tournament. Against a strong entry from the United States, Canada needed a tie to win their group. Downie set up Boyd for the game-tying goal, then, with American goalie Cory Schneider pulled for an extra attacker late in the game, sent in Canadian

Bourdon and his Val-d'Or teammate Kris Letang keyed a defence that surrendered only six goals in the tournament, capped by a shutout victory over Russia in the final.

Andrew Cogliano picked up a pair of assists in the 5–0 gold-medal-game victory over Russia. Cogliano injected open-ice speed into Canada's offence by committee.

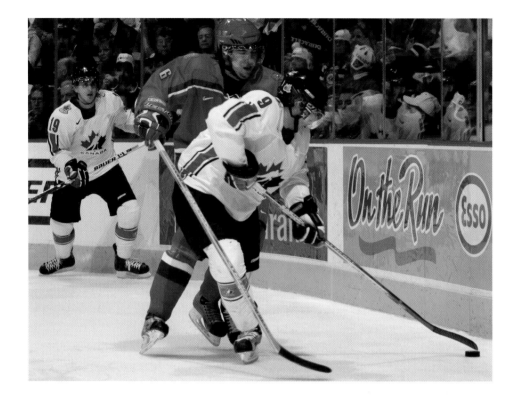

Defenceman Marc Staal thumped Evgeni Malkin in the gold-medal game. Staal and blue-line partner Ryan Parent shut down and thoroughly frustrated Malkin and the favoured Russians.

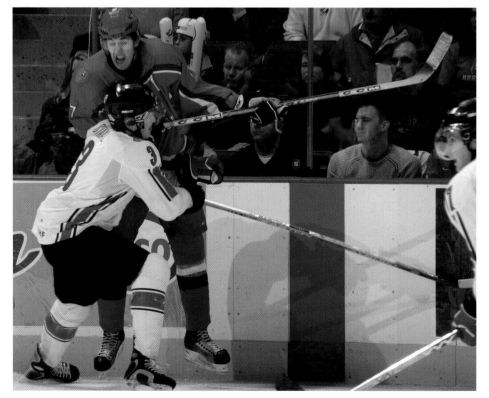

captain Kyle Chipchura for the game-winning goal about the same time as Team U.S.A.'s Jack Johnson was throwing a flying elbow at Downie's noggin.

None the worse for wear, Downie came back for the 4–0 win over Finland in the semifinal, then scored the first goal against Russia in the gold-medal game and drew back-to-back penalties in the second period that led to Canada's fourth goal.

The tournament final, in fact, would provide the canvas for Sutter's most enduring work in his two years with the Canadian juniors. The Russians were stacked. Malkin was among the best players, period, in the KHL. His supporting cast included Nikolai Kulemin, Alexander Radulov, Enver Lisin, and Ilya Zubov. The Russians had also demolished the Americans 5–1 in the other semifinal.

"We were facing a much stronger team with a superstar like Malkin," said Letang. "But it was a chance to show everyone what kind of team we had."

And they did every bit of that. Downie set the tone, blasting Russian rearguard Denis Bodrov in the opening minutes and taking a charging penalty for his troubles. The Russians would outshoot Canada 15–3 over the first 15 minutes of the first period but Pogge stood tall. Downie then beat Malkin behind the Russian net and sifted a roller through goalie Anton Khudobin to open the scoring. Less than two minutes later, defenceman Marc Staal picked off a pass in the neutral zone and set up Comeau for the second goal.

The Russians would have a goal disallowed early in the second and were still carrying the play when Michael Blunden scored a backbreaking third goal on the power play. Blunden would add another power-play goal. Chipchura would add the fifth goal with three minutes left and, in a celebration that presaged the gold-medal game at the 2010 Winter Olympics in the same arena, Canadian fans stood for the final two minutes of the game and saluted their young heroes.

"The whole focus was on winning the gold," said Sutter. "Everyone on that team was focused on that moment."

The summer before the WJC, the Vancouver Canucks had taken Luc Bourdon with their first pick, 10th overall, and there was considerable buzz about the young blueliner as the tournament opened. Bourdon had enjoyed an impressive training camp with the Canucks and almost made the NHL team as an 18-year-old. As it was, he became fast friends with the Canucks' Alex Burrows before returning to Val-d'Or.

He would be traded to Moncton during the WJC, where he played in the Memorial Cup that spring.

"We worked out together for a solid week," says Burrows. "That's really where we started to become great friends. He came from a small town and didn't know a

Michael Blunden (number 21 with stick raised) picked up two power-play goals in the second period of the gold-medal game. Russia had outshot Canada 15–4 in the first period, but Blunden's second goal made the score 4–0.

lot about the big city. I'd been around the team and I think he was comfortable with me."

Bourdon would enjoy a solid WJC. Staal was named the tournament's outstanding defenceman, but Bourdon was one of the focal points of the team. Choruses of "Luuuuc, Luuuuc" would rattle around the building every time he made a play. He would also be named to the tournament all-star team, and it seemed the WJC represented just the first of many memorable moments for the big blueliner in Vancouver.

"It was really exciting for him," says Letang. "It was pretty much his building. For him, it was a chance to show them he was going to be ready to play in the NHL. He was already a leader."

The next season, Letang and Bourdon would again win gold for Team Canada at the WJC in Sweden. The year after, Bourdon split the season between Manitoba and the Canucks while Letang played 63 games with the Penguins. Letang was with the Penguins in the Stanley Cup final against Detroit when he heard he'd lost his friend. Luc Bourdon had just turned 21 when he died.

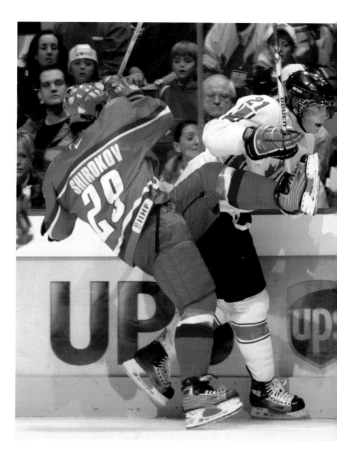

Blunden (here hammering Sergei Shirokov) and his Canadian teammates surrendered scoring chances to the Russians through the first two periods but were the more physical team throughout the game.

"It's always fresh in my mind," says Letang. "It's hard when the month of May comes around. I try to think about him every day. It's something you don't forget."

So he keeps the friendship alive. Letang makes a point of talking to Bourdon's mother, Suzanne Boucher, a couple of times a year. He also sees her at the annual Luc Bourdon Golf Classic. Before he passed, Bourdon donated $10,000 to sports groups in Shippagan. Boucher has since established the Luc Bourdon Foundation to help students and athletes from the area.

Burrows, meanwhile, is also involved in the tournament. He and his wife, Nancy, remain close to Charlene, Bourdon's fiancée, who is attending medical school.

In the Canucks first game of the 2008–09 season, a permanent display honouring Bourdon was unveiled at GM Place (now known as Rogers Arena). As a video tribute played, Canadian recording artist Tom Cochrane sang "Big League" with bandmate Ken Greer. Vancouver fans then chanted "Luuuuc" one more time before the game started with the Calgary Flames.

Burrows would score twice in that game. After each goal, he mimed pulling an arrow from his back and shooting it into the sky. That was for Bourdon.

"He was my friend," says Burrows. "He'll always be my friend."

2007

LEKSAND
THE TENSE VICTORY

GARE JOYCE

Jonathan Toews (here taking a faceoff against U.S. rival Peter Mueller) did it all for Canada in the 2007 tournament, leading the team in scoring and notching three goals in the shootout victory over the Americans in the semifinal.

For sustained suspense, no single game matches it in the history of the Program of Excellence. Sixty minutes of regulation couldn't settle it, nor could 10 minutes of sudden death. The semifinal between Canada and the United States at the 2007 world juniors had to go to a shootout. And even the shootout had to go into overtime.

The cliffhanger was so dramatic that Canada's 4–2 win over Russia in the final seemed anticlimactic.

The images that are burned in the memories of most who watched the semifinal feature the two best Canadian players in Leksand, Sweden: Jonathan Toews and Carey Price.

Toews was in his second turn with the under-20 team. As the youngest Canadian player in Vancouver the year before, Toews served on the checking line and flew under the radar, picking up just a couple of assists. In Sweden, however, he centred the first line, worked the first power play and penalty-killing units, and was expected to do everything but drive the team bus. He was at something of a disadvantage—he was playing through a shoulder injury and his season at the University of North Dakota had been a disappointment to that point. Still, Toews led the Canadians in scoring with four goals and three assists in six games—none of his teammates had more than two goals. Still, what people remember most about Toews in that

Defenceman Ryan Parent was the loneliest player on the ice when the United States went on the power play in overtime of the semifinal game. Parent and blue-line partner Marc Staal reprised their roles from Vancouver as Canada's shutdown defence pairing.

tournament were three goals that don't show up on the stats sheet: the three goals that Toews scored on goaltender Jeff Frazee in the shootout victory over the Americans.

It seemed like the U.S., with players like Patrick Kane, Peter Mueller, and Kyle Okposo, had an advantage over Canada in the skills department going into the shootout. At the outset of the tournament, the conventional wisdom had been that the Canadians were going to be gritty, disciplined, and defensively sound but offensively challenged, that they could count on Toews for goals but would have to scramble to find others to chip in. That's pretty well how it played out when Canada went undefeated in the opening round. Toews keyed the most crucial win in that round, a 6–3 victory over the United States in which he scored two goals, the second being a winner on a penalty shot.

Before the semifinal, the Canadians were at risk of a false sense of confidence with that win and the Americans' unimpressive run through the opening round—a loss to Germany meant that the U.S. needed an overtime win over Sweden just to avoid heading to the relegation games. The Americans, however, saved their best effort and most effective play for this showdown against their rivals and, for the Canadian teenagers in the lineup and thousands of fans who travelled to Sweden, comfort gave way to anxiety.

After a close-checking and scoreless first period, the U.S. took a lead on a power play with an attempted pass by Taylor Chorney banking off Canadian defenceman Marc Staal's skate and eluding Price. The defending champions were still trailing by that single goal deep into the third period but pulled even on a power-play goal by Luc Bourdon with less than 8 minutes in regulation.

When the game went to four-on-four in the 10-minute overtime period, it looked tense. And when a high-sticking penalty to Kris Letang gave the U.S. a power play, it looked tenser still, especially from the penalty box where the fretful defenceman sat. Letang called it "the longest two minutes of my life." Coach Craig Hartsburg sent out his designated shutdown defencemen, Ryan Parent and Marc Staal, who were reprising their roles from Vancouver a year before. They had been teammates on the Ontario under-17 team and in the Canadian under-18 program. Parent and Staal were the blue line's bedrock and a good fit. Both hailed from northern Ontario, Parent from remote Sioux Lookout, Staal from Thunder Bay. Both played in the Ontario Hockey League, Parent for Guelph, Staal for Sudbury. It was a tough test for the two and the forward out there with the game on the line, Tom Pyatt, who had grown up playing with Marc Staal in Thunder Bay.

The American power-play unit (Mueller and Jack Johnson on the blue line and Patrick Kane and Kyle Okposo up front) controlled play for the entire two minutes and the Canadian penalty killers could neither get the puck out of their zone nor get close enough to the bench for a line change. Parent was completely stranded on the opposite side of the ice, 180 feet from the Canadian bench. Others might have panicked, but Parent, Staal, and Pyatt went about their business. "It was lonely out there," Parent said. "They had possession, but we could have got into trouble if we chased them and overcommitted. We were doing what we needed to do, pushing them out to the perimeter. Our job was to deny them the areas they had a chance to score from."

Over the course of the 10-minute overtime period, the Canadians never mustered a serious scoring chance and Price had to make 12 saves compared to two by Frazee.

The anxiety was ratcheted up during the shootout. Many players on the Canadian bench kept their heads down almost prayerfully when their teammates took their turns. Any prayers weren't answered in Canada's first two turns, with Frazee turning aside Steve Downie and Bryan Little. When it came to the Americans' second attempt, Mueller deked and beat Price. After he gave the U.S. the 1–0 lead, Mueller skated by the Canadian bench and gave a shrug with uplifted palms, as if to say that it was all too easy.

Thereafter, Jonathan Toews took charge. On the very next attempt, Canada's third, he wired a low wrist low past Frazee, the first of five consecutive attempts that would beat the U.S. goaltender. Because of the vagaries of the IIHF's rules on shootouts, coach Hartsburg could send out shooters for more than one attempt. He sent Bryan Little back out in the fourth round and this time he beat Frazee. In the fifth round, Toews picked the top corner. In the sixth, Andrew Cogliano's wrist shot again found the net. And finally, in the seventh round, Toews deked and beat Frazee—remarkably, it seemed like each of Toews's goals in the shootout was more sure-handed than the previous one. The last made it 5–4 for Canada, with the Americans owning the last shot.

Price needed to turn aside a shot and secure a berth in the finals. It was poetic justice that his save in the seventh round came on Peter Mueller. A high-scoring centre with Everett in the Western Hockey League, Mueller was a known quantity to Price. What's more, Mueller tried a move on Price that he had used on a breakaway in a WHL regular-season game. Like Toews, Mueller had scored in his first two attempts in the shootout and it looked like this third might slip through Price's pads,

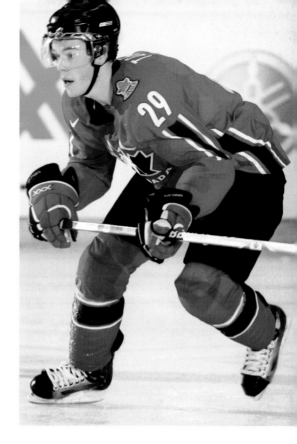

Toews was the undisputed leader of the 2007 Canadian team, but he had come into the tournament with a shoulder injury and had not enjoyed much success to that point in his season with the University of North Dakota.

but the puck disappeared into or under the goalie's pads within a hair of the goal line. Afterwards the Americans would protest that it at least merited video review, and some would claim it was in. No matter; Canada advanced to final against Russia.

"I can't put it into words," Price said. "Playing hockey, I usually don't get nervous. But this was really nerve-racking."

For Price, who gave up only seven goals in six games, the 2007 world juniors were vindication. He had gone to the evaluation camp in December '05 hoping to make the Canadian team defending the championship in his home province. Instead of a Team Canada sweater he was handed a bus ticket back to the Tri-City Americans. "I play for a team in the States so I didn't really even get to watch the tournament," Price said afterwards. "The one thing about getting cut is that you don't give up. I wasn't going to give up. I wanted to show the doubters. There are always doubters," he said. "They're out there."

Winger Darren Helm, here pushing a Czech opponent off the puck, brought strong two-way play and a physical presence to Canada's checking line.

Though he wouldn't name the doubters, it was clear to whom he was referring: Those who criticized the Montreal Canadiens for selecting him with the fifth pick in the first round of the 2005 NHL draft, and those who cut him from the Canadian junior team the year before.

Like any victory, the win over the U.S. wasn't a solo or even duo effort and it was full of subtexts, not the least of them Hartsburg's decision to go with Toews three times in the shootout, a strategy that would have been ruthlessly second-guessed if the outcome had been different.

There was still work to do. In the final the Canadian juniors would face a skilled and swift Russian team that had rolled over the host Swedes in their semifinal.

The defending champions came out in the first period as if on an adrenaline high carrying over from their shootout victory over the U.S. Again it was Toews who set the stage. Canada had jumped out in front 1–0 on a goal by Andrew Cogliano in the first period, but the lead didn't look safe at all. A few minutes before the intermission Toews drew a holding minor on Artem Anisimov and Bryan Little scored on the ensuing power play. On the next shift, with the Russians reeling, Toews scored the prettiest goal of the game, a roof-shot over goalie Semyon Varlamov's right shoulder, to make it 3–0 for Canada. Six minutes into the second period, Toews set up Brad Marchand to extend the lead.

After the fourth goal, the Canadians' energy level dropped. Toews said it was "natural to let up with a lead like that." It was also inevitable, given the frenetic pace of the game.

The second half of the game belonged to Price. The Russians beat him twice on

10 second-period shots, which on paper looks like a mediocre performance. It was anything but.

Late in the second period, he made the save of the tournament, one that will be up there with anything you see in any hockey season. Andrei Kiryukhin, the Russians' most dangerous forward, was parked off the edge of the crease, on Price's glove side. With Price kneeling and committed to the far post, the puck came over to Kiryukhin, who one-timed it. You could hear the air being sucked out of the arena, which was filled with Canadian fans who had travelled to Sweden. They were sure the Russians had scored once again. Kiryukhin seemed ready to raise his stick. And Danny Kurmann, the Swiss referee, was looking in the back of the net for the puck. Price was the only one on the ice and maybe the only person in the arena who knew he had it in his glove. "I couldn't look," forward Ryan O'Marra said. "I had my head in my gloves on the bench. I couldn't believe it when I looked up and heard the Canadian fans cheering." That save would have been reason enough to make the Russians believe it wasn't going to be their day.

After the medal presentation, Jonathan Toews and Carey Price stood outside the dressing room.

Toews was smiling—no, beaming—through the pain. He had a welt under his right eye, a cut across the bridge of his nose, and a patch of tender skin under one nostril where he'd had stitches removed days before. There was a big blotch of blood on the right sleeve of a sweater he has saved and never washed.

Carey Price was unmarked but subdued, keeping his emotions in check, as he did throughout. He had silenced Peter Mueller and the Americans and then the Russians. He almost meditatively took it all in, quiet satisfaction—his resolve issued from that silent bus ride out of Vancouver the year before.

The Canadian juniors stormed out to a 4–0 lead in the gold-medal game but had to hold off a surge from the Russians to secure the title.

2008

PARDUBICE
THE NARROW ESCAPE

DONNA SPENCER

Seventeen-year-old Steven Stamkos started out as a small part of the Canadian team's game plan in the 2008 WJC, but his smooth skating and smart defensive play earned him more ice time in the medal round.

Canada was distinctly lacking in humility upon the team's arrival in Pardubice, Czech Republic, for the 2008 world junior hockey championship. The players felt bulletproof.

Canada was riding an 18-game winning streak in the tournament. The golden run had survived a serious challenge the previous year in Leksand, Sweden. Most of the players on the 2008 team had thumped rival Russia a couple of months earlier in the Super Series, an eight-game set commemorating the 35th anniversary of the 1972 Summit Series. The Super Series was hardly super-competitive, with Canada outscoring Russia 39–13.

Head coach Craig Hartsburg preached to his players how hard it would be to win the country's fourth straight gold medal at the world junior championship. It was a tough sell, maybe an impossible one. He could see them nodding their heads and his words going in one ear and out the other.

"We knew at the start it was going to be a battle with young kids and a younger team," Hartsburg recalled. "The core group of kids went through that summer program without a real challenge.

"They had to experience that there were some good teams in this tournament and a lot better teams than the Russians in the summer."

Brad Marchand (number 17) was Canada's player of the game in the gold-medal victory over Sweden. Kyle Turris, about to take the faceoff, was the Canadians' leading scorer in the tournament.

One player who might have had a modicum of humbleness was Brad Marchand. He and defenceman Karl Alzner were the only two returning players from the previous year's squad.

As a veteran, Marchand was expected to be in the lineup again and put that experience to work. But coach Brent Sutter benched him in the final game of the Super Series for his lack of discipline and told Marchand he wouldn't play for Canada again if he didn't clean up his act.

Marchand was named to the team but still hadn't lost his swagger.

"After we dominated the Super Series, I think we thought we were going to walk through the world juniors," Marchand said.

Alzner, named the team's captain, felt the weight of the expectations created by three straight gold medals.

"Right away I felt a little bit more pressure because I didn't want to be the captain of a team that broke that streak," Alzner says now. "I know it's not a big deal, but to me it was."

This Canadian team was similar in makeup to the young squad that emerged victorious in Vancouver in 2006 despite having one returning player from the previous year. The 2008 group faced the additional challenges of taking it on the road to Europe and onto the bigger ice surface.

Three exhibition wins and then back-to-back shutouts against the host Czechs and Slovakia to open the tournament reinforced Canada's sense of invincibility. The players were so self-assured, the chatter in the dressing room between periods touched on non-hockey topics.

Their third game against Sweden was following the script in the Canadians' heads. They led 2–0 early in the third. What happened next was akin to a sucker punch in the solar plexus—and Canada would not recover easily from it.

When the Swedes had needed a 5–4 win over Belarus five years earlier to avoid relegation, it galvanized their hockey federation into examining what was missing in the development of their junior-aged players. Officials convened a summit conference to plot a new strategy. Better coaching for young goaltenders and fostering a more physical and aggressive game were identified as primary goals.

Those changes were manifested in the Swedish junior program by 2008. Sweden had 12 NHL draft picks on their WJC roster that year.

The biggest, fastest, and toughest Swedish team Canada had faced in years scored three unanswered goals starting at 5:14 of the third period to take a 3–2 lead.

Momentum swung hard to the Swedes on their second goal, when Tony Lagerstrom's shot from behind the goal line went off the back of goaltender Jonathan Bernier's skate.

Canada's Claude Giroux managed to tie the game at 16:18 with a power-play goal, but the Canadians were scrambling in the face of Sweden's pressure. Tobias Forsberg scored the winner for the Swedes with seven seconds left.

More than their inability to protect a lead, the Canadians were stunned by the discovery they had chinks in their armour.

When Alzner and assistant captains Marchand, Logan Pyett, Brandon Sutter, and Stefan Legein met with the coaching staff to analyze video the following day, they saw the room they gave Sweden's speed down the middle, breakdowns in coverage, missed backchecks, and turnovers.

While Canada generated more even-strength chances on offence than in their first two games, they also gave up more scoring chances to the Swedes.

With an average age of 18 years, 11 months, it was Canada's fifth-youngest team at the tournament. Their composure rattled, they faced the task of having to win a quarter-final en route to gold.

In the six years the tournament format awarded each pool winner a bye to the semifinal, only Russia in 1999 had won gold via a win in the quarters.

The loss to Sweden marked a sea change in Canada's attitude. It started to sink in that gold was not assured.

"We thought we were a little bit invincible before then," said Alzner. "We turned into a team that knew we had to be desperate every single game."

There was the danger, however, that the young team would not recover its confidence in time for the games to follow.

When they weren't at the rink, the Canadian players spent most of their time back at the hotel scanning the internet and reading email. After the loss to Sweden, the players read comments from some people at home doubting their ability to win another gold. That galvanized the team and drew them closer together in an us-against-the-world mentality.

"That struck a chord with everybody and kind of fired us up," Alzner recalled. "We were all more focused after that. We turned it up and were snapping the puck a little bit more."

Canada scored a 4–1 win over minnow Denmark in their next game. Even though their subsequent 4–2 quarter-final win over Finland booked Canada into the semis, there was a sense they were playing with white knuckles. The chemistry and confidence still wasn't quite there.

Swedish goaltender Jhonas Enroth stones Steven Stamkos in the gold-medal game. Canada struggled to get the puck to the Swedish net, managing only 20 shots in regulation time.

There wasn't any non-hockey talk in the dressing room now.

A subplot to the tournament was Hartsburg's decision to go with Steve Mason in goal for the medal round, even though some hockey pundits felt he should put Bernier in net.

Canada rarely had goaltending controversies extending into the tournament, as one of the two goalies usually established himself as the starter either during camp or in pre-tournament games.

The day of Canada's semifinal against the United States was tumultuous for Mason, who found out before the game that the London Knights had traded him to Kitchener. The timing couldn't have been worse, and Mason's focus was going to be even further tested.

Mason persevered. So did the team in front of him. Cockiness was a character flaw of this team, but it was balanced out by emotional resiliency.

Even when it looked doubtful Canada was strong enough to win gold again and the goaltending question loomed over the team, the players seemed unaffected off the ice.

They were still enjoying the experience of playing for their country. When it came to dealing with the media, they were a bunch of chatterboxes and relished the attention.

"We had a colourful group of guys," agreed Alzner. "When you get back to the hotel, you talk about the game for half an hour and then it's about having fun and being buddies. That's something that really helped us. We were tight-knit.

"You look at the guys now, where they are in their career, they're still talking lots and still letting that colourful attitude and personality come through."

Canada was also buoyed by the ever-growing army of fans from home who followed them to Europe. If Canadians didn't make up the majority of people in the stands, their raucous support made them the loudest of any country's contingent.

A 4–1 semifinal win over the United States put the Canadians back on firmer ground emotionally. They regained confidence, but not the arrogance they'd brought with them to the tournament. Mason quieted his critics with a 33-save performance against the Americans.

Craig Hartsburg made the toughest call a coach might face late in an international tournament: switching starting goaltenders. Hartsburg decided to go with Steve Mason (shown here) in place of Jonathan Bernier during the medal round.

Shawn Matthias crashes into goaltender Jhonas Enroth just as Matt Halischuk slides the puck into the net for the golden goal in the fourth minute of overtime.

"All we needed was to realize we could beat the good teams again," Alzner said.

But once again, Canada would face Sweden—now established as the tournament favourite with a fast, dangerous attack. Hartsburg was ill with the flu and had just 24 hours to prepare his team for the gold-medal game the next day.

The Canadians were ready for payback versus the Swedes. They'd matured over the course of the world junior tournament, but they would be pushed to the limit to get the gold.

Canada lost Legein to a shoulder injury in the first period, but led 2–0 after two periods on goals from Marchand and Giroux.

There was a sense of déjà vu in the third, however, as Jonathan Carlsson scored at 5:13 and Thomas Larsson tied it up with 38 seconds remaining in regulation and the Swedish net empty.

The extra game Canada had played in the quarter-final was taking its toll by the end of the championship game, as the Swedes outshot Canada 14–3 in the third period.

"We were literally halfway through the third period and it was like a switch went on for them and turned off for us," recalled Kyle Turris, Canada's scoring leader in the tournament.

Hartsburg had a job to do in the dressing room before overtime to calm down his distraught players.

"The first thing was to get them off thinking 'Well, we just blew the gold medal,'" Hartsburg said. "We had to get them settled down because there were kids who were devastated by it and they were pretty close to tears. We needed one shot and we talked about that immediately."

And as it turned out, it was just one shot. After Mason made three saves on the Swedes, Matt Halischuk swarmed their net and shovelled the puck past Jhonas Enroth at 3:36 of overtime. Canada's post-game celebration was a whirl of joy, gratitude, and relief.

Halischuk's goal will go down in history as one of the many big ones a Canadian has scored in the world junior championship. But as a defining moment, Canada might not have won without the dose of humility served to them in their earlier loss to the Swedes.

"You hate to say when you lose it's good, but it was the best thing that happened to the team," Hartsburg said.

Riley Holzapfel waves the maple leaf after the gold-medal win over Sweden. In the last six minutes of regulation time, a tired Canadian team had given up a two-goal lead.

Marchand was named player of the game for Canada in the final. He'd taken only two minor penalties the whole tournament and finished second in team scoring behind Turris with four goals and two assists.

Marchand agreed that both he and his teammates grew up during the 2008 championship.

"I think we thought it was going to come way too easy for us," Marchand said. "After that loss, we realized we had to suck it up and do everything we can to win the tournament."

Alzner often thinks about that roller coaster of a world junior tournament now that he's playing in the NHL.

"I look back on things like that, big games in tournaments like world juniors, for help sometimes when we do get into a sticky situation on the ice and I personally need something to propel me to play a little bit better," he says.

2009

OTTAWA
THE LAST GASP

GORD MILLER

In his second trip to the world juniors, 18-year-old John Tavares provided offensive skill up the middle for the Canadian team in Ottawa.

Jordan Eberle didn't have time to think about how his life was about to change, or about how close he was to scoring one of the most famous goals in Canadian hockey history. His only concern was how much time was left on the clock in the semifinal game of the 2009 world junior championship against Russia.

To be exact, at the moment the puck went into the net there were 5.4 seconds left.

Eberle had tied the score at five, gathering up a bouncing puck on a centring pass from John Tavares that had caromed off a Russian defender and onto his waiting stick. Seeing that Russian netminder Vadim Zhelobnyuk had gone down, Eberle went to his favourite move: forehand, backhand, up.

The Ottawa crowd exploded, and Eberle was mobbed by jubilant teammates. "I don't remember much," Eberle said, recalling the moments after the goal. "Except that P. K. Subban slammed into me pretty hard. My shoulder was sore for a while."

"I looked around and saw the Russians kneeling on the ice," Tavares said. "They were absolutely crushed."

In the broadcast booth high above the ice, I could feel the building shake from the roar of the crowd. There was no time to react, so I said the first words that came to mind: "CAN ... YOU ... BELIEVE IT!"

It was more of a statement than a question, because the truth was, I couldn't believe it.

In a motel room near Comox, British Columbia, Al Murray, watching the game on television, smiled. The chief scout for Hockey Canada had known Eberle for years, having coached and later scouted him in their native Regina. Murray had seen that move countless times before, most often in the Eberle family driveway.

"My son Jake and Jordan went to school together and were teammates in all kinds of sports," Murray remembered. "We'd swing by Jordan's house and there he'd be in the driveway, with a stick and a tennis ball, going forehand, backhand, roof, over and over again."

Despite having such a close relationship with the chief scout, Eberle's spot on the 2009 national junior team was far from guaranteed. A prolific scorer in minor hockey, Eberle was often overlooked—his hometown Regina Pats didn't take him until the seventh round of the WHL draft.

Even with Murray in charge of player selection, Eberle wasn't invited to try out for the 2008 world junior team, one of the few highly ranked prospects for the NHL draft who wasn't there. The following summer, when Eberle was invited to the August evaluation camp in Ottawa, he struggled.

Eberle had just been drafted in the first round by Edmonton, and seemed anxious to prove that his new-found status was deserved. When the coaching staff finished the evaluations from the camp, Eberle was rated last among the 44 players in attendance. "He was awful," Murray said later, laughing.

Like so many memorable moments for Canada at the world junior championships, Eberle's magical goal was the product of some hard work and more than a little good luck.

The road to a fifth straight gold medal began with a bumpy summer. Two weeks after the evaluation camp, head coach Benoit Groulx unexpectedly stepped down, taking a job with the AHL's Rochester Americans.

Picking one assistant over the other to be the head coach would be awkward, and finding someone on short notice outside the program wouldn't be easy either, since the coach would be asked to leave his junior team for nearly a month.

And so, Hockey Canada president Bob Nicholson picked up the phone and once again called an old friend: Pat Quinn.

Quinn was already one of Canada's most decorated international coaches, having guided the Canadian men's team to gold at the 2002 Olympics in Salt Lake City.

In addition, he had answered the call in the spring of 2008, coaching the Canadian under-18 team to gold in the World Championship in Kazan, Russia.

Picking Quinn to coach the under-18s was a surprising choice to say the least. While Quinn had a wealth of experience, his years in the NHL had been marked by whispers that he didn't get along with young players.

Now, fresh off another gold medal and two years removed from his last NHL job, Quinn once again accepted Nicholson's invitation. "I wanted to put that whole thing about young players behind me," he said. "And besides, I was bouncing off the walls."

Quinn's 2009 Canadian junior team included six players who had been with him the previous spring in Kazan. One of the six was Eberle, who had played well for Quinn on the under-18 team and had overcome his bad August camp with a blistering start to his season in Regina.

This Team Canada was younger than usual, as eight players, including Steven Stamkos and Drew Doughty, had not been released by their NHL teams. On the eve of the tournament, chief scout Al Murray made a bold prediction.

"He's not the biggest guy or the fastest skater," Murray said. "But when it's all said and done, I think Jordan Eberle will score some big goals for this team."

―――――――――

After three games, it didn't seem as if any heroics would be required in Ottawa, because drama was in short supply. Canada opened with an 8–1 win over the Czechs, beat Kazakhstan 15–0, and then won 5–1 against Germany. The aggregate score of 28–2, combined with the fact that Canada had won the previous four world junior tournaments, had critics wondering if the competition had become too one-sided.

But on New Year's Eve Canada faced the United States in the first tough test of the tournament—and almost failed it miserably.

Less than 13 minutes in, the Americans had seized a 3–0 lead, silencing the Ottawa crowd and forcing Quinn to call a time out. "Have you forgotten how to play?" Quinn asked his bewildered players. But he calmed them, and urged them to get back to basics.

"He has this unbelievable presence," Eberle said later. "Everything about him is big: his head, his hands, his voice."

But Quinn was more than just a figurehead; he was also a veteran NHL coach who knew how to run a bench. He immediately began double-shifting his best player, John Tavares of the Oshawa Generals. Tavares was a breakout star in the 2008 tournament in the Czech Republic, and now was one of only four returning players in Ottawa.

Two explosive first-period goals by John Tavares led a rally from an early 3–0 deficit to a key opening-round victory over the United States.

Tavares scored two quick goals, and Eberle scored before the end of the period to tie the score at three. The game was fiercely contested the rest of the way before Canada scored two empty-net goals to win 7–4.

"We hadn't really been challenged to that point," Eberle remembered. "We were way too jacked up at the start of that game. It was a good lesson for us."

It was already being called a classic, the most exciting game Canada had ever played at the WJC. It was inconceivable that just three days later, the team would play in an even better one.

"Right from the start, that Russia game was wild," Eberle said. "We'd score, and they'd come right back, and every time we thought we were finally in control, they'd come back again."

A last-minute icing call in the third period against the Russians set in motion events that led to one of the most memorable goals in the history of Canadian hockey: Jordan Eberle's tally with 5.4 seconds left that took the 2009 semifinal into overtime. Here, the puck comes to Eberle at the edge of Vadim Zhelobnyuk's crease.

Canada took a quick 1–0 lead, but the Russians answered, a chain of events that would repeat itself four times, as Canada took leads of 2–1, 3–2 (on a goal by Eberle), and 4–3, only to see the Russians come back every time.

Now, with 2:20 to go, there was a scramble to the right of Canadian goaltender Dustin Tokarski. Russia's Dimitri Klopov poked home the loose puck for his second score of the game and the Russians led for the first time, 5–4. The Ottawa crowd fell silent.

As he did against the United States, Quinn tried to steady his team. When Russia's Dmitri Kugryshev iced the puck with 1:24 left, Quinn called a time out and pulled Tokarski from the Canadian goal.

Quinn normally left tactics to his assistants, but this time he ran the time out himself, at one point telling Eberle, "If the puck is on the right hand side, get to the net." It was a play Quinn had used countless times in the final minutes of games in the NHL. (Later, he was asked how many times it had worked. "Not very often," he said with a chuckle.)

With 41 seconds left, Klopov gained control of the puck in his own zone. Despite having time and space to move the puck ahead, he fired down the ice at the empty Canadian net, perhaps looking for the hat trick. He missed. It was icing, and the faceoff came back to the Russian zone. Far from being distraught, Klopov and his Russian teammates were laughing as they prepared for the faceoff.

"When I saw that, I was really hoping it would come back and bite them," Eberle said.

After Canada had won a third straight faceoff in the Russian zone, Cody Hodgson got a good shot away with 24 seconds left, but Zhelobnyuk kicked it to the corner. The puck went to Nikita Filatov, who tried to clear it on his backhand, but Ryan Ellis read the play and moved to cut it off. Ellis slammed into the boards, actually knocking the puck down with his shoulder to keep it in. Instead of blindly throwing the puck toward the goal, Ellis squeezed it by two Russian defenders along the boards.

In the ensuing scramble, Tavares poked the puck free. Russian defenceman Vyacheslav Voinov went to clear it, but Hodgson deftly lifted his stick. The puck went back to Tavares, who saw three Russian players around him. "I knew there wasn't much time left, and when I saw all those Russians along the wall, I just threw it blindly toward the net, thinking maybe there was an opening," he recalled.

Jordan Eberle was sliding across the goalmouth on his knees when he answered Canadian fans' prayers against the Russians.

Goaltender Dustin Tokarski had won a Memorial Cup with Spokane in the spring of 2008 before landing the starter's job with the Canadian juniors. Coach Pat Quinn gave Tokarski a vote of confidence despite his struggles in games against the United States and Russia.

Remembering Quinn's instructions, Eberle left the battle along the boards and moved to the slot. When Russian defenceman Dmitri Kulikov tried to block the shot, the puck bounced off his shin pad and went right to Eberle, whose momentum was carrying him to the front of the Russian goal. Forehand, backhand, up. Tie game.

———————

Unlike Paul Henderson's goal in the 1972 Summit Series, Mario Lemieux's goal in the 1987 Canada Cup, or Sidney Crosby's gold-medal clincher in Vancouver in 2010, Jordan Eberle's goal didn't win the game for Canada. Pat Quinn thinks that's why it's so widely remembered.

"If Henderson doesn't score, or Lemieux or Crosby don't score, those games continue, and who knows what happens," Quinn said. "If Jordan Eberle doesn't score, the game is over and there's no gold medal."

The rest of the game was something of an anticlimax. Canada dominated the OT but didn't score, sending the game to a shootout. Tavares and Eberle scored on the first two shots for Canada, while Russian coach Sergei Nemchinov mysteriously left his best player, Filatov, to shoot third. He never got the chance. Tokarski stopped the first two Russian shooters and the game was over.

Two days later, Eberle had three points as Canada beat Sweden 5–1 to win a fifth straight goal medal.

———————

Jordan Eberle isn't much for collecting souvenirs. The puck he put in the Russian net went back into play and was never recovered. Eberle kept using the same stick in the OT, the shootout, the gold-medal game, and even two more games in the WHL until the shaft finally snapped. Eberle discarded the stick, but the Pats equipment man, knowing it was the one he had used to score the now famous goal, retrieved it and kept it for him.

Eberle's biggest thrill came two months later, when he met Paul Henderson, who welcomed him into the exclusive club of Canadians who had scored iconic international goals. "Congratulations, Jordan," Henderson said. "You'll be talking about that goal for the rest of your life."

———————

Of all the moments I have called, the one I am asked about most is "the Eberle goal." More than a year after he scored it, I was walking through my neighbourhood and

came across a bunch of kids playing road hockey. Sure enough, one of them went forehand, backhand, roof and looked over at me, smiling.

"C'mon," he said. "Say it."

"CAN … YOU … BELIEVE IT!" I boomed, my voice echoing down the street. The kids raised their sticks, roaring their approval.

Even now, it gives me chills.

Eberle's goal against Russia wasn't a game-winner, but it was a game-saver and kept Canada's hopes alive for a fifth straight gold medal.

2010

SASKATOON
THE END OF THE GOLDEN RUN

ROY MacGREGOR

Brayden Schenn goes airborne to deck U.S. forward Derek Stepan in the neutral zone. Two tight games between Canada and the United States kept fans in Saskatchewan on the edge of their seats.

Crunch!

Crunch!

Crunch!

These are not the sounds of the game being played—though there was much physical contact, as usual, at the 2010 world junior hockey championship—but the sound of people walking to and from the rink, the sound of heavy boots on hard, frozen snow, the sounds that carry at –30°C and below.

Welcome to the true home of the winter game. It is not an actual place—not Windsor, Nova Scotia; not Kingston, Ontario; not Montreal, all of which claim to have been the true birthplace of hockey—but a climate, the game Canadian weather created born of necessity where one must find a way to keep warm as well as keep moving over ice as slippery as a soaped glass.

"In a land so inescapably and inhospitably cold," Bruce Kidd and John Macfarlane wrote many years ago, "hockey is the dance of life, an affirmation that despite the deathly chill of winter we are alive."

And nowhere is the game more alive than on the Canadian prairies. Here is where the hockey rink became the natural community gathering place for towns otherwise fragmented by immigrants arriving from Europe with different languages

Jake Allen won the starting job, but he was pulled from the Canadian goal in the third period of the gold-medal game.

and different churches. Here—just on the outside of Saskatoon—is where little Floral once stood, the small community where a neighbour returned Katherine Howe's kindness during the Great Depression by dropping off a gunny sack containing a pair of old skates. Katherine's awkward son, Gordie, tried them out on the pond back of the house, "fell in love with hockey that day"—and the rest is history.

Those who love hockey could not help but love a WJC held in Regina and Saskatoon in the dead of Canadian winter. Crunching snow, early dark, battery jumps in the parking lots, 50/50 draws worth as much as a new home, volunteers happily paying $50 apiece for the "privilege" of giving up their holiday time in exchange for long days at the rink helping stage this remarkable event.

Team Canada even arrived with its own compelling storyline from the Prairies: Travis Hamonic, a 19-year-old defenceman with the Moose Jaw Warriors who had grown up in little St. Malo, Manitoba, and who used to drive to the rink on his Ski-Doo, hockey bag thrown over the back and sticks held across the handlebars. Hamonic was the youngest of four children and hoped, one day, to be like older brother Jesse, who played. Their father, Gerald, had been head of the local minor hockey system until he died suddenly of heart failure. Travis had been only 10 at the time and had dedicated his junior career to his father's memory. Deeply religious, he wore No. 3 to honour the Holy Trinity—Father, Son, and Holy Spirit—and before each game would write a private message to his father on the blade of his stick, quickly taping over the secret words before anyone else could see.

The City of Saskatoon itself even offered a charming connection between the national game and local politics, with Mayor Don Atchison having once been the goaltender for the local junior team, the Saskatoon Blades, and later enjoying a brief minor-league professional career in which he tended net for the Johnston Jets, the wonky team that inspired *Slap Shot*, the 1977 cult movie about hockey. Atchison's locker was next to Ned Dowd's, a player who took notes for his sister Nancy, who wrote the Hollywood screenplay. Dowd took Atchison's crazy sense of humour and the personality of the team's other goalie, Louis Levasseur, and out of that created Denis Lemieux ("You feel shame"), a character as beloved as Paul Newman's Reggie

Dunlop and the infamous Hanson Brothers. "Everything in that movie is true," claims the mayor of Saskatoon.

A much more evident truth is that the "world juniors" has come to mean something very, very special to all Canadians—especially when played in Canada. It has become as much a part of the annual Christmas break as Boxing Day sales and New Year's hangovers. It is an 11-day festival that begins the day after Christmas and extends into the heart of winter itself, as the game of cold and ice should. It also helps, of course, that Canada wins the tournament often, thereby calming the insecurities that fly up each time the country that gave the world this game has to give the world credit for playing it as well as, even sometimes better than, Canadians themselves.

Team Canada came to Saskatoon with a chance to mark its sixth successive victory in the championship. Victory in Saskatoon on the final day would mean that this string would surpass the record five in a row that Canada set in the 1990s and matched in Ottawa in 2009. Canada's success had already proved to be a remarkable accomplishment—five gold, four silver, and three bronze over the past 12 championships—and stood as a powerful statement that the game at the youth level has never been in as excellent shape as it is today.

The Canadian team rallied around Travis Hamonic, who had to watch the final from the sidelines with a separated shoulder.

The pride Canadian players bring is obvious. "When you pull on a world junior jersey," Team Canada forward and Regina native Jordan Eberle, the hero of the gold-medal victory in Ottawa, said when he came to his home province, "you're expected to win gold. That's just how it is. For me and for every kid on this team, we grew up watching this tournament. It's a special event. Kids grow up dreaming of playing in it."

"These kids are all prospects for the NHL," added Taylor Hall, the Windsor Spitfires star many were predicting (accurately, it turned out) would go first overall in the NHL draft the following June. "I think fans have an interest in watching that. When I was a little kid, there was nothing better than watching the world juniors with my buddies on Boxing Day. It's something special to Canadians. It's a combination of hockey, for sure, and holidays. I find it attracts even non–hockey fans."

Willie Desjardins, the Saskatchewan-born coach of the Canadian team, tried to put it all into perspective when he said one beauty of the tournament is that, each year, it contains "a little bit of the unknown and a little bit of the unexpected." And while the outcome could often be a surprise, the interest in the tournament is no surprise at all. "It's the time of year," Desjardins said. "Everybody's home with their families and it's something they do together.

"It's hockey and it's Canada."

The 2009 WJC had been decided in Ottawa by that 6–5 final, a score held to be almost sacred in Canadian hockey circles when it came to discussing the greatest of games ever played in hockey. Paul Henderson's dramatic last-minute goal in the 1972 Summit Series had given Canada a 6–5 victory over the Soviet Union. Wayne Gretzky's pass to Mario Lemieux and Lemieux's rifle shot had given Canada the 1987 Canada Cup by a 6–5 score. It seemed only fitting that one of the greatest WJC games ever played should also end 6–5.

Even before the medal round, Saskatoon had enjoyed a world junior match between Canada and the United States that set the stage, brilliantly, for the final. Before a record crowd of 15,171 at Credit Union Centre—the stands bleeding red with screaming Canadian fans—Team U.S.A. and Team Canada fought to a 4–4 tie that ultimately went to a shootout. It had been a game for the ages so far as early-round matches go, the lead changing twice, the swift Americans scoring two short-handed goals, the determined Canadians coming back from being down 4–2 and scoring short-handed to tie the game in the dying minutes. Canada's Jordan Eberle, the previous year's hero, had scored twice, Stefan Della Rovere once, and Alex Pietrangelo had delivered the tying goal by intercepting a clearing pass and roofing a shot just under the crossbar. Philip McRae, Jordan Schroeder, Tyler Johnson, and Danny Kristo had all scored for Team U.S.A.

In the wild shootout that was held to settle matters, Canada scored on all three

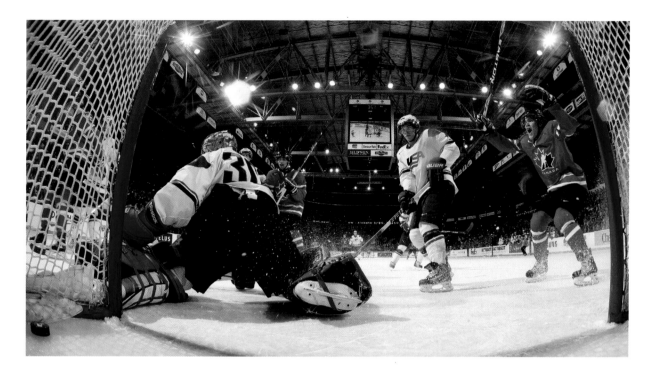

of its shots (Eberle, Nazem Kadri, and Brandon Kozun), while the Americans matched goal for goal (Kristo and Jeremy Morin) until the final shooter of the night (Schroeder) failed to score when Canadian goaltender Jake Allen scissored his pads closed to deny the shot.

It was clear, by this game, that the Americans had become the new rivals to the Canadians—two teams perfectly matched on the ice and two countries forever rubbing up against each other off the ice. It was fitting that the two North American rivals were meeting in a gold-medal game held in—as hockey promoter Bill Hunter put it years ago when Saskatoon was wooing the St. Louis Blues—the very *heart* of the continent. As Canadian poet Al Purdy had once said, victory in hockey, especially against the United States, serves "as a Canadian specific to salve the anguish of inferiority at being good at something the Americans aren't."

The shootout victory over Team U.S.A. gave Canada a bye into the semifinals. The Americans now had to play Finland in order to survive. And survive the Americans did, defeating Finland to advance against pre-tournament favourite Sweden and then winning that match 5–2 to reach the final. Canada, on the other hand, had a skate in the park by comparison, as they next met unheralded Switzerland, the tournament surprise when they bumped out Russia with a 3–2 overtime victory. Drained and missing their best defenceman to injury, the Swiss had fallen easily to Canada, 6–1.

It set up a rematch that was jokingly referred to as "Groundhog Day in Saskatoon"—the Canadians and Americans meeting again on the same ice to settle

Taylor Hall celebrates Greg Nemisz's goal that tied the score 2–2 in the first period of the gold-medal game.

the score once and for all. "A shootout loss is not really a loss," rationalized Team U.S.A.'s Kristo. "It shows up as a loss, but it's not really a loss."

If the Americans found inspiration in avenging that shootout, then the Canadians had theirs in Travis Hamonic. The young defenceman from little St. Malo, Manitoba, had gone down with a separated shoulder in the final moments of the semifinal. He wouldn't be suiting up in the game he had worked so hard to get to, and he wouldn't be playing for the gold medal he had dreamed since childhood of winning. This time he wouldn't be writing that private message to his late father before the game and then taping over the blade so only he would know what he said. Now, the message was for him, and completely public. "We're going to try and go out there and win it for him," said Canadian forward Brayden Schenn.

The Canadians scored on their first shot, and then their fifth, while the Americans

Jordan Eberle scored eight goals in six games in the 2010 tournament, but there would be no repeat of 2009's magical goal in his second bid for gold.

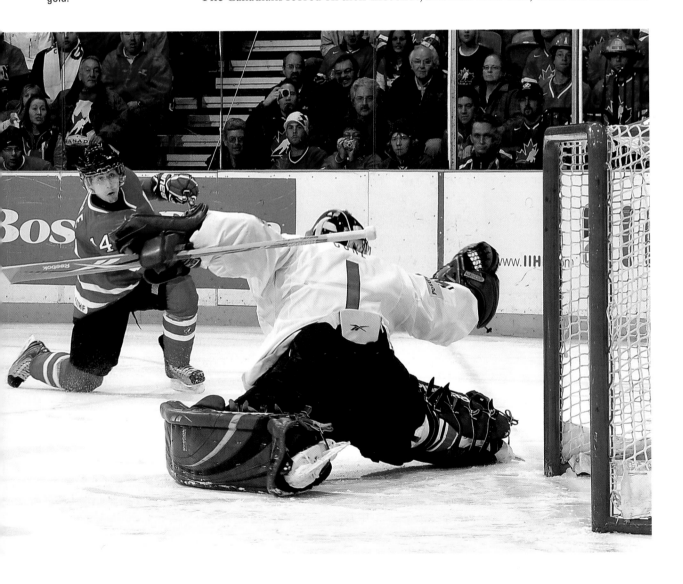

matched the Canadian goals and then moved ahead to take a 3–2 lead. When Canada tied the game at 3–3 early in the second period, the American side pulled goaltender Mike Lee in favour of Jack Campbell, who had played so well in the New Year's classic that Canada had finally taken 5–4 in the shootout. Campbell was an instant standout, continually stopping what seemed, at times, a Canadian stampede to the American net.

It was not to be the only goaltending change, though, with Canada pulling Jake Allen after the Americans scored twice in the third period and replacing Allen with Martin Jones. The change seemed to fire up the Canadians, with Jordan Eberle once again the Canadian hero as he scored twice on the brilliant Campbell in a span of 2:49 to, once again, force overtime in the gold-medal game. Eberle's two, combined with Canadian goals from Luke Adam, Greg Nemisz, and Taylor Hall, matched the five goals from five different Team U.S.A. players: Chris Kreider, Jordan Schroeder, John Carlson, Jerry D'Amigo, and Derek Stepan.

But there would be no shootout this time. And no sixth straight gold medal for Canada. Instead, the dramatic game was ended at 4:21 of the overtime when Team U.S.A. broke up ice on a three-on-one break and rushing defenceman Carlson, with his second goal of the night, beat Jones fairly with a hard blast from the left circle.

Final score, 6–5. Just like all the great games ever played.

And Travis Hamonic, shoulder in a sling, had a medal for his father—just not the gold one he had prayed for.

American John Carlson's overtime goal silenced the crowd in Saskatoon and denied the Canadians a sixth consecutive gold medal.

2011

BUFFALO
THE BORDER CROSSING

ROY MacGREGOR

Carter Ashton hoists an opponent along the boards in Canada's 10–1 romp over Norway. The Canadians had things their own way throughout the tournament up to the third period of the gold-medal game.

It is shortly after midnight, January 6, 2011. Traffic is still heavy on the Peace Bridge that spans the Niagara River between Fort Erie, Ontario, and Buffalo, New York. Vehicles holding red-jerseyed, face-painted, hoarse Canadians who, earlier in the evening, had packed the HSBC Arena to witness the most astonishing collapse in world junior championship history are slowly making their way home.

In one car sits Dan Visentin, the driver, who refuses to turn on the radio because he knows only too well what they will be saying and he does not wish to hear the one word that is bouncing about the airwaves: "choke," the ultimate curse word in hockey. Besides Dan, the car holds Liz, his wife, like Dan a schoolteacher, and his parents, Italo and Rita, who decades ago immigrated to Canada and found their dream life in Niagara Falls. They were now following the great dream of their grandson, Mark, and had just witnessed its shattering.

The green light signalled them up to the booth. Dan rolled down the window, preparing to hand over the four passports.

"How ya doing tonight?" the Canadian border guard asked.

"Depressed," Dan answered.

The guard flicked through the top passport, paused and looked up, surprised.

"You're a Visentin," he said.

Canadian goaltender Mark Visentin knew all about the loneliest position in the game.

"I'm the father."

The guard handed back the passports. "Don't worry," he said. "You have a great kid there—you got to be proud of him."

"We are."

"He's going to be a great goalie one day."

"We know."

———

The first time Mark Visentin tried playing goal, he "fell in love with it." His hero was "CuJo"—Curtis Joseph of the Toronto Maple Leafs—and he tried to emulate Joseph's style. He played on backyard rinks and driveways and in the street in little Waterdown, Ontario. He even played with the family dog, Sheeba, the golden retriever who had grown up with him, changing from a puppy who happily chased balls that missed the net Mark was guarding to a faithful old dog, herself a teenager now, who was simply content to get a pat on the head and her ears scratched. There was no one in her life as important as Mark, her lifelong playmate.

Goaltenders, as the entire hockey world has long known, are both different people and special people. The great Russian goaltender Vladislav Tretiak called it the most "noble" position in all of sport. Gump Worsley argued it was "not a job that would interest any normal, straight-thinking human." Hall of Famer Jacques Plante once asked, "How would you like it if you were sitting in your office and you made one little mistake. Suddenly, a big red light went on and 18,000 people jumped up and started screaming at you, calling you a bum and an imbecile and throwing garbage at you."

Mark Visentin's a reflective young man who possesses an understanding of the potential rewards and gut-wrenching risks that his position entails. "The goaltender can be a game-changer," he says, "and that is a great feeling. But if you're going to do that, you have to accept the ups and downs."

Heading into the 2011 world junior championship, it had been all ups. A brilliant minor hockey goaltender, he had made the leap to major junior at 16. At 17, six weeks short of his 18th birthday, he became a first-round draft pick (chosen 27th overall) of the Phoenix Coyotes. He was already a junior star with the Niagara IceDogs and hoped to have a professional career, but as he was also an excellent student he had a backup plan: a degree at nearby Brock University. He had a girlfriend, Harmony, and life could hardly be better for a kid just turned 18.

Team Canada 2011 came to Buffalo with tremendous promise and a few questions. The team had been selected with an eye to assembling a roster of, as head coach Dave Cameron put it, "200-foot players." He did not, fortunately, mean height, but rather style. Cameron and management wanted solid, working-class players who were comfortable at both ends of the ice. With a number of flashier juniors left off the team, there were naturally questions raised concerning who would do the scoring, but there were also questions raised as to who would stop the scoring from the other side. From a list of top junior goaltenders the choice came down to two: Olivier Roy, a 19-year-old native of Causapscal, Quebec, playing for the Acadie-Bathurst Titan, and 18-year-old Mark Visentin.

Roy, the more experienced of the two, had been chosen to start Canada's first three games, but when Canada lost a 6–5 shootout to another pre-tournament favourite, Sweden, the decision was made to give Visentin a chance the next game—which would be Switzerland and a game that, of course, Canada could be expected to win handily.

It was not an auspicious debut. The Canada-Switzerland game was barely a minute old when, back of the Canadian net, two Swiss forwards came up with a puck that should already have been cleared safely away by the Canadian defence. Inti Pestoni came around the net and flipped a soft shot that somehow slipped in between Visentin's right pad and the post.

Ooooooooooooooops.

It was, however, the only goal the pesky Swiss could manage. Canada went on to a 4–1 victory and the chance to meet nemesis Team U.S.A.—the gold-medal winner in Saskatoon only the year before—in the 2011 semifinal. Visentin, who had stopped the 21 other shots directed his way, was philosophical about the first. "I didn't want that to happen," he said. "But it's over and you can't change that."

He talked about how he had been working on his "mental focus" as much as his angles. He had been learning not to get down on himself, not to doubt—the debilitating bug that all goaltenders must fight off from time to time. "There were 59 minutes left," he told himself. More than enough time to repair matters.

He talked about the possibility of him now facing the Americans. A year earlier he had watched the championship being played out in Saskatoon and the final had been "a heartbreaker." He wanted to be a part of the avenging of Saskatoon.

He got his wish. Visentin started against the arch-rival Americans and played well, with Canada winning 4–1 to advance once again to the key gold-medal match. What was surprising was the opponent: Russia. The Russians had barely been on the radar heading into the tournament, losing their first two matches to Canada (6–3) and Sweden (2–0), but they had since fashioned the two most remarkable comebacks of 2011. Down 3–1 against the Finns, they had won 4–3 in overtime, then had tied the Swedes in the dying seconds of Sunday's semifinal game to force overtime and get to a shootout, which they won.

Instead of the anticipated United States–Canada match, the gold medal had come down to Canada vs. Russia.

———

These Russians could not be taken lightly—not after such dramatic comebacks against Finland and Sweden—and the Canadians did not take them lightly. Team Canada captain Ryan Ellis opened the scoring with a blast from the point on an early Canadian power play. Before the first period was over, Canada was up 2–0 on big Carter Ashton's goal. When Brayden Schenn made it 3–0—a seemingly insurmountable lead—it marked Schenn's 18th point of the tournament, tying him for the all-time Team Canada single tournament scoring lead with Dale McCourt, who had set the mark in 1977—back before Hockey Canada had established the Program of Excellence.

To gain some sense of the shock to come, it is worth noting that those who were voting on the tournament's top players handed in their ballots at the end of the second period. Schenn, to no surprise, was named tournament MVP as well as best forward. Ellis was named the top defenceman. And top goaltender title went to Team U.S.A.'s Jack Campbell.

And then it happened. In less than five minutes of play, the Russians managed six shots on young Visentin and scored three times—and the period was not even half over. You could almost see the blood drain from the red-painted faces of the Canadian fans who had packed the HSBC Arena to cheer on what had appeared a certain Canadian victory.

The Russians moved ahead 4–3 when Artemi Panarin managed to elude three Canadian checkers to slip the puck past Visentin and scored again in the dying moments to make it 5–3, all five Russian goals coming in a third period that was already being tagged "a monumental collapse." Many were even saying the word that losing players and coaches most dread: "choke."

In his second trip to the tournament, Brayden Schenn racked up 18 points, more than any other player in the history of the Program of Excellence.

Who, people wanted to know, was to blame for this humiliation? Cameron for failing to pull his goalie as the Russians had done? Team Canada scouts and officials for failing to add snipers? Or Mark Visentin, the goaltender who couldn't stop the Russian flood? As Jacques Plante so eloquently put it more than half a century earlier, the goalie gets the blame, no matter what.

The Russian national anthem was played, and the Canadians, silver medals hanging like albatrosses around their necks, left the ice and hurried through the media availability without even looking up. Mark Visentin had sobbed openly on the ice and cried some more in the dressing room. He heard Hockey Canada's André Brin asking some of the other players if anyone was ready to speak to the waiting media.

"I'll come out," he volunteered, surprising Brin.

The gathered media were even more surprised. Here was this 18-year-old kid who had just been at the centre of a crushing turn of events and he was ready to talk. A few in the media noted how clear his eyes were: shouldn't he be off somewhere crying?

And yet he stood there, towering over the microphones and notepads, head held high, and he spoke for as long as there were questions—even though no language could possibly provide equal answers.

———

Mark Visentin dressed slowly, still processing what had happened. The teammates said their goodbyes—painful and poignant—and Mark found Harmony waiting outside, as arranged, and the two began the long drive back in the dark. He knew his parents and grandparents would have already crossed over and he made it through without comment, without a border guard recognizing his name. He drove slowly

Left: Canadian captain Ryan Ellis brought savvy puck-handling skills to the blue line in his third WJC.

Above: Defenceman Maxim Berezin lines up Carter Ashton in the final. With the gold medal on the line, the older, bigger Russians physically wore down the Canadians.

Mark Visentin is beaten for a goal in the third period against the Russians. He showed dignity beyond his years in the wake of a wrenching defeat in the gold-medal game.

back to his parents' home in Waterdown. No radio for them, either. He didn't need to hear his own words played back to him.

"I like to get stuff done and not leave it," he told me a couple of days later.

He put no blame on the defence that, at times, let him down, no blame on the forwards who had their own breakdowns. He took full responsibility.

"I'm not the guy who blames his team," he said. "You really wish you could have provided a couple of saves when they were needed."

He had felt the tide turning. He watched the spark go into the Russians and knew that it had gone out of his own team. "We pushed the panic button a bit," he said. "We tried to get back but.…

"No one to blame but me. I try to make myself accountable for what happens."

He was, however, being held accountable by others, perhaps too shocked or too angry to allow for perspective. Hockey means so much to Canadians, and success has been so regular, that only success seems acceptable. People who might not expect their own teen to clean up his room or take out the garbage were not only expecting, but demanding, that these teenagers take on the best hockey teams in the world and remain, always, the best hockey team in the world.

Yet even those who knew this made no sense were concerned. What, they wondered, would be the long-term effect of such an experience? They needed to be reminded that in Game 5 of the 1972 Summit Series, the original Team Canada had been up 4–1 in the third period in Moscow only to have the Soviets score four unanswered goals and win. The goaltender in net for that "monumental collapse" was Tony Esposito, who was in the prime of his Hall of Fame career.

"People lose perspective," Dan Visentin said of his son a few days after the game. "Mark will be fine. He's got his whole future in front of him."

Mark, however, had driven home that night in silence, thinking more on his past. "It was weird," he remembered. "There was just so much to take in." He thought about former coaches, teammates. He was grateful for his relationship with his family, with Ben Vanderklok, a coach with the Niagara IceDogs who had been working so hard with Mark on the importance of personal mental toughness.

"It was a tough pill to swallow," he said of what had happened. "But I think I'm a better person for it."

If he could handle this, he knew, he could handle anything. He knew now that he was strong enough to leave it behind him, to move on. There would be more "ups" coming.

No one was up when Mark came through the front door that evening. But then, almost immediately, came the sound of an old dog's nails moving along the floor. Sheeba, still going strong at 14, came hurrying toward him, wiggling and tail wagging.

"She was just happy to see me," he said.

And he her, considering the day he had just put in at the most noble position in the game.

EPILOGUE

BOB NICHOLSON,
PRESIDENT AND CEO,
HOCKEY CANADA

The Program of Excellence has grown by our willingness to learn. When we've made mistakes, we've learned from them. When we've had successful approaches, we've tried to repeat them. That said, we had to make sure that we didn't settle for the same old thing. We haven't stayed in one place with our program. We couldn't. We've had to keep evolving, after our victories and our defeats. It's not change for change's sake. We've been forced to adjust because other programs have learned from us and they improve every year. The world junior championship was always a tough tournament to win, but it's tougher now than ever before. The last two tournaments prove the point.

Sweden won its lone WJC title back in 1981, the season before the launch of our Program of Excellence. The Swedes have won world championships and Olympic gold and sent scores of stars to the NHL. They often failed to live up to expectations at the WJC. That, however, has not been the case in recent years. The Swedish Ice Hockey Association has placed a greater emphasis on its junior program and the teams wearing the Tre Kronor are at or near the front of the pack in virtually every season. The Swedes beat our team in the qualifying rounds in Pardubice in the 2008 WJC and, in the rematch with the gold medal on the line, a hard-fought contest went to overtime before Matt Halischuk scored the golden goal.

Through the WJC's first 20 years, U.S. teams were only occasionally a factor. Over the last decade, however, the United States has come away with two golds,

the most recent when they beat our team in overtime of the 2010 gold-medal game in Saskatoon. We know from experience that a gold is hard to win on the road and hardest in the other team's building. You have to give Team U.S.A. full credit for what they were able to do. We go into every tournament now knowing that the United States is going to have a strong team.

Russian teams were the dominant force in the tournament back before the Program of Excellence and almost always a gold-medal threat. Some people have thought that Russia's junior program has been in a downturn because there haven't been breakthrough Russian stars in the NHL since Alexander Ovechkin and Evgeni Malkin. Maybe people have forgotten that it took a last-second goal by Jordan Eberle just to send the semifinal into overtime in 2009. It hardly looked like the Russian program was on hard times when its team stormed back on us in the third period of the gold-medal game in Buffalo.

Those were narrow wins and tough losses, but the greater lesson to learn goes deeper than the gold-medal games: nothing can be taken for granted. No tournament. No game. We saw it in the game the Americans lost to Slovakia in the quarters in Ottawa, and in the Russians' loss to Switzerland in Saskatoon. Any gaps between the teams in this tournament have closed dramatically. Other countries are dedicating more resources and more money to the development of young players. They've moved aggressively and I think that makes what we've accomplished in the last 10 years with the Program of Excellence look all the more impressive. I know that it is going to make our next 10 years an even greater challenge.

I don't think it's a coincidence that our program produced some of Team Canada's greatest moments after our biggest disappointments.

When we were disqualified from the 1987 WJC in Piestany because of the bench-clearing brawl, we came back the next year with a highly disciplined squad and beat a great Soviet team in Moscow. We instilled in our players a better sense of what it was going to take to win, not just technically but also emotionally. Over the years it's been a message we deliver to all the players who come through the program. That said, we don't avoid players who might seem like risks because of their histories in major junior. When Steve Downie came to us for the first time back in December 2005, we told him that he would have to check a lot of his emotions or impulses at the door. The same applied with Steve Ott a few years earlier. Both players and others like them appreciated our position of having open minds about them and they played very well for us.

When we lost in Füssen in 1992, we tried to do something different in the run-up to the tournament. We added players to the lineup on the eve of the round robin, ignoring what we had learned about assembling a team and establishing good chemistry. Our poor result in that tournament forced us to take a long, hard look—not at the players, but at ourselves. We had forgotten how valuable our team building had been to our success. We tried to take a shortcut and the loss fell on us. What might have worked out with a team over the course of a hockey season is tougher to pull off in a short tournament. There's no time for a learning curve. The team has to be ready to play immediately, from the first shift of the first period of the first game. In Füssen, we thought the players would come together—but they simply did not have enough time.

Our greatest assets going forward aren't anything money can buy. They are our people. When I say this, I'm not talking about our players being superior. No, I'm talking about the Canadian Hockey League executives we've developed excellent working relationships with and the coaches who've learned and grown in Hockey Canada's programs over the years. I'm talking about physicians, sports psychologists, trainers, and technical staff who volunteer their time for us. And I'm talking about grass-roots supporters who have contributed in hundreds of different ways to the development of the players who represent this nation at the WJC.

There isn't a particular profile that we seek out for the Program of Excellence. There isn't a "company man." We've had a wide range of characters and they've displayed their mettle at the tournament. They've faced a variety of challenges and been forced to respond to them in ways they could not have anticipated.

Perry Pearn has always been thought of as a tactician and technical coach rather than a fiery, emotional presence. He had to break that mould in Sweden in 1993. Perry's players seemingly had no gas left in the tank when they made it to the gold-medal game. He came up with an emotional speech that many would have thought was out of character. Later, he placed his championship ring on a table and walked out of the dressing room. Those are inspired coaching moments, spontaneous decisions made in the heat of battle.

Brent Sutter faced an entirely different set of challenges with the teams he coached in 2005 and 2006. In his first go-round at the WJC, Brent had a powerhouse team. His challenge was to keep his players focused and any egos in check. The next year, however, was a very different set of circumstances: a team that went into the gold-medal game as an underdog in the minds of many. Instead of worrying about egos, Brent had to be concerned about nerves and self-doubts. The result was the same—in fact, our team's performance in the 2006 gold-medal game might have been more impressive than the final the year before. The work of Brent and his staff in Vancouver certainly was.

In the wake of victories it's easy to forget just how difficult many big decisions were along the way. Our two most recent WJC gold medals came after our coaches made incredibly tough decisions about their goaltenders. In '08, Craig Hartsburg went with a hunch late in the tournament, going with Steve Mason in the medal round. In '09, Pat Quinn stayed with Dustin Tokarski despite three first-period goals scored by Team U.S.A. late in the round robin—on that occasion his own assistant coaches were sure he'd make the switch. Both Mason and Tokarski were key to their teams' victories.

Everyone who has been involved in the Program of Excellence doesn't just give it his all for a few weeks, or even a season. There's a sense of loyalty and kinship there and an incredible willingness to share and give back. Those who have coached or played another role always come back to help out and work with those who are coming up through the ranks. That includes coaches who went on to helm Stanley Cup winners: Mike Babcock, Ken Hitchcock, and Claude Julien. That includes hockey people like Pat Quinn, who has worked in the game for more than four decades, and others like Guy Boucher, who is barely four decades old.

When Murray Costello and Dennis McDonald founded the Program of Excellence, I don't know if they fully intended its name to work on so many levels. Our WJC program draws on gifted, industrious, tireless people who would never settle for less than excellence and puts them in situations that demand excellence. Good isn't good enough. Excellence is what we aspire to but will never settle for because we believe we can be even better next year. And we know that we have to be better every year.

TEAM ROSTERS

1982

#	NAME	P	S	HT	WT	BORN	HOMETOWN	CLUB	DRAFT STATUS
14	Scott Arniel	F	L	6'1"	170	09/17/62	Kingston, Ont.	Cornell (ECAC)	WPG '81 (2, 22)
5	Paul Boutilier	D	R	5'11"	189	05/03/63	Halifax, N.S.	Sherbrooke (QMJHL)	NYI '81 (1, 21)
10	Garth Butcher	D	R	5'11.5"	181	08/03/63	Regina, Sask.	Regina (WHL)	VAN '81 (1, 10)
1	Frank Caprice	G	L	5'9"	150	05/12/62	Hamilton, Ont.	London (OHL)	VAN '81 (9, 178)
19	Paul Cyr	F	L	5'11"	185	10/31/63	Victoria, B.C.	Victoriaville (QMJHL)	1982 Draft
24	Bruce Eakin	F	L	5'11"	185	09/28/62	Winnipeg, Man.	Lethbridge (WHL)	CGY '81 (10, 204)
16	Marc Habscheid	F	R	5'11"	172	03/01/63	Wymark, Sask.	Victoriaville (QMJHL)	EDM '81 (6, 113)
4	Gord Kluzak	D	L	6'4"	216	03/04/64	Climax, Sask.	Billings (OHL)	1982 Draft
12	Moe Lemay	F	L	5'11"	185	02/18/62	Ottawa, Ont.	Ottawa (OHL)	VAN '81 (5, 105)
30	Mike Moffat	G	L	5'11"	170	02/04/62	Mississauga, Ont.	Kingston (OHL)	BOS '80 (8, 165)
26	Mike Moller	F	R	6'1"	189	06/16/62	Red Deer, Alta.	Lethbridge (WHL)	BUF '80 (2, 41)
2	Randy Moller	D	R	6'2"	205	08/23/63	Red Deer, Alta.	Lethbridge (WHL)	QUE '81 (1, 11)
23	Dave Morrison	F	R	6'1"	189	06/12/62	Kingston, Ont.	Peterborough (OHL)	LA '80 (2, 34)
17	Mark Morrison	F	R	5'8"	150	03/11/63	Tsawwassen, B.C.	Victoriaville (QMJHL)	NYR '81 (3, 51)
21	Troy Murray C	F	R	5'11"	189	07/31/62	St. Albert, Alta.	North Dakota (WCHA)	CHI '80 (3, 57)
3	Gary Nylund	D	L	6'4"	207	10/28/63	North Delta, B.C.	Portland (WHL)	1982 Draft
9	James Patrick	D	R	5'9"	165	06/14/63	Winnipeg, Man.	North Dakota (WCHA)	NYR '81 (1, 9)
7	Pierre Rioux	F	R	5'9"	165	02/01/62	Quebec City, Que.	Shawinigan (QMJHL)	Undrafted
11	Todd Strueby	F	L	6'1"	192	06/15/63	Humboldt, Sask.	Saskatoon (WHL)	EDM '81 (2, 29)
20	Carey Wilson	F	R	6'1"	192	05/11/62	Winnipeg, Man.	IFK Helsinki (FIN)	CHI '80 (4, 67)

Head coach: Dave King

Assistant coach: Georges Larivière

Assistant coach: Sherry Bassin

1983

#	NAME	P	S	HT	WT	BORN	HOMETOWN	CLUB	DRAFT STATUS
15	Dave Andreychuk	F	R	6'2"	159	09/29/63	Hamilton, Ont.	Oshawa (OHL)	BUF '82 (1, 16)
5	Paul Boutilier	D	R	5'10.5"	189	05/03/63	Halifax, N.S.	St-Jean (QMJHL)	NYI '81 (1, 21)
2	Joe Cirella	D	R	6'0.5"	189	05/09/63	Stoney Creek, Ont.	Oshawa (OHL)	COL '81 (1, 5)
19	Paul Cyr	F	L	5'11"	185	10/31/63	Port Alberni, B.C.	Victoriaville (QMJHL)	BUF '82 (1, 9)
12	Dale Derkatch	F	L	5'5"	140	10/17/64	Winnipeg, Man.	Regina (WHL)	1983 Draft
8	Mike Eagles	F	L	5'11"	161	03/07/63	Sussex, N.B.	Kitchener (OHL)	QUE '81 (6,,116)
20	Pat Flatley	F	R	6'0.5"	194	10/03/63	Toronto, Ont.	Wisconsin (WCHA)	NYI '82 (1, 21)
4	Gary Leeman	D	R	5'11"	168	02/19/64	Toronto, Ont.	Regina (WHL)	TOR '82 (2, 24)
24	Mario Lemieux	F	R	6'0.5"	176	10/05/65	Montreal, Que.	Laval (QMJHL)	1983 Draft
17	Mark Morrison	F	R	5'8"	159	03/11/63	Delta, B.C.	Victoriaville (QMJHL)	NYR '81 (3, 51)
9	James Patrick C	D	L	6'0.5"	178	06/14/63	Winnipeg, Man.	North Dakota (WCHA)	NYR '81 (1, 9)
1	Mike Sands	G	L	5'7"	154	04/06/63	Mississauga, Ont.	Sudbury (OHL)	MIN '81 (2, 31)
7	Brad Shaw	D	R	5'11"	159	04/28/64	Cambridge, Ont.	Ottawa (OHL)	DET '82 (5, 86)
21	Gord Sherven	F	R	5'10.5"	183	08/21/63	Mankota, Sask.	North Dakota (WCHA)	MIN '81 (10, 197)
11	Tony Tanti	F	L	5'9"	189	09/07/63	Mississauga, Ont.	Oshawa (OHL)	CHI '81 (1, 12)
3	Larry Trader	D	L	6'0.5"	194	07/07/63	Barry's Bay, Ont.	London (OHL)	DET '81 (5, 86)
10	Sylvain Turgeon	F	L	5'10.5"	161	01/17/65	Rouyn-Noranda, Que.	Hull (QMJHL)	1983 Draft
18	Pat Verbeek	F	R	5'7"	174	05/24/64	Sarnia, Ont.	Sudbury (OHL)	NJ '82 (3, 43)
30	Mike Vernon	G	L	5'8"	150	02/24/63	Calgary, Alta.	Calgary (WHL)	CGY '81 (3, 56)
14	Steve Yzerman	F	R	5'9"	172	09/05/65	Nepean, Ont.	Peterborough (OHL)	1983 Draft

Head coach: Dave King

Assistant coach: Michel Morin

Assistant coach: Doug Sauter

1984

#	NAME	P	S	HT	WT	BORN	HOMETOWN	CLUB	DRAFT STATUS
30	Allan Bester	G	L	5'7"	150	03/26/64	Hamilton, Ont.	Brantford (OHL)	TOR '83 (3, 48)
20	Lyndon Byers	F	R	6'1"	185	02/29/64	Nipawin, Sask.	Regina (WHL)	BOS '82 (2, 39)
6	Bruce Cassidy	D	L	6'1"	180	05/20/65	Ottawa, Ont.	Ottawa (OHL)	CHI '83 (1, 18)
22	Sylvain Côté	D	R	6'0"	175	01/19/66	Quebec City, Que.	Quebec (QMJHL)	1984 Draft
21	Yves Courteau	F	L	6'1"	185	02/29/64	Pointe-aux-Trembles, Que.	Laval (QMJHL)	DET '82 (2, 23)
9	Russ Courtnall C	F	R	5'10"	175	06/03/65	Victoria, B.C.	Victoriaville (QMJHL)	TOR '83 (1, 7)
3	J.J. Daigneault	D	L	5'11"	181	10/12/65	Montreal, Que.	Canadian National Team	1984 Draft
26	Dale Derkatch	F	L	5'5"	140	10/17/64	Winnipeg, Man.	Regina (WHL)	EDM '83 (7, 140)
23	Gerald Diduck	D	R	6'2"	202	04/05/65	Sherwood Park, Alta.	Lethbridge (WHL)	NYI '83 (1, 16)
11	Dean Evason	F	R	5'10"	175	08/22/64	Brandon, Man.	Kamloops (WHL)	WSH '82 (5, 89)
17	Dave Gagner	F	L	5'10"	185	12/11/64	Chatham, Ont.	Brantford (OHL)	NYR '83 (1, 12)
12	Randy Heath	F	L	5'8"	165	11/11/64	Vancouver, B.C.	Portland (WHL)	NYR '83 (2, 33)
16	Dan Hodgson	F	R	5'11"	170	08/29/65	Fort McMurray, Alta.	Prince Albert (WHL)	TOR '83 (5, 83)
27	Garry Lacey	F	L	5'11"	178	05/24/64	Falconbridge, Ont.	Toronto (OHL)	NYI '82 (3, 63)
19	Gary Leeman	D	R	5'11"	170	02/19/64	Toronto, Ont.	Regina (WHL)	TOR '82 (2, 24)
8	John MacLean	F	R	6'0"	194	11/20/64	Oshawa, Ont.	New Jersey (NHL)	NJ '83 (1, 6)
10	Kirk Muller	F	L	6'0"	189	02/08/66	Kingston, Ont.	Guelph (OHL)	1984 Draft
5	Mark Paterson	D	L	6'0"	195	02/22/64	Nepean , Ont.	Ottawa (OHL)	HFD '82 (2, 35)
4	Brad Shaw A	D	R	5'10"	170	04/28/64	Cambridge, Ont.	Ottawa (OHL)	DET '82 (5, 86)
1	Ken Wregget	G	L	6'1"	182	03/25/64	Brandon, Man.	Lethbridge (WHL)	TOR '82 (3, 45)

Head coach: Brian Kilrea

Assistant coach: Terry Simpson

Assistant coach: Georges Larivière

1985

#	NAME	P	S	HT	WT	BORN	HOMETOWN	CLUB	DRAFT STATUS
14	Bob Bassen	F	L	5'10"	181	05/06/65	Calgary, Alta.	Medicine Hat (WHL)	Undrafted
19	Yves Beaudoin	D	R	5'9"	180	01/07/65	Pointe-aux-Trembles, Que.	Shawinigan (QMJHL)	WSH '83 (10, 195)
2	Brad Berry	D	L	6'2"	190	04/01/65	Bashaw, Alta.	North Dakota (WCHA)	WPG '83 (2, 29)
25	Jeff Beukeboom	D	R	6'4"	210	03/28/65	Lindsay, Ont.	Sault Ste. Marie (OHL)	EDM '83 (1, 18)
1	Craig Billington	G	L	5'10"	155	09/11/66	London, Ont.	Belleville (OHL)	NJ '84 (2, 23)
8	Brian Bradley	F	R	5'9"	183	01/21/65	Kitchener, Ont.	London (OHL)	CGY '83 (3, 51)
6	Wendel Clark	F	L	5'11"	187	10/25/66	Kelvington, Sask.	Saskatoon (WHL)	1985 Draft/Rep.
9	Shayne Corson	F	L	6'2"	185	08/13/66	Barrie, Ont.	Hamilton (OHL)	MTL '84 (1, 8)
11	Adam Creighton A	F	L	6'5"	205	06/06/65	Welland, Ont.	Buffalo (NHL)	BUF '83 (1, 11)
5	Bobby Dollas	D	L	6'3"	210	01/31/65	Montreal, Que.	Winnipeg (NHL)	WPG '83 (1, 14)
30	Norm Foster	G	L	5'7"	175	02/10/65	Vancouver, B.C.	Michigan State (CCHA)	BOS '83 (11, 222)
24	Dan Gratton	F	L	6'0"	182	12/07/66	Brantford, Ont.	Oshawa (OHL)	1985 Draft/Rep.
16	Dan Hodgson C	F	R	5'11"	175	08/29/65	Fort McMurray, Alta.	Prince Albert (WHL)	TOR '83 (5, 83)
12	Jeff Jackson	F	L	6'1"	190	04/24/65	Dresden, Ont.	Hamilton (OHL)	TOR '83 (2, 28)
10	Greg Johnston	F	R	6'1"	205	01/14/65	Barrie, Ont.	Toronto (OHL)	BOS '83 (2, 42)
21	Claude Lemieux	F	R	6'1"	208	07/16/65	Montreal, Que.	Verdun (QMJHL)	MTL '83 (2, 26)
3	John Miner	D	R	5'11"	187	08/28/65	Regina, Sask.	Regina (WHL)	EDM '83 (11, 220)
7	Selmar Odelein	D	R	6'1"	201	04/11/66	Quill Lake, Sask.	Regina (WHL)	EDM '84 (1, 21)
23	Stéphane Richer	F	R	6'2"	185	07/07/66	Ripon, Que.	Granby (QMJHL)	MTL '84 (2, 29)
26	Jim Sandlak	F	R	6'3"	202	12/12/66	Kitchener, Ont.	London (OHL)	1985 Draft/Rep.

Head coach: Terry Simpson

Assistant coach: Ron Lapointe

1986

#	NAME	P	S	HT	WT	BORN	HOMETOWN	CLUB	DRAFT STATUS
1	Craig Billington	G	L	5'10"	160	09/11/66	London, Ont.	Belleville (OHL)	NJ '84 (2, 23)
30	Sean Burke	G	L	6'3"	195	01/29/67	Windsor, Ont.	Toronto (OHL)	NJ '85 (2, 24)
2	Terry Carkner	D	L	6'4"	202	03/07/66	Winchester, Ont.	Peterborough (OHL)	NYR '84 (1, 14)
27	Al Conroy	F	R	5'7"	165	01/17/66	Calgary, Alta.	Medicine Hat (WHL)	Undrafted
9	Shayne Corson	F	L	6'1"	187	08/13/66	Barrie, Ont.	Hamilton (OHL)	MTL '84 (1, 8)
24	Alain Côté	D	R	6'0"	201	04/14/67	Matane, Que.	Boston (NHL)	BOS '85 (2, 31)
22	Sylvain Côté	D	R	6'0"	177	01/19/66	Quebec City, Que.	Hartford (NHL)	HFD '84 (1, 11)
10	Peter Douris	F	R	6'0"	195	02/19/66	Toronto, Ont.	New Hampshire (ECAC)	WPG '84 (2, 30)
22	Jeff Greenlaw	F	L	6'2"	195	02/28/68	Aylmer, Ont.	Canadian National Team	1986 Draft
8	Derek Laxdal	F	R	6'2"	189	02/21/66	Stonewall, Man.	Brandon (WHL)	TOR '84 (8, 151)
20	Scott Mellanby	F	R	6'1"	200	06/11/66	Islington, Ont.	Wisconsin (WCHA)	PHI '84 (2, 27)
5	Dave Moylan	D	L	6'2"	201	08/13/67	Tillsonburg, Ont.	Sudbury (OHL)	BUF '85 (4, 77)
14	Joe Murphy	F	L	6'1"	170	10/16/67	London, Ont.	Penticton (BCHL)	1986 Draft
19	Joe Nieuwendyk	F	L	6'2"	187	09/10/66	Oshawa, Ont.	London (OHL)	CGY '85 (2, 27)
7	Selmar Odelein	D	R	6'1"	190	04/11/66	Quill Lake, Sask.	Regina (WHL)	EDM '84 (1, 21)
12	Gary Roberts	F	L	6'1"	187	05/23/66	Whitby, Ont.	Ottawa (OHL)	CGY '84 (1, 12)
15	Luc Robitaille	F	L	6'1"	185	02/17/66	Montreal, Que.	Hull (QMJHL)	LA '84 (9, 171)
26	Jim Sandlak C	F	R	6'3"	207	12/12/66	Kitchener, Ont.	London (OHL)	VAN '85 (1, 4)
25	Mike Stapleton	F	R	5'10"	175	05/05/66	Strathroy, Ont.	Cornell (ECAC)	CHI '84 (7, 132)
3	Emmanuel Viveiros	D	L	5'11"	171	01/08/66	St. Albert, Alta.	Prince Albert (WHL)	EDM '84 (6, 106)

Head coach: Terry Simpson

Assistant coach: Michel Parizeau

1987

#	NAME	P	S	HT	WT	BORN	HOMETOWN	CLUB	DRAFT STATUS
4	Steve Chiasson C	D	L	6'0"	205	04/14/67	Peterborough, Ont.	Detroit (NHL)	DET '85 (3, 50)
9	Yvon Corriveau	F	L	6'1"	200	02/08/67	Welland, Ont.	Washington (NHL)	WSH '85 (1, 19)
15	Pat Elynuik	F	R	6'0"	181	10/30/67	Foam Lake, Alta.	Prince Albert (WHL)	WPG '86 (1, 8)
10	Theoren Fleury	F	R	5'10"	160	06/29/68	Russell, Man.	Moose Jaw (WHL)	1987 Draft
2	Greg Hawgood	D	L	5'9"	185	08/10/68	St. Albert, Alta.	Kamloops (WHL)	BOS '86 (10,202)
6	Kerry Huffman	D	L	6'2"	185	01/03/68	Peterborough, Ont.	Guelph (OHL)	PHI '86 (2, 22)
5	Chris Joseph	D	R	6'2"	194	09/10/69	Burnaby, B.C.	Seattle (WHL)	1987 Draft
11	Mike Keane	F	R	5'10"	179	09/25/67	Winnipeg, Man.	Moose Jaw (WHL)	Undrafted
22	David Latta	F	L	6'0"	187	01/03/67	Thunder Bay, Ont.	Kitchener (OHL)	QUE '85 (1, 15)
14	Dave McLlwain	F	L	6'0"	176	06/09/67	Seaforth, Ont.	North Bay (OHL)	PIT '86 (9,172)
16	Scott Metcalfe A	F	L	6'0"	192	01/06/67	Mississauga, Ont.	Kingston (OHL)	EDM '85 (1, 20)
19	Steve Nemeth A	F	L	5'9"	176	02/11/67	Calgary, Alta.	Canadian National Team	NYR '85 (10, 196)
8	Luke Richardson	D	L	6'3"	197	03/26/69	Ottawa, Ont.	Peterborough (OHL)	1987 Draft
21	Stéphane Roy	F	L	6'0"	182	06/29/69	Quebec City, Que.	Granby (QMJHL)	MIN '85 (3, 51)
12	Everett Sanipass	F	L	6'2"	198	02/13/68	Moncton, N.B.	Verdun (QMJHL)	CHI '86 (1, 14)
18	Brendan Shanahan	F	R	6'3"	206	01/23/69	Mimico, Ont.	London (OHL)	1987 Draft
1	Shawn Simpson	G	L	5'11"	157	08/10/68	Ottawa, Ont.	St-Hyacinthe (QMJHL)	WSH '86 (3, 60)
20	Pierre Turgeon	F	L	6'1"	204	08/02/69	Rouyn-Noranda, Que.	Granby (QMJHL)	1987 Draft
30	Jimmy Waite	G	L	5'11"	162	04/15/69	Sherbrooke, Que.	Chicoutimi (QMJHL)	1987 Draft
3	Glen Wesley	D	L	6'1"	192	10/02/68	Red Deer, Alta.	Portland (WHL)	1987 Draft

Head coach: Bert Templeton

Assistant coach: Pat Burns

1988

#	NAME	P	S	HT	WT	BORN	HOMETOWN	CLUB	DRAFT STATUS
17	Warren Babe	F	L	6'3"	192	09/07/68	Bow Island, Alta./	Minnesota (NHL)	MIN '86 (1, 12)
16	Rob Brown	F	L	5'11"	188	04/10/68	St. Albert, Alta.	Pittsburgh (NHL)	PIT '86 (4, 67)
26	Dan Currie	F	L	6'0"	178	03/15/68	Burlington, Ont.	Sault Ste. Marie (OHL)	EDM '86 (4, 84)
21	Eric Desjardins	D	R	6'0"	182	06/14/69	Rouyn-Noranda, Que.	Granby (QMJHL)	MTL '87 (2, 38)
18	Rob DiMaio	F	R	5'10"	187	02/19/68	Calgary, Alta.	Medicine Hat (WHL)	NYI '87 (6, 118)
10	Theoren Fleury C	F	R	5'10"	160	06/29/68	Russell, Man.	Moose Jaw (WHL)	CGY '87 (8, 166)
15	Adam Graves	F	L	6'1"	191	01/14/68	Toronto, Ont.	Windsor (OHL)	DET '86 (1, 22)
	Jeff Hackett	G	L	6'0"	183	06/01/68	London, Ont.	Oshawa (OHL)	NYI '87 (2, 34)
2	Greg Hawgood	D	L	5'9"	190	08/10/68	St. Albert, Alta.	Kamloops (WHL)	BOS '86 (10,202)
12	Jody Hull	F	R	6'2"	200	02/02/69	Cambridge, Ont.	Peterborough (OHL)	HFD '87 (1, 18)
5	Chris Joseph	D	R	6'0"	195	09/10/69	Burnaby, B.C.	Canadian National Team	PIT '87 (1, 5)
20	Sheldon Kennedy	F	R	5'10"	170	06/15/69	Elkhorn, Man.	Swift Current (WHL)	1988 Draft
3	Marc Laniel	D	L	6'1"	190	01/16/68	Scarborough, Ont.	Oshawa (OHL)	NJ '86 (3, 62)
10	Trevor Linden	F	R	6'2"	177	04/11/70	Medicine Hat, Alta.	Medicine Hat (WHL)	1988 Draft
7	Wayne McBean	D	L	6'2"	200	02/21/69	Calgary, Alta.	Los Angeles (NHL)	LA '87 (1, 4)
6	Scott McCrady	D	R	6'2"	190	10/30/68	Calgary, Alta.	Medicine Hat (WHL)	NYI '87 (2, 35)
14	Mark Pederson	F	L	6'1"	192	01/14/68	Medicine Hat, Alta.	Medicine Hat (WHL)	MTL '86 (1, 15)
8	Mark Recchi	F	L	5'10"	188	02/02/69	Kamloops, B.C.	Kamloops (WHL)	Undrafted
19	Joe Sakic	F	L	5'11"	185	07/07/69	Burnaby, B.C.	Swift Current (WHL)	QUE '87 (1, 15)
30	Jimmy Waite	G	L	6'0"	163	04/15/69	Sherbrooke, Que.	Chicoutimi (QMJHL)	CHI '87 (1, 8)

Head coach: Dave Chambers

Assistant coach: Jean Bégin

Assistant coach: Ken Hitchcock

1989

#	NAME	P	S	HT	WT	BORN	HOMETOWN	CLUB	DRAFT STATUS
20	Rod Brind'Amour	F	L	6'0"	190	08/09/70	Campbell River, B.C.	Michigan State (CCHA)	STL '88 (1, 9)
25	Andrew Cassels	F	L	5'11"	187	07/23/69	Bramalea, Ont.	Ottawa (OHL)	MTL '87 (1, 17)
27	Rob Cimetta	F	L	6'1"	191	02/15/70	Toronto, Ont.	Toronto (OHL)	BOS '88 (1, 18)
6	Eric Desjardins C	D	R	6'1"	190	06/14/69	Rouyn-Noranda, Que.	Montreal (NHL)	MTL '87 (2, 38)
29	Stéphane Fiset	G	L	6'0"	174	06/17/70	Montreal, Que.	Victoriaville (QMJHL)	QUE '88 (2, 24)
4	Corey Foster	D	L	6'3"	203	10/27/69	Ottawa, Ont.	Peterborough (OHL)	NJ '88 (1, 12)
7	Martin Gélinas	F	L	5'11"	195	06/05/70	Shawinigan. Que.	Hull (QMJHL)	LA '88 (1, 7)
21	Sheldon Kennedy A	F	R	5'10"	170	06/15/69	Elkhorn, Man.	Swift Current (WHL)	DET '88 (4, 80)
24	Dan Lambert	D	L	5'7"	173	01/12/70	St. Malo, Man.	Swift Current (WHL)	Undrafted
28	Jamie Leach	F	R	6'1"	185	08/25/69	Winnipeg, Man.	Niagara Falls (OHL)	PIT '87 (3, 47)
10	Darcy Loewen	F	L	5'10"	185	02/26/69	Calgary, Alta.	Spokane (WHL)	BUF '88 (3, 55)
8	John McIntyre	F	L	6'1"	182	04/29/69	London, Ont.	Guelph (OHL)	TOR '87 (3, 49)
1	Gus Morschauser	G	L	5'9"	163	03/26/69	Kitchener, Ont.	Kitchener (OHL)	Undrafted
14	Rob Murphy	F	L	6'3"	203	04/07/69	Hull, Que.	Vancouver (NHL)	VAN '87 (2, 2)
16	Yves Racine	D	L	6'0"	194	02/07/69	Matane, Que.	Victoriaville (QMJHL)	DET '87 (1, 11)
26	Mike Ricci	F	L	6'1"	191	10/27/71	Scarborough, Ont.	Peterborough (OHL)	1990 Draft
18	Reginald Savage	F	L	5'10"	185	05/01/70	Montreal, Que.	Victoriaville (QMJHL)	WSH '88 (1, 15)
22	Darrin Shannon	F	L	6'2"	190	12/08/69	Barrie, Ont.	Windsor (OHL)	PIT '88 (1, 4)
5	Geoff Smith	D	L	6'3"	191	03/07/69	Edmonton, Alta.	North Dakota (WCHA)	EDM '87 (3, 63)
2	Steve Veilleux	D	R	6'0"	200	03/09/69	Lachenaie, Que.	Trois-Rivieres, Que./QC	VAN '87 (3, 45)

Head coach: Tom Webster

Assistant coach: Alain Vigneault

1990

#	NAME	P	S	HT	WT	BORN	HOMETOWN	CLUB	DRAFT STATUS
28	Stu Barnes	F	R	5'11"	175	12/25/70	Spruce Grove, Alta.	Tri-City (WHL)	WPG '89 (1, 4)
24	Patrice Brisebois	D	R	6'2"	172	01/27/71	Montreal, Que.	Laval (QMJHL)	MTL '89 (2, 30)
16	Dave Chyzowski C	F	L	6'1"	192	07/11/71	Edmonton, Alta.	NY Islanders (NHL)	NYI '89 (1, 2)
15	Mike Craig	F	R	6'1"	167	06/06/71	London, Ont.	Oshawa (OHL)	MIN '89 (2, 28)
19	Kris Draper	F	L	5'10"	189	06/24/71	West Hill, Ont.	Canadian National Team	WPG '89 (3, 62)
29	Stéphane Fiset	G	L	6'0"	178	06/17/70	Montreal, Que.	Victoriaville (QMJHL)	QUE '88 (2, 24)
6	Kevin Haller	D	L	6'2"	180	12/05/70	Trochu, Alta.	Regina (WHL)	BUF '89 (1, 14)
5	Jason Herter	D	R	6'1"	196	10/02/70	Hafford, Sask.	North Dakota (WCHA)	VAN '89 (1, 8)
1	Trevor Kidd	G	L	6'1"	168	03/26/72	Dugald, Man.	Brandon (WHL)	1990 Draft
88	Eric Lindros	F	R	6'4"	218	02/28/73	Toronto, Ont.	Oshawa (OHL)	1991 Draft
4	Stewart Malgunas	D	L	5'11"	184	04/21/70	Prince George, B.C.	Seattle (WHL)	Undrafted
21	Kent Manderville	F	L	6'3"	193	04/12/71	Victoria, B.C.	Cornell (ECAC)	CGY '89 (2, 24)
14	Mike Needham	F	R	5'10"	196	03/25/70	Fort Saskatchewan, Alta.	Kamloops (WHL)	PIT '89 (6, 126)
10	Dwayne Norris	F	R	5'10"	178	01/08/70	St. John's, N.L.	Michigan State (CCHA)	Undrafted
18	Scott Pellerin	F	L	5'11"	195	01/09/70	Shediac, N.B.	Maine (Hky East)	NJ '89 (3, 47)
7	Adrien Plavsic	D	L	6'1"	195	01/13/70	Dollard, Que.	Peoria (IHL)	STL '88 (2, 30)
2	Dan Ratushny A	D	R	6'1"	202	10/29/70	Nepean , Ont.	Cornell (ECAC)WPG	'89 (2, 25)
9	Mike Ricci A	F	L	6'1"	190	10/27/71	Scarborough, Ont.	Peterborough (OHL)	1990 Draft
12	Steven Rice	F	R	6'1"	209	05/26/71	Waterloo, Ont.	Kitchener (OHL)	NYR '89 (1, 20)
13	Wes Walz	F	R	5'11"	181	05/15/70	Calgary, Alta.	Lethbridge (WHL)	BOS '89 (3, 57)

Head coach: Guy Charron

Assistant coach: Dick Todd

Assistant coach: Perry Pearn

1991

#	NAME	P	S	HT	WT	BORN	HOMETOWN	CLUB	DRAFT STATUS
24	Patrice Brisebois	D	R	6'2"	181	01/27/71	Montreal, Que.	Drummondville (QMJHL)	MTL '89 (2, 30)
15	Mike Craig	F	R	6'0.5"	181	06/06/71	London, Ont.	Minnesota (NHL)	MIN '89 (2, 28)
18	Dale Craigwell	F	L	5'11"	181	04/24/71	Oshawa, Ont.	Oshawa (OHL)	Undrafted
19	Kris Draper	F	L	5'11"	189	05/24/71	West Hill, Ont.	Ottawa (OHL)	WPG '89 (3, 62)
4	Karl Dykhuis	D	R	6'3"	201	07/08/72	Sept-Îles, Que.	Canadian National Team	CHI '90 (1, 16)
9	Pat Falloon	F	R	5'11"	189	09/22/72	Foxwarren, Man.	Spokane (WHL)	1991 Draft
7	David Harlock	D	L	6'2"	205	03/16/71	Toronto, Ont.	Michigan (CCHA)	NJ '90 (2, 24)
8	Greg Johnson	F	L	5'11"	183	03/16/71	Thunder Bay, Ont.	North Dakota (WCHA)	PHI '89 (2, 33)
1	Trevor Kidd	G	L	6'2"	185	03/26/72	Dugald, Man.	Brandon (WHL)	CGY '90 (1, 11)
26	Martin Lapointe	F	L	5'11"	201	09/12/73	Ville St-Pierre, Que.	Laval (QMJHL)	1991 Draft
88	Eric Lindros	F	R	6'5"	223	02/28/73	Toronto, Ont.	Oshawa (OHL)	1991 Draft
21	Kent Manderville	F	L	6'3"	205	04/12/71	Victoria, B.C.	Cornell (ECAC)	CGY '89 (2, 24)
2	Jason Marshall	D	R	6'2"	196	02/22/71	Cranbrook, B.C.	Tri-City (WHL)	STL '89 (1, 9)
10	Brad May	F	L	6'0.5"	207	11/29/71	Markham, Ont.	Niagara Falls (OHL)	BUF '90 (1, 14)
28	Scott Niedermayer	D	L	6'0"	196	08/31/73	Cranbrook, B.C.	Kamloops (WHL)	1991 Draft
29	Félix Potvin	G	L	6'0.5"	174	06/23/71	Anjou, Que.	Chicoutimi (QMJHL)	TOR '90 (2, 31)
12	Steven Rice C	F	R	6'0.5"	214	05/26/71	Waterloo, Ont.	Kitchener (OHL)	NYR '89 (1, 20)
22	Pierre Sévigny	F	L	6'0"	185	09/08/71	Trois-Rivières, Que.	St-Hyacinthe (QMJHL)	MTL '89 (3, 51)
16	Mike Sillinger	F	R	5'11"	189	06/29/71	Regina, Sask.	Regina (WHL)	DET '89 (1, 11)
27	John Slaney	D	L	5'11"	189	02/07/72	St. John's, N.L.	Cornell (ECAC)	WSH '90 (1, 9)
6	Chris Snell	D	L	5'11"	201	07/12/71	Oshawa, Ont.	Ottawa (OHL)	Undrafted
11	Scott Thornton	F	L	6'3"	205	01/09/71	London, Ont.	Toronto (NHL)	TOR '89 (1, 3)

Head coach: Dick Todd

Assistant coach: Perry Pearn

Assistant coach: Alain Vigneault

1992

#	NAME	P	S	HT	WT	BORN	HOMETOWN	CLUB	DRAFT STATUS
55	Brad Bombardir	D	L	6'0.5"	196	05/05/72	Powell River, B.C.	North Dakota (WCHA)	NJ '90 (3, 56)
2	Jassen Cullimore	D	L	6'5"	220	12/04/72	Simcoe, Ont.	Peterborough (OHL)	VAN '91 (2, 29)
14	Kimbi Daniels	F	R	6'1.5"	174	01/19/72	Brandon, Man.	Philadelphia (NHL)	PHI '90 (3, 44)
24	Karl Dykhuis	D	R	6'3"	201	07/08/72	Sept-Îles, Que.	Canadian National Team	CHI '90 (1, 16)
	Mike Fountain	G	L	6'0"	168	01/26/72	Gravenhurst, Ont.	Oshawa (OHL)	Undrafted
9	Ryan Hughes	F	L	6'2"	189	1/1/72	Montreal, Que.	Cornell (ECAC)	QUE '90 (2, 22)
11	Steve Junker	F	L	6'0"	189	06/25/72	Castlegar, B.C.	Spokane (WHL)	NYI '91 (5, 92)
18	Paul Kariya	F	L	5'10.5"	150	10/16/74	North Vancouver, B.C.	Penticton (BCHL)	1993 Draft
1	Trevor Kidd	G	L	6'2"	185	03/26/72	Dugald, Man.	Canadian National Team	CGY '90 (1, 11)
22	Martin Lapointe A	F	R	5'11"	201	09/12/73	Ville St-Pierre, Que.	Laval (QMJHL)	DET '91 (1, 10)
88	Eric Lindros C	F	R	6'5"	225	02/28/73	Toronto, Ont.	Oshawa (OHL)	QUE '91 (1, 1)
13	Richard Matvichuk	D	L	6'2.5"	187	02/05/73	Edmonton, Alta.	Saskatoon (WHL)	MIN '91 (1, 8)
7	Jeff Nelson	F	L	5'10.5"	189	12/18/72	Prince Albert, Sask.	Prince Albert (WHL)	WSH '91 (2, 36)
44	Scott Niedermayer	D	L	6'0"	203	08/31/73	Cranbrook, B.C.	Kamloops (WHL)	NJ '91 (1, 3)
8	Chad Penney	F	R	6'0.5"	196	09/18/73	St. John's, N.L.	North Bay (OHL)	1992 Draft
19	Patrick Poulin	F	R	6'0.5"	212	04/23/73	Vanier, Que.	St-Hyacinthe (QMJHL)	HFD '91 (1, 9)
17	Andy Schneider	F	L	5'9"	150	03/29/72	Edmonton, Alta.	Swift Current (WHL)	Undrafted
77	John Slaney	D	L	5'10.5"	192	02/07/72	St. John's, N.L.	Cornell (ECAC)	WSH '90 (1, 9)
23	Turner Stevenson	F	R	6'2.5"	209	05/18/72	Port Alberni, B.C.	Seattle (WHL)	MTL '90 (1, 12)
16	David St-Pierre	F	R	6'0"	181	03/26/72	Montreal, Que.	Verdun (QMJHL)	CGY '91 (8, 173)
5	Darryl Sydor A	D	L	6'0"	198	05/13/72	Edmonton, Alta.	Los Angeles (NHL)	LA '90 (1, 7)
12	Tyler Wright	F	R	5'10.5"	176	04/06/73	Kamsack, Sask.	Swift Current (WHL)	EDM '91 (1, 12)

Head scout: Sheldon Ferguson

Head coach: Rick Cornacchia

Assistant coach: Tom Renney

Assistant coach: Gary Agnew

1993

#	NAME	P	S	HT	WT	BORN	HOMETOWN	CLUB	DRAFT STATUS
3	Adrian Aucoin A	D	R	6'1"	194	07/03/73	Gloucester, Ont.	Canadian National Team	VAN '92 (5, 117)
11	Jeff Bes	F	L	6'0"	187	07/31/73	Tillsonburg, Ont.	Guelph (OHL)	MIN '92 (3, 58)
14	Joël Bouchard	D	L	6'0"	185	01/23/74	Montreal, Que.	Verdun (QMJHL)	CGY '92 (6, 129)
19	Alexandre Daigle	F	L	6'0"	170	02/07/75	Laval, Que.	Victoriaville (QMJHL)	1993 Draft
10	Jason Dawe	F	L	5'10.5"	192	05/29/73	Scarborough, Ont.	Peterborough (OHL)	BUF '91 (2, 35)
31	Philippe DeRouville	G	L	6'1"	189	08/07/74	Victoriaville, Que.	Verdun (QMJHL)	PIT '92 (5, 115)
32	Martin Gendron	F	R	5'9"	192	02/15/74	Valleyfield, Que.	St-Hyacinthe (QMJHL)	WSH '92 (3, 71)
7	Chris Gratton	F	L	6'3.5"	203	07/05/75	Brantford, Ont.	Kingston (OHL)	1993 Draft
9	Ralph Intranuovo	F	L	5'9"	170	12/11/73	Scarborough, Ont.	Sault Ste. Marie (OHL)	EDM '92 (4, 96)
18	Paul Kariya	F	L	5'10.5"	150	10/16/74	North Vancouver, B.C.	Maine (Hky East)	1993 Draft
21	Nathan Lafayette	F	R	6'1"	189	02/17/73	Mississauga, Ont.	Newmarket (OHL)	STL '91 (3, 65)
22	Martin Lapointe C	F	R	5'11"	201	09/12/73	Ville St-Pierre, Que.	Laval (QMJHL)	DET '91 (1, 10)
30	Manny Legace	G	L	5'9"	181	02/04/73	Alliston, Ont.	Niagara Falls (OHL)	Undrafted
16	Dean McAmmond	F	L	6'0"	187	06/15/73	Grande Cache, Alta.	Prince Albert (WHL)	CHI '91 (1, 22)
23	Rob Niedermayer	F	L	6'2"	201	12/28/74	Cranbrook, B.C.	Medicine Hat (WHL)	1993 Draft
6	Chris Pronger	D	L	6'6"	190	10/10/74	Dryden, Ont.	Peterborough (OHL)	1993 Draft
33	Mike Rathje	D	L	6'5"	203	05/11/74	Medicine Hat, Alta.	Medicine Hat (WHL)	SJ '92 (1, 3)
29	Jeff Shantz	F	R	6'1"	194	10/10/73	Duchess, Alta.	Regina (WHL)	CHI '92 (2, 36)
15	Jason Smith	D	R	6'3.5"	201	11/02/73	Calgary, Alta.	Regina (WHL)	NJ '92 (1, 18)
2	Brent Tully	D	R	6'3.5"	189	03/26/74	Peterborough, Ont.	Peterborough (OHL)	VAN '92 (4, 93)
4	Darcy Werenka	D	R	6'0.5"	209	05/13/73	Beaumont, Alta.	Brandon (WHL)	NYR '91 (2, 37)
12	Tyler Wright A	F	R	5'11"	170	04/06/73	Kamsack, Sask.	Swift Current (WHL)	EDM '91 (1, 12)

Head scout: Sheldon Ferguson

Head coach: Perry Pearn

Assistant coach: Joe Canale

Assistant coach: Dave Siciliano

1994

#	NAME	P	S	HT	WT	BORN	HOMETOWN	CLUB	DRAFT STATUS
8	Jason Allison	F	R	6'3"	201	05/29/75	North York, Ont.	London (OHL)	WSH '93 (1, 17)
34	Chris Armstrong	D	L	6'0"	194	06/26/75	Whitewood, Sask.	Moose Jaw (WHL)	FLA '93 (3, 57)
5	Drew Bannister	D	R	6'0.5"	205	04/09/74	Sudbury, Ont.	Sault Ste. Marie (OHL)	TB '92 (2, 26)
23	Jason Botterill	F	L	6'3"	205	05/19/76	Winnipeg, Man.	Michigan (CCHA)	1994 Draft
24	Joël Bouchard	D	L	6'0"	192	01/23/73	Montreal, Que.	Verdun (QMJHL)	CGY '92 (6, 129)
20	Curtis Bowen	F	L	6'0.5"	201	03/24/74	Kenora, Ont.	Ottawa (OHL)	DET '92 (1, 22)
19	Anson Carter	F	R	6'0.5"	181	06/06/74	Scarborough, Ont.	Michigan State (CCHA)	WSH '92 (10, 220)
12	Brandon Convery	F	R	6'0"	187	02/04/74	Kingston, Ont.	Niagara Falls (OHL)	TOR '92 (1, 8)
9	Yanick Dubé	F	R	5'9"	170	06/14/74	Gaspé, Que.	Laval (QMJHL)	Undrafted
30	Manny Fernandez	G	L	5'10.5"	163	08/27/74	Sherbrooke, Que.	Laval (QMJHL)	QUE '92 (3, 52)
25	Jeff Friesen	F	L	6'0"	185	08/05/76	Meadow Lake, Sask.	Regina (WHL)	1994 Draft
22	Aaron Gavey	F	L	6'0.5"	181	02/22/74	Sudbury, Ont.	Sault Ste. Marie (OHL)	TB '92 (4, 74)
32	Martin Gendron	F	R	5'9"	198	02/15/74	Valleyfield, Que.	Hull (QMJHL)	WSH '92 (3, 71)
18	Rick Girard	F	L	5'10.5"	176	05/01/74	Edmonton, Alta.	Swift Current (WHL)	VAN '93 (2, 46)
10	Todd Harvey *A*	F	R	5'10.5"	203	02/17/75	Sheffield, Ont.	Detroit (OHL)	DAL '93 (1, 9)
4	Bryan McCabe	D	L	6'2"	201	06/08/75	Calgary, Alta.	Spokane (WHL)	NYI '93 (2, 40)
28	Marty Murray	F	L	5'9"	165	02/16/75	Lyleton, Man.	Brandon (WHL)	CGY '93 (4, 96)
27	Mike Peca	F	R	5'10.5"	174	03/26/74	Toronto, Ont.	Ottawa (OHL)	VAN '92 (2, 40)
14	Nick Stajduhar	D	L	6'2"	205	12/06/74	Kitchener, Ont.	London (OHL)	EDM '93 (1, 16)
1	Jamie Storr	G	L	6'0.5"	161	12/25/75	Brampton, Ont.	Owen Sound (OHL)	1994 Draft
2	Brent Tully *C*	D	R	6'3.5"	201	03/26/74	Peterborough, Ont.	Peterborough (OHL)	VAN '92 (4, 93)
6	Brendan Witt *A*	D	L	6'0"	212	02/20/75	Humboldt, Sask.	Seattle (WHL)	WSH '93 (1, 11)

Head coach: Joe Canale

Assistant coach: Dan Flynn

Assistant coach: Mike Johnston

1995

#	NAME	P	S	HT	WT	BORN	HOMETOWN	CLUB	DRAFT STATUS
3	Chad Allan	D	L	6'1"	190	07/12/76	Davidson, Sask.	Saskatoon (WHL)	VAN '94 (3, 65)
9	Jason Allison *A*	F	R	6'3"	192	05/29/75	North York, Ont.	London (OHL)	WSH '93 (1, 17)
5	Nolan Baumgartner	D	R	6'1"	187	03/23/76	Calgary, Alta.	Kamloops (WHL)	WSH '94 (1, 10)
21	Jason Botterill	F	L	6'4"	209	05/19/76	Winnipeg, Man.	Michigan (CCHA)	DAL '94 (1, 20)
30	Dan Cloutier	G	L	6'1"	182	04/22/76	Sault Ste. Marie, Ont.	Sault Ste. Marie (OHL)	NYR '94 (2, 26)
8	Larry Courville	F	L	6'2"	184	04/02/75	Timmins, Ont.	Oshawa (OHL)	WPG '93 (5, 119)
19	Alexandre Daigle	F	L	6'0"	185	02/07/75	Laval, Que.	Victoriaville (QMJHL)	OTT '93 (1, 1)
24	Eric Daze	F	L	6'5"	204	07/02/75	Montreal, Que.	Beauport (QMJHL)	CHI '93 (4, 90)
22	Shean Donovan	F	R	6'1"	170	01/22/75	Timmins, Ont.	Ottawa (OHL)	SJ '93 (2, 28)
25	Jeff Friesen	F	L	6'0"	183	08/05/76	Meadow Lake, Sask.	Regina (WHL)	SJ '94 (1, 11)
10	Todd Harvey *C*	F	R	6'0"	200	02/17/75	Sheffield, Ont.	Detroit (OHL)	DAL '93 (1, 9)
14	Ed Jovanovski	D	L	6'2"	210	06/26/76	Windsor, Ont.	Windsor (OHL)	FLA '94 (1, 1)
4	Bryan McCabe *A*	D	L	6'1"	200	06/08/75	Calgary, Alta.	Spokane (WHL)	NYI '93 (2, 40)
28	Marty Murray	F	L	5'9"	168	02/16/75	Lyleton, Man.	Brandon (WHL)	CGY '93 (4, 96)
17	Jeff O'Neill	F	R	6'0"	186	02/23/76	King City, Ont.	Guelph (OHL)	HFD '94 (1, 5)
23	Denis Pederson	F	L	6'2"	194	09/10/75	Prince Albert, Sask.	Prince Albert (WHL)	NJ '93 (1, 13)
6	Wade Redden	D	L	6'1"	193	06/12/77	Lloydminster, Sask.	Brandon (WHL)	1995 Draft
12	Jamie Rivers	D	L	6'1"	185	03/16/75	Ottawa, Ont.	Sudbury (OHL)	STL '93 (3, 63)
20	Ryan Smyth	F	L	6'2"	183	02/21/76	Banff, Alta.	Moose Jaw (WHL)	EDM '94 (1, 6)
7	Lee Sorochan	D	L	6'2"	205	09/09/75	Gibbons, Alta.	Lethbridge (WHL)	NYR '93 (2, 34)
1	Jamie Storr	G	L	6'1"	174	12/28/75	Brampton, Ont.	Owen Sound (OHL)	LA '94 (1, 7)
16	Darcy Tucker	F	L	5'10"	163	03/15/75	Endiang, Alta.	Kamloops (WHL)	MTL '93 (6, 151)

Head coach: Don Hay

Assistant coach: Mike Johnston

Assistant coach: Alain Rajotte

1996

#	NAME	P	S	HT	WT	BORN	HOMETOWN	CLUB	DRAFT STATUS
7	Chad Allan *A*	D	L	6'1"	196	07/12/76	Davidson, Sask.	Saskatoon (WHL)	VAN '94 (3, 65)
5	Nolan Baumgartner *C*	D	R	6'1"	200	03/23/76	Calgary, Alta.	Kamloops (WHL)	WSH '94 (1, 10)
19	Jason Botterill *A*	F	L	6'3"	205	05/19/76	Winnipeg, Man.	Michigan (CCHA)	DAL '94 (1, 20)
11	Curtis Brown	F	L	6'0"	182	02/12/76	Seniac, Sask.	Moose Jaw (WHL)	BUF '94 (2, 43)
31	Marc Denis	G	L	6'0"	187	08/01/77	Montreal, Que.	Chicoutimi (QMJHL)	COL '95 (2, 25)
17	Hnat Domenichelli	F	L	5'11"	179	02/17/76	Edmonton, Alta.	Kamloops (WHL)	HFD '94 (5, 83)
9	Christian Dubé	F	R	5'11"	180	04/25/77	Quebec City, Que.	Sherbrooke (QMJHL)	NYR '95 (2, 39)
21	Denis Gauthier	D	L	6'2"	210	10/01/76	Montreal, Que.	Drummondville (QMJHL)	CGY '95 (1, 20)
16	Robb Gordon	F	R	6'0"	195	01/13/76	Surrey, B.C.	Kelowna (WHL)	VAN '94 (2, 39)
3	Jason Holland	D	R	6'2"	200	04/30/76	Morinville, Alta.	Kamloops (WHL)	NYI '94 (2, 38)
12	Jarome Iginla	F	R	6'1"	193	07/01/77	St. Albert, Alta.	Kamloops (WHL)	DAL '95 (1, 11)
14	Daymond Langkow	F	L	5'10"	170	09/27/76	Edmonton, Alta.	Tri-City (WHL)	TB '95 (1, 5)
23	Brad Larsen	F	L	6'0"	200	06/28/77	Vernon, B.C.	Swift Current (WHL)	OTT '95 (3, 53)
8	Alyn McCauley	F	L	5'11"	185	05/29/77	Gananoque, Ont.	Ottawa (OHL)	NJ '95 (4, 79)
24	Craig Mills	F	R	5'11"	190	08/27/76	Toronto, Ont.	Belleville (OHL)	WPG '94 (5, 108)
4	Chris Phillips	D	L	6'2"	200	03/09/78	Fort McMurray, Alta.	Prince Albert (WHL)	1996 Draft
22	Jason Podollan	F	R	6'1"	181	02/18/76	Vernon, B.C.	Spokane (WHL)	FLA '94 (2, 31)
6	Wade Redden	D	L	6'2"	196	06/12/77	Lloydminster, Sask.	Brandon (WHL)	NYI '95 (1, 2)
1	José Théodore	G	L	5'10.5"	174	09/13/76	Laval, Que.	Hull (QMJHL)	MTL '94 (2, 44)
30	Rhett Warrener	D	L	6'1"	209	01/27/76	Saskatoon, Sask.	Florida (NHL)	FLA '94 (2, 27)
18	Mike Watt	F	L	6'1"	214	03/31/76	Egmondville, Ont.	Michigan (CCHA)	EDM '94 (2, 32)
10	Jamie Wright	F	L	5'11"	172	05/13/76	Elmira, Ont.	Guelph (OHL)	DAL '94 (4, 98)

Head coach: Marcel Comeau

Assistant coach: Terry Bangen

Assistant coach: Blair MacKasey

1997

#	NAME	P	S	HT	WT	BORN	HOMETOWN	CLUB	DRAFT STATUS
1	Martin Biron	G	L	6'2"	165	08/15/77	Lac St-Charles, Que.	Beauport (QMJHL)	BUF '95 (1, 16)
14	Daniel Brière	F	R	5'9"	160	10/06/77	Gatineau, Que.	Drummondville (QMJHL)	PHX '96 (1, 24)
31	Marc Denis	G	L	6'1"	193	08/01/77	Montreal, Que.	Chicoutimi (QMJHL)	COL '95 (2, 25)
19	Boyd Devereaux	F	L	6'2"	190	04/16/78	Seaforth, Ont.	Kitchener (OHL)	EDM '96 (1, 6)
4	Jason Doig	D	R	6'3"	216	01/29/77	Montreal, Que.	Granby (QMJHL)	WPG '95 (2, 34)
9	Christian Dubé *A*	F	R	5'11"	186	04/25/77	Sherbrooke, Que.	NY Rangers (NHL)	NYR '95 (2, 39)
3	Hugh Hamilton	D	L	6'1"	175	02/11/77	Leask, Sask.	Spokane (WHL)	HFD '95 (5, 113)
28	Dwayne Hay	F	L	6'1"	192	02/11/77	London, Ont.	Guelph (OHL)	WSH '95 (2, 43)
12	Brad Isbister	F	R	6'3"	225	05/07/77	Calgary, Alta.	Portland (WHL)	WPG '95 (3, 67)
24	Richard Jackman	D	L	6'2"	176	06/28/78	Brampton, Ont.	Sault Ste. Marie (OHL)	DAL '96 (1, 5)
23	Brad Larsen *C*	F	L	6'0"	200	06/28/77	Vernon, B.C.	Swift Current (WHL)	OTT '95 (3, 53)
17	Trevor Letowski	F	R	5'10"	175	04/05/77	Thunder Bay, Ont.	Sarnia (OHL)	PHX '96 (7, 174)
10	Cameron Mann	F	R	6'0"	190	04/20/77	Balmertown, Ont.	Peterborough (OHL)	BOS '95 (4, 99)
18	Alyn McCauley *A*	F	L	5'11"	185	05/29/77	Gananoque, Ont.	Ottawa (OHL)	NJ '95 (4, 79)
7	Chris Phillips *A*	D	L	6'2"	200	03/09/78	Fort McMurray, Alta.	Prince Albert (WHL)	OTT '96 (1, 1)
22	Cory Sarich	D	R	6'3"	175	08/16/78	Bladworth, Sask.	Saskatoon (WHL)	BUF '96 (2, 27)
27	Peter Schaefer	F	L	6'0"	187	07/12/77	Yellow Grass, Sask.	Brandon (WHL)	VAN '95 (3, 66)
25	Joe Thornton	F	L	6'4"	186	07/02/79	St. Thomas, Ont.	Sault Ste. Marie (OHL)	1997 Draft
34	Jesse Wallin	D	L	6'2"	186	03/10/78	North Battleford, Sask.	Red Deer (WHL)	DET '96 (1, 26)
33	Jeff Ware	D	L	6'4"	225	05/29/77	Toronto, Ont.	Toronto (NHL)	TOR '95 (1, 15)
35	Trent Whitfield	F	L	5'11"	180	06/17/77	Alameda, Sask.	Spokane (WHL)	BOS '96 (4, 100)
20	Shane Willis	F	R	6'1"	185	06/13/77	Sylvan Lake, Alta.	Prince Albert (WHL)	TB '95 (3, 56)

Head coach: Mike Babcock

Assistant coach: Mike Pelino

Assistant coach: Réal Paiement

1998

#	NAME	P	S	HT	WT	BORN	HOMETOWN	CLUB	DRAFT STATUS
11	Steve Bégin *A*	F	L	6'0"	188	06/04/78	Trois-Rivières, Que.	Val-d'Or (QMJHL)	CGY '96 (2, 40)
7	Sean Blanchard	D	L	6'0"	201	03/29/78	Garson, Ont.	Ottawa (OHL)	LA '97 (4, 99)
28	Matt Bradley	F	R	6'1"	188	06/13/78	Stittsville, Ont.	Kingston (OHL)	SJ '96 (4, 102)
3	Eric Brewer	D	L	6'3"	196	04/17/79	Kamloops, B.C.	Prince George (WHL)	1998 Draft
12	Matt Cooke	F	L	6'1"	195	09/07/78	Belleville, Ont.	Windsor (OHL)	VAN '97 (6, 144)
15	Daniel Corso	F	L	5'10"	161	04/03/78	St-Hubert, Que.	Victoriaville (QMJHL)	STL '96 (7, 169)
18	Jean-Pierre Dumont	F	L	6'0"	195	04/01/78	Montreal, Que.	Val-d'Or (QMJHL)	NYI '96 (1, 3)
2	Brad Ference	D	R	6'3"	190	04/02/79	Calgary, Alta.	Spokane (WHL)	VAN '97 (1, 10)
32	Mathieu Garon	G	R	6'0.5"	192	01/09/78	Chandler, Que.	Victoriaville (QMJHL)	MTL '96 (2, 44)
21	Josh Holden	F	L	6'0"	170	01/18/78	Calgary, Alta.	Regina (WHL)	VAN '96 (1, 12)
5	Zenith Komarniski	D	L	6'2"	190	08/13/78	Edmonton, Alta.	Spokane (WHL)	VAN '96 (3, 75)
14	Vincent Lecavalier	F	L	6'4"	180	04/21/80	Île-Bizard, Que.	Rimouski (QMJHL)	1998 Draft
1	Roberto Luongo	G	L	6'2"	185	04/04/79	Montreal, Que.	Val-d'Or (QMJHL)	NYI '97 (1, 4)
6	Manny Malhotra	F	L	6'1"	210	05/18/80	Mississauga, Ont.	Guelph (OHL)	1998 Draft
16	Brett McLean	F	L	5'10"	187	08/14/78	Comox, B.C.	Kelowna (WHL)	DAL '97 (9, 242)
22	Cory Sarich *C A*	D	R	6'3"	190	08/16/78	Bladworth, Sask.	Saskatoon (WHL)	BUF '96 (2, 27)
19	Alex Tanguay	F	L	6'0"	180	11/21/79	Ste-Justine, Que.	Halifax (QMJHL)	1998 Draft
10	Daniel Tkaczuk	F	L	6'0"	195	06/10/79	Mississauga, Ont.	Barrie (OHL)	CGY '97 (1, 6)
26	Mike Van Ryn	D	R	6'2"	186	05/14/79	London, Ont.	Michigan (CCHA)	1998 Draft
4	Jesse Wallin *C A*	D	L	6'2"	190	03/10/78	North Battleford, Sask.	Red Deer (WHL)	DET '96 (1, 26)
20	Jason Ward	F	R	6'2"	193	01/16/79	Oshawa, Ont.	Erie (OHL)	MTL '97 (1, 11)
24	Brian Willsie	F	R	6'0"	179	03/16/78	London, Ont.	Guelph (OHL)	COL '96 (6, 146)

Head coach: Réal Paiement

Assistant coach: Peter DeBoer

Assistant coach: Terry Bangen

1999

#	NAME	P	S	HT	WT	BORN	HOMETOWN	CLUB	DRAFT STATUS
28	Bryan Allen	D	L	6'4"	206	08/21/80	Kingston, Ont.	Oshawa (OHL)	VAN '98 (1, 4)
20	Blair Betts	F	L	6'2"	200	02/16/80	Sherwood Park, Alta.	Prince George (WHL)	CGY '98 (2, 33)
31	Tyler Bouck	F	L	6'0"	185	01/13/80	Camrose, Alta.	Prince George (WHL)	DAL '98 (2, 57)
5	Kyle Calder	F	L	6'0"	180	01/05/79	Mannville, Alta.	Regina (WHL)	CHI '97 (5, 130)
14	Brian Campbell	D	L	5'11"	190	05/23/79	Strathroy, Ont.	Ottawa (OHL)	BUF '97 (6, 156)
23	Jason Chimera	F	L	6'2"	190	05/02/79	Edmonton, Alta.	Medicine Hat (WHL)	EDM '97 (5, 121)
19	Harold Druken	F	L	6'0"	205	01/26/79	St. John's, N.L.	Plymouth (OHL)	VAN '97 (2, 36)
9	Rico Fata	F	L	6'0"	205	02/12/80	Sault Ste. Marie, Ont.	Calgary (WHL)	CGY '98 (1, 6)
27	Andrew Ference	D	L	5'11"	190	03/27/79	Sherwood Park, Alta.	Portland (WHL)	PIT '97 (8, 208)
2	Brad Ference	D	R	6'3"	195	04/02/79	Calgary, Alta.	Spokane (WHL)	VAN '97 (1, 10)
32	Brian Finley	G	L	6'3"	185	03/07/81	Sault Ste. Marie, Ont.	Barrie (OHL)	1999 Draft
12	Simon Gagné	F	L	6'0"	180	02/29/80	Ste-Foy, Que.	Quebec (QMJHL)	PHI '98 (1, 22)
35	Brad Leeb	F	R	5'11"	180	08/27/79	Red Deer, Alta.	Red Deer (WHL)	Undrafted
1	Roberto Luongo	G	L	6'2"	193	04/04/79	Montreal, Que.	Acadie-Bathurst (QMJHL)	NYI '97 (1, 4)
17	Adam Mair *A*	F	R	6'1"	190	02/15/79	Hamilton, Ont.	Owen Sound (OHL)	TOR '97 (4, 84)
36	Kent McDonnell	F	R	6'1"	195	03/01/79	Cornwall, Ont.	Guelph (OHL)	CAR '97 (9, 225)
33	Brenden Morrow	F	L	6'0"	205	01/16/79	Carlyle, Sask.	Portland (WHL)	DAL '97 (1, 25)
24	Robyn Regehr	D	L	6'3"	220	04/19/80	Rosthern, Sask.	Kamloops (WHL)	COL '98 (1, 19)
7	Brad Stuart	D	L	6'2"	217	06/11/79	Rocky Mountain House, Alta.	Regina (WHL)	SJ '98 (1, 3)
10	Daniel Tkaczuk *A*	F	L	6'1"	190	06/10/79	Mississauga, Ont.	Barrie (OHL)	CGY '97 (1, 6)
26	Mike Van Ryn *C*	D	R	6'1"	195	05/14/79	London, Ont.	Michigan (CCHA)	NJ '98 (1, 26)
20	Jason Ward	F	R	6'3"	190	01/16/79	Oshawa, Ont.	Windsor (OHL)	MTL '97 (1, 11)

Head coach: Tom Renney

Head scout: Barry Trapp

Assistant coach: Stan Butler

Assistant coach: Claude Julien

2000

#	NAME	P	S	HT	WT	BORN	HOMETOWN	CLUB	DRAFT STATUS
16	Mark Bell	F	L	6'3"	198	08/05/80	St. Paul's, Ont.	Ottawa (OHL)	CHI '98 (1, 8)
33	Mathieu Biron A	D	R	6'6"	220	04/29/80	Lac St-Charles, Que.	NY Islanders (NHL)	NYI '98 (1, 21)
12	Tyler Bouck A	F	L	6'0"	200	01/13/80	Camrose, Alta.	Prince George (WHL)	DAL '98 (2, 57)
3	Jay Bouwmeester	D	L	6'4"	195	09/27/83	Edmonton, Alta.	Medicine Hat (WHL)	2002 Draft
7	Éric Chouinard	F	L	6'3"	200	07/08/80	Cap Rouge, Que.	Quebec (QMJHL)	MTL '98 (1, 16)
1	Brian Finley	G	L	6'3"	180	07/03/81	Sault Ste. Marie, Ont.	Barrie (OHL)	NSH '99 (1, 6)
11	Dany Heatley	F	L	6'3"	195	01/21/81	Calgary, Alta.	Wisconsin (WCHA)	2000 Draft
20	Barret Jackman	D	L	6'1"	203	03/05/81	Fruitvale, B.C.	Regina (WHL)	STL '99 (1, 17)
2	Matt Kinch	D	L	5'11"	185	02/17/80	Red Deer, Alta.	Calgary (WHL)	BUF '99 (5, 146)
31	Jamie Lundmark	F	R	6'0"	185	01/16/81	Edmonton, Alta.	Moose Jaw (WHL)	NYR '99 (1, 9)
6	Manny Malhotra C	F	L	6'2"	210	05/18/80	Mississauga, Ont.	NY Rangers (NHL)	NYR '98 (1, 7)
18	Steve McCarthy	D	L	6'0"	205	02/03/81	Trail, B.C.	Kootenay (WHL)	CHI '99 (1, 23)
10	Chris Nielsen	F	R	6'2"	193	02/16/80	Goodlands, Man.	Calgary (WHL)	NYI '98 (2, 36)
30	Maxime Ouellet	G	L	6'1"	195	06/17/81	Beauport, Que.	Quebec (QMJHL)	PHI '99 (1, 22)
26	Matt Pettinger	F	L	6'1"	205	10/22/80	Victoria, B.C.	Denver (WCHA)	2000 Draft
25	Brandon Reid	F	R	5'8"	165	03/09/81	Kirland, Que.	Halifax (QMJHL)	Undrafted
35	Mike Ribeiro	F	L	5'11"	164	02/10/80	Montreal, Que.	Montreal (NHL)	MTL '98 (2, 45)
9	Brad Richards	F	L	6'0"	180	05/02/80	Murray Harbour, N.L.	Rimouski (QMJHL)	TB '98 (3, 64)
24	Kyle Rossiter	D	L	6'2"	220	06/09/80	Edmonton, Alta.	Spokane (WHL)	FLA '98 (2, 30)
21	Joé Rullier	D	R	6'4"	203	01/28/80	Montreal, Que.	Rimouski (QMJHL)	LA '98 (5, 133)
27	Michael Ryder	F	R	6'0"	190	03/31/80	Bonavista, N.L.	Hull (QMJHL)	MTL '98 (8, 216)
19	Jason Spezza	F	R	6'3"	195	06/13/83	Mississauga, Ont.	Mississauga (OHL)	2001 Draft

Head coach: Claude Julien

Assistant coach: Todd McLellan

Assistant coach: Dean Clark

2001

#	NAME	P	S	HT	WT	BORN	HOMETOWN	CLUB	DRAFT STATUS
33	Alex Auld	G	L	6'3.5"	198	01/07/81	Thunder Bay, Ont.	North Bay (OHL)	FLA '99 (2, 40)
4	Jay Bouwmeester	D	L	6'4"	207	09/27/83	Edmonton, Alta.	Medicine Hat (WHL)	2002 Draft
34	Brad Boyes	F	R	6'0"	181	04/17/82	Mississauga, Ont.	Erie (OHL)	TOR '00 (1, 24)
29	Mike Cammalleri	F	L	5'8.5"	174	06/08/82	Richmond Hill, Ont.	Michigan (CCHA)	2001 Draft
5	Dan Hamhuis	D	L	6'0.5"	194	12/13/82	Smithers, B.C.	Prince George (WHL)	2001 Draft
23	Jay Harrison	D	L	6'3"	205	11/03/82	Whitby, Ont.	Brampton (OHL)	2001 Draft
15	Dany Heatley	F	L	6'2"	205	01/21/81	Calgary, Alta.	Wisconsin (WCHA)	ATL '00 (1, 2)
2	Barret Jackman A	D	L	6'0.5"	201	03/05/81	Fruitvale, B.C.	Regina (WHL)	STL '99 (1, 17)
22	Jason Jaspers	F	L	5'10.5"	183	04/08/81	Thunder Bay, Ont.	Sudbury (OHL)	PHX '99 (4, 71)
17	Jamie Lundmark	F	R	6'0"	185	01/16/81	Edmonton, Alta.	Seattle (WHL)	NYR '99 (1, 9)
16	Derek MacKenzie	F	L	5'11"	178	06/11/81	Sudbury, Ont.	Sudbury (OHL)	ATL '99 (5, 128)
7	Steve McCarthy C	D	L	6'0"	196	02/03/81	Trail, B.C.	Chicago (NHL)	CHI '99 (1, 23)
12	David Morisset	F	R	6'1.5"	203	04/06/81	Langley, B.C.	Seattle (WHL)	STL ' 00 (2, 65)
21	Steve Ott	F	L	6'0"	181	08/19/82	Stoney Point, Ont.	Windsor (OHL)	DAL '00 (1, 25)
30	Maxime Ouellet	G	L	6'1.5"	198	06/17/81	Beauport, Que.	Rouyn-Noranda (QMJHL)	PHI '99 (1, 22)
27	Mark Popovic	D	L	6'1.5"	189	10/11/82	Stoney Creek, Ont.	Toronto St. Michael's (OHL)	2001 Draft
25	Brandon Reid A	F	R	5'9"	170	03/09/81	Kirkland, Que.	Val-d'Or (QMJHL)	VAN '00 (7, 208)
3	Nick Schultz	D	L	6'0.5"	194	08/25/82	Strasbourg, Sask.	Prince Albert (WHL)	MIN '00 (2, 33)
9	Jason Spezza	F	R	6'0.5"	209	06/13/83	Mississauga, Ont.	Windsor (OHL)	2001 Draft
19	Jarret Stoll	F	R	6'0.5"	198	06/24/82	Neudorf, Sask.	Kootenay (WHL)	CGY '00 (2, 46)
28	Raffi Torres	F	L	5'11.5"	209	10/08/81	Markham, Ont.	Brampton (OHL)	NYI '00 (1, 5)
10	Mike Zigomanis	F	R	6'0.5"	194	01/17/81	North York, Ont.	Kingston (OHL)	BUF '99 (2, 64)

Head scout: Barry Trapp

Head coach: Stan Butler

Assistant coach: Kevin Dickie

Assistant coach: Mike Kelly

2002

#	NAME	P	S	HT	WT	BORN	HOMETOWN	CLUB	DRAFT STATUS
34	Jared Aulin	F	R	6'0"	187	03/15/82	Calgary, Alta.	Kamloops (WHL)	COL '00 (2, 47)
4	Jay Bouwmeester	D	L	6'4"	207	09/27/83	Edmonton, Alta.	Medicine Hat (WHL)	2002 Draft.
17	Brad Boyes	F	R	6'0"	187	04/17/82	Mississauga, Ont.	Erie (OHL)	TOR '00 (1, 24)
13	Mike Cammalleri A	F	L	5'9"	181	06/08/82	Richmond Hill, Ont.	Michigan (CCHA)	LA '00 (2, 49)
8	Carlo Colaiacovo	D	L	6'0.5"	183	01/27/83	Toronto, Ont.	Erie (OHL)	TOR '01 (1, 17)
5	Dan Hamhuis	D	L	6'0.5"	198	12/13/82	Smithers, B.C.	Prince George (WHL)	NSH '01 (1, 12)
23	Jay Harrison	D	L	6'3.5"	209	11/03/82	Whitby, Ont.	Brampton (OHL)	TOR '01 (3, 82)
21	Chuck Kobasew	F	R	5'11.5"	194	04/17/82	Osoyoos, B.C.	Kelowna (WHL)	CGY '01 (1, 14)
31	Pascal Leclaire	G	L	6'1.5"	183	11/07/92	St-Gabriel-de-Brandon, Que.	Montreal (QMJHL)	CBJ '01 (1, 8)
18	Jay McClement	F	L	6'0.5"	198	03/02/83	Kingston, Ont.	Brampton (OHL)	STL '01 (2, 57)
30	Olivier Michaud	G	L	5'10.5"	163	09/14/83	Beloeil, Que.	Shawinigan (QMJHL)	Undrafted
10	Garth Murray	F	L	6'0.5"	207	09/17/82	Regina, Sask.	Regina (WHL)	NYR '01 (3, 79)
38	Rick Nash	F	L	6'1.5"	170	06/12/84	Brampton, Ont.	London (OHL)	2002 Draft
14	Steve Ott	F	L	6'0"	178	08/19/82	Stoney Point, Ont.	Windsor (OHL)	DAL '00 (1, 25)
37	Nathan Paetsch	D	L	6'0"	201	03/30/83	Leroy, Sask.	Moose Jaw (WHL)	WSH '01 (2, 58)
27	Mark Popovic	D	L	6'1.5"	189	10/11/82	Stoney Creek, Ont.	Toronto St. Michael's (OHL)	ANA '01 (2, 35)
7	Nick Schultz A	D	L	6'1.5"	203	08/25/82	Strasbourg, Sask.	Minnesota (NHL)	MIN '00 (2, 33)
9	Jason Spezza	F	R	6'2"	209	06/13/83	Mississauga, Ont.	Windsor (OHL)	OTT '01 (1, 2)
16	Jarret Stoll C	F	R	6'1.5"	198	06/24/82	Neudorf, Sask.	Kootenay (WHL)	CGY '00 (2, 46)
20	Brian Sutherby	F	L	6'3"	196	03/01/82	Edmonton, Alta.	Moose Jaw (WHL)	WSH '00 (1, 26)
19	Scottie Upshall	F	L	5'10.5"	178	10/07/83	Fort McMurray, Alta.	Kamloops (WHL)	2002 Draft
22	Stephen Weiss	F	L	6'0"	185	04/03/83	Markham, Ont.	Plymouth (OHL)	FLA '01 (1, 4)

Head coach: Stan Butler

Assistant coach: Marc Habscheid

Assistant coach: Mike Kelly

Goaltending consultant: Andy Moog

2003

#	NAME	P	S	HT	WT	BORN	HOMETOWN	CLUB	DRAFT STATUS
7	Brendan Bell	D	L	6'0.5"	207	03/31/83	Ottawa, Ont.	Ottawa (OHL)	TOR '01 (3, 65)
16	Pierre-Marc Bouchard A	F	L	5'11"	165	04/27/84	Boucherville, Que.	Minnesota (NHL)	MIN '02 (1, 8)
11	Gregory Campbell	F	L	5'10.5"	187	12/17/83	Tillsonburg, Ont.	Kitchener (OHL)	FLA '02 (3, 67)
8	Carlo Colaiacovo	D	L	6'0.5"	187	01/27/83	Toronto, Ont.	Erie (OHL)	TOR '01 (1, 17)
2	Steve Eminger A	D	R	6'1.5"	187	10/31/83	Woodbridge, Ont.	Washington (NHL)	WSH '02 (1, 12)
1	Marc-André Fleury	D	L	6'1.5"	170	11/28/84	Sorel, Que.	Cape Breton (QMJHL)	2003 Draft
27	Boyd Gordon	F	R	6'0"	185	10/18/83	Regina, Sask.	Red Deer (WHL)	STL '02 (1, 17)
29	Brooks Laich	F	L	6'0"	183	06/23/83	Wawota, Sask.	Seattle (WHL)	OTT '01 (6, 193)
31	David LeNeveu	D	L	6'0.5"	170	05/23/83	Fernie, B.C.	Cornell (ECAC)	PHX '02 (2, 46)
15	Joffrey Lupul	F	R	6'1.5"	194	09/23/83	Fort Saskatchewan, Alta.	Medicine Hat (WHL)	ANA '02 (1, 7)
18	Jay McClement	F	L	6'1.5"	194	03/02/83	Kingston, Ont.	Brampton (OHL)	STL '01 (2, 57)
6	Nathan Paetsch	D	L	6'0.5"	194	03/30/83	Leroy, Sask.	Moose Jaw (WHL)	WSH '01 (2, 58)
10	Daniel Paille	F	L	6'0"	201	04/15/84	Welland, Ont.	Guelph (OHL)	BUF '02 (1, 20)
25	Pierre-Alexandre Parenteau	F	R	5'11.5"	178	03/24/83	Boucherville, Que.	Chicoutimi (QMJHL)	ANA '01 (9, 264)
3	Alexandre Rouleau	D	L	6'0.5"	189	07/29/83	Mont-Laurier, Que.	Val-d'Or (QMJHL)	PIT '01 (3, 96)
21	Derek Roy	F	L	5'8.5"	187	05/04/83	Rockland, Ont.	Kitchener (OHL)	BUF '01 (2, 32)
14	Matt Stajan	F	L	6'1.5"	187	12/19/83	Mississauga, Ont.	Belleville (OHL)	TOR '02 (2, 57)
22	Jordin Tootoo	F	R	5'8.5"	185	02/02/83	Rankin Inlet, Nun.	Brandon (WHL)	NSH '01 (4, 98)
19	Scottie Upshall C	F	L	5'11.5"	178	10/07/83	Fort McMurray, Alta.	Kamloops (WHL)	NSH '02 (1, 6)
28	Kyle Wellwood	F	R	5'9.5"	189	05/16/83	Oldcastle, Ont.	Windsor (OHL)	TOR '01 (5, 134)
17	Ian White	D	R	5'9.5"	183	06/04/84	Steinbach, Man.	Swift Current (WHL)	TOR '02 (6, 191)
4	Jeff Woywitka	D	L	6'3"	216	09/01/83	Vermilion, Alta.	Red Deer (WHL)	PHI '01 (1, 27)

Head scout: Blair MacKasey

Head coach: Marc Habscheid

Assistant coach: Mario Durocher

Assistant coach: Mike Kelly

2004

#	NAME	P	S	HT	WT	BORN	HOMETOWN	CLUB	DRAFT STATUS
37	Shawn Belle	D	L	6'1"	184	01/03/85	Edmonton, Alta.	Tri-City (WHL)	STL '03 (1, 30)
8	Tim Brent A	F	R	6'0"	186	03/10/84	Cambridge, Ont.	Toronto St. Michael's (OHL)	ANA '02 (2, 37)
22	Brent Burns	F	R	6'4"	200	09/03/85	Barrie, Ont.	Minnesota (NHL)	MIN '03 (1, 20)
9	Jeff Carter	F	R	6'3"	202	01/01/85	London, Ont.	Sault Ste. Marie (OHL)	PHI '03 (1, 11)
29	Braydon Coburn	D	L	6'5"	217	02/27/85	Shaunavon, Sask.	Portland (WHL)	ATL '03 (1, 8)
21	Jeremy Colliton	F	R	6'1"	194	01/13/85	Blackie, Alta.	Prince Albert (WHL)	NYI '03 (2, 58)
28	Sidney Crosby	F	L	5'10"	185	08/07/87	Cole Harbour, N.S.	Rimouski (QMJHL)	2005 Draft
27	Nigel Dawes	F	L	5'8"	176	02/09/85	Winnipeg, Man.	Kootenay (WHL)	NYR '03 (5, 149)
24	Stephen Dixon	F	L	5'11"	188	09/07/85	Halifax, N.S.	Cape Breton (QMJHL)	PIT '03 (7, 229)
1	Marc-André Fleury	G	L	6'1.5"	173	11/28/84	Sorel, Que.	Pittsburgh (NHL)	PIT '03 (1, 1)
15	Ryan Getzlaf	F	R	6'3"	206	05/10/85	Regina, Sask.	Calgary (WHL)	ANA '03 (1, 19)
5	Josh Gorges	D	L	6'0"	188	08/14/84	Kelowna, B.C.	Kelowna (WHL)	Undrafted
35	Josh Harding	G	R	6'1"	183	06/18/84	Regina, Sask.	Regina (WHL)	MIN '02 (2, 38)
6	Kevin Klein	D	R	6'0.5"	197	12/13/84	Kitchener, Ont.	Guelph (OHL)	NSH '03 (2, 37)
2	Derek Meech	D	L	5'11"	194	10/21/84	Winnipeg, Man.	Red Deer (WHL)	DET '02 (7, 229)
20	Daniel Paille C	F	L	6'0"	203	04/04/84	Welland, Ont.	Guelph (OHL)	BUF '02 (1, 20)
3	Dion Phaneuf	D	L	6'2"	205	04/10/85	Edmonton, Alta.	Red Deer (WHL)	CGY '03 (1, 9)
18	Michael Richards	F	L	5'11"	195	02/11/85	Kenora, Ont.	Kitchener (OHL)	PHI '03 (1, 24)
32	Brent Seabrook	D	R	6'2"	225	04/20/85	Tsawwassen, B.C.	Lethbridge (WHL)	CHI '03 (1, 14)
12	Anthony Stewart	F	R	6'1"	230	01/05/85	Scarborough, Ont.	Kingston (OHL)	FLA '03 (1, 25)
25	Maxime Talbot A	F	L	5'10"	181	02/11/84	St-Bruno, Que.	Gatineau (QMJHL)	PIT '02 (8, 234)
19	Jeff Tambellini	F	L	5'10"	190	04/13/84	Port Moody, B.C.	Michigan (CCHA)	LA '03 (1, 27)

Head scout: Blair MacKasey

Head coach: Mario Durocher

Assistant coach: Dean Chynoweth

Assistant coach: Jim Hulton

Goaltending coach: Ian Clark

2005

#	NAME	P	S	HT	WT	BORN	HOMETOWN	CLUB	DRAFT STATUS
25	Cam Barker	D	L	6'3"	220	04/04/86	Winnipeg, Man.	Medicine Hat (WHL)	CHI '04 (1, 3)
35	Réjean Beauchemin	G	L	6'2"	198	05/03/85	Winnipeg, Man.	Prince Albert (WHL)	PHI '03 (6, 191)
4	Shawn Belle	D	L	6'1"	229	01/03/85	Edmonton, Alta.	Tri-City (WHL)	STL '03 (1, 30)
37	Patrice Bergeron A	F	R	6'1"	186	07/24/85	Quebec City, Que.	Providence (AHL)	BOS '03 (2, 45)
7	Jeff Carter A	F	R	6'4"	207	01/01/85	London, Ont.	Sault Ste. Marie (OHL)	PHI '03 (1, 11)
29	Braydon Coburn	D	L	6'5"	220	02/27/85	Shaunavon, Sask.	Portland (WHL)	ATL '03 (1, 8)
21	Jeremy Colliton	F	R	6'1"	202	01/13/85	Blackie, Alta.	Prince Albert (WHL)	NYI '03 (2, 58)
9	Sidney Crosby	F	L	5'10"	193	08/07/87	Cole Harbour, N.S.	Rimouski (QMJHL)	2005 Draft
17	Nigel Dawes	F	L	5'8"	187	02/09/85	Winnipeg, Man.	Kootenay (WHL)	NYR '03 (5, 149)
14	Stephen Dixon	F	L	5'10"	198	09/07/85	Halifax, N.S.	Cape Breton (QMJHL)	PIT '03 (7, 229)
11	Colin Fraser	F	L	6'1"	187	01/28/85	Surrey, B.C.	Red Deer (WHL)	PHI '03 (3, 69)
15	Ryan Getzlaf	F	R	6'3"	209	05/10/85	Regina, Sask.	Calgary (WHL)	ANA '03 (1, 19)
33	Jeff Glass	G	L	6'1"	180	11/19/85	Cochrane, Alta.	Kootenay (WHL)	OTT '04 (3, 89)
19	Andrew Ladd	F	L	6'1"	202	12/12/85	Maple Ridge, B.C.	Calgary (WHL)	CAR '04 (1, 4)
17	Clarke MacArthur	F	L	6'0"	187	04/06/85	Lloydminster, Alta.	Medicine Hat (WHL)	BUF '03 (3, 74)
24	Corey Perry	F	R	6'2"	198	05/16/85	Peterborough, Ont.	London (OHL)	ANA '03 (1, 28)
3	Dion Phaneuf A	D	L	6'2"	216	04/10/85	Edmonton, Alta.	Red Deer (WHL)	CGY '03 (1, 9)
18	Michael Richards C	F	L	5'10"	198	02/11/85	Kenora, Ont.	Kitchener (OHL)	PHI '03 (1, 24)
2	Brent Seabrook	D	R	6'1"	224	04/20/85	Tsawwassen, B.C.	Lethbridge (WHL)	CHI '03 (1, 14)
12	Anthony Stewart	F	R	6'1"	233	01/05/85	Scarborough, Ont.	Kingston (OHL)	FLA '03 (1, 25)
20	Danny Syvret	D	L	5'10"	200	06/13/85	Millgrove, Ont.	London (OHL)	Undrafted
6	Shea Weber	D	R	6'3"	220	08/14/85	Sicamous, B.C.	Kelowna (WHL)	NSH '03 (2, 49)

Head scout: Blair MacKasey

Head coach: Brent Sutter

Assistant coach: Peter DeBoer

Assistant coach: Jim Hulton

Assistant coach: Rob Cookson

Goaltending coach: Ian Clark

#	NAME	P	S	HT	WT	BORN	HOMETOWN	CLUB	DRAFT STATUS
25	Cam Barker *A*	D	L	6'3"	220	04/04/86	Winnipeg, Man.	Medicine Hat (WHL)	CHI '04 (1, 3)
22	Daniel Bertram	F	R	5'11"	175	01/14/87	Calgary, Alta.	Boston College (Hky East)	CHI '05 (2, 54)
21	Michael Blunden	F	R	6'3"	213	12/15/86	Gloucester, Ont.	Erie (OHL)	CHI '05 (2, 43)
19	David Bolland *A*	F	R	5'11"	176	06/05/86	Mimico, Ont.	London (OHL)	CHI '04 (2, 32)
6	Luc Bourdon *A*	D	L	6'2"	199	02/16/87	Shippagan, N.B.	Val-d'Or (QMJHL)	VAN '05 (1, 10)
16	Dustin Boyd	F	L	6'0"	185	07/16/86	Winnipeg, Man.	Moose Jaw (WHL)	CGY '04 (3, 98)
17	Kyle Chipchura *C*	F	L	6'1"	209	02/19/86	Vimy, Alta.	Prince Albert (WHL)	MTL '04 (1, 18)
9	Andrew Cogliano	F	L	5'9"	178	06/14/87	Woodbridge, Ont.	Michigan (CCHA)	EDM '05 (1, 25)
14	Blake Comeau *A*	F	R	6'1"	207	02/18/86	Meadow Lake, Sask.	Kelowna (WHL)	NYI '04 (2, 47)
7	Steve Downie	F	R	5'10"	189	04/03/87	Queensville, Ont.	Peterborough (OHL)	PHI '05 (1, 29)
30	Devan Dubnyk	G	L	6'5"	200	05/04/86	Calgary, Alta.	Kamloops (WHL)	EDM '04 (1, 14)
20	Guillaume Latendresse	F	L	6'2"	222	05/24/87	Ste-Catherine, Que.	Drummondville (QMJHL)	MTL '05 (2, 45)
12	Kristopher Letang	D	R	5'11"	190	04/24/87	Laval, Que.	Val-d'Or (QMJHL)	PIT '05 (3, 62)
23	Ryan O'Marra	F	R	6'1"	194	06/09/87	Mississauga, Ont.	Erie (OHL)	NYI '05 (1, 15)
4	Ryan Parent	D	L	6'2"	183	03/17/87	Sioux Lookout, Ont.	Guelph (OHL)	NSH '05 (1, 18)
33	Justin Pogge	G	L	6'3"	205	04/22/86	Penticton, B.C.	Calgary (WHL)	TOR '04 (3, 90)
36	Sasha Pokulok	D	L	6'5"	230	05/25/86	Vaudreuil-Dorion, Que.	Cornell (ECAC)	WSH '05 (1, 14)
37	Benoit Pouliot	F	L	6'3"	179	09/29/86	Ottawa, Ont.	Sudbury (OHL)	MIN '05 (1, 4)
27	Tom Pyatt	F	L	5'11"	180	02/14/87	Thunder Bay, Ont.	Saginaw (OHL)	NYR '05 (4, 107)
10	Kris Russell	D	L	5'10"	166	05/02/87	Caroline, Alta.	Medicine Hat (WHL)	CBJ '05 (3, 67)
3	Marc Staal	D	L	6'3"	196	01/13/87	Thunder Bay, Ont.	Sudbury (OHL)	NYR '05 (1, 12)
29	Jonathan Toews	F	L	6'2"	185	04/29/88	Winnipeg, Man.	North Dakota (WCHA)	2006 Draft

Head coach: Brent Sutter

Assistant coach: Craig Hartsburg

Assistant coach: Clément Jodoin

Goaltending coach: Ian Clark

#	NAME	P	S	HT	WT	BORN	HOMETOWN	CLUB	DRAFT STATUS
3	Karl Alzner	D	L	6'2"	209	09/24/88	Burnaby, B.C.	Calgary (WHL)	2007 Draft
22	Dan Bertram	F	R	5'10"	183	01/14/87	Calgary, Alta.	Boston College (Hky East)	CHI '05 (2, 54)
6	Luc Bourdon	D	L	5'5"	211	02/16/87	Shippagan, N.B.	Moncton (QMJHL)	VAN '05 (1, 10)
11	Marc-André Cliche	F	R	6'0.5"	187	03/23/87	Rouyn-Noranda, Que.	Lewiston (QMJHL)	NYR '05 (2, 56)
9	Andrew Cogliano	F	L	5'9"	186	06/14/87	Woodbridge, Ont.	Michigan (CCHA)	EDM '05 (1, 25)
7	Steve Downie *A*	F	L	5'10.5"	203	04/03/87	Queensville, Ont.	Peterborough (OHL)	PHI '05 (1, 29)
26	Cody Franson	D	R	6'3"	204	08/08/87	Sicamous, B.C.	Vancouver (WHL)	NSH '05 (3, 79)
38	Sam Gagner	F	R	5'10.5"	190	08/10/89	Oakville, Ont.	London (OHL)	2007 Draft
15	Darren Helm	F	L	6'0"	183	01/21/87	St. Andrews, Man.	Medicine Hat (WHL)	DET '05 (5, 132)
31	Leland Irving	G	L	6'0"	177	04/11/88	Swan Hills, Man.	Everett (WHL)	CGY '06 (1,26)
5	Kristopher Letang *C*	D	L	5'11.5"	207	04/24/87	Ste-Julie, Que.	Val-d'Or (QMJHL)	PIT '05 (3, 62)
20	Bryan Little	F	R	5'10.5"	201	11/23/87	Cambridge, Ont.	Barrie (OHL)	ATL '06 (1, 12)
17	Brad Marchand	F	L	5'9"	183	05/11/88	Hammonds Plains, N.S.	Val-d'Or (QMJHL)	BOS '06 (3, 71)
12	Kenndal McArdle	F	L	5'11.5"	205	01/04/87	Burnaby, B.C.	Vancouver (WHL)	FLA '05 (1, 20)
19	James Neal	F	L	6'2.5"	203	09/03/87	Whitby, Ont.	Plymouth (OHL)	DAL '05 (2, 33)
23	Ryan O'Marra	F	R	6'2"	207	06/09/87	Mississauga, Ont.	Saginaw (OHL)	NYI '05 (1, 15)
4	Ryan Parent	D	L	6'2"	194	03/17/87	Sioux Lookout, Ont.	Guelph (OHL)	NSH '05 (1, 18)
1	Carey Price	G	L	6'2"	217	08/16/87	Anahim Lake, B.C.	Tri-City (WHL)	MTL '05 (1, 5)
27	Tom Pyatt *A*	F	L	5'11"	186	02/14/87	Thunder Bay, Ont.	Saginaw (OHL)	NYR '05 (4, 107)
10	Kris Russell	D	L	5'10"	162	05/02/87	Caroline, Alta.	Medicine Hat (WHL)	CBJ '05 (3, 67)
14	Marc Staal *A*	D	L	6'4"	207	01/13/87	Thunder Bay, Ont.	Sudbury (OHL)	NYR '05 (1, 12)
29	Jonathan Toews *A*	F	L	6'1.5"	203	04/29/88	Winnipeg, Man.	North Dakota (WCHA)	CHI '06 (1, 3)

Head scout: Jim Hammett

Head coach: Craig Hartsburg

Assistant coach: Curtis Hunt

Assistant coach: Clément Jodoin

Goaltending coach: Corey Hirsch

#	NAME	P	S	HT	WT	BORN	HOMETOWN	CLUB	DRAFT STATUS
27	Karl Alzner *C*	D	L	6'2"	209	09/24/88	Burnaby, B.C.	Calgary (WHL)	WSH '07 (1, 5)
1	Jonathan Bernier	G	L	6'0"	185	08/07/88	Laval, Que.	Lewiston (QMJHL)	LA '06 (1, 11)
11	Zach Boychuk	F	L	5'9"	176	10/04/89	Airdrie, Alta.	Lethbridge (WHL)	2008 Draft
8	Drew Doughty	D	R	6'0"	190	12/08/89	London, Ont.	Guelph (OHL)	2008 Draft
18	Colton Gillies	F	L	6'4"	189	02/12/89	Surrey, B.C.	Saskatoon (WHL)	MIN '07 (1, 16)
28	Claude Giroux	F	R	5'11"	172	01/12/88	Ottawa, Ont.	Gatineau (QMJHL)	PHI '06 (1, 22)
2	Josh Godfrey	D	R	6'0"	187	01/15/88	Kingston, Ont.	Sault Ste. Marie (OHL)	WSH '07 (2, 34)
32	Matt Halischuk	F	R	5'11"	173	06/01/88	Mississauga, Ont.	Kitchener (OHL)	NJ '07 (4, 117)
4	Thomas Hickey	D	L	5'11"	182	02/08/89	Calgary, Alta.	Seattle (WHL)	LA '07 (1, 4)
21	Riley Holzapfel	F	L	5'11"	185	08/18/88	Regina, Sask.	Moose Jaw (WHL)	ATL '06 (2, 43)
21	Stefan Legein *A*	F	R	5'9"	170	11/24/88	Oakville, Ont.	Niagara (OHL)	CBJ '07 (2,37)
17	Brad Marchand *A*	F	L	5'9"	183	05/11/88	Hammonds Plains, N.S.	Val-d'Or (QMJHL)	BOS '06 (3, 71)
30	Steve Mason	G	R	6'3"	186	05/29/88	Oakville, Ont.	London (OHL)	CBJ '06 (3, 69)
22	Shawn Matthias	F	L	6'4"	213	02/19/88	Mississauga, Ont.	Belleville (OHL)	DET '07 (2, 47)
3	Logan Pyett *A*	D	R	5'10"	199	05/26/88	Milestone, Sask.	Regina (WHL)	DET '06 (7, 212)
15	Luke Schenn	D	R	6'2"	210	11/02/89	Saskatoon, Sask.	Kelowna (WHL)	2008 Draft
34	Wayne Simmonds	F	R	6'2"	175	08/26/88	Pickering, Ont.	Owen Sound (OHL)	LA '07 (2, 61)
10	Steven Stamkos	F	R	6'0"	183	02/07/90	Unionville, Ont.	Saginaw (OHL)	2008 Draft
23	P.K. Subban	D	R	5'11"	204	05/13/89	Toronto, Ont.	Belleville (OHL)	MTL '07 (2, 43)
12	Brandon Sutter *A*	F	R	6'3"	170	02/14/89	Red Deer, Alta.	Red Deer (WHL)	CAR '07 (1, 11)
20	John Tavares	F	L	6'0"	196	09/20/90	Oakville, Ont.	Oshawa (OHL)	2009 Draft
19	Kyle Turris	F	R	6'2"	170	08/14/89	New Westminster, B.C.	Wisconsin (WCHA)	PHX '07 (1, 3)

Head scout: Al Murray

Head coach: Craig Hartsburg

Assistant coach: Curtis Hunt

Assistant coach: Clément Jodoin

Goaltending coach: Corey Hirsch

#	NAME	P	S	HT	WT	BORN	HOMETOWN	CLUB	DRAFT STATUS
32	Keith Aulie	D	L	6'6"	215	06/11/89	Rouleau, Sask.	Brandon (WHL)	CGY '07 (4, 116)
24	Jamie Benn	F	L	6'1.5"	202	07/18/89	Victoria, B.C.	Kelowna (WHL)	DAL '07 (5, 129)
11	Zach Boychuk *A*	F	L	5'10"	175	10/04/89	Airdrie, Alta.	Lethbridge (WHL)	CAR '08 (1, 14)
28	Patrice Cormier	F	L	6'1.5"	201	06/14/89	Cap-Pele, N.B.	Rimouski (QMJHL)	NJ '08 (2, 54)
15	Stefan Della Rovere	F	L	5'11"	200	02/25/90	Maple, Ont.	Barrie (OHL)	WSH '08 (7, 204)
25	Chris DiDomenico	F	R	5'11"	170	02/20/89	Woodbridge, Ont.	Saint John (QMJHL)	TOR '07 (6, 164)
14	Jordan Eberle	F	R	5'10"	181	05/15/90	Regina, Sask.	Regina (WHL)	EDM '08 (1, 22)
8	Ryan Ellis	D	R	5'9.5"	176	01/03/91	Freelton, Ont.	Windsor (OHL)	2009 Draft
22	Tyler Ennis	F	L	5'8"	165	10/06/89	Edmonton, Alta.	Medicine Hat (WHL)	BUF '08 (1, 26)
7	Angelo Esposito	F	L	6'1"	180	02/20/89	Montreal, Que.	Montreal (QMJHL)	PIT '07 (1, 20)
17	Cody Goloubef	D	R	6'1"	194	11/30/89	Oakville, Ont.	Wisconsin (WCHA)	CBJ '08 (2, 37)
4	Thomas Hickey *C*	D	L	5'11"	194	02/08/89	Calgary, Alta.	Seattle (WHL)	LA '07 (1, 4)
18	Cody Hodgson *A*	F	R	5'11"	189	02/18/90	Markham, Ont.	Brampton (OHL)	VAN '08 (1, 10)
29	Evander Kane	F	L	6'1"	180	08/02/90	Vancouver, B.C.	Vancouver (WHL)	2009 Draft
3	Tyler Myers	D	R	6'7.5"	213	02/01/90	Calgary, Alta.	Kelowna (WHL)	BUF '08 (1, 12)
31	Chet Pickard	G	L	6'1"	216	11/29/89	Winnipeg, Man.	Tri-City (WHL)	NSH '08 (1, 18)
10	Alex Pietrangelo	D	R	6'2.5"	204	01/18/90	King City, Ont.	Niagara (OHL)	STL '08 (1, 4)
12	Brett Sonne	F	L	6'0"	187	05/16/89	Maple Ridge, B.C.	Calgary (WHL)	STL '07 (3, 85)
5	P.K. Subban *A*	D	R	5'11"	206	05/13/89	Toronto, Ont.	Belleville (OHL)	MTL '07 (2, 43)
20	John Tavares *A*	F	L	6'0"	203	09/20/90	Oakville, Ont.	Oshawa (OHL)	2009 Draft
2	Colten Teubert	D	R	6'3"	189	03/08/90	White Rock, B.C.	Regina (WHL)	LA '08 (1, 13)
30	Dustin Tokarski	G	L	5'11"	189	09/16/89	Watson, Sask.	Spokane (WHL)	TB '08 (5, 122)
16	Dana Tyrell	F	L	5'9.5"	182	04/23/89	Airdrie, Alta.	Prince George (WHL)	TB '07 (2, 47)

Head scout: Al Murray

Head coach: Pat Quinn

Assistant coach: Dave Cameron

Assistant coach: Willie Desjardins

Assistant coach: Guy Boucher

Goaltending coach: Frédéric Chabot

2010

#	NAME	P	S	HT	WT	BORN	HOMETOWN	CLUB	DRAFT STATUS
20	Luke Adam	F	L	6'2"	201	06/18/90	St. John's, N.L.	Cape Breton (QMJHL)	BUF '08 (2, 44)
1	Jake Allen	G	L	6'1"	191	08/07/90	Fredericton, N.B.	Montreal (QMJHL)	STL '08 (2, 34)
7	Gabriel Bourque	F	L	5'9"	183	01/25/91	Squatec, Que.	Baie-Comeau (QMJHL)	NSH '09 (5, 132)
26	Jordan Caron	F	L	6'2"	200	11/02/90	Sayabec, Que.	Rimouski (QMJHL)	BOS '09 (1, 25)
28	Patrice Cormier *C*	F	L	6'1.5"	201	06/14/90	Cap-Pelé, N.B.	Rimouski (QMJHL)	NJ '08 (2, 54)
22	Jared Cowen	D	L	6'5"	226	01/25/91	Allan, Sask.	Spokane (WHL)	OTT '09 (1, 9)
24	Calvin de Haan	D	L	6'0"	182	05/09/91	Carp, Ont.	Oshawa (OHL)	NYI '09 (1, 12)
19	Stefan Della Rovere *A*	F	L	5'10.5"	200	02/25/90	Maple, Ont.	Barrie (OHL)	WSH '08 (7, 204)
14	Jordan Eberle *A*	F	R	5'10"	181	05/15/90	Regina, Sask.	Regina (WHL)	EDM '08 (1, 22)
6	Ryan Ellis *A*	D	R	5'9.5"	184	01/03/91	Freelton, Ont.	Windsor (OHL)	NSH '09 (1, 11)
4	Taylor Hall	F	L	6'0"	181	11/14/91	Kingston, Ont.	Windsor (OHL)	2010 Draft
3	Travis Hamonic	D	R	6'0"	219	08/16/90	St. Malo, Man.	Moose Jaw (WHL)	NYI '08 (2, 53)
12	Adam Henrique	F	L	5'11"	188	02/06/90	Burford, Ont.	Windsor (OHL)	NJ '08 (3, 82)
31	Martin Jones	G	R	6'3.5"	187	01/10/90	North Vancouver, B.C.	Calgary (WHL)	Undrafted
9	Nazem Kadri *A*	F	L	6'0"	174	10/06/90	London, Ont.	London (OHL)	TOR '09 (1, 7)
17	Brandon Kozun	F	R	5'7"	156	03/08/90	Calgary, Alta.	Calgary (WHL)	LA '09 (6, 179)
15	Brandon McMillan	F	L	5'11"	185	03/22/90	Delta, B.C.	Kelowna (WHL)	ANA '08 (3, 95)
16	Greg Nemisz	F	R	6'3"	199	06/05/90	Courtice, Ont.	Windsor (OHL)	CGY '08 (1, 25)
27	Alex Pietrangelo *A*	D	R	6'3"	207	01/18/90	King City, Ont.	St. Louis (NHL)	STL '08 (1, 4)
5	Marco Scandella	D	L	6'2.5"	217	02/23/90	Montreal, Que.	Val-d'Or (QMJHL)	MIN '08 (2, 55)
10	Brayden Schenn	F	L	6'0"	194	08/22/91	Saskatoon, Sask.	Brandon (WHL)	LA '09 (1, 5)
2	Colten Teubert *A*	D	R	6'3"	195	03/08/90	White Rock, B.C.	Regina (WHL)	LA '08 (1, 13)

Head scout: Al Murray
Head coach: Willie Desjardins
Associate coach: Dave Cameron
Assistant coach: Steve Spott
Assistant coach: André Tourigny
Goaltending coach: Ron Tugnutt

2011

#	NAME	P	S	HT	WT	BORN	HOMETOWN	CLUB	DRAFT STATUS
25	Carter Ashton	F	L	6'3"	219	04/01/91	Saskatoon, Sask.	Tri-City (WHL)	TB '09 (1, 29)
22	Tyson Barrie	D	R	5'10"	190	07/26/91	Victoria, B.C.	Kelowna (WHL)	COL '09 (3, 64)
11	Casey Cizikas	F	L	5'11"	191	02/27/91	Mississauga, Ont.	Mississauga St. Michael's (OHL)	NYI '09 (4, 92)
28	Brett Connolly	F	R	6'2"	181	05/02/92	Prince George, B.C.	Prince George (WHL)	TB '10 (1, 6)
7	Sean Couturier	F	L	6'3"	192	12/07/92	Bathurst, N.B.	Drummondville (QMJHL)	2011 Draft
2	Jared Cowen *A*	D	L	6'5"	227	01/25/91	Allan, Sask.	Spokane (WHL)	OTT '09 (1, 9)
24	Calvin de Haan *A*	D	L	6'0"	189	05/09/91	Carp, Ont.	Oshawa (OHL)	NYI '09 (1, 12)
3	Simon Després	D	L	6'4"	222	07/27/91	Laval, Que.	Saint John (QMJHL)	PIT '09 (1, 30)
21	Cody Eakin	F	L	6'0"	187	05/24/91	Winnipeg, Man.	Swift Current (WHL)	WSH '09 (3, 85)
6	Ryan Ellis *C*	D	R	5'10"	184	01/03/91	Freelton, Ont.	Windsor (OHL)	NSH '09 (1, 11)
17	Marcus Foligno	F	L	6'1"	200	08/10/91	Sudbury, Ont.	Sudbury (OHL)	BUF '09 (4, 104)
5	Erik Gudbranson	D	R	6'4"	211	01/07/92	Orleans, Ont.	Kingston (OHL)	FLA '10 (1, 3)
16	Curtis Hamilton	F	L	6'3"	202	12/04/91	Kelowna, B.C.	Saskatoon (WHL)	EDM '10 (2, 48)
12	Quinton Howden	F	L	6'2"	192	01/21/92	Oak Bank, Man.	Moose Jaw (WHL)	FLA '10 (1, 25)
19	Ryan Johansen	F	R	6'2"	193	07/31/92	Port Moody, B.C.	Portland (WHL)	CBJ '10 (1, 4)
9	Zack Kassian	F	R	6'3"	226	01/24/91	LaSalle, Ont.	Windsor (OHL)	BUF '09 (1, 13)
20	Louis Leblanc	F	R	5'11"	181	01/26/91	Kirkland, Ont.	Montreal (QMJHL)	MTL '09 (1, 18)
4	Dylan Olsen	D	L	6'2"	223	01/03/91	Calgary, Alta.	Minnesota-Duluth (WCHA)	CHI '09 (1, 28)
31	Olivier Roy	G	L	5'11"	186	07/12/91	Causapscal, Que.	Acadie-Bathurst (QMJHL)	EDM '09 (5, 133)
10	Brayden Schenn *A*	F	L	6'0"	199	08/22/91	Saskatoon, Sask.	Brandon (WHL)	LA '09 (1, 5)
8	Jaden Schwartz	F	L	5'10"	184	06/25/92	Wilcox, Sask.	Colorado College (WCHA)	STL '10 (1, 14)
30	Mark Visentin	G	L	6'1"	198	08/07/92	Waterdown, Ont.	Niagara (OHL)	PHX '10 (1, 27)

Head scout: Kevin Prendergast
Head coach: Dave Cameron
Assistant coach: Ryan Huska
Assistant coach: André Tourigny
Assistant coach: George Burnett
Goaltending coach: Ron Tugnutt

CONTRIBUTORS

MIKE BABCOCK coached the Detroit Red Wings to the Stanley Cup in 2008 and the Canadian men's hockey team to an Olympic gold medal in 2010.

BRENDAN BELL has played for the Toronto Maple Leafs, the Phoenix Coyotes, and the Ottawa Senators. He was a first-team all-star in the Ontario Hockey League with the Ottawa 67's.

MURRAY COSTELLO was president of Hockey Canada and president of the Canadian Amateur Hockey Association. He played for the Chicago Blackhawks, Boston Bruins, and Detroit Red Wings, in a 163-game NHL career. He was inducted into the Hockey Hall of Fame in 2005 as a builder.

DAMIEN COX is the *Toronto Star*'s hockey columnist and a regular on Sportsnet's radio and television broadcasts. He has written and co-written several books about hockey.

DEAN EVASON is an assistant coach with the Washington Capitals. He played over 800 games in the NHL and also coached in the Western Hockey League.

SHELDON FERGUSON is director of amateur scouting for the Carolina Hurricanes.

TERRY KOSHAN writes about the NHL and major junior hockey for the *Toronto Sun*. He has covered many Memorial Cup tournaments and world junior championships since joining the paper in 1996.

STÉPHANE LEROUX covers junior hockey at RDS.

ROY MacGREGOR has been a columnist at *The Globe and Mail* for the last decade. His book *Home Team: Fathers, Sons and Hockey* was shortlisted for a Governor General's Award.

BOB McKENZIE has been a hockey commentator on TSN since the late 1980s. He first covered the world juniors on air in 1990.

GORD MILLER joined TSN in 1990 and has been the network's lead NHL play-by-play announcer since 2002. His work at the 2008 world junior championship earned him a Gemini nomination.

STEVE MILTON is a long-time columnist with *The Hamilton Spectator*. He covered the 1985 WJC.

DAVE MORRISON is head of the amateur scouting department for the Toronto Maple Leafs. He played professional hockey for 18 seasons before retiring in 1999.

BOB NICHOLSON has been the president and CEO of the Canadian Hockey Association since 1998 and serves as Canada's representative to the International Ice Hockey Federation. In the years since he was named senior vice-president of the association in 1992, the Program of Excellence has won ten gold medals, six silver, and two bronze at the IIHF world under-20 tournament.

FRANK ORR is a member of the media wing of the Hockey Hall of Fame. He has covered many Stanley Cups and international tournaments for the *Toronto Star*.

MIKE SANDS is a retired professional hockey player who played six games in the NHL with the Minnesota North Stars and has worked for the NHL Central Scouting Bureau. He currently serves as the director of amateur scouting for the Calgary Flames.

DONNA SPENCER has covered the world junior championships and other major international tournaments for the Canadian Press for over a decade. She is based in Calgary.

JESSE WALLIN is the coach of the Red Deer Rebels. He is a former first-round draft pick of the Detroit Red Wings.

TOM WEBSTER is a retired professional hockey player and head coach. He currently serves as an amateur scout for the Calgary Flames.

TIM WHARNSBY writes about hockey for CBC.ca. He previously worked for the *Toronto Sun* and *The Globe and Mail*.

ED WILLES joined *The Province* (Vancouver) as its general sports columnist in 1982, and has worked for newspapers in western Canada for three decades. He has also written two hockey books.

INDEX

PHOTO CREDITS

Pages xi–xii: SebStock
Pages 13–14: The Canadian Press/TASS
Pages 16–17: The Canadian Press/TASS
Page 19: AP/Karl-Inge Lindberg
Page 60: LEHTIKUVA/Ari-Veikko Peltonen
Page 61: LEHTIKUVA/Juha Kärkkäinen
Page 62: LEHTIKUVA/Matti Björkman
Page 63: LEHTIKUVA/Heikki Saukkomaa
Page 67: LEHTIKUVA/Heikki Saukkomaa
Page 79: S. Levy/Bruce Bennett/Getty Images
Page 80: B. Bennett/Getty Images Sport/Getty Images
Page 82: Paul Bereswill/Hockey Hall of Fame
Pages 90–95: The Canadian Press/Dave Buston
Pages 129–131: The Canadian Press/Kevin Frayer
Pages 134–135: The Canadian Press/Kevin Frayer
Page 137: The Canadian Press/Kevin Frayer
Page 140 (top): The Canadian Press/Kevin Frayer
Page 143: The Canadian Press/Kevin Frayer
Pages 145–149: The Canadian Press/Tom Hanson
Page 220: The Canadian Press

All interior images not listed here courtesy of Hockey Canada the Spanish sun glowed in the golden skins of the ladies; par-rakeet-like, they chattered an incomprehensible farago; their blue-black hair a mass of coloured ribbons, they capered to the flute and tambourine, springing ingeniously into the warm evening air;[2] under their arms nestled sucking pigs whose collars were also composed of the gayest ribbons.

As the river Bidassoa fell behind, a landscape almost lunar in its desolation was unfolded. A high tableland, white beneath the sun; here and there a crag, crowned not with some elegant castle as would have been the way in France or England, but by a shepherd's poor hut. Little moved save for the goats and the few muscular sheep that cropped the bitter grass, the sails of the great windmills in La Mancha, or an occasional cloud advancing majestically across the wide and sparkling sky.

Where in the valleys the soil was tilled, there were but few more signs of life. Only at harvest time did the fields and vineyards fill with clamour — and even that, more often than not, was of an alien sort. For the harvesting throughout a great part of Spain was the work of French occasional labour — gangs of peasants from Guyenne and Languedoc who yearly took good money out of the countryside; while the Spanish farmer sat in a smoky hut, strumming his guitar, and growing each autumn a little poorer.

The towns occasionally huddled round fortresses and cathedrals, or in the shadow of ruined Roman aqueducts, were thronged with no greedy crowds. Under the arcades one caught a glimpse of a few dark figures; in the shadow of some fountain or of a church door, bundles of rags tossed fitfully. But so long as the sun was high, life seemed to be arrested in full course, an elaborate piece of clockwork held back by its ratchet till the appointed hour. Then in the green dusk which turned cork trees into dark stalagmites, the catch was released, the machine

[2] For this and many details in following pages see Mme d'Aulnoys' *Voyage d'Espagne*.

started; the bundles of rags became so many beggars, while from the colonnades and shadowy doorways there stalked, with the gravity of automata, the gentlemen of the town.

The Spanish Captains out of Callot's engravings evoke somewhat the aspect of these strange beings; their get-up was a marriage of current fashion misunderstood, and of tradition distorted. Upon their noble — and for the most part empty — heads were cocked enormous black felt hats. These and the wigs extravagantly full and over-curled, almost hid the sallow faces; and as if overwhelming pride were not enough to keep those heads high and stiff, the necks were encased in gigantic ruffs starched to an iron hardness, and permitting scarce a movement in any direction. These ruffs, called golillos, were the object of an extraordinary national affection; the discomfort they caused was as nothing beside the disgrace of rufflessness.

The suits were invariably black (for gravity was all the rage), and cut in a manner that travestied the tastes of bygone ages: with jackets absurdly short, and sleeves of extreme fullness; while from the belts swung long thin swords, generally of Toledo steel, but growing a trifle rusty these days.

In the luminous twilight those strange beings paced, bowing to one another as graciously as the cruel ruffs would permit; and to swell the black tide, there hurried to and fro a horde of priests, prosperous in the enjoyment of their privileges. There were at this time more than 4,000 religious establishments in Spain, and almost as many clerics to laymen as are to be found nowadays in Tibet.

To the noble crowd stalking the plaza, the sound of a boisterous life would be blown from the taverns. There in the courtyards the muleteers would be eating tortillas and garlic, using for tables their recumbent mules, whose flanks would afterwards serve as bony pillows. Within, two or three score candles no bigger than matches served rather to suffocate than to illumine; as a partridge turned slowly on the spit, some arrogant gipsy scraped a guitar, while his wild-haired girl, decked out with huge glass beads, sang in a manner which recalled to the ear of one particular French traveller the caterwauling of a lascivious puss.

Within the palaces of the nobility, behind façades heavy with escutcheons and Moors' heads, the ladies, even their shoulder blades rouged, sat on the floor the late afternoon through. The galleries where they met might be hung with the finest arras; between the windows, as like as not, on silver stands there reposed cabinets of the rarest woods, from the Philippines, the Viceroyalties of Peru or of New Granada; the endless collations of spiced chocolate and dried fruits were served in vessels of such a gleaming richness as was rarely encountered in England or in France. But for all that there would be not a chair to be seen.

The languorous eyes were heavily mascaraed; they sheltered behind spectacles which varied in size with the nobility of the wearers (those affected by grandees and their women were almost as big as tea-cups). Everyone of consequence wore spectacles; they were yet another aid to gravity, and the right to wear them was often a reward for merit; young women of the finest beauty would even be sculpted in them. The Venetian Government, it was said, had played a cruel trick upon the members of the Spanish State Council, when it presented them with enormous spectacles which were really burning glasses as powerful as Murano could manufacture.

As dusk fell, there would enter the major-domo. Striking with his staff upon the parquet, he would cry, "All praise to the Holy Sacrament." "For ever," the company would answer, "and for ever." Then two by two the pages would bring in the lights, great columns of silver with silver reflectors, and filled with olive or almond oil. When the last lamp was disposed, casting an aromatic cone of light that set the mirrors uneasily

7

trembling in the darkness, and made the wings of some Mexican hummingbird flash once again in a dusty workbox: then would come a noise like starlings in October, and all the ladies in their cages of tyrannical silk and whalebone would rise and curtsy, sighing "Bless you" to each other, as if someone had been so vulgar as to sneeze.

With the darkness, conversation would take a gallant turn: whispers, shocked laughter at what had happened that morning in church — for the churches were the notorious haunts of pleasure. In their recesses, filled with jasmine and orange trees, where tropic birds fluttered among the preserved tears of forgotten saints, and fountains watered an artificial sward, the poor duennas had a despairing duty. Their charges, soft and well spoken as pigeons, had vanished in a trice behind some jasmine bush, to turn there into amorous turtles and fly with their gallants for a fierce ten minutes into some near-by house. Then they would reappear, demure as you please, eyes cast down behind the enormous spectacles, and fob the duennas off with tales of extra paternosters.

In this topsy-turvy country, austerity was reserved for the play. Lope de Vega and the glories of the contemporary Spanish theatre were almost unknown outside of Madrid. Instead, in barn-like halls, riddled with the wind's salvoes, there were presented interminable pieces dealing with some edifying subject, the life of St. Francis Xavier, perhaps, or the forty-eight Jesuit Martyrs of Nagasaki. The audience would follow each word with devout attention, crying whenever a saint's name was mentioned: "Ora pro nobis," and dropping now and then from their hard benches on to their knees with a "Culpa mea, culpa mea maxima." All through the auditorium would then be heard the click of rosaries.

Madrid, of course, enjoyed a life organized on a pattern more familiar, more closely approaching the European norm. The administration of a vast Empire, the periodical arrival of

Indian riches, lent to the streets of the capital, after midday at any rate, a certain briskness. There was a proper theatre, too, with ladies behind gilded trellises in boxes, and strumpets brazening it in the pit: operas, Italian comedies just as in Paris, pretty actresses kept by the quality. In the sharp Madrilleno dusk all the town took a turn through the Prado gardens, as it might have been St. James's Park.

Behind this polite façade, however, fantasy reigned little less absolute than in the provinces. French fashions were considered scandalous; women walking assumed a stilted action which, with their extreme slenderness, gave them an air of floating wraiths; the purpose of this gait was to ensure the invisibility of the feet beneath the immense skirts in every circumstance. What Spanish poet would have been so licentious as to sing of little feet that darted in and out like mice beneath the petticoat? Here, the feet of all Spanish women must be kept inviolate from the gaze of men; a mistress would concede to her lover the most fantastic freedoms before she let him see her ankles; such a favour was a declaration of passion so violent as to frighten any casual gallant from the scene.

In Lent, there was the peculiar excitement afforded by the Penitentes. Wild young nobles, in white gowns and pointed hoods with eye-slits, paraded the streets of Madrid accompanied by friends and servants, thrashing themselves industriously. In the narrow streets the ladies watched, compassionate but admiring; happy the mistress to be spattered with her lover's blood, or see him faint at her feet!

The oddest spectacle of all was the court. The misfortune which had afflicted the great monarchy of Spain was, in some degree, reflected in her monarchs. Since Philip II, the royal eyes with each generation had grown paler, their glance wilder; as if to escape annihilation beneath the pendant lower lip of the Habsburgs, the chin lengthened till now it measured a whole third of the long narrow head, from the top of which

9

the spare Flemish hair steadily retreated with each despairing reign: until the sovereign with whom we are first concerned, His Catholic Majesty King Charles II, the last Habsburg to sit on the Spanish throne, looked like a caricature of one of his own family portraits — an impression heightened by his out-moded dress.

The last surviving son of the unlucky Philip IV, he had ascended the throne in 1665, a sickly child of four, Habsburg on both sides. His reign had been a chronicle of continued private ill-health and public misfortune; as the flame burnt low in the grey royal body, so the shadow of death crept further across the might of Spain. The poor gentle King was quite incapable of arresting either his own or the national decline. A portrait of him by Carreño at Guadalupe shows an odd, sadly submissive gaze wavering above the pale expanse of lower face. Melancholy submission was the mainspring of his con-duct, submission to his mother and her German confessor Nitard, then to his bastard half-brother, John, and lastly to his two Queens. The first one, a pretty daughter of "Monsieur," Duc d'Orléans, and of "Minette" (she was thus a niece of our own Charles II), had made him happy.[3] On her death — some said murder — in 1690, he had married Anna Marie of Neuburg, sister to the Empress, and to the Duchess of Parma. The new Queen turned out to be a nagging, superstitious busy-body. Charles wore out the days in fevers and fits, leaving her to queen it in a world of muttering dwarfs, parrots, musical clocks, and monkeys. The policy of the grandest monarchy in

[3] It is by no means so certain that she was. It is supposed that she had a fancy for her cousin, the Dauphin. Louis XIV when telling her she was to be Queen of Spain added: "I couldn't have done better for my own daughter." "Yes," she is said to have answered, "but you could for your niece."

When she said good-bye to the Dauphin, he merely wished her luck, and enjoined her not to forget to send him parcels of turrones, a delicious Span-ish sweetmeat made with almonds, sugar, and honey, upon which he doted. Parting from the court in Fontainebleau Forest, she sprang into her carriage without saying a word to the Dauphin. Who can blame her?

Europe was now decided by the vision of some gipsy in coffee grounds, or in the vapours that issued from a newly opened bottle of champagne.

The King's hypochondria tended towards insanity. Descending to the tombs of his ancestors in the Escorial, he would gaze upon the body of his late Queen, which was but lightly touched by corruption; he would burst into tears at the sight of the beloved, still distinguishable features, and cry that he would soon be with her. . . .

His behaviour was but little less extravagant than that of the Duke of Alba. Deserted by a mistress upon whom he doted, he caused innumerable Masses to be said for her return. Then he took to his bed, and lay still upon his right side, vowing not to move till he had recovered her. The most brilliant society called to look at this strange penance; his mistress never came back, and he died at last, in cramped fidelity, well into the new reign. Only in his son's time was an Alba seen once again about the Court.

The administration was no less moribund and fantastic. The lifeblood of government was clogged and curdled by half a dozen antiquated councils — those of Castille and the Indies for example — "damned areopagi" we shall hear them later called. The noble dotards who composed them thought far less of the State than of their own wretched privileges — symbolized by the right of each member to an empty coach that followed the sedan chair in which he went abroad. These venerable nuisances could be trusted to defeat any measure which implied change, however necessary.

A labyrinth of taxes bemused legitimate trade. The Church, exempt from taxation, gathered to itself much of the wealth that should have reached the government, and sent it to stiffen the sparkling accoutrements of some holy image. Another large share of the Indies' tribute stuck in predatory grandee claws; it was metamorphosed not into artillery, or good roads, or bridges; but into immense services for noble parties that were never given. (The Duke of Infantado, for instance, possessed more than fifteen hundred plates in Potosí silver, yet never asked a soul across the doorstep.)

The Spanish fleet, formerly glorious, had almost ceased to exist. The galleons of the Indies squadron were an easy prey for heretic pirates; the galleys rotted at their encrusted moorings. The King of Spain was so poor, his coachmen, long unpaid, at last refused to drive him even for a turn into the country. His infantry, once the terror of Europe, had never recovered from the confusion into which the young Condé had flung them at Rocroy in 1643. They now begged before the palace, a rabble of scarecrows.

Going north-eastwards from Madrid, over the proud uplands of Aragon, and the rebellious plains of Catalonia: over the Pyrenees and the Alps gleaming like some monstrous sherbet, one came at last to a city wall, circumscribed by a crazy parapet of bones. It was Vienna, and the bones were the monument to Sobieski's recent victory over the Turks. Within those walls the Emperor Leopold dreamed of reviving the dominion of Charles V;[4] despite his piety, his ambitions were relentless, nor was he over-nice in his methods of advancing them. The French, at least, believed that the first consort of the distracted Spanish King had been a victim of Austrian poisons.[5]

Returning across the Alps, one beheld the last word in modern cities rising at Turin, broad avenues of decent palaces and at the end of every vista a view of the encircling mountains, inevitable as a latrine, or an old nurse's wisdom. Pungent water from the hills incessantly scavenged the new streets, and in his bright palace the artful Duke Victor-Amadeus lay uneasy. His

[4] His least unattractive trait was perhaps his passion for music: he played ably upon the spinet, and also composed. He lived 1640–1705.
[5] The poison is supposed to have been given in oysters.

little dominion astride the Alps, reaching up to Chambéry and east to the Milanese, could only survive by trickery. With this he was well endowed. Until recently an ally of England, he had been bought into treachery by the marriage of his eldest daughter with Louis XIV's eldest grandson, the Duc de Bourgogne, second heir to the French throne. Victor-Amadeus was at present the client of France, cossetted by Versailles; but loyalty was a luxury which no prince so precariously placed as he might long afford; nor could Victor-Amadeus forget that his subjects, mindful of old injuries, remained stubbornly opposed to France.

In Milan, in the ugly shadow of the unfinished cathedral, there were the spectacles and gravity again to remind the traveller that this was a Spanish dominion.[6] Next door at Brescia the Venetian Republic began a sort of spider's web of pleasure, with the knowing old monster of a city at its centre sucking into its silver-pink belly the young coxcombs and wantons of Europe — the Montmartre, the Palm Beach of the day, but invested by beauty and elegance with an insidious potency which never for a moment ebbed. Roses jostling offal in the dust cart, the fatuousness of the empty bottle, or of a tired bitter face in the drunken dawn, were hardly known in Venice. A moss of prettiness softened the stark contours of vice — masks and sighs and gondolas slipping home through the mist from guilty ridotti. Industries languished; the East like some wilful mistress had slipped away to other arms; occasional wars with Turkey were but an excuse for the luxury of partings. Only the Carnival remained, extended till one wore the beak-like mask the whole year through — save of course for the few weeks in high summer when the quality lolled in some Palladian colonnade by the Brenta. Pleasure, shrewdly exploited, reigned unassailable. The smallest piazzetta was a theatre for jugglers or for a pyramid of acrobats.[6] The churches, so many sea-shells, echoed

[6] See Addison's *Remarks on Several Parts of Italy, 1701–3.*

not with the sound of the ocean but with the strains of amorous fiddles.

South-eastward lay Mantua, little now save a coral image in the marshy water. In their vast pink palace the ducal family were dwindling to the stature of the dwarfs that had been about them since Mantegna's day. The Gonzaga blood flowing obscurely through the royal veins of Europe has helped, as much as anything perhaps, to destroy the medieval conception of a monarch who towers physically above his subjects. "Every inch a King," we say. Before the dwarfs of Mantegna were thought of, kingship could be reckoned in feet.

Florence slept supine under the shadow of Brunelleschi's vernal dome, a city of empty houses. "It appears so dispeopled," wrote Bishop Burnet after a visit in 1685, "that one cannot but wonder to see a country that hath been the scene of so much . . . now so forsaken and poor." Clerics were everywhere. They thronged the Grand Duchy of Tuscany, profiting from the piety of the Grand Duke Cosimo who collected papal honours as if they were so many exotic butterflies, and was never happier than when on some journey of penance.

As Florence languished, so did the Grand Ducal line. Cosimo's son and heir, Prince Ferdinando, married in 1689 to a Bavarian princess, had after many efforts got her with nothing better than a severe attack of syphilis. He had then passed off into a fatal coma. The second heir, Gian Gastone, retching at the coarseness of his Bohemian consort, was now sunk into barren luxury, beguiled by the society of handsome actors and cut-purses.

In Rome the Vatican steered an ingenious course between French and Austrian pretensions. Clement XI stood in perpetual awe of his venal nephews, and tearfully altered course with every changing puff of the European wind. Outside, among the overgrown ruins of Imperial days, there was no sound save the cropping of sheep, the rooting of swine, or the murmur of some ruddy English antiquary. Religious establishments abounded — particularly convents, where the veils weighed as light as feathers, and ladies of quality languished behind the flimsiest of bars.

Especially renowned was the cell of the former Duchess of Bracciano: Born in 1642 of the turbulent Tremouille family,[7] she had married a Talleyrand, the Comte de Chalais, who in 1662 was exiled from France for fighting a duel. The young couple in no great affluence fled to Spain; there they found a courteous welcome but small hope of advancement. They moved on to Italy; leaving his wife in Naples, Chalais set off to offer his sword to the Venetian Republic, but incontinently died before reaching the end of his journey, of a fever caught in the swamps round Mestre. The widow fixed herself in Rome, and quickly passed into the most elegant society of the Vatican.

French diplomacy was then bent upon acquiring an ascendancy in Rome; and this noble widowed Frenchwoman, with her beguiling charm, was a perfect instrument of this policy. The French married her in 1675 to the elderly Duke of Bracciano, an Orsini; she was thus able to exercise a powerful Gallophile influence in the highest Roman society. But Bracciano had died lately; his title, with his castle, had been sold to the Colonnas to pay his debts; and she had taken the name of Principessa degli Orsini, or Princesse des Ursins, by which history now knows her. She waited in Rome, rising sixty but still making gallants sigh, leaving her destiny to a fate which she knew to be momentous.

Against the plumed stage-set of Vesuvius, Naples seethed and bubbled with turbulent life. The saturnine face of Alessandro Scarlatti would be glimpsed for an instant, as he struck and urged his harpsichord, turning it under his satyr hands into some divine and ferocious machine. The balconies were heavy with gossiping women, or strong voluptuous flowers that

[7] Almost all her relatives had been involved in the Fronde.

seemed to resemble them. Down the dark alley-ways, beyond which the sea always gleamed like a happy ending, the fruit hawkers plied their wares: "Pears like ladies' thighs! Grapes that have follied with the sun!" . . .

Northward again lay the Duchies of Parma and Piacenza, in the very centre of Italy which the Romans called Æmilia. The Æmilian plains have ever been known for their tomatoes and artichokes, their succulent sausages, and, above all, Parmesan cheese and ham. The Via Æmilia, running like a taut string above the luxurious plains, disclosed a prospect of intense husbandry: field upon closely cultivated field, meadows where prosperous swine and cattle cropped in abundance. No more well-favoured country, one would have said, could exist under the sun; the sturdy, cynical peasants, with their laughter and their heroic appetites, were surely the favoured of God. But in fact, all this richness served not their bellies but their Duke.[8]

The Farnesi rulers of the two Duchies sprang from the union of a bastard grandson of Pope Paul V with a bastard daughter of the Emperor Charles V. Once they had been great men of action; Alexander Farnese was the principal glory of Habsburg arms in their heyday; as far north as Breda his name still clings to many a forgotten earthwork or stagnant moat. But they had gone to seed in the general decadence of the Italian world. An unlucky marriage with an Aldobrandini girl had brought upon the Farnese line the curse of an almost legendary fatness. The heir to the Duchies, Prince Odoardo, had

[8] "Their subjects would live in great plenty amidst so rich and well cultivated a soil, were not the taxes and impositions so very exorbitant; for the courts are much too splendid and magnificent for the territories that lie about them, and one cannot but be amazed to see such a profusion of wealth laid out in coaches, trappings, tables, cabinets, and the like precious toys in which there are few princes of Europe who equal them, when at the same time they have not had the generosity to make bridges over the rivers . . . for the convenience of their subjects." (Addison's description of Parma in his *Remarks on Several Parts of Italy 1701-3*.)

16

died in 1690, "stifled so to speak," as the local chronicler says, "by his own bulk, suffocated by his extraordinary obesity."

The family was distinguished by an extraordinary wit, and a taste which had made their art-collection famous throughout Europe. But this sensibility carried with it a certain price. The baroque age is said to have begun with Correggio's "Hash of Frogs" on the dome of Parma Cathedral; and Parma had certainly become with time the archetype of a baroque city. The ducal wealth through successive generations was expended on enchanting spectacle and luxurious buildings; the theatre, for instance, annexed to the rosy palace at Parma, is one of the highest expressions of Sette Cento ingenuity.

The pink streets, where the fine flower of the new architecture jostled graceful baptisteries of the thirteenth century, were thronged with priests, soldiers, nobles, theologians and adventurers, in such profusion as no small state could easily support. Amid this glittering and expensive hurly-burly might have been discerned at this time a hurrying figure, slightly plump and carrying with it for all its gracefulness some rustic remembrance of the surrounding farms. This was the Abbé Giulio Alberoni, whom we may term the chief figure, if not the hero, of this work.

He was born at Piacenza on the 21st of March 1664, in a poor quarter which now proudly calls itself the "Vicolo Alberoni." The very same day he was baptized in the parish church of Santi Nazaro e Celso, which would seem to suggest that nobody had any great faith in his chances of survival. Nor was this to be wondered at. His father was a poor gardener, his mother a seamstress disturbed by frequent pregnancies. Amid all the plenty of Piacenza, the six Alberoni children could rarely fill their hungry little bellies. It must have been a tantalizing thing to starve among the mysterious artichokes, the smoked hams that the quality cut fine as lawn, the spiced sausages with their almost liturgical taste.

In 1674 the father died. The mother was helplessly pregnant, and the young Alberoni had to shift for the family. He seems to have got work as bell-ringer to the monks of St. Maria di Valverde. To feel the clangorous serpent of a bell-rope live and die in his young hands, to hear the chimes of his creation sing and jump among the Placentian domes and encircling gardens, was his first taste of power. Beside this, the scrap of food, the few pence that he earned must have counted for little.

Next he is said to have become clerk of the Sacristy in St. Nazaro, the church of his baptism. There he caught the fancy of some benevolent priests, who taught him to read and write. Then the Barnabite fathers in the neighbouring parish of Santa Brigita took him in, gave him the rudiments of Latin and the humanities.

All trace of him now vanishes until 1680, his seventeenth year, when the young peasant is found studying philosophy in the elegant Jesuit college of St. Pietro. How he contrived to enter there is a mystery. It was, after all, an establishment normally reserved for the nobility. But this early mingling with his betters, as if by right, set the tone for the whole of his strange career.

The charm which had saved him from the tedium of a kitchen-garden, or a sacristy at best, here gained for young Alberoni the favour of the Placentian quality. For all his taking ways, however, throughout his life he showed a remarkable loyalty to his friends. At the seminary of St. Pietro this talent received its first test. Alberoni had apparently struck up a great friendship with a certain Dr. Ignazio Gardini, a lawyer from Ravenna who practised in the criminal courts of Piacenza. For a time the youth would seem to have acted in his spare time as assistant to Gardini in the courts. Then, early in 1685, when Alberoni was rising twenty-one, came calamity. For reasons

THE FORTRESS–PRISON OF SEGOVIA

LOS PENITENTES

VENETIAN MASKED FOR THE CARNIVAL
Drawing by Giambattista Tiepolo

into which, stolidly declares the local chronicler, it is neither necessary nor desirable to go, Gardini was suddenly banished from the Parmesan territories.

Alberoni resolved to accompany him into exile. Certain historians have suggested that this act was far from voluntary; Alberoni, they hint, was himself involved in some unsavoury financial business that imposed upon him a rapid flight from the Duchy. There is no evidence to support this theory, and his whole behaviour in after life belies it. A thirst for money, got at any cost, never distinguished him; and while he never entirely lost the amoral ingenuity of the gutter, there are no grounds for supposing that other reasons than affection drove him away from the hair-splitting ease of his life at Piacenza.

For a time the exiles tramped the neighbouring towns. Then, like an abandoned cat, Gardini made for his native Ravenna. The young Alberoni went with him.

A fashionable taste for the Byzantine had lately revived the ancient capital of Justinian's Exarchy. But in the late seventeenth century it lay among its bitter marshes, peeling and tarnished by the acrid sea wind. In the Church of St. Apollinare in Classe the mosaics, which depict the radiance of Theodora and her court, dissolved into mildew and verdigris. At the tomb of Galla Placidia, that jewel of early Christendom, the light seeping through the alabaster windows fished the glittering angels, like a school of Indian sea-monsters, out of the dark mosaic sea. But the monument lay forlorn in the middle of a cabbage patch. No doubt it seemed barbarously Gothic to men of that age. For them indeed Ravenna was the very pinnacle of boredom.

Nobody chafed more at it than Monsignore Giorgio Barni, Papal Vice-Legate and ruler of the town; he seems to have been a typical cleric of his age, with a taste for his comforts, smart society (he was greatly petted in Rome), and for company. The last he unexpectedly found in the young exile. We do not know how the acquaintance was struck up, nor is any echo of Alberoni's quips borne to us across the ages by the salty winds of Ravenna. But no doubt they contrived to distract the poor Vice-Legate, for when in 1688 as luck would have it he was raised to the Bishopric of Parma, Alberoni went home with him to be Master of his Household.

There then followed the most obscure period in Alberoni's history. Later he was to show himself pre-eminent in administration and in the good ordering of a household. Yet in the Bishop's establishment he was no success; the appointment was soon ended, though with no sort of rancour.

An even less explicable misadventure follows. About this time the young man was ordained a priest in Parma Cathedral. A year or so later, the parroco of Santi Nazaro e Celso, Prevosto Gianbernardo degli Uomini, who had baptized Alberoni, felt that his incumbency was too heavy for his advancing years; under the influence of the Duchess Maria Maddalena Farnese, who had begun to interest herself in the ingenious young priest, he decided to cede the living to him. In January 1691 the change was formally made with the approval of the parishioners; it seemed as if the days of wandering and of the gaieties that had once enchanted Bishop Barni's table were past.

Alberoni, however, had been but a few days installed in his parish when the former priest and parishioners of St. Nazaro revoked their decision. There exists no inkling of their motives; perhaps his flock could not forget that Alberoni had once been a starving guttersnipe and the object of their charity. Whatever the cause, he lost the living, and the future for a time must have seemed drab enough to him.

Throughout his career, reverses were ever the heralds of fortune. Before long, Bishop Barni had appointed him as tutor to a certain young nephew, Count Gianbattista Barni, who was destined for Holy Orders.

As a priest of quality, young Barni, the uncle hinted, would be less concerned with the care of vulgar souls than with government, and particularly diplomacy. A good grounding in history, law, philosophy, and theology was also a course essential; nor must he be lacking in the graces of a courtier. Alberoni, to whom there still clung something of the rich Parmesan earth, may have seemed hardly an obvious choice for his preceptor. But the abbé had a rare way with him. A voice melodious and thrilling; a fine commanding eye subdued, even at this early day, all but his late parishioners; and he would appear to have brought his young charge no less completely under his dominion than was the uncle.

In 1696 young Barni was packed off to Rome; Alberoni went with him. A choleric and inexact English historian – Mr. George Moore – writing in 1814, suggests that "if the young gentleman did not make much profit in classical or ecclesiastical knowledge he was better amused. He found in his preceptor a ready and dexterous go-between with those kind beauties who at Rome as well as other places are not inexorable to the addresses of the young rich."

Only a few scraps of gossip, hawked about by one or two unreliable Spanish historians, can support this charge of pimping; nor is there any reason to suppose that young Barni did not get real profit from his stay in Rome. It is certain that Alberoni did. He learnt French there, which was to make his fortune, and all the graces of movement and address that, with his voice, were to render people his slaves even when his shape had become swollen and monstrous.

In 1698 he returned to Parma, his employment as tutor was over, and he took up in the cathedral his canon's stall which the unending benevolence of Bishop Barni had procured him. Then began for him one of the most agreeable periods of his life. His mother had lately died; the rest of the family were, one gathers, now independent of his charity, and his small stipend took care of all ordinary needs. His wit, his scholarship, the easy affable manners which the company of the great in Rome had given him, opened for Alberoni the closest doors of Parma. The great officers of the court welcomed him into their intimate circle, and the evenings passed in a conviviality so sparkling that it seemed to rival the very sky.

Parmesan society had not yet hardened into the sort of narrow despotism which to the south, in near-by Florence, bored itself into a coma. There was plenty of strong aromatic wine to hoist up one's spirit, the finest cooking in the peninsula, and liberty freely to advance all ideas, however chimerical. It must have been a pleasant enough life, with all the good things of the Parmesan to eat, aubergines, white truffles, served with a "fondua" of cheese piping hot, crayfish from the sea at Sestri de Levante, partridges and plump quails that from the manner of their cooking seemed to evoke the Æmilian vineyards. And afterwards extravagant conversations till the dawn, or fireworks with brilliant set pieces showing the True Church triumphant over Heresy or Prometheus stealing Fire; operas of Monteverdi in the Duke's great theatre with His Highness almost bursting out of his box, and the heartrending arias fluttering like so many silver pheasants among the wooden draperies. Into this strange still world there swept in the second year of the eighteenth century a vast European war, to catch up in its wind the plump sociable Abbé Alberoni and blow him back and forth until at last it dropped him into fortune in Spain.

## II

WAR ABOUT SPAIN

Like the German cloud across the last fifty years, the shadow of French tyranny fell blackly on the end of the seventeenth century. Wandering through some glade at Versailles it is hard to remember that this place of fountains no longer time-troubled, of dusty windows blinking like some old cat's eyes, was the Berchtesgaden of the baroque world.

The supremacy of France was in part fortuitous. The wars of the Fronde, for all their farce, had dragooned the French nation into a state of obedience unique in Europe. Fear of a palace revolt curved the despotic sway of a Romanov Emperor, or of the Sultan; Charles II of England must squander his talents in squabbles with a tight-fisted Parliament; the King of Spain was plagued by a dozen such jealous bodies, scattered through his kingdoms; in the Estates of Holland and the Polish Diet so many spoke their mind that decision was paralyzed.

The ruin of the German world in the recent Thirty Years' War also assisted France's rise. Europe between the Rhine and the Vistula had been reduced to something like a desert; and the race which had fathered Dürer and Cranach was now sunk into an uncouth turbulence, from which it was never to recover. By playing off one jealous German prince against another, the young Louis XIV could march where he wished, and arbitrarily advance his frontiers eastward.

Nor did he at first meet serious opposition from any other quarter. The impotence of Spain has already been noted. England, exhausted by internal squabbles, was from 1672 to 1688 a

23

French dependency, no more than occasionally recalcitrant. The ingenuity of Charles II, it is true, preserved for us some measure of independence; but James II, while clamouring for subsidies and French troops, could only assert his dignity in lengthy arguments on the niceties of diplomatic precedence. "Le roi, mon frère, est fier," Louis XIV would murmur drily, "mais il aime les pistoles de France."

The ambitions of the French Crown were by no means confined to the European scene. Louis's boundless spirit, anticipating the destiny of his country, brooded over the Barbary Coast, and toyed with the idea of a Suez Canal. In Constantinople a powerful French Embassy informed and abetted Turkish policy; at Pondicherry, upon the Malabar shore, amid orchids and clanging palms that had been somehow pruned into a classic order, plans were laid for a great empire. An increasing traffic with Cochin-China and Siam had influenced Parisian fashions for a whole winter. By handsome subsidies, and a gift of astronomical instruments, the Jesuit missionaries at Peking, who held the great office of Court Astrologers, were encouraged to bind the humanist Manchu Emperor K'ang Hsi to the French cause; while the New World from the Arctic Circle to the Gulf of Mexico was being fashioned by ardent French priests and trappers into yet another Bourbon dominion.

With a war against the Pope himself, Louis had begun to disturb the peace of Europe, in the year of Alberoni's birth. He continued to do so with brilliant success, except for one unhappy attempt upon Holland, and even the general conflict that ensued he turned to his advantage.

Before the menace of this power apprehension rose in Europe with a sluggishness strange to the modern mind. For years Holland alone had fully realized the danger. In those days there was no complicated and sensitive machine of international trade to record the slightest shock, and transmit it to all its members. Harvesting, the chase, vinting, the arrival of spice- or treasure-fleet, were events that proceeded normally in peace or war, until the enemy was upon your fields, burning your cities. At the same time — and here Louis XIV had the advantage of modern dictators — the pre-eminence of France in the arts and sciences, in the very graces of humdrum life, seemed to invalidate all criticism; some petty German prince shivering before the mouths of French batteries would yet ruin his little state to build a minor Marly, or set his generals to play Racine in togas.

Grown over-confident, Louis in the last decade of the seventeenth century overplayed his hand. The Protestant world, and even the Pope himself, were outraged by the revocation of the Edict of Nantes, the consequent submission of French Protestants to extreme miseries, and the persecution of their brethren, the Barbets, in obscure mountain valleys of Savoy, beyond the French frontiers.[1]

The rising resentment of European princes was, a few years later, heightened by Louis's wanton ravishing of the Palatinate, on a claim trumped-up in the name of his sister-in-law, the Palatine Duchesse d'Orléans, known to history as "Madame." She was the last woman to wish disaster upon her darling country, and when the invading French troops began their careful devastation of it, her anguish knew no bounds, the corridors of Versailles and Meudon rang with her lamentations. Meanwhile, Heidelberg and Mannheim dissolved into dust; their inhabitants were shot down as they cowered among the debris. Out in the countryside, castles and manors flared into the June sky; while the Pfalz vines, cradles of such delicate pleasure, were uprooted, and flung to burn with some peasant's dirty bed.

When the French had finished, there was little left whole in

[1] After a few weeks' campaign the French general could report that nothing had been left alive in these valleys.

the Palatinate save some Electoral family portraits, which were brought home as a present for "Madame." To this attention she proved sadly indifferent.

These horrors, if wrought now, would rouse in us but half an hour's pang; in the seventeenth century they provoked an appalled reaction which before long had ranged half Europe in war against Louis XIV. After the revolution of 1688 England, under William of Orange, became the main animator of resistance to French power.

The noise of war as it rolled across Piedmont and the Milanese no doubt echoed among the airy colonnades of Parma; but for Alberoni and his friends it can have meant little more than a topic for conversation; nor could any fear of French tyranny be strong enough to offset the hatred that all the Parmesan, and nobody more fiercely than Alberoni, felt for the traditional enemy of the French — the barbarous Germans.[2] By this sentiment his life was to be dominated; whether the hatred came from any personal experience is hard to say; most probably it was the instinctive revulsion which every decent Italian feels for his northern neighbour in normal times.[3]

The war ended at last, somewhat to the outward advantage of France. But though Louis might boast of having defied half Europe with success, the country was exhausted, encumbered with what was for those days a huge war debt — expenditure was now some four times as great as revenue — and starving from a succession of bad harvests. Trade, too, was in a sorry way. Cruel taxation, the loss of the English market for silks,

[2] "That infamous race which has remained untouched by so many centuries of civilization in its primordial state as speculators and professionals of war" (Alberoni's letters).

[3] Not many years ago the writer was driving through Bologna in a car bearing Austrian numbers; we had occasion to stop in some side street, and the usual gaping crowd assembled. Suddenly a plump brown baby pointed at a little silver pig on the radiator cap that served for a mascot, and: "Porco, porco, come loro!" he proclaimed gravely. All the company nodded in agreement with this estimate of the barbarian swine from beyond the mountains. . . . So did Alberoni feel."

dimities and wines, a swollen and interfering bureaucracy, the regimenting of agriculture for purposes of war — whole areas suited only to the vine had been put under corn — all this had brought France very low. And there was work for but a fraction of the disbanded troops; the towns were crowded with hungry wretches, the roads infested with footpads; riding from Lyons to Paris, for example, the traveller saw swinging from each gibbet some veteran of Steenkirk or Landen whom despair had driven into petty crime.

Conditions were little better in England. The Tory squires squealed at a land tax of five shillings in the pound; the Whig merchants wept for lost markets, and for the ravages worked among their shipping by Jean Bart and the lesser French privateers; while the reduction in the army, much more drastic here than in France, increased the general misery.

Though they nursed for each other a hatred far more savage than anything they felt for the King of France, Whig and Tory were at one in their detestation of a standing army. For the former it was the symbol and instrument of royal, for the latter of demagogic, tyranny; and so, despite King William's protests, some seventy thousand of his eighty-four thousand veterans were flung upon the streets. The main roads of England became more dangerous than they had ever been for a century; many of the quality suffered disagreeable experiences while travelling to Newmarket for the Spring Meeting of 1698; and it was found necessary to provide a strong cavalry escort for the new French Ambassador, Marshal Tallard, when he proceeded from London to join the King on the Heath. The middle-classes of England felt scant responsibility for the misery and crime which they themselves had provoked; it merely justified their contention, long repeated, that soldiers, beside debauching daughters and putting the horns on worthy husbands, were also thieving murderous rascals.

The reduction of our armed forces was not, however, entirely prompted by frivolous prejudice. There was a genuine belief, current alike in France and England — an idea common enough indeed after almost every vast conflict of modern times — that mankind had learnt its lesson, that so bloody an expedient as war would not again be lightly employed. International disputes must in future be resolved by arbitration and collaboration between the Great Powers — between France and England in short, since the Emperor again had his hands full with the Turks, the vast Empire of Spain counted for little, and Russia was but beginning to stir from her cruel and snowy sleep.

King William had come out of the war the recognized equal of King Louis. The English monarchy was no longer an importunate pensioner of France. Louis exchanged with his inveterate enemy and official cousin expressions of the highest mutual respect. All peace-loving men now waited for the two great sovereigns peaceably to order the affairs of Europe.

A special English embassy proceeded to Versailles. A glittering affair, it was led by King William's old crony, Bentinck, who had lately become an English earl, with the title of Portland and huge estates confiscated from English and Irish Jacobites. For years he had served as an unsmiling buttress between his master and the spiteful, frivolous English; he had been the supreme confidant, the invariable companion of the austere royal pleasures; now his place was being reft from him by a young compatriot, Keppel, Lord Albemarle: reft away in a manner so delicate, the forthright Bentinck felt impotent against the attack. He was glad therefore to hide his discomfiture in this embassy to Paris. True, his English staff, with their dissolute ways, filled him with horror; one of his secretaries, an ingenious young poet called Matthew Prior, though a good enough diplomat, inspired him with particular suspicion; for Prior was always turning out jaunty poems about nymphs utterly devoid of good Dutch virtues and religion, or of doves that flew down ladies' dresses for no proper reason; though his anxious questions were deflected with a quip and a respectful bow, Portland remained gravely concerned for his secretary's spiritual health. . . .

Large and small cares were, however, lost in the brilliant welcome at Versailles. Never before had a foreign envoy been received with such exceptional marks of favour. In the hunt, in the chosen assemblies at Marly, the King was continually summoning Portland to his side; at Versailles in that almost hieratic ritual, there was conferred upon him an honour to which no diplomat, no peer of France, could rightfully aspire; when the King undressed for the night, Portland would be admitted within the balustrade about the royal bed, among the "enfants de France" and princes of the blood, to hold for a sublime second a nightshirt, or some humbler but no doubt useful object.

It was not long before the purpose of these unusual favours was declared. Delicately, with a world of circumspection, the courtiers hinted that King Louis desired to negotiate with King William a settlement of the Spanish succession. It was a question which might at any moment become acute. Charles II of Spain now showed the most hopeful signs of dissolution. Never had his frame been more wasted, or his behaviour more extravagant; the very sight of his German Queen, her clumsy efforts to rule him, stung him to fury. He would put out his tongue at her, like any street-urchin; and then the long pale face would be suddenly suffused with blood, he would go off into a sort of epileptic fit, against which in no way availed the warm entrails of pigeons placed on his forehead and navel. When he did at last recover, he was always a little weaker, a shade less coherent than before; the periods during which he could swallow nothing but human milk steadily lengthened.

For years like some wounded maddened hare he had evaded Death; Death instead had turned aside to take off the hunters one by one; till it seemed that the King of Spain was invested with a sort of sickly immortality. But the race was nearly run now; all Europe knew it and no one so well as the tragic King himself.

As his strength failed, the problem of his succession came to obsess him. People mocked at him because of his prayers for guidance, his appeals to the Holy Father for a judgement, his hobnobbing with witches and soothsayers in the mountains. But the poor tortured brain was after all confronted with a problem more complex than that which Versailles failed to solve in 1919 — the transfer of sovereignty over an empire that embraced almost half the earth — in Europe, Spain itself, the Low Countries, the Milanese, Naples and Sicily: in America, all the Southern continent save Brazil, the whole central isthmus, Mexico, the southern part of what is now the United States and most of the islands of the Caribbean seas; across the Pacific Ocean lay his Philippines, and further on, in Africa, many valuable trading posts.

In his agony of doubt Charles was moved by a single principle — the inviolability of his dominions. At all costs he was determined to transmit them intact to his chosen successor. It was the fashion to regard the Spanish Empire as polyglot and unhomogeneous and therefore ripe for partition — like the view taken of the Turkish and Austrian Empires in recent times. But for Charles, as for most of his subjects, the various parts of his heritage, however diverse in speech, were joined by a common spirit, a common way of life, into a sacred whole.

There is something to be said for this view. Anglo-Saxon civilization with its plumbing, its clubs, the tearooms kept by dainty gentlewomen, the neo-Gothic and ferro-concrete, remains a substance distinct from any culture upon which it is imposed. Its only chance of taking root abroad lies in such territories as Canada or Australia, from whence the indigenous culture has long since vanished. Elsewhere it rarely contrives to penetrate the soil. A Hong-Kong Chinese, a British West Indian, a Rajput chief or a Gold Coast stevedore, what have they in common save a claim upon His Majesty's Government for protection? Nothing: and they would be highly incensed if anyone thought otherwise. But Spanish culture has seeped into and metamorphosed every land that it has touched; and though in the last century and a half the former Empire of Charles II has been parcelled out among more than a score of states, a peculiarly harsh enchantment, sometimes ravishing, sometimes monstrous, pervades them all — the note of a guitar cutting like glass through the Mexican night, a Filipino gallant crooning over his fighting cock before its battle, the hooded penitentes of Furnes flagellating themselves among the Belgian dunes; a certain rhythm, an inflexion of a street song, that seems to sway across the world from Palermo to Potosí.

Such considerations, however cogent in Spain, had little force with the hard-headed Western powers. Visions of ancient grandeur were immaterial figments for them if not borne upon hard cash; in this the Spanish realm, a potential Eldorado, was woefully lacking. Maladministration, it was obvious, must be the cause of so grievous a state; in the interests of Progress (a divinity the English and French were just beginning to honour), and of handsome profits, it was desirable that at least some part of the sumptuous Spanish world pass into hands worthy of it. Among the merchants of London the new device of the joint-stock company was already breeding a "capitalistic" mentality. Upon France, whose economy was still State-controlled, the impact of this new ideal would not be fully exerted for another twenty years, not till the frenzied era of Law and the Mississippi bubble. Nevertheless these considerations were not entirely absent from the minds of the French negotiators in the hagglings which now ensued.

There were five possible claimants to the Spanish throne; only three of them were important, the Dauphin of France, the Bavarian Electress, and the Holy Roman Emperor Leopold.[4] The Dauphin had obviously the strongest claim by blood, for his mother had been the Infanta Maria Theresa, the eldest sister of the moribund Spanish King. The Infanta had however made very formal renunciations of her rights in Spain, when she married Louis XIV; the pretext of an unpaid dowry, on the other hand, was now advanced to invalidate this renunciation.

Maria Theresa had been a dim enough figure; her ardent temperament did not easily bear the King's neglect of her. When he did condescend to the duties of the marriage-bed, she was filled with a sense of triumph that lasted far beyond the night. Next morning, gay as a bird, singing, snapping her fingers, she would indicate her late felicity by a thousand little coynesses. Those the court remembered, and how her teeth had been discoloured by incessant drinking of chocolate. Little more could be recalled of her; but now posthumously her rights as an Infanta of Spain assumed formidable importance.

Then there were the claims of the Bavarian Electress, the Emperor Leopold's only child by his first marriage with the Spanish King's other sister, claims that had never been renounced; and the Emperor's own more indirect interest as the next male Habsburg. But conscious that Europe would never stomach the union of the Spanish realm with the Empire, Leopold made known his readiness to delegate all his expectations to the Archduke Charles, his second son by a later marriage.

Over the pretensions advanced by Victor-Amadeus of Savoy, and by "Monsieur," Duc d'Orléans, the bedizened brother of Louis XIV, we need hardly linger, though the Orleanist claim was later to provoke some heartburning, as we shall see in due course. During the negotiations that now ensued, William and Louis found themselves at one in their respect for the delicate equilibrium of Europe. The First Parti-

[4] See genealogical table at end of book.

tion Treaty of October 1698, negotiated over the furious heads of the Spanish and Austrian monarchs, awarded the bulk of the Spanish inheritance to the little Bavarian Electoral Prince; the French and Austrian claimants were to be suitably compensated; an eventual union of Spain and Bavaria could, it was obvious, menace nobody.

But once again Charles II cheated the hunt; in February 1699 there died not this royal half-corpse, but the Bavarian boy. Rarely has the snuffing out of so brief a life brought more dire consequences; at one stride the phantom of war moved into terrifying eminence. Yet the negotiators did not despair; a Second Partition Treaty was concluded in March 1700, giving most of the Spanish territories to the Archduke Charles; the Dauphin was to receive Charles's Italian possessions and the Basque province of Guipuzcoa.

The new treaty was received with rage at Madrid. The Queen is reported to have smashed the furniture in her apartments, wreaking particular vengeance upon the mirrors which came from Louis XIV's factory at St. Gobin. The Spanish King all but had a stroke; he then made a will leaving his dominions in their entirety to the Archduke Charles.

With triumph in their hands, the Austrian Habsburgs now jettisoned all tact, refusing the most trifling condition which Charles II might make. Tempers grew warm; the Archduke was supposed to call his future subjects by a contemptuous name; the Spanish Ambassador in Vienna publicly described the Austrian ministers as "small, hard, and twisted like the horns on the goats in my country."

Harcourt, the adroit French Ambassador at Madrid, was quick to profit by these blunders; he persuaded the hapless King that remedy lay only in the bequest of his Empire to France. France, powerful and progressive, he argued, alone could nurse Spain back to health. The Pope's support of these audacious plans was discreetly secured, and in October 1700 the tormented Spanish King was induced to make a fresh will, bequeathing the whole of his dominions to the Duc d'Anjou, second son of the Dauphin. Then Charles rallied; family ties tugged at him once more; he seemed about to reverse the testament. But it was too late. While the priests, like Tibetan lamas, tried by their chantings to exorcize the King's devils, the unsteady life ended, that had kept all Europe on tenterhooks.

In London the solution provided by the late King's will was generally considered preferable to the unpopular Partition Treaties; only in the immediate circle of King William was there any apprehension. Through Hyde Park the poor devils of half-pay officers wandered, out at elbows; how should they know salvation was so close? . . .

In Paris the talk was all of the treasures which the barque *Amphitrite* had just brought back from China; Amphitrite muslins, celestial conceits absorbed attention; the Carnaval next year at Versailles, it was said, would be largely Chinese in inspiration. . . .

There was enough notice taken of the happenings in Spain, however, to inspire a lampoon:

> "Ci-gît l'infirme roi d'Espagne
> Qui de ses jours ne fit compagne.
> Point de conquêtes, point d'enfants.
> Que fit-il donc pendant trente ans
> Qu'on vit régner ce faible prince?
> Il posséda mainte province;
> Mais, pour le dire franchement,
> Il ne fit rien qu'un testament."

On November 27th 1700 Louis XIV formally accepted the testament, and a shy boy of sixteen was precipitated on to a throne he had never coveted; for nearly half a century he was to occupy it, with abdication foremost in his mind for most of that time. In face of Austrian intransigence war was probably inevitable whatever France did. Louis, however, hesitated a week before agreeing to the step which meant a violation of his solemn engagements; and emerging from the fateful council, he declared with some truth to the Princesse de Conti that he would be blamed, whatever course he took.

As if to bear out these words, Tallard suddenly appeared from London, gravely distressed at the violation of the Partition Treaty in which he had had so large a hand. He felt his personal honour engaged, and when nobody would listen, he was to be seen wandering among the fountains, hat over eyes, declaiming with wild gestures against the King's imprudence. The more his advice was ignored, the more the habit of these soliloquies grew. One evening he went to dine at a friend's house; believing himself unobserved he began before a mirror in the hall to rehearse a violent remonstrance, which no doubt he would never have dared address to his master. A peal of laughter from the spying company cut him short. He turned upon them an agitated gaze obscured by tears. Did he see through the future to the bloody field of Blenheim, his own son killed, and he himself imprisoned in Marlborough's coach? . . .

The new King of Spain, the young Duc d'Anjou, possessed little of that humdrum gusto which distinguished his father, or Louis XIV, his grandfather. His mother, a melancholy Bavarian princess, had incurred the King's displeasure for her failure to acquire French graces. She had been too frightened of him ever to confess to the ill-health which racked her, and finally carried her off in a moment so busy, the court had hardly noticed her disappearance.[5]

The Duc d'Anjou was a monument to her melancholy. There was little enough of her in Bourgogne's imperious na-

---

[5] According to "Madame," she was killed by unkindness: "on l'a tuée comme si on lui avait tiré un coup de pistolet."

35

ture, or in the light-hearted malice of her youngest son, Berry; but to Anjou she had bequeathed a sombre temper which seemed eminently to fit him for the throne of Spain.

He was not, however, trained to rule. Too often had French kings been harmed by the turbulence of younger brothers. Every step had therefore been taken to ensure that Anjou should never vex Bourgogne. The results of this care exceeded all expectations. "He has never," reported his tutor, as if with some regret, "given me a moment's uneasiness or contradiction."

Let us observe him at this sudden moment of eminence, a pale, not unhandsome youth, silent and liking few things save hunting, or the fairy tales that flowed from "Madame's" lips. He sat for hours at her feet, listening to the accounts she had brought with her from Germany of deep pine forests, and ruined castles where princesses lay enchanted. Left alone, he lapsed into silent vacancy; the full mouth, a Habsburg legacy no doubt, would slowly open till he was gaping like a young carp. Madame de Maintenon might chide him, and the mouth closed again; but not for long; a few moments, and it was yawning wide once more, to show a pale tongue not far removed in colour from the teeth. . . .

The rights to all the splendours of Spain were willingly passed on to him by his father, the Dauphin. That sharp-tongued, unaccountable nonentity had been systematically held off by his father from any share in public business, till the very thought of authority disgusted him.[6] One day, as yet comfortably remote, he would become King of France. That was a good enough heritage for anyone, without additional complications. Meanwhile he was happy to overeat prodigiously — his gluttony had brought on a stroke a few years before — and

6 "Il . . . ne craignait rien au monde tant que d'être un jour roi . . . car il était d'une paresse extrême . . . il aurait préféré ses aises à tous les empires et royaumes" (Memoirs of "Madame").

to live in decorous bliss with an actress, La Chouin. To this good creature, renowned chiefly for her bad breath, he was reputed to be married. Occasionally he would favour her with a strange endearment; lightly slapping her majestic bosom, he would cry to his courtiers: "Sounds just like cymbals, don't it?"

Vermilion face suffused with pride, he was now happy to puff about after his son, according him regal honours; happy too in the thought of being one king's son, and the father of another. No doubt he had forgotten the prophecy made by a gipsy long before, that he would never be a king himself. . . .

Philip V, as Anjou was now known, was bewildered by the congratulations, the leave-takings and Spanish lessons; he shrank from the embarrassing necessity of henceforward addressing his grandfather as "My Brother," and of leaving the life he loved, the hunting and the fairy tales, for a glory that already frightened him.

He set out for Spain early in 1701. Heavy with admonitions, the grandfather escorted him as far as Sceaux outside Paris; Bourgogne and Berry accompanied him to the Pyrenees. There were grandiloquent addresses that made him yawn, and fireworks swirling in the sombre skies. At Fuentarrabia, where Harcourt awaited him, the prince took leave of his brothers, whom he was never to see again. After a turn through the kingdom, they would regain the dear familiar world, the fortress that was their grandfather, green hunts, and laughter. For Philip, as he uneasily crossed the Bidassoa, there was only the prospect of a stern unknown land, where, as Harcourt warned him, he must always be on his guard against poison, even in gloves or flowers.

In the spring war broke out with the Empire. The court of Vienna had refused to recognize Philip as King of Spain. Little Louis XIV cared, for without England, what could the Empire do? And England, he believed, would merely bluster. In vain did Tallard warn him that the recent seizure of Belgium by French troops, the elbowing of British interests out of Mexico and Peru by Franco-Spanish monopolies were souring the English temper. Tallard after all was given to prophesying woe.

In April 1701 a French force entered North Italy, to support Victor-Amadeus of Savoy against the Empire. The first French commander there, Catinat, was paralyzed by the confused instructions which poured upon him from Versailles. In his old age, now that the martial giants of his youth were dead, Louis XIV had become a dangerous arm-chair strategist. He would conduct his own campaigns — from the comfort of the Maintenon's fireside. Of an evening, before the ritual of feeding his dogs distracted him, he would pore over the maps, pricking them with knowing little flags. Then he would dictate an order which as like as not destined a thousand or so of his poor devils to manure some Lombardian pasture.

Villeroy next had the Italian command. He owed his marshal's baton to the chance of having been brought up with the King. Nothing could shake Louis's affection for him; and he gave back to the King a devotion which was perhaps the only eminent quality in his kindly, trivial nature. It informs the last view we have of him, fifteen years later, the withered guardian of the infant Louis XV, tasting every regal cup of soup or chocolate, lest it had been poisoned by the wicked Regent. All this is far away, however, from a Lombardian autumn in 1701 where only the shaven fields proclaim the sun's departure, and the smoke of burning farms the advance of the enemy under the terrible Prince Eugene.

For Villeroy the campaign seemed at first like some party at Versailles such as he excelled in arranging. The pompous ritual of command enchanted him. But his enjoyment was short-lived; the charm, fine leg, and noble voice were blown like so much chaff before the hot whirlwind of Eugene's attack. Discomforted again and again, the bewildered marshal was driven out of Venetia, back to Cremona. There, early in 1702, he underwent a supreme humiliation. By means of a disused culvert Eugene found his way into the city and surprised the garrison one winter's dawn. The attack miscarried, but the retreating Austrians took away with them Villeroy himself, whom they had caught as he ran out indignant to condemn the early noise.[7]

Suddenly there came fresh hope for the dispirited French troops. The great Duc de Vendôme, who shared with Villars the heritage of Condé and Turenne, was to replace poor, absurd Villeroy. The spring running like a green flame across the sedate countryside no longer meant a renewal of calamity, but triumph almost inevitable.

Louis-Joseph de Vendôme was the great-grandson of Henri IV and the enchanting Gabrielle d'Estrées. But for the hazard of a poisoned wine-glass, which had put an end to Gabrielle on the eve of her wedding to her lover, Vendôme might have been King of France.

Two generations of his family had despised and betrayed the legal heirs to the Crown, the pale issue of Henri IV's political marriage with Marie de Medici. But with this latest prince the itch for rebellion had died out; he gave to his King a rare and selfless loyalty, and Louis XIV in return was devoted to him, according him precedence immediately after the princes of the blood.

But Vendôme was something more than a mere semi-royal magnate. He was unquestionably one of the greatest commanders of his day, a match for Eugene, and finding his master

---

[7] Lampoons like this commemorated the ridiculous episode:

> "Français, rendez grace à Bellone,
> Votre bonheur est sans égal.
> Vous avez conservé Crémone,
> Et perdu votre général."

only in Marlborough. He had been fighting since his childhood without thinking much of it; complimented at the age of fourteen by Louis XIV for his coolness in some action, he answered, out of simplicity as much as pride: "Am I not the descendant of Henri IV?"

## III

ALBERONI TAKES THE FIELD

THE LITTLE COURT OF PARMA was in some embarrassment. The Austrians, trumping up some antique feudal rights over the Farnese territories, had occupied several Parmesan towns. At French headquarters a nasty rumour was abroad of Parmesan complicity in the Cremona disaster, and there was talk of reprisals. Uncertain which way to turn, the Duke of Parma resolved to send an informal delegation on an attempt to avert Vendôme's wrath. It was led by the aged Bishop Roncovieri; as the author of a portentous work upon the reign of Louis XIII, he was supposed to be expert in French affairs and ways. But the bishop suffered from gout, besides being no chicken; and so, to assist him in his arduous duties, he took with him as secretary his ingenious young friend, the Abbé Alberoni.

After the decorums of Parma, the French headquarters were a queer enough world for an ecclesiastic to enter. The turbulence of his forebears had with Vendôme been metamorphosed into an eccentricity, better suited perhaps to the sixteenth than the eighteenth century. His headquarters were less camp than court, with poets, musicians, and prostitutes of both sexes rubbing shoulders. And his military methods were hardly more orthodox than his private life. Unlike Marlborough, he was not a man inspired and exhilarated by the very smell of war. His instinct was to lie in bed till afternoon, and then rise rather for a debauch than a battle; and his late rising would often oblige his men to set out on gruelling marches at the hottest part of the day, so that "les fraîcheurs du duc de Vendôme" had become proverbial. Not that the soldiers minded. His easy manners, his general care of them, a sweetness of temper, a natural charity and lack of pomp inspired a unique devotion. As Voltaire says, the troops fought for Vendôme; they would give their lives to rescue him from any pass. And he did not fail them; for just as catastrophe seemed imminent, he would rise from his tumbled bed or luxurious table; filled with divine powers he would drop like a thunderbolt upon the enemy, and gain in an hour far more than he had ever lost in a month of vicious inactivity.

He had of course many detractors; not the least of them was the jealous young Duc de Saint-Simon, who had just begun to keep a diary, and who was to bring down upon the unheeding head of Vendôme, and upon Alberoni too for that matter, the opprobrium of history. So large a part has Saint-Simon played in forming the conventional estimate of posterity upon his age, the lineaments of that strange small genius must now be sketched.

His father, who came of a respectable but undistinguished family, as a page had caught the eye of Louis XIII by his neat handling of a royal stirrup; the King's favour had before long brought him a dukedom.

He was rising seventy when he begat his heir; the boy betrayed all the foibles of an old man's son. The extravagance and fervours of youth were never given any normal vent. His own master at an early age, he married his wife for political reasons, without looking at her. The notice of his marriage which he himself probably inserted in the *Mercure Galant* is quick to point out that the bridegroom knows everything necessary for a man of quality, and adds as an afterthought that the bride is blonde, with a pretty figure and bosom and a rather long nose. She bore him the children he wanted, and toward her he maintained perfect fidelity.

It was not in love or the bottle that he found oblivion, but in the pages of his diary, where with the dispensation of his confessor he castigated humanity every night. Thus he achieved the only greatness he was ever to know — and that posthumously. His attempts to cut a figure in the army or in politics ended in nothing but disappointment, and though during the Regency he knew some small importance, his feverish little activities, his cloak of self-importance gave pleasure to few save the lampooners.[1]

His whole mentality was affected by an inordinate passion for his order, an obsession natural enough perhaps in the second holder of a title. His dukedom was the one important thing in his life; to defend its most trivial privileges, he was ready to insult the King, sacrifice all prospects of advancement. Now in Saint-Simon's eyes Vendôme was guilty of two crimes: he had achieved military eminence without much effort, and by his precedence over the dukes had degraded their order. Therefore he must be traduced, destroyed. Saint-Simon's loathing of him burns with an awful constancy throughout the diary, though it was completed some forty years after Vendôme's death. We have a view of the diarist at the end of it, during his embassy to Spain in 1721, gloating over Vendôme's poor corpse as it putrefies in the Escorial. Meanwhile no chance is lost of concocting the portrait of a filthy and incompetent monster, which too many historians have taken for a likeness.

The caricature of Alberoni, as he now enters Saint-Simon's treacherous pages, is drawn with an equal venom. Bishop Ron-

[1] "D'où vient tant de gloire,
Dis-moi, petit Simon
Boudrillon?
Nous n'avons dans l'histoire
Jamais trouvé ton nom.

Il remue, il cabale,
Fait le fui et le bon
Boudrillon.
Il jappe avec scandale
En toute occasion."

43

covieri's embassy to Vendôme was an entire success; Parmesan innocence in the affair of Cremona was effectively proved, and the French troops turned away from the duchies. In the course of his duties, Alberoni was presented to the Commander-in-Chief by Campistron, a hack poet who drafted the despatches with some inefficiency, and whom Alberoni had once rescued from footpads. Vendôme seems to have taken immediately to the young abbé. No doubt his favour was prompted by nothing more complicated than delight in a nimble tongue.

But to Saint-Simon, the liking of a great man for a plebeian could only spring from some monstrous root; and so of Alberoni's first meeting with that strange hero who was to transform his life, Saint-Simon recounts a story which has been swallowed uncritically by many a shocked generation of historians. He depicts Vendôme receiving the Parmesan envoys as he sits upon the privy; to proclaim his estimate of them, he rises and turns toward them his bare backside. Bishop Roncovieri is supposed to have withdrawn forthwith, and abandoned his mission in disgust; while Alberoni found fortune by rushing forward with a cry of "Que culo d'angelo!"

In fact, Roncovieri presided for nearly two years over his mission, on excellent terms with the French commander.[2] And when at the end of 1703 he resigned his appointment into Alberoni's care, it was because of his gout, and a tumour that caused intermittent fevers. Since Saint-Simon's story is so inaccurate in these main respects, what credence can be extended to its details?

Alberoni quickly identified himself with the French cause. For him Vendôme became the venerated hero, "le bon compaire, le grand général." "Our army," he reported to Parma in May 1703, "is advancing straight into the territories of the Venetians. I don't know how those crooks will take it. Monsieur de Vendôme is despatching a detachment of fifteen thou-

[2] His despatches are at Parma.

44

HIS CATHOLIC MAJESTY KING CHARLES II OF SPAIN
AND THE INDIES

QUEEN ANNA MARIA OF SPAIN
by Luca Giordano

sand men into the Tyrol to burn the countryside, and make those poor devils pay tribute. . . ."

It was intoxicating to think of the Germans being driven out of Italy, and of their own Tyrol being invaded. Vendôme even talked of linking up with the Bavarian Elector, who had lately come over to the French side; the Franco-Bavarian army would then sweep on to Vienna. A magnificent prospect; yet the ravaging of a quiet countryside, the browbeating of bemused peasants — even if they did speak German — filled the abbé with dismay. A peasant himself, he understood what it meant for crops and house to be burnt, cattle stolen, in a cause far beyond their rustic understanding. The glitter of war always enchanted him — a regiment well presented, with standards flying, or the French officers, exquisitely mounted, with their wigs rising in two great horns above their heads, as if to remind them of absent dear ones. Yet he was galled by the mischief such splendid creatures could wreak upon decent quiet people who asked for no more than sun and rain, each at its auspicious time.

A fresh treachery of Victor-Amadeus interrupted all these plans. Though his eldest daughter was the Duchesse de Bourgogne, and his second, Maria Louisa, two years before had married the new King of Spain, Versailles had long nursed suspicions of his good faith. With England, which had entered the war in 1702, he now began negotiations; through the British Minister's indiscretion, the plot was soon known, and Vendôme came storming back across the Alps to bring Savoy-Piedmont to heel.

A swift chastisement would probably have scotched the danger; the stage seemed set for it, so that Alberoni as a humane man could not forbear from crying: "Unlucky country that is about to suffer the fate of the Palatinate!" But the blow never fell. True, Nice was occupied, and what is now French Savoy was overrun; yet by the King's orders Vendôme was compelled to hold off from Turin. It seems probable that these galling restraints were the work of the enchanting little Duchesse de Bourgogne. Vendôme had long suspected her of treachery, and "Madame" declares it was proved after her death.[3] At all events Louis XIV could refuse her little. Between a bathe in the lake, and a flight to some masked ball in Paris, she would float into the old King's cabinet, perch on the arm of his chair, cast her eye over a few despatches, or successfully implore mercy for her native land; then she would stroke the drooping chin and drift off again on a wave of endearments. . . .

Whatever the cause, Turin was not attacked until it was too late. Meanwhile the dream of a march upon Vienna faded; in August 1704 it was finally dissipated on the field of Blenheim.

Within the narrow scope of his instructions however, Vendôme was uniformly successful. Gradually he herded the relieving Austrian armies away from Savoy-Piedmont (whose defection was now open) and pinned them into the Alpine foothills. At Cassano in the spring of 1705 he inflicted upon Prince Eugene a severe drubbing, in an encounter which he won in his own particular fashion. He dallied over his lunch until disaster seemed inevitable, then rose from the table, came on to the field like a fury and snatched victory out of the late afternoon.

In his report of the victory, Vendôme drew the particular attention of Louis XIV to "son cher, cher abbé" who had, he declared, done so much toward the defeat of the Germans. This encomium brought from the King a respectable pension, which, alas! was not paid regularly. It was only right that

---

[3] "Cet enfant, si séduisant et si cher au roi, n'en trahissait pas moins l'état, en instruisant son père, alors duc de Savoie et notre ennemi, de tous les projets militaires qu'elle trouvait le moyen de lire. Le roi en eut la preuve par les lettres qu'il trouva dans la cassette de cette princesse après sa mort. 'La petite coquine,' dit-il à Madame de Maintenon, 'nous trompait.'" (Memoirs of Duclos.)

Alberoni should receive some mark of favour, for by now he was acting in his spare time as a staff officer and private secretary to his hero. Before long Vendôme was reporting that no Frenchman existed more devoted than the Parmesan abbé.

Not however by clerkly diligence alone did he win the friendship of the army; he delighted them with a thousand frivolous but agreeable attentions. Did they lack wigs? He found them wigmakers of talent. After Cassano there was a cry for a portrait-painter. The abbé had the very man to hand, a certain Giovanni della Piana, who was summoned to the camp forthwith. Inspired by the princely extravagance of the French, the artist fell to work like a demon. His portraits of the heroes (no doubt they corresponded in quality to the elaborate "pictorial reconstructions" which certain illustrated periodicals still affect) may have disappeared; but it is not difficult to imagine elaborate perruques untroubled by the cannon-ball's wind, radiant breast-plate set off by reeking howitzer, and a brisk cavalry action in the smoke of the background. A couple of centuries earlier one corner of the canvas would have shown a peasant quietly ploughing, remote from the schoolboy fury; but with the advance in the arts of war, the peasant's plough had been broken, the landscape cleared to heighten the majesty of battle. . . .

Then there were the culinary delights of Italy, which a fervent patriot like Alberoni was proud to show off. The French officers in their ignorance complained they were never given anything worth eating. The abbé confounded them with a fine cheese from old Bishop Roncovieri, which showed the French "there are still things in Lombardy to tempt gourmands." To advance the interests of Parma, the Duke put at Alberoni's disposal the Palazzo Landi at Piacenza, stocked with wines from his cellars and delicacies from his kitchens. Thither the abbé would carry a bright company of officers and regale them handsomely.

As like as not the dishes would be cooked by his own hand. For about this time he began to display that great talent in the kitchen which was to inform all his subsequent career. It was of course a fashion of the age to dabble in cookery. Did not Madame de Maintenon devise an excellent method of dressing veal cutlets "en papillotte"? Would not young Orléans, afterwards Regent of France, one day devise a masterpiece with carps' roes? But of the great figures who two centuries ago haunted their own kitchens, Alberoni was probably the most accomplished and professional. . . .

Life was not however all cooking and banquets. While the abbé never forgot his duties to his Parmesan master, Vendôme now treated him as one of his staff officers. Were the quick-witted Italian not at hand, the C.-in-C. would fume. "I've ridden today," Alberoni wailed on one occasion, "forty miles on my buttocks, and by a vile road." He arrived in camp to find Vendôme in a fury of impatience; only Alberoni's evident exhaustion won him forgiveness.

Once, crossing a torrent he fell in. Thereafter his clothes looked shabbier than ever; the merest groom in the French army, he reported ruefully to Parma, was better turned out than he; and he lost, into the bargain, his one decent wig. He ordered another from Parma, but it was a long time in coming; meanwhile he was forced to make do with a cheap one from Cremona that fitted vilely. "Pray remember about my wig," he entreated the Prime Minister of Parma, "for if I fall again into the water, I shall be obliged to don a dragoon's bonnet."

Then he was continuously worried by the turbulence of a groom furnished by the Master of the Horse at Parma. This bully was always brawling with the French troops and the abbé's muleteers. When his master reproved him, he became as "furious as a horse."

However the war might be going for France elsewhere, in Italy the campaign of 1706 began brilliantly. At Calcinato

Vendôme was again triumphant. Pinning the Austrians behind the River Adige, the French were now free to extinguish at Turin the last flickers of Allied resistance. Alas! The reduction of Victor-Amadeus's capital was entrusted to the cocksure young Duc de la Feuillade (whose chief military recommendation was his being married to "the cruelly ugly" daughter of Chamillart, the Minister for War). And a nice muddle La Feuillade made of it.

Meanwhile Villeroy, exchanged against some other important prisoner, and entrusted with the command in Flanders, risked battle with Marlborough at Ramillies (May 1706). In a couple of bloody hours all Belgium was lost; there was no rallying of wits or units until the French had been pushed back almost on to their sacred frontiers. Once again Villeroy had blundered. Would Vendôme be called in to avenge Ramillies as he had avenged Cremona? "The Duc de Vendôme," Alberoni commented, "is the only person who serves the King out of the goodness of his heart and from friendship; otherwise that Prince is badly served." Because he was jealous of Vendôme's success at Calcinato, Villeroy had let himself be beaten "like a dog." "God, if he could go to Flanders, how 'le bon compaire' would lead that army!" Suddenly at the end of June, Alberoni's prayers were granted. Vendôme was recalled to save France.

His successor in Italy, the young Duc d'Orléans, requested the appointment of Alberoni to his headquarters. Instead the abbé followed his hero to France. Saint-Simon, and most of the historians who follow him, have not bothered to analyse the motives which inspired Alberoni to this step, and to the fourteen years' absence from his beloved Italy. They notice how he emerges at the French headquarters more as one of Vendôme's assistants than as a foreign diplomatic envoy; and they straightway assume that like so many of his countrymen he is seeking preferment abroad.

In actual fact, Alberoni was no base adventurer, deserting his old master for a better one. Although for the next six years he was to present to the outside world the figure of a staff officer in the French service, and then after a short interval was to become Prime Minister of Spain, he still maintained his fundamental quality of Parmesan representative; with him the Duke of Parma's orders were to override all others. Even though his loyalty was to be rewarded with ingratitude and treachery, he never dreamed of deserting the Parmesan service.

In the present instance, it was at the orders and expense of the Parmesan court that Alberoni now proceeded to France. After Ramillies secret peace negotiations had been set on foot. It was believed that a peace conference would follow, where no doubt Vendôme, as the one successful French commander, would play a leading part. At that conference who better could protect the interests of the Parmesan than the abbé?

The two friends were still on the road when the consequences of their leaving the Italian theatre were made evident. Prince Eugene broke out of the barriers behind which Vendôme had confined him; marching rapidly, he appeared not long afterwards in front of Turin, where the fatuous La Feuillade was dallying over his siege. Battle was joined with the French forces under the divided command of young Orléans, the unlucky Maréchal de Marsin, who held him in leading-strings, and La Feuillade. The upshot was a defeat in which poor Marsin lost his life, and which swept the Franco-Spanish forces out of the peninsula for the rest of the war. But it took a little time for the full gravity of the news to penetrate Alberoni's consciousness. He was too busy helping Vendôme reform a scattered army in the wet, green fields round Mons.

There was great depression at Versailles when they passed through there. Nowhere was the war going well for France. An Anglo-Austrian force had invaded Spain, and captured

Madrid. Vazet, Philip V's valet, the only man who could make the King smile, arrived in Paris with the Spanish crown jewels and sad tales of the little Queen Maria Louisa cramped into lodgings at Burgos to which the lordly sun could only struggle through ranks of tattered washing. All seemed lost in Spain, the origin and cause of the war; there was much support for old Vauban's project, to pack Philip off to a new throne in the New World, and let the Habsburgs have Madrid.

No better was the spirit of the tattered force of which Vendôme assumed command at Lille in August 1706; cowering among the fortresses that marked the Franco-Belgian border, it watched with rising despondency and impotence Marlborough's steady advance southward. It was as if nobody any longer believed that the great English commander could be held; there was even a tendency, Vendôme reported, for officers to doff their hats when the name of Marlborough was mentioned.

With Alberoni at his side, Vendôme worked miracles. The remnants of Villeroy's fine army were quickly brought into Lille and somehow given fresh spirit; within a few weeks the Army of Flanders was in being again, sadly reduced of course, but at least such a proper field force as had not been seen for three months. By September the cavalry were in so good fettle, there was talk of hazarding an encounter with the enemy in the plains round Ath, where horsemen could be used to advantage. But the King would not sanction such a move, however Vendôme might entreat and storm. All hope of peace had vanished; the campaign must continue next year; it would be folly therefore to risk the revived, precious army. Nevertheless it was galling to be held in check while fortress after fortress fell to Marlborough.

At the end of October, just when it seemed as if Vendôme might have a chance of striking, orders came from Versailles to disperse into winter quarters. Alberoni's disappointment was not lifted by the news which had at last filtered through from Italy. For months there had been only obscurity; now suddenly the curtain was drawn aside and the plight of the beloved fatherland disclosed. As if the triumph of the hated enemy were not enough, several rivers had burst their banks. "God must be enraged against us," the abbé wrote to Parma; his heart bled for the poor country, exposed to every sort of horror at once.

To the rage of Saint-Simon, Vendôme's reception at Versailles was most warm. The King acclaimed the preserving of France's northern frontier, and the refashioning of an army.

This winter lull was the time for deserved pleasures. Crozat, the financier and patron of Watteau, received Vendôme and Alberoni sumptuously. A dozen other great houses were no less welcoming; and the eminent people the abbé met there he quickly charmed with a host of graceful services. Did they want Venetian goblets? Presto! Their tables glittered with them. Did some memory of Italian travel foster a taste for those delicious spiced sausages from Florence (without garlic of course, for that would not be practical at court)? In a trice the cherished dish was conjured up. Seeds of Italian flowers, masks from Venice, the curiosities and luxuries of Italy, were used to gain powerful friends for Parma and for himself.

In the spring, before leaving for the new campaign, Vendôme gave a sumptuous party at Anet, his principal seat. Diane de Poictiers once lived there; her sickle moon and stags still adorn the gateway; but a disastrous invocation of her memory has recently spoiled the château beyond all aid. In the gardens however are still to be seen some of Vendôme's felicities which caused La Fontaine to break into song:

"Clio sur son giron à l'exemple d'Homère
Vient de les retoucher, attentif à vous plaire.

On dit qu'elle et ses sœurs, par l'ordre d'Apollon,
Transportent dans Anet tout le sacré vallon."

Anet lies in the lush valley of the Eure, which pours its tribute into the Seine near Rouen. It is a world of rich turf and
docile water which, by their interplay, attain a fuguelike pattern. The dramatic use of water, as of staircases to embellish
existence, was among the supreme achievements of the baroque age. If in Italian hands the grand staircase — la scala
nobile — attained audacious powers, the streams and cascades
of the humid north sired a heroic "wasserkunst" — the art of
embellishing life with tossing fountains and discreet canals.
The gardens of Versailles may have set the standard of water-
art; but Anet had a moist verdant harmony exquisitely suited
to a place of pleasure. Meudon and Marly from their plans
must have possessed a similar quality, but their watery decorations are for the most part choked up or vanished.

Down the alley-ways, where the early spring sailed on the
spray, the glistening throng would parade, thankful to escape
for a moment the splendid tedium of the court. National disasters, royal deaths, would soon drive the last pretences of
pleasure from Versailles, even from Marly; but already the surviving vestiges of it, the order that allowed the courtier his personal liberty only in moments of royal gout, were intolerable
to the new generation that had come in with the eighteenth
century. For them pleasure must be intimate and easy. The
Duchesse du Maine with her home-made operas and games
of hide-and-seek among the sweet-smelling mazes of Sceaux
normally provided their best refuge; now while Vendôme was
home for an instant from the wars, lovely Anet was open to
their carefree laughter.

For the occasion Campistron wrote an opera, *Galathée*. No
doubt it was decked out with the fashionable conceits, ballets

of satyrs amid thunder, gods descending upon unsteady clouds to prophesy for the Dauphin — all too inaccurately — a prosperous reign.

Alberoni was at special pains to captivate the Dauphin; "a courtier," he wrote complacently to Parma, "tells me that Monseigneur [i.e., the Dauphin] has shown particular favour to our friend the abbé. He [i.e., Alberoni] gave him a macaroni soup prepared with butter and cheese, that Monseigneur found much to his taste. The abbé was in despair because of the Parmesan cheese, which was not in prime condition. Nevertheless it's certain he's made a good impression on all those Princes, and he has reason to be grateful for so favourable an opportunity that was arranged with particular care by the Duc de Vendôme. . . ."

A few days later the two friends were off to the wars again. Prospects were infinitely better than in the previous years; the Army of Flanders had been reinforced by thousands of the troops from Italy — Vendôme's old veterans whom Louis XIV had been able to withdraw from beyond the Alps by agreement with the Emperor, greatly to Marlborough's irritation. "France," Alberoni wrote joyfully to Parma, "is still capable of biting, if she wants to. . . . The Allies will be greatly surprised, for they never expected to see such a great effort."

In the bare Hainault plains the two great armies faced each other with not above eight or nine miles between them; hardly a ditch or copse to cover a sudden movement; the slightest stir in either camp must surely provoke a mighty clash. The prospect filled the abbé with excitement; gone was his usual humanity; as with many another nature fundamentally gentle, exasperation at the intolerable delays of war had made him almost bloodthirsty. Let there occur one decisive battle, and then be done with it all. "I believe this campaign will be decisive . . ." he wrote exultant, ". . . it'll be a pretty sight to see thirty thousand horse on our side, and almost as many on the other, not counting about ninety battalions in each army. . . . If a battle takes place, it'll be a very bloody one. I'll try to watch it from a distance, where I won't be disturbed by that cursed animal, the cannon. . . ."

But there was no battle. After the meagre spring it came on to rain; the heavens opened, never, it seemed, to close again. The rain was a vertical extension of the flat, endless mud.

It was now high summer; in Parma one panted for air during the day; at night one would walk the luminous piazza till it was cool enough to sleep. Here, summer was the wet candles of some chestnut-tree that flashed for an instant through the waving rain, the corn so black and laid, the devastations of war seemed superfluous. Beneath the arches of a Spanish belfry the doves opened their feathers like indignant umbrellas. The Flemish youths, debarred from exploring the fertility of the girls among the swaying reeds, tried instead the edges of their knives, as they swallowed their gin, glaring with equal fury at one another and the bursting drain-pipes.

Throughout the long wetness of those summer days Vendôme and Marlborough sat in the Belgian mud watching each other and events elsewhere. Disasters in Spain weakened Marlborough,[4] drawing away from his command troops that he could ill spare. King Louis was however not yet in any mood to risk a battle; he was watching too with excited attention the sapping of Marlborough's position with Queen Anne, by the smooth Abigail Hill, and the mole-like Harley. The main purpose for which the Tory squires of England had gone to war, the humbling of French military power, had been achieved; as the land-tax swelled, the interminable struggle lost for the English public all purpose save the recapture of Spanish markets. To this object that would benefit the Whig merchants alone, the landed gentry saw no reason to be sacrificed.

[4] Notably the defeat of an Allied force at Almanza (April 25, 1707).

In July moreover an Anglo-Savoyard invasion of Provence obliged Vendôme to send reinforcements thither and sheared him of that numerical superiority which he had momentarily enjoyed. The Englishman tried to turn the situation to his advantage. Securing a grudging measure of liberty from the Dutch Field-Deputies he sought by a sudden movement to outflank the French and cut their communications through Mons with the French frontier. But Vendôme, warned in time, splashed after him with equal speed through the sodden countryside.

The heavy fieldpieces stuck in the glutinous mud, wigs lost their curl, hung lank about the dirty faces, the English red, the French white coats took on a common dun smirch, gold lace turned blacker than the vicious sky. As night came on after a day's fast marching, but a couple of miles separated the two armies; Marlborough tried to fall upon the French rearguard; in the wet obscurity the plan miscarried; moving always with great agility Vendôme slipped away and sat down in front of Mons, his communications safe again. The last chance of mauling him had vanished; "Our Prince," commented Alberoni, "is a great general. . . . Battles are for desperate men, and not for people who have much to defend."

Gone was the bellicose mood of a few months back. Perhaps it had been washed away by the despairing rains that did not cease until well into September, too late in the year to permit of any great enterprise. The pugnacious thoughts of the Parmesan priest now flew to another quarter, to Italy, where the supineness of the Vatican in the face of an Austrian advance toward Naples aroused in him torments of indignation. All this floundering through the northern damp had little purpose if his dear fatherland were to be ravaged by those transalpine barbarians, if the Holy Father were to forget his duties as a good Italian and as a temporal prince of the peninsula. For as the Austrians came southward, Clement XI alternated between a bombardment of excommunications and fulsome cajoleries, furnishing the invaders with all sorts of rations.

The spectacle moved Alberoni with a contempt for the Pontiff that he was never to lose. "The gentry from beyond the mountains," he wrote to Rocca, "don't stand in much awe of excommunications, and if you want me to speak frankly, this is no time to use them. . . . With all his threats he'll be lucky if they leave him as parson of Rome, for he's never shown the least sign of the qualities of a Pope. Why claim the dignity of a temporal prince, when he's powerless to defend his subjects? He'd best give it up, and take himself off to say Masses and chant homilies and visit churches. You'll say perhaps that I talk like a soldier, but I can assure you that I wouldn't think otherwise if I followed another calling."

By this time he had come to regard himself primarily as a military official; but his own advancement seems to have been of little moment to him; it was for the other Italians in the army, such men as Albergotti, who had risen to the rank of lieutenant-general, to serve the Bourbons out of ambition; with him it was a question of contributing to a French victory, not out of love for the French, but to bring about the expulsion of the Germans from Italian soil.

The armies went into winter quarters toward mid-October. Vendôme, declared Alberoni to Parma, had reason to be satisfied with the campaign, "glorious for him and useful to the kingdom. He has found the secret of amusing a superior army during the Allied invasion of Provence, which obliged us to detach some of our troops for its defence."

An attack of dysentery delayed the abbé at Lille, so that he was unable to witness the honours and affection with which the King welcomed Vendôme back to Versailles. In January 1708, however, he came in for his share of them. Vendôme presented him to the old monarch, who was graciousness itself, increased his pension by 3000 francs, and declared, "I'm delighted to be

57

agreeable to you, the more so as I know of no better way to please your colonel, who has so much friendship and esteem for you." A few months later the abbé was able to announce that the King of Spain in his turn had granted him a pension of yet another 3000 francs payable upon the Asiento, or traffic in African slaves to America. The faithful Alberoni was quick to assure his government that he was now in a position to serve them without any pay. He continued whenever occasion offered to advance the interests of Parma with the French; far from forgetting his old friends he did them a thousand favours, securing commissions for their sons in smart French regiments, buying fine table linen for them, or tapestries "of an enchanting beauty" after designs by Teniers. They retaliated by taking from him his house at Piacenza, the Palazzo Landi, where he had been wont to receive Vendôme. They excused themselves by his long absence. Such behaviour, he warmly retorted, might well cause him to stay away still longer. But he recovered from his anger, before leaving for the front. "All the misfortunes," he declared, "that may come upon me will not make me forget my friends and patrons. . . ."

❧ IV ❧

OUDENARDE AND TEMPORARY
DISGRACE

THERE WAS THE usual last party at Anet, particularly splendid this year — the Dauphin and a gay company appeared as usual . . . then it was Flanders once more. Vendôme was no longer his own master in the field. That bigwig the Duc de Bourgogne had been put in nominal command, with Vendôme as his mentor. A more unfortunate combination it would have been hard to devise; on the one hand an inhibited young prince, making up for military inexperience by a mass of ill-conceived theories; on the other, a shameless atheist of great talent, who had been fighting since childhood, and had little use for amateurs, or for those who thought it a sin to seek their pleasure outside the marriage-bed.

Bourgogne's high moral tone did not always inspire the behaviour of his nimble young duchess. She might criticize the disorder of Vendôme's conduct. But what of her rolling about on her bed in the arms of her pretty, wanton ladies, kissing and petting them? She dared to rate Vendôme for coarse habits, she who would take a clyster in the old King's very cabinet, with the court present, and pretending not to notice it. She might have turned pious of late, but it was largely, people said, to curry favour with the Maintenon. As for Bourgogne himself, Vendôme was not impressed by the young man's painful virtue. It was born, he believed, largely from fear, that fear of hellfire with which the Bishop of Cambrai had inspired him. Did he find attractions in some girl other than his wife, he would squint at her, to repel her, and remove temptation from him.

To Vendôme, in short, everything that Bourgogne represented was odious. From the very opening of the campaign, dissension paralyzed the French headquarters.

The war that year began by the armies resuming the elaborate sort of counter-dance of the previous campaign. The French advanced towards Brussels; Marlborough fell back to near Louvain, and for a time there was inaction. In his letters to Parma Alberoni could find nothing more exciting to mention than Bourgogne's liking for a Parmesan cheese of remarkable flavour — one out of Alberoni's own stock — that Vendôme had presented to the prince. Nevertheless the French headquarters were sternly occupied. Belgian discontent with the Dutch occupation was to be exploited; early in July the French, taking Marlborough apparently by surprise, struck rapidly toward Bruges and Ghent, whose gates were joyfully opened to them.

There is a fashion, of which Saint-Simon was the first and Mr. Winston Churchill is the latest protagonist,[1] to give credit for this operation to Bourgogne, and to blame Vendôme for the disaster that occurred at Oudenarde not long afterwards. Alberoni of course maintained that the reverse was entirely due to Bourgogne's stupidity and wilfulness. This contention he amplified in a published letter that was to play a great part in the controversy, and which inspires Mr. Churchill to some invective. There are few exercises more tedious than pettifogging controversy over dead battles. Lee's miscalculations at Gettysburg, von Kluck's hesitations in front of Paris, serve only to emphasize the essential futility of militarism, which is hardly tolerable even in success. But in fairness to Alberoni's hero, it can incontestably be said that at Oudenarde, his only important reverse, a large part of the French army was never

[1] *Marlborough and His Times*, vol. iii.

brought into action — and that through Bourgogne's recalcitrance. At a critical moment of the engagement, Vendôme sent a message to the young prince, asking him to bring up the French left wing. Wrongly believing the ground ahead of him to be marshland, Bourgogne disregarded the appeal. The staff-officer charged with conveying this decision to Vendôme was killed on his way to headquarters, and Vendôme for long remained ignorant of the inaction on his left. An admirable opportunity to destroy the van of the British attack was lost, Vendôme and his finest regiments were practically surrounded; only nightfall and his prompt action saved them from annihilation.

Bourgogne and his brother Berry were swept off the field by their terrified lackeys, and drew breath again only at Huysse, far to the rear, where they fell in with the furious Vendôme; using terms that scandalized Saint-Simon, he upbraided the heir presumptive to the throne, and proposed to resume the action on the morrow with the large force that had not yet been engaged.

He was however overridden, and compelled to withdraw behind the Ghent-Bruges canal, where he strongly entrenched. Having made his dispositions he immediately offered his resignation to the King.[2] But the King would have none of it. Bourgogne meanwhile spent much time in prayer. "You may," remarked an officer to him one day, "for all I know possess the Kingdom of Heaven, but as for the earthly one, Eugene and Marlborough fare better than you do!"

At Versailles there were furious recriminations. Alberoni's letter was in every hand; he did not mince his words; "there are too many bigwigs and courtiers [in this army]; they are

[2] "Since," he wrote, "I find myself of no use to Y.M. surrounded as I am by people who defer neither to my rank nor to my experience, and who oppose me on all critical occasions, I humbly beg that Y.M. will be pleased to let me resign, and thus spare a veteran general the shame of being no more than a melancholy witness of reverses. . . ."

the ruin of princes and of states. . . . If it hadn't been for the courage and resolution of H.H. [i.e., Vendôme] the unfortunate engagement near Oudenarde, which as it turns out is an affair of little consequence, might have had results as disastrous as those of Ramillies." The expression of his opinion, printed by the thousand, found its way into every café in France, reached even the scarlet paws of the fishwives and the vegetable-sellers of the Halles, among whom there existed a traditional affection for the Vendôme family. To the people it seemed at least strange that their hero should have been beaten on the one occasion he was under the orders of an inexperienced prince.

Marlborough meanwhile moved upon Lille, the second town of France, and one of the strongest fortresses in Europe. Every effort was first made, however, to tempt Vendôme out of Ghent, and thus loosen his hold upon the waterways, the all-important means of communication in those days of abominable roads. Vendôme refused to budge, and it became necessary to bring overland from Brussels in an immense convoy all the material for which the siege called. It was widely supposed that the French would interfere with the convoy, but here again, if Saint-Simon is to be believed, Bourgogne forbade any move.

Early in September, Bourgogne and Vendôme, reinforced by Berwick from the Rhine, moved south to the attempted relief of Lille. A great battle seemed imminent, and Versailles was taut with anxiety; the Duchess de Bourgogne set a fashion in prayer that was followed by many ladies whose lovers or husbands were with the army; for once a thousand courtly eyes were not strained after a regal smile, a quick revelation of favour; instead they stared, so long as it was light, out of the palace windows, to glimpse the first feather of dust that would announce a new courier from Flanders. But even when the

courier had arrived, curiosity could not be slaked before nightfall, till the King was back from the hunt. That no misfortune
might disturb. Only then would the despatches, however momentous, be opened.

The King was not alone in this mood of apparent indifference. The Dauphin could hardly be persuaded to listen to the
reading of the despatches, however much they might concern
the repute of his eldest son; they must not interfere with his
Homeric meals, nor with the endless monologues on venery or
upon the peculiar names of certain stretches of the forest, that
now exasperated even his devoted Princesse de Conti. But he
let it get about that he was none too pleased with Bourgogne;
at bedtime, when the breeches were being tenderly slipped
down his shapely legs, he would grumble that Bourgogne was
vilely self-willed; why, at Bourgogne's age, when he had gone
campaigning, he would never have dared to question the judgement of a soldier so experienced and eminent as Vendôme.
Then he would speak with pride of his youngest son, Berry;
there was a prince with sense; and gay, too; none of that psalm-
singing nonsense; as for the second one, Spain, his eye kindled
when he spoke of him; his favourite, and he would probably
never see him again. . . .

The court might have spared its anxiety; no great action
took place; there were tense conferences to which Chamillart,
the Minister of War, came in person; as a consequence of
them, Vendôme was overruled, and the enemy's position
voted too strong to attack. The rest of the campaign dragged
itself out in similar hesitations and quarrels which arose out
of Vendôme's fruitless attempts to assert his will.

The spirit of the army began to suffer; the common soldiers
would have followed Vendôme anywhere; there was no tight-
laced popinjay but a professional warrior whose judgement
they could trust; yet when they saw his resolution confused in

a maze of incomprehensible intrigues, the stuffing went out of those fine troops who not many months later at Malplaquet were to fight like demons.

That year the campaign was prolonged far beyond the usual time, into the very beginning of winter. "Here we are," wrote Alberoni philosophically, "campaigning through Flanders in winter; it's a fashion that comes from Italy. These fine gentlemen, who aren't accustomed to it, take it hardly. I must say, if instead of being a poor officer, I were a bigwig, well in at court, I should very much object to being forced to make war in winter. . . ."

After the fall of Lille a last desperate stroke was hazarded; the Elector of Bavaria appeared from the Rhine at Vendôme's headquarters, and led a sudden raid upon Brussels, counting for his success upon the popularity he had won when Governor of Belgium; the main army masked the operation by guarding the passages of the Scheldt, on the far side of which Marlborough lay. But once again Bourgogne failed in his duty; a good night's sleep, a heavy breakfast, a game of tennis were allowed to delay his marching at the critical moment; the Allied army passed the river, and Max-Emmanuel of Bavaria could only save himself by racing back to the cover of Mons.

Raiding parties of the enemy were soon despoiling northern France; a mood of dark resignation now seized the old King at Versailles; his grandsons, impatient for the pleasures of court had little difficulty in persuading him that further resistance that year was vain, and he incontinently decreed a dispersal into winter quarters. While Bourgogne and Berry hurried back to Versailles, Vendôme was for continuing the campaign, from the formidable line that united Ghent with Bruges; thence, he argued, he could raid even into Holland itself, and paralyze the enemy's attack. Alberoni, whom he had already sent once to plead his views at court, he now despatched to Paris in a vain endeavour to put some spirit into the government. The abbé

arrived toward the end of November, and stopped with Chamillart. His visit, however, excited more curiosity than courage;
against the defeatism of the Bourgogne faction he could do
nothing. Before going back to the front, he prophesied to
Parma that they would soon hear of Ghent and Bruges falling.
And so it happened; the last strongholds of French power in
Belgium, the only fruits of this disastrous campaign, passed
tamely back into Allied hands for want of spirit at Versailles.

There Berry, with his gay laughter, was greeted joyfully.
Bourgogne's welcome was hardly so cordial; tales of his delin-
quencies had been bruited about. His wife grew anxious;
through the Maintenon, she began a subtle attack upon Vendôme's position in the old King's esteem.

When the unfortunate hero at last appeared, Louis's reception of him was no less affectionate than usual; but under the
insistent nagging of the two women, the fear of his family
being disrupted by controversy, he began to waver in his loyalty to his most distinguished general. No doubt, neither Vendôme nor Alberoni was slow to notice what was amiss. When
Saint-Simon came upon them in one of the corridors, the first
evening of their return, he noticed with quiet satisfaction that
they seemed put out. Their enemies were soon in full cry. Even
Alberoni's appearance at Mass in the Royal Chapel was taken,
for all his cloth, as an act of supreme effrontery; the Marquis
d'O, who a few weeks before had been as hot as anybody
against Bourgogne, said to Vendôme one day, "You see what
comes of never going to Mass! Look at our disasters!" "Do you
imagine," Vendôme retorted, "that Marlborough goes to it any
more than I do?"

It was more than a man of spirit could stand. At an interview
with the King, who was all graciousness, Vendôme reverted
to his offer of resignation. The King's grandson wished to see
him removed from the command in Flanders; very well; he
would go of his own free will. Feebly the King offered him the

Rhine command instead. But he would have none of it. He sold his military equipment, and the two friends went off to Anet. Anticipating his admirer Voltaire, Alberoni counselled the fallen hero to cultivate his garden. Seeds of fennel and of a particularly succulent runner bean were solicited from Parma. The abbé, heedless of his own heavy heart, filled the idle days with horticulture and bright hunting parties.[3] At all costs Vendôme must be rid of his cares; an attack of gout had stricken him down after Oudenarde, and contributed in the last months of the campaign to the lassitude and depression which had now overcome him. The early months of 1709 Alberoni spent therefore in fortifying his hero for the new tasks which, he was convinced, lay ahead. Alberoni himself had of course no friend to comfort him, no wealth in which to take refuge. Indeed, funds from Italy had run out, and when he was not with Vendôme at Anet or La Ferté Alais, he seems to have come near to starving. To make matters worse, his sausages from Italy arrived flaccid, and the cheeses spoilt. But not even this misfortune could discourage the abbé. "Tempo e pazienza," he cried, "everything has an end: it needs great blows to bring down great oak trees."

Then, in that winter of 1708–9 — when in England Lord Shaftesbury was annunciating the principle of a benign and ever-virtuous Nature — an idea that was to revolutionize the thought of succeeding generations and inaugurate the age of nature-worship in which we still live — there occurred one of the cruellest cold bouts within human memory. It began the eve of Twelfth Night; within a few days even the Channel

---

[3] In the following lines the *Mercure Galant* was later to comment upon this retirement from the battlefield to the kitchen-garden and the chase:

> "Vraiment c'eut été grand dommage
> De voir Vendôme en son village
> S'amuser à planter les choux,
> A tirer aux canards, à courre après les loups,
> Comme nous l'avons vu la dernière campagne."

was frozen for several miles out. A brief thaw served only to rob the land of its protective snow; then the frost gripped it more fiercely than ever; livestock died by the thousand, ink turned solid, liqueurs burst like grenades from their bottles. Even when they had discharged their soft white burden, the skies grew no lighter, continued to hang like a still black cloth over the land, stifling all ordinary noise. Little was to be heard but the complaint of famished birds or the crack of falling vines. Victorious England, it is true, had still spirit enough to set up fairs on the ice; but their music echoed dully through the mortal black quiet.

Next came a cold unceasing rain that killed the puny harvest. The distribution of grain was muddled. At one moment France seemed to be on the verge of famine, and Alberoni reported to Parma that hunger had brought in more recruits to the army than it could absorb. Beneath the windows of Versailles angry crowds chanted angry lampoons.[4]

Early in the spring negotiations for peace were begun at The Hague; they came to nothing however, and it was resolved somehow to resume the struggle. When the King distributed the various commands, it was found that Vendôme had been

---

[4] "Le grandpère est un fanfaron,
Le fils un imbécile,
Le petit-fils un grand poltron.
'Oh! La belle famille!
Que je vous plains, pauvres Français,
Soumis à cette empire!
Faites comme ont fait les Anglais.
C'est assez vous en dire!"
               or
"Après les cruelles horreurs
D'un hiver effroyable,
Nous croyions goûter les douceurs
D'un printemps agréable.
Le vent, la grêle, les brouillards
Causent mille désastres;
N'est-ce pas quelque Chamillart
Qui gouverne les astres?"

67

passed over. The exultation of his enemies knew no bounds. Madame de Bourgogne indeed insulted him publicly at Marly, made it almost impossible for him to come to court. Next the clique turned against Alberoni; they inflamed the King against him for his criticisms of Bourgogne; and urged the Duke of Parma to recall him, to save him from a term in the Bastille. Indeed they even spread reports at the Parmesan court that he was already in prison. But: "We're not dead yet!" Alberoni cried, and put every obstacle in the way of his recall. The truth was, he had no intention of leaving Vendôme's side, for he had a new plan.

Like so many of his later strokes it was born of misfortune. His French pension had been stopped for lack of funds, and now payment of the Spanish one too was suddenly suspended. Through Count Pighetti, Parmesan Minister in Paris, he took up the matter with the Spanish Ambassador, the Duke of Alba, the son of the Duke whose strange end we have already recorded.[5] This younger Alba had fewer foibles than his father; true, he was at times consumed with passion for some particularly ugly woman; then he would purge himself cruelly to acquire a pallor proper to a lover. But for the most part he was a sensible man who had distinguished himself in his Embassy, though at the cost of falling heavily into debt. While not vulgarly ambitious, he now yearned for some preferment in Spain, to which his birth, devotion, and parts seemed to entitle him. Spain lacked a first minister; she also lacked a general to pursue the war, even if French support were withdrawn. To Alberoni it seemed a miraculous opportunity. Securing therefore a free hand from Vendôme, he hinted to the Ambassador that Spain's salvation lay in his becoming Prime Minister, with Vendôme as Commander-in-Chief. The flattered Alba passed on the idea to Madame des Ursins [6] in Madrid; Madame des

[5] Page 11.
[6] See pages 77–8 re Madame des Ursins's position at the Spanish court.

DEATH OF CHARLES II OF SPAIN

THE REARGUARD
by Antoine Watteau

Ursins, through the Queen, worked upon Philip V; in July there arrived at Versailles an official appeal from him for Vendôme's services.

There were fresh *pourparlers* for peace about this time. The Allies in their pride were demanding that Louis be responsible for the expulsion of his own blood from Spain. To so odious a condition he would not subscribe, but even in his moments of most violent revolt he hesitated to lend to Spain a general of Vendôme's eminence. It would, the majority of his Council held, be a direct act of provocation. Moreover, it would probably cause an outburst from behind the heavy grey veils of his wife. The King declared therefore that it did not suit his interests for the Duc de Vendôme to go to Spain.

In September occurred Malplaquet, an encounter honourable enough for French arms, but a defeat nevertheless, which hardly encouraged a prolongation of the war. At Gertruydenburg, the obscure Dutch town where peace conversations dragged on through the early months of 1710, it was rather a question, even on the French side, of evicting Philip V from Spain, than of sending him generals of talent. Nevertheless, Alberoni did not lose hope. By now, it would seem, he was treating direct with the Spanish sovereigns; and the official demand for Vendôme's services was soon renewed.

But it was above all at the French court that the abbé's powers of blandishment were deployed. His Italian delicacies were themselves once more; they embellished the tables of all his potential allies; though they arrived in profusion from Italy, there was never enough of them. "It's small presents for the table," Alberoni reminded Parma one day, "that make the French remember you, and keep them friendly."

The isolation to which the court had condemned Vendôme was gradually ending. The quality were slipping back to lovely Anet, and to his hunting château, La Ferté Alais, drawn by the elegance of the fêtes that Alberoni organized to distract him;

Orléans lent him his pack of hounds; even the gates of Versailles, for all Madame de Bourgogne's intrigues, were soon to open to him once more.

To the discredit of the Allies, and particularly of England, the peace negotiations at Gertruydenburg were allowed to break down. Louis agreed to abject terms, the surrender of Alsace, his strongest fortresses in northern France, Newfoundland and the Hudson Bay, even to defraying the cost of expelling Philip V from Spain. In England there had been growing for some time past an impatience with the war. Nobody felt it more strongly than the Queen. She was tired to death of the strain and the intrigues that the continued conflict bred, of Sarah Marlborough and Abigail with their ceaseless talk of politics. The news of Oudenarde had made her cry, "Will this bloodshed never cease?" When, a few months later, her good silly husband had died, she had shut herself up for a fortnight alone in his room. Sarah assumed she was closeted with Abigail. Abigail, tortured with apprehension, had believed Anne once more to be in the clutches of Sarah. In fact, the Queen was taking refuge from both intriguing women.

The Queen's mood mirrored, in the main, that of her kingdom. But the Whig Junto, who now ruled at Westminster, were drunk with victory. England, with two bad harvests forcing up the cost of living, with an ugly weight of taxation upon her, needed peace hardly less than did France; and could have had it that winter of 1710, upon glorious terms. But the Whigs put forward the preposterous proviso that Louis should with his own troops drive his grandson from Spain.

No self-respecting nation, laid however low, could accept such conditions. Rightly did Torcy, the French Foreign Minister, declare that it would wound the honour of his master to make war on his own flesh and blood, and on a prince who had always obeyed him. Marlborough's conduct in the affair was far from admirable. He as much as anyone had been responsible for the Whig catchphrase "No peace without Spain"; he must have known that Louis could never accept the monstrous Whig conditions; yet he did nothing to save the conference from deadlock. To some of his Tory enemies it seemed as if he wished the war to go on, that he might continue to draw his handsome pay and perquisites; and his attempt to secure the office of captain-general to himself for life did little to remove these suspicions. More likely is it that his supine conduct sprang from a fundamental defect of character. In war he was one of the greatest leaders that the world has ever seen; but when he had gained the victory, he was at a loss. He could put the awful machine of battle into motion, and by a thousand shifts keep it running till its purpose was achieved; he had, however, no notion how then to stop it.

In March the King of Spain renewed his demand for Vendôme. The moment seemed more favourable; before the outrageous conditions of the Allies, the old King had stiffened, resolved once more to fight. It seemed as if all Alberoni's faithful machinations might triumph. Within a few weeks he was able proudly to report that the talk of Paris was of Vendôme going to take command in Spain. But in May reverses inflicted by Marlborough caused once again a sudden change in policy; at The Hague the French representatives prostrated themselves, consenting to the use of force against Philip V, and offering from the exhausted treasury of France the finances necessary for the measure. At this late hour the abbé's schemes now seemed once more confounded. But he was not particularly worried. In his bones he knew that peace would never be made at the cost of Philip's departure from Spain. "If peace," he wrote to Parma in May 1710, "absolutely depends upon Philip V's leaving Spain, it may, I think, be still very remote. . . ." He knew the Spanish sovereign's intentions well enough; he

71

was even then concerting with Madrid a further appeal for the loan of Vendôme.

The subject of these rumours and intrigues remained lost in rural and luxurious obscurity. He was absorbed too in the arrangements for his coming marriage to Mademoiselle d'Enghien, the minute grand-daughter of the Great Condé, "Monsieur-le-Prince le Héros" as he was called to distinguish him from his son and her father, the unheroic fantastic "Monsieur le Prince." Mademoiselle d'Enghien had suffered from her father's foibles. He was capable of spending fortunes upon some exquisite fête that he would organize at Chantilly ostensibly in the King's honour, but really to delay the departure for Italy of some pretty woman after whom he sighed; at enormous expense he would hire in Paris a whole street of houses for the secrecy of his amorous encounters; the fountains and glades of his beloved Chantilly might have been his mistresses, such splendours did he lavish upon them. But outside love and gardening he was a miser and a recluse, who had kept his unfortunate little daughter in half-starved spinsterhood far beyond the time when any young woman so ill-favoured could still hope for a husband. There had once been a question of a match with a Duke of Mantua. The project had been ruined by her father; but he had at last died in 1709, and she was now free to marry as she wished. The suit of Vendôme had been pressed by the Maines, and indeed it had many advantages. He was still a very important personage, and immensely rich. For that matter she was no pauper, with, as Alberoni complacently reported to Parma, excellent expectations from her mother, who was worth about eight million francs in her own right. For Vendôme it was a highly convenient union. Plain though she might be, she was after all a princess of the blood; by his marriage with her, Vendôme at the very moment of his apparent ruin was to all intents and purposes legitimized into the royal circle of the Bourbon family. As Alberoni said on the eve of the ceremony, the house of Vendôme would be put by it "into a great elevation." [7]

No sentiment was allowed to disturb the perfection of the arrangement. A few days after the marriage, which took place under the Maines' elegant roof at Sceaux, the bridegroom was back at his beloved Anet, without his diminutive bride, who was only too glad to enjoy her new liberty at court. "You will be surprised by this," Alberoni wrote to Parma, "but you must understand that almost all marriages in France are on a similar basis. Husbands and wives here see each other occasionally and go about together as friends do in our own country. It's not just, they say, that a man and a woman, merely because they're married to each other, should be inconvenienced. . . . I don't know whether it's from logic or lubriciousness that they live in this way. . . ."

Vendôme's favour was now rapidly restored. On June 4th 1710, the King summoned him to Versailles; "they say," Alberoni reported, "that all the squabbles will be ended by his visit, and that it's an expedient invented by the King, who wishes that everybody should live in peace." The abbé was obliged to admit a few days later that "les deux mégères" (Mesdames de Bourgogne and de Maintenon) were continuing to diffuse their poison; but it had lost its strength. Madame de Bourgogne's own sister, the heroic young Queen of Spain, wrote at this moment to Louis XIV entreating him to send Vendôme to her without delay, as an essential proof of her hus-

[7] The marriage provoked the following lampoon, in allusion to the eccentric personal habits with which gossip credited the bridegroom:

> "Préparons, dessus nos musettes,
> Pour Vendôme nos chansonnettes
> Il donne dans le sacrement,
> L'épouse sera bien baisée
> S'il est sur elle aussi souvent
> Qu'il est sur la chaise percée!"

band's determination to defend his throne. Meanwhile the Allies in their tragic folly had finally rejected the French offer to foot the bill for a war against Philip V; they continued to insist that the operation should be carried out by French troops. At last the French representatives were recalled from The Hague. They arrived at Marly on July 30th 1710; a council was immediately held, which resolved to accede to the Spanish sovereign's entreaties. Alberoni had triumphed.

A few days later Louis XIV received the reinstated Vendôme to discuss the forthcoming campaign. They conferred in the regal apartments, then walked in the gardens. Since money was tight, the fountains were dead save where the King passed; without his fountains, particularly on a summer's day, he would have been undressed; it was arranged therefore that they should come to life just in front of him, rise to full majesty over the regal head, which never was so indelicate as to look back upon the jets sinking away behind; so that it was as if a flashing great plume of spray were fixed in the King's hat while he walked with his general among the statues, talking of affairs in Spain.

The King mentioned the sum of 50,000 écus that had been set aside for personal expenses during the campaign; Vendôme proudly refused them, saying that they should be kept for those who could not cut a figure in their King's service without a subsidy. For his part he did not propose to cost his sovereign a penny, even in Spain. He did not mention that he had sold his princely house in Paris, near where the Hotel Ritz now stands, to defray his Spanish expenses.

"You will have heard," wrote Alberoni with pride to Parma, "that H.H. is to take the command in Spain. I am to have the honour of accompanying him. You can suspend the presents of sausages and cheeses. You will redouble them on our return, if God be pleased to bring us back safe and sound."

But habit was too strong; the very day, August 28th, 1710,

that he left Paris with Vendôme for the Spanish front, the abbé wrote to Parma: "I don't doubt that you'll receive the order for the cheese and the sausages. In France they say that gifts foster friendship. It's not much that I take the liberty of asking you. . . ."

THE FREEING OF SPAIN, AND VENDÔME'S DEATH

Wʜɪʟᴇ Vᴇɴᴅᴏ̂ᴍᴇ and Alberoni chew their impatience in the slow prison of a coach, let us fly ahead of them to Spain, to cast an eye on that stage which must now be set for their entrance, and on the court which they are expected to rescue.

We last saw the King of Spain, a bewildered young French prince, sadly crossing the Bidassoa to his inheritance. His troubles had begun at the frontier. Most Spaniards had believed that their country was now placed under the direct government of Louis XIV; he would, of course, spend a part of the year in Madrid; bullfights were already being organized in honour of his arrival; naturally, he would arrange to come at the season when the bulls were at their best. . . . Instead, the pride of Spaniards was injured by the solitary appearance of a shy and sulky child.

Though he affected the golillo and a taste for Spanish cooking, Philip for his part could not conceal his misery. He would arrive hours late in council, peer at the clock, yawn and rush off to shoot at the first decent opportunity. It was his only pleasure; when not at it, he would burst into tears, and on the shoulder of his ingenious friend, the Marquis de Louville, sob for the bright woods and diverse pleasures of France.

In the spring of 1701, however, he had been married to little Maria Louisa of Savoy, and had discovered a pleasure keener than that of the chase. From his first leap into the marriage-bed, his uxoriousness provoked titters throughout Europe.[1] He quickly surrendered the government into the hands of his thirteen-year-old bride, and of her Camarera Mayor or Lady of the Bedchamber, Madame des Ursins, whom Louis XIV had brought out of the cell where last we saw her languishing,[2] and had set up in Spain as the very corner-stone of French policy.

In the spring of 1702, the young King made a tour of his Italian dominions. The little Queen stayed behind in Spain as Regent, and the youth in consequence was a nervous wreck by the time he reached Naples. Nor did the portents help matters; the Neapolitan crowds withheld from Philip their impudent affection; though by letters patent he allied St. Januarius to St. James as protector of the Spanish Crown, the holy blood refused to liquefy so long as the King was in the shrine.[3]

There then descended upon him the first shrouds of that melancholy, bordering at times upon dementia, which he was never entirely to put off, and which was sensibly to influence the history of Europe. Refusing to leave the dark palace in Naples, he passed his days with the dwarfs who muttered in every cranny, or shot unceasingly at sparrows from his bedroom window. Though he mooned after Maria Louisa, he could hardly bring himself to write to her; it was the faithful Louville who composed his letters. Louville was at his wits' ends; he even offered a pretty girl to his master; but the King was scandalized, for his conscience was as excessive as his lusts. He combined the nature of a priapist with religious scruples of the narrowest sort. Louville was soon to pay for his temerity with his place.

During Maria Louisa's Regency in Spain, while Philip was

[1] ". . . pourvu qu'il ait une femme dans son lit, il n'en demande pas davantage" (Memoirs of "Madame").

[2] See page 15.

[3] It had liquefied docilely enough at the ceremony of proclaiming Philip as King in the previous year. That stout Protestant, Joseph Addison, who happened to witness the episode, was not impressed.

77

shooting his Neapolitan sparrows, Madame des Ursins established her permanent dominion over the little Queen, and became through her the real ruler of the country. It was a situation which Louis XIV at first welcomed, for Madame des
Ursins, an intimate friend of the Maintenon, stood in high favour at Versailles. When she stayed there, she was accorded
a precious honour: the bedroom door of an ordinary guest bore
unadorned their ordinary style, as "Maréchale de Villeroy," or
"Duc de Chevreuse"; upon hers would magically be inscribed
"*Pour* Madame la Princesse des Ursins" — an honour compara-
ble to the right of passing in your carriage under the central
arch of the Horse Guards' Parade, which Palmerston valued
more highly than an Irish Viscountcy. . . .

Though over sixty, she had kept in her armoury many of
the charms which had once subdued lay and other princes; blue
eyes that could express pleasure with rare eloquence, a grace
that allowed her even to blow her nose with distinction, and
a vernal bosom she would display with not unjustifiable pride;
indeed at the age of a grandmother she affected décolletages
daring even for Spain, where the backs of evening dresses
would often be cut down almost to the waist. With this foible
went some arrogance and formidable powers of malice.

She was the only link with the outside world, through the
mob of old Spanish ladies round the Queen. The Savoyard
household had been turned back at the frontier; the Spanish
dowagers chilled Maria Louisa's young heart; untiring and
grave, they clicked their rosaries for ever; devout Spanish
women were said to continue the practice even as they lent
themselves to their lovers' follies.

Did a French dish appear at table, it was swept on to the
floor; when Maria Louisa moved to suppress the long dusty
trains, the hoops under innumerable petticoats that made all
doors too narrow for a lady of quality, the dowagers shrieked
that their feet would be exposed, a prospect more shameful to

78

their husbands than the horns; it could hardly have been more remote.

By Madame des Ursins's enchantments all these difficulties were exorcized; and her wisdom seemed to dissipate the problems of government for the wonderful child who was Maria Louisa. Under the tuition of her camarera mayor, she took to politics as if they were her most cherished dolls. The young Queen's charm and dexterity were a delight to her instructress. When the senile Council of Regency sought to bury all projects of reform beneath interminable discussions on privilege, Madame des Ursins with pride would observe Maria Louisa bring out her needlework, and fall so heedlessly to irrigating a verdant landscape with a tinsel river, some old dotard would be shamed into ending his useless harangue.

Of an evening the Queen would play at "Blind Man's Buff" with her younger ladies — a diversion of which Madame des Ursins could approve, for had she not seen Louis XIV stoop to it with poor lovely "Minette" long years ago? Later at night it was the fashion to jog along the dry bed of the Manzanares in your carriage. There the Queen would stay until three o'clock in the morning perhaps, sustained by the sour beauty of guitars, and a light supper. Music, cold chicken, and stars brighter than any stone from the New World. . . . The only inconvenience were those hideous familiar dwarfs, who spied by day at her door, and as she went out at night forced their way into her carriage. . . . When the Queen and her camarera mayor returned to the cavernous palace, they would remember the threats of assassination that whirled about Madrid; their resolute hearts would stumble as they heard a near-by lock being tried; but it would be only a blundering lover on his way to the room of some lady-in-waiting.

Those were serene days; they ended when the King came back from Italy in 1703, with most of his handsome hair lost through an attack of measles. And a fine to-do there was to fit him out with a wig; the grandees must be assured that every hair bore a distinguished origin; otherwise, who knew what harm might be done to the State?

For Madame des Ursins life now became a matter of blundering about in the dark of the royal bedroom with the young sovereign's chamber-pots and candles; or unending quarrels with the coxcombs who in a bewildering succession followed the sagacious Harcourt as Louis XIV's Ambassador, if not Viceroy, in Spain. Madame des Ursins's war with the French Embassy, in the course of which she was banished for a time from Spain for tampering with the diplomatic bag, ended in her emergence as dictatress of the country, and the collapse of the attempt to govern Spain from Versailles (1705–10).

War in the meantime had broken out, and the English were preparing to invade the country in the name of the Austrian Archduke Charles, whom they proclaimed as "King Charles III of Spain and the Indies." In 1702 there was an attempt upon Cadiz, when the English troops looted churches and shrines, and generally left behind them, as a local English merchant put it, "Such a filthy stench among the Spaniards that a whole age will hardly blot it out."

Save for the loss of Gibraltar, which the English took during 1704, in a mood of vague exasperation, the Bourbon rule in Spain was not seriously threatened until the autumn of 1705, when the great port of Barcelona fell to an Anglo-Austrian force, and the turbulent Catalans welcomed the Archduke Charles as their King.

The main animator of this campaign, which nearly turned Philip out of Spain, was the famous Peterborough.[4] Part inspired buffoon, part peevish eccentric, Peterborough stands

[4] Charles Mordaunt, 3rd Earl of Peterborough (1654–1735), general, politician and friend of the wits. Swift described him as "a person of great talents, but dashed with something restless and capricious, and a sort of person who may give good advice which wise men may reasonably refuse to follow."

out from among the fantastic nonentities of the Spanish war; he was not far removed from the concept which, as Voltaire records, the Spanish women cherished of him — the embodiment of a hero out of some romantic novel.

The storming of Monjuich fortress, just when the Anglo-Austrian force had despaired of success, and the subsequent reduction of Barcelona itself were as much as anything due to Peterborough's ingenuity, his wonderful talent for turning even accidents to account. In the disorders that followed, it was only right that to him, with his kindling eye for a pretty shape, should have come the felicity of rescuing from a brutal crowd the lovely Duchess of Popoli. She fled to his protection through the burning street; her beautiful hair fell loose down her back, and her terror, in the eye of an officer who accompanied Peterborough, seemed only to enhance her charms. "I stayed behind," he adds, "while the Earl conveyed the distressed Duchess to her requested Asylum; and I believe it was much the longest part of an hour before he returned. . . ."

A splendid pageant commemorated the liberation of Catalonia from Castilian tyranny. The Archduke was on a balcony with Peterborough beside him throwing dollars to the crowd. A great car with an aviary on top stopped beneath the balcony. At the appropriate moment a catch was released, a flock of gaudy birds winged their way into the frosty sky. This symbolism was widely applauded.

There now ensued perhaps the most extravagant phase of Peterborough's career. With a little band of men, ill-equipped and ill-fed — for funds were low, and Peterborough more often than not pledged his own credit to pay the army — he turned southward into Valencia at the end of 1705, and reduced the province within a few weeks. Superior forces might come against him; he would head out his little band, tantalize the grave Spaniards with a dozen artifices, each one more preposterous than the last, until they thought their armies endangered, and their sanity too. The lemon groves and painted hills would then witness the curious spectacle of important bodies of troops flying in disorder before a few hundred thirsty Englishmen, and three or four squadrons of half-starved Catalan irregulars.

With the province of Valencia won, he could rest for a moment to enjoy his spoils. Valencia has long been famed for its amenities, and particularly for its enchanting women. According to the proverb, Valencia would make a Jew forget Jerusalem. It certainly dispelled from Peterborough's mercurial head all disagreeable thoughts of the Archduke Charles, with his sloth and his comical passion for ceremony, or of the lying "Vienna crew" who advised him.

Peterborough was at this moment incensed against almost all his associates; Cifuentes, the Spanish irregular leader he trounced as "the Spanish pimp." Conyngham, his second-in-command was a "screech owl" who must be removed to another theatre. Meanwhile there were bullfights to be arranged for the friendly Valencians, and a hundred dark-eyed temptations down each street. "The only tolerable thing here," he wrote to Sarah Marlborough, "is Your Grace's sex, and that attended by the greatest danger."

Early in 1706 there was an attempt to recapture Barcelona. The situation of the Allied garrison was one of considerable peril. From among his Valencian pleasures Peterborough advised the Archduke to leave the beleaguered city; let the tedious youth join Lord Galway, who was preparing to invade western Spain from the Portuguese side. Reinforced, however, by the fanatic devotion of the Catalans, and a vision of the Virgin with two angelic supporters, Charles displayed considerable energy and resolution; his presence stiffened the defence, until that day early in May when the English squadron with Peterborough on board swept into the harbour to raise the siege. The French commander, the charming Tessé, retreated toward the French border, sped on his way by the disastrous news of Ramillies, and an eclipse that seemed to punish the French King for his temerity in taking the sun as his emblem.

Catalan irregulars cut off the road to Madrid; an Anglo-Portuguese force was advancing from the west into the heart of the country; to Maria Louisa, a refugee in dirty Burgos lodgings, to Philip, who could only rejoin her by a detour along the Pyrenees, through French territory, there came a moment of despair.

Indeed, at that time a little speed and resolution might have given Spain to the Archduke Charles. Instead, he and the "Vienna Crew" squandered their advantage in the niceties of ceremony, and tiffs with Peterborough. The Englishman retired in disgust to the pleasures of Italy, prophesying woe, while the Allied forces under Lord Galway went on to occupy Madrid, in apparent triumph.

But only the hot, mocking air, and the fat flies buzzed an acclamation; every dark alley hid a cutpurse, with a knife for such redcoats as sought the perilous shade; the furious whores of the Albaicin established a camp beyond the Manzanares, and sent back their most diseased sisters to decimate the enemy. When these syphilitic Judiths returned, the account of their triumphs would set the whole company screaming and dancing a mad fandango round their bonfires.

Gradually Madrid became untenable; Galway withdrew to Toledo. All her Habsburg sympathies aroused, the Dowager Queen, who had been exiled to that town, entertained the army; for a brief while her dark palace blazed with ten thousand candles; its long passages echoed with sounds more aimiable than the abuse of aging parrots. Then, by easy stages the Allies fell back to winter in Valencia; decision was paralyzed by the Archduke's incessant squabbles with Galway, and in the following spring the inevitable disaster occurred. At Almanza, Galway was outmanœuvred and overwhelmed, the Archduke was driven back into Catalonia, and the Bourbon cause established more solidly than ever.

When Maria Louisa towards the end of 1706 came back in triumph to Madrid, the eavesdropping dwarfs and terrible dowagers were for the most part sent packing. No longer could the Queen be pestered save by her husband and by pregnant women; immemorial custom gave them the right to force their way into anybody's presence, and the Queen's in particular, there to finger clothes, or pinch and pat reluctant flesh.[5] For that matter, the Queen herself suddenly became pregnant. There were great rejoicings, for no royal birth had occurred in Spain during the better half of a century. The happy delivery of a Prince of the Asturias in the summer of 1707 [6] strengthened Philip's position; the gaping sad-eyed young man at whom they had once mocked was now the darling of the Spaniards; every impudent attempt of foreigners to unseat him inflamed Spanish loyalty.

By now, of course not only the English and the Austrians, but even the French, wanted him gone from Spain. His renunciation of the Spanish throne seemed after Oudenarde the easiest price that France could pay for peace. Only at his grandfather's orders had Philip mounted the Spanish throne; it was now his grandfather's wish that he should step down from it. But the tedious youth, when France lay prostrate, and Marlborough's scouts menaced the sacred groves of Marly, forgot he existed only to further the interests of his family, prated of honour, conscience, his duty to the Spanish people. Louis began to withdraw his troops from Spain. His frightened old wife, when the enemy grew impatient, talked openly of the coming campaign beyond the Pyrenees to knock some sense

[5] Gallants would often take the disguise of pregnant women, to gain admission to their mistresses' rooms.

[6] Subsequently Luis I (ob. 1724).

84

into Philip's head. In Spain there surged in turn a sudden tide of feeling against France; they banished Frenchmen from the country; grandees were heard telling startled French diplomats that for very little Spain would join with the Allies to carry the war into Guyenne and Languedoc.

The attempt to absorb Spain into the French administrative system had failed; no longer was the French Ambassador admitted — as he had been in the first days of Philip's reign — to the inner secrets of the Spanish Cabinet. As the artists who imported new fashions into Spain, Hans of Cologne, the Silöe family, El Greco himself, were at length conquered by the Spanish genius, so now the French prince, his half-French consort, and their French mentor, ceasing to be regents in Spain for Louis XIV, became the jealous guardians of Spanish independence.

The common rage against France was hardly allayed by the imprudent behaviour of the Duc d'Orléans,[7] who had taken over command of the Bourbon forces in Spain, on the morrow of Almanza. At first, all had gone well; in the field he was consistently successful; at court, he was on the best of terms with the Spanish monarchs, his cousin, and his step-niece. He imported the latest fashions from Paris for the little Queen, and new comedies to beguile the tedium of her confinements. The malicious even suspected an intrigue. But in fact with a fidelity that hardly foreshadowed the promiscuities of middle age, he adored his mistress, Madame d'Argenton. He sought for her a place as lady-in-waiting to Maria Louisa; Mesdames des Ursins and Maintenon frustrated his plan. Orléans was at no pains to conceal his anger. One evening, when drink was flowing, he raised his glass. "Buvons," he exhorted his officers, "au c— capitaine, et au c— lieutenant!" The objects of his toast,

---

[7] Philippe, Duc d'Orléans and later Regent of France (1674-1723), son of Louis XIV's brother "Monsieur" and of his second wife, Charlotte-Elisabeth of Bavaria, "Madame."

quickly informed, henceforward became his implacable enemies.

He soon gave them an opportunity to destroy him. After Oudenarde, when the question arose of Philip's renouncing his throne, certain grandees conceived the idea of putting Orléans in his place. Orléans, it will be remembered, possessed something of a claim to the Spanish throne. To what degree he was now disloyal to Philip V remains obscure; it is certain that there ensued discreet *pourparlers* with General Stanhope, the new English commander in Spain.[8] Stanhope seems to have hinted that a valiant, enlightened Prince like Orléans, known for his love of the British constitution, would be infinitely more appetizing than the heavy Habsburg candidate; even Louis XIV apparently favoured the idea.

The intrigue was still-born. In 1709, when Orléans was on leave in France, two agents he had left behind in Spain, Flotte and Regnault, talked too much; for this indiscretion they were sent to languish six years long in Segovia prison. A tempest burst upon Orléans's large head. Nor was he accused of treachery alone; his fondness for chemical experiments was recalled, and the motive for them was now supposed to stand revealed. Obviously he was a poisoner; he was plotting to do away with the Spanish monarch.

This absurd idea came to obsess Philip V; he would hardly touch a dish till his dogs had tried it; and he conceived a hatred for Orléans which for long was to hang over European affairs like an evil fog. There was talk of Orléans being committed to the Bastille; though Louis XIV scotched the cruel slander, the reputation of an intending murderer clung to the unfortunate Duke, driving him into an exile that was to warp his brilliant gifts. Topers, trollops, and fortune-tellers now became his

8 (1673–1721): son of Alexander Stanhope, former British Minister to Spain. Under George I he became Secretary of State and later First Lord of the Treasury. Created first Earl Stanhope; connected by marriage with the Pitts.

constant companions; he surrounded himself with incessant noise to drive off his regrets — regrets for the talents he must squander as an outcast, regrets for his lost Spanish command, a post that had given him perfect happiness, though the Spanish sun might have spoiled his eyes, and burnt his face to a permanent vermilion.

The war in Spain was now dormant for a year. Peterborough reappeared for an instant, very jaunty from his Italian pleasures. "Col. Breton and myself," he wrote to the harassed Stanhope, "intend to mortify you with the account of our happy days in Italy — of the nights we will say nothing — but I must say I am impatient to be passing them there." He wandered homeward soon after, to become the hero of the Tories, a stick to beat Marlborough with.

Next year, in 1710, fighting flared up again. The Whig James Stanhope had set his heart on winning the country before the Tories came to power with their plans for peace.[9] Under his fiery exhortations, the Archduke Charles and Stahremberg, the Austrian commander, agreed to a cautious advance into Aragon. At Almenara, on the Aragonese border, the Bourbon forces were badly mauled in late July, thanks mainly to a charge by Stanhope at the head of "a very pretty body of English horse and dragoons"; a month later, outside Saragossa, they were finally broken and scattered down the rocky valley of the Ebro. His dark face blackened by the sweat of victory, Stanhope could pause from his tending of the wounded, to reflect that he had avenged Almanza. The following day he swept the reluctant Archduke into a decision to march upon Madrid. It was the very moment when Vendôme and Alberoni were setting out for Spain. . . .

Catalonia, with its great exchanges, its handsome Gothic churches, was still the familiar world; but when they crossed

[9] In fact he had in principle been superseded by the Duke of Argyll when he was defeated at the end of the year.

the Ebro, the English found themselves in a hostile continent. An infinity of towers that were half minarets: exhortations to Allah secreted by Mudéjar workmen among Gospel inscriptions; the closed houses and whispering alleys all seemed to proclaim the cruel Barbary Coast; the very sunsets enfolded the stark hills in a vast unfriendly cataclysm.

The Allies found Madrid half-empty and sullen; most of the inhabitants had accompanied the King and Queen to Valladolid; one ancient marquess even followed the monarchs in his glass coffin. The Archduke took one look at his tepid subjects, worshipped once before the jewel-clad Lady of Atocha ("but the saint remained neuter; both Kings had been her adorers," as an English officer drily remarked). Then he fled from the heavy enmity of the streets to some villa in the country.

At Bayonne, Vendôme and Alberoni first got news of the Saragossa disaster. Louis XIV had changed his mind again, and the Duc de Noailles arrived with orders from him to his grandson to abdicate. Vendôme scotched the idea. With a few troops, he told Verailles, he could still make things uncomfortable for Stahremberg. "He's a lion for courage, spirit, and resolution," Alberoni reported; "you can't imagine with what acclamations and joy these people of the frontier have received H.H., and are reassured by his arrival."

At Valladolid, the Spanish monarchs greeted Vendôme with all affection, and resolved under his guidance to continue the war. Noailles went back to France with no edict of abdication, but instead with a project for a diversion into Catalonia from Rousillon, to threaten the enemy's communications. Meanwhile, in Spain Vendôme's lack of pretension, his gay courage, won the affection and raised the hearts of the Bourbon partisans. Within a few weeks, he built up out of nothing a disciplined force of 15,000.

In London, dining at Harley's house one night, when all the

talk was of Stanhope's triumph, Peterborough declared that Spain would be lost by Christmas. It was a shrewd estimate; the success of Stanhope's impetuous march to Madrid depended upon a rapid junction with an Anglo-Portuguese force advancing from the west. But after dawdling several weeks, Stanhope set off on a leisurely march down the Tagus. At the Bridge of Almaraz, where the Estremaduran mountains begin to close in upon the river, as if to prevent its escape toward Lisbon and the oblivion of the sea, he hoped to effect the meeting. Instead, to his dismay, he found Vendôme waiting for him with a powerful force.

The new Bourbon army had left Valladolid early in October, and gone down by forced marches to Salamanca. (Philip V trailed after them; like an orchard honouring the passage of the sun, Salamanca to recall his visit blossomed under the care of the Churriguerra family into a luxuriance of domes and vibrating façades.) Vendôme hurried across the Sierra de Gata, past strange and long-abandoned castles, down to Plasencia with its unfinished cathedral, and quickly on to the Bridge.

A few weeks before, Spain had been virtually without an army; now a new body had sprung miraculously into being, not only to disappoint Stanhope of help from the west, but even to drive him back in ignominy towards Toledo. Without a shot, the whole complexion of the war had changed. "Your Majesty," Vendôme pointed out to Philip, "has gained more by the possession of the Bridge at Almaraz than did the Archduke by the Battle of Saragossa!"

Gradually it became clear that Madrid was untenable. "The country," cried Stanhope in desperation, "is our enemy; and we are not masters in Castile of more ground than we can encamp on!" Irregulars constantly interrupted communications, penetrating into the very suburbs of the capital. Nothing could wean the Madrillenos from their furtive hostility; memories of our behaviour at Cadiz, and the arrival of Anglican

prayer-books in large quantities, convinced them that we menaced the true faith. In revenge, they refused to supply food,
and the health of the army suffered. "Our soldiers," wrote an
English observer, "are not good for to suffer heat and want of
victuals, and besides being the most disorderly in the world,
great devourers of fruit, and that could not abstain from wines
when they came their way, which would fling them into fluxes
and calentures. . . ."

So Madrid was abandoned, and the army tried to winter in
Toledo. But Vendôme advanced inexorably up the Tagus, and
Noailles drove into Catalonia from the north. The Archduke
hurried back to Barcelona with 2,000 precious cavalry; while
Stanhope and Stahremberg with the rest of the forces began a
leisurely retreat, early in December.

They imagined Vendôme to be still at Talavera, fifty miles
away; in fact he entered Madrid the very day they took the
road for Catalonia. He tore the King from his obeisances at the
Atocha shrine, dragged him through floods, and over frosty
hills, to the town of Brihuega, where he had caught Stanhope.
The Englishman had halted there to bake bread; and he was so
confident that Vendôme was still miles away, he put out no
patrols to watch the surrounding hills, and maintained precarious touch with Stahremberg, who lay at Cifuentes, two hours'
ride off.

Not till Vendôme had come up with the bulk of his army
did Stanhope realize what was afoot. Outnumbered and lacking artillery, he nevertheless put up a good fight, which might
have saved him, had Stahremberg been less sluggish an ally. As
it was, the English did not capitulate until half Brihuega was
lighting up the bare winter's sky. The next day Vendôme met
the tardy Austrians on the plain of Villaviciosa, and drove
them off in confusion. They hardly stayed their flight till they
reached Barcelona.

Seated on a drum, in all the chaos of victory, Vendôme wrote his report to Versailles. While his officers took their choice of the rich equipment that littered the field, he perceived a small dog cowering among the wreckage. Enticing the poor creature to him, he named her "La Déroute," and wanted no other booty. "You, Sire," he cried to the dazed Spanish King, "have vanquished your enemies, and I have vanquished mine!" Night was coming on, and Philip complained that in the speed of the advance his bed had been left behind. "Your majesty," Vendôme assured him, "shall have the most splendid couch that ever a king has lain upon," and under some tree that had survived the day, he piled captured standards as a royal mattress.

For Alberoni, the victories were the justification of all his work and hopes. "H.H. is crowned with glory," he cried; "his courage, his resolution, his actions have put the crown back on the head of Philip V; and what is most surprising, at a moment when everything was lacking, and everyone plunged into utter despair." With what satisfaction did he recount how old King Louis, when he heard the news, had cried, "See what comes of having one extra man in Spain — when the man is Vendôme!" Even the Bourgognes had the grace to send a word of congratulation. Vendôme was once more the hero of France, however much Saint-Simon might strain his ingenuity to prove that nobody in the know gave him credit for the success.

In England, the unhappy Whigs were flung into consternation. Power was slipping hourly from their baffled hands, now into the bargain they had lost the dearest object of their war. By repeating their own catchphrases they had hypnotized themselves into the belief that confirmation of Philip V upon the throne of Spain meant the closing of the New World to English enterprise, and the ultimate ruin of our country. They saw the Mediterranean shut to our vessels, the Levantine silk trade, and the valuable Portuguese market lost to us, only the French enjoying access to Eldorado. The Whig pamphleteers in their clamour for a new Spanish expedition outdid each other in making the public flesh creep.[10] "How wretched," wrote one, "will be the condition of those gay ladies who sparkle every afternoon in the Ring, or blaze every night in the Boxes? How will those soft hands be made to work? How will those complections agree with Morning air? And yet Hunger will not let them sleep. . . . And lastly, what will become of the Race of the finest fox-hunters in the world? They may even feed their dogs with their horses; and when they have done, they may hang up all their dogs. It will be no time for Sport and Diversions, when they shall be entertained everywhere with Scenes of Horror; when they shall be no where able to turn their eyes, without seeing the Ruin and Desolation of their Country, and yet shall be no where able to see more miserable Creatures than themselves."

The Tories on the other hand found the discomfiture of the Allied cause in Spain highly convenient. For them the Habsburgs and the Germanic body were infinitely more hateful than France and the Bourbons. A few weeks before Brihuega they had secretly resumed the negotiations broken off at Gertruydenburg; and now they decided to expend no more British strength upon the establishment of a Habsburg in Spain. If they could secure the monopoly of the Asiento (which meant in practice not only the African slave traffic, but the whole carrying trade to the Spanish American world), then they would acquiesce in the establishment of a Bourbon line in Spain. To this inclination strength was added by the death just after Easter 1711 of the Habsburg Emperor Joseph; his brother, the heavy Archduke Charles, succeeded.

But to persist in supporting the new Emperor in his claim to the Spanish throne would be to work for the restoration of Charles V's terrifying hegemony in Europe; and though Stanhope in his captivity might assure Alberoni that the Grand Alliance would continue, it was in fact already dead.

[10] *A Project for humbling Spain,* London, 1710.

There was a State entry into Madrid; despite the scarf that hid the marks of the King's Evil on her poor neck little Queen Maria Louisa was likened to Venus by the newspapers, and her long-faced King invoked now as Adonis, now as Mars.[11] There was such a glitter of plate, it seemed, said the account, as if the Indies mines had been bled dry; the Royal Palace "usurped the jurisdiction of the day. . . ."

At the end of January 1711 there was a similar ceremony at Saragossa. To Alberoni fell the honour of conducting the Spanish sovereigns into their Aragonese capital. The Queen was particularly gracious. "Well, Abbé Alberoni," she cried on seeing him, "we meet in very different circumstances from those of Valladolid. This magnificent and astounding change we owe to God and to the Duc de Vendôme."

The virtual quartermaster of the army, Alberoni was already treated by her as one of her ministers; from the first she seems to have used every device to bind him to the Spanish interest; a pension upon the revenues of Toledo archbishopric was followed a few months later by honorary Spanish naturalization. Alberoni answered these favours by a warm championing of everything Spanish; it was his pride to equip the army largely from Spanish resources: Spain, he reported, was a country of great possibilities; there was no need for dependence upon those rogues of French army contractors.

Te Deums were silenced, and preparations for further vic-

[11] "Llegaron Sus Majestades al Real Convento de Atocha, entre dos y tres de la tarde. . . . Cantòse en la Real Capilla de N.S. de Atocha el 'Te Deum' y la 'Salve'. . . . Venia el Rey muestro señor montado en un arrogante cavallo, arrimado al estrivo derecho del coche, siendo entonces el mas bello Adonis de la mas hermosa Venus, el que en la campaña sabe ser el mas valiente Marte. . . . Lo suntuoso y adornado de las calles retrataba en su hermosa variedad à la belleza de los jardines de chipre. Su riqueza era tanta, y tan mucha la plata de que se viò adornada la Plateria, que parecia averse desangrado las minas de entrambas Indias.

"Con esta pompa, cortejo, lucimiento y acclamaciones entraron Sus Majestades à la nochezer en su Real Palacio, el qual estaba tan lleno de luzes, que parecia se avia usurpado la jurisdicion al Dia."

tories disturbed by a sudden illness of the young Queen. At Valladolid the swollen glands in her neck pained her so sorely, there had been talk of a cure at Bagnères in the Pyrenees, to be followed by a visit to her sister, Madame de Bourgogne, at Marly. But the glands had subsided, the plan was forgotten in the delirium of victory; now the trouble revived, more virulently than ever.

A dozen doctors worked untiringly upon her tired person; her pretty hair was cut away, fresh pigeon's blood applied to the scalp. Nothing seemed to avail, and the King was in despair. Suddenly, miraculously she recovered. One morning, April 8th, 1711, Alberoni was writing nervously, "For the last few days the Queen has suffered from a light fever. . . . God keep her, for she would be an irreparable loss. . . . She is an adorable Queen, adorable because of her ways, her conduct, her wisdom, and her spirit." Then, that same day at noon he unexpectedly reported in a joyful postscript: "Thank God, the Queen has no more fever." Though it returned momentarily a few weeks later, she was dancing at a court ball before the summer was out.

Saragossa was a nursery of great hopes that winter: all Spain should be brought back into allegiance by the summer; Alberoni and his hero would then descend upon Naples, and begin the liberation of Italy from the detestable German yoke. At last the two friends would return triumphant to Versailles: the old King must die soon, and the Dauphin would reign, with his admired Vendôme as first Minister, and his abbé beside him.

Alas! All these prospects were confounded by jealousies and death. The mood of national exaltation and unity soon passed: action was paralyzed by Noailles's hatred of Vendôme, by fear that Vendôme might become a military dictator, by Madame des Ursins's general mistrust of everyone, and by the sudden death of the Dauphin at Easter 1711.

94

In immortal pages Saint-Simon has described how the un-happy prince caught smallpox from a funeral, how the Bur-gundy faction, and the diarist himself with them, exulted. Then the patient rallied, there was a moment of consternation, except for the fishwives of the Halles, who came in hired carriages from Paris to fling themselves, transported with happiness, at the foot of the sickbed — for they adored this heavy nonentity. Suddenly a relapse set in, there was time only for a mumbled confession to a village priest; as the poor prince lay dying, court and incompetent doctors lost their heads, fled howling from the château, leaving the swelling corpse alone with Made-moiselle Chouin and her honest tears. . . . When the news reached Saragossa, "H.H. is penetrated with grief," wrote Al-beroni; "it's a terrible loss for him." Indeed it was; there was little more hope of an ultimate triumph in France. From this moment Alberoni's whole ambitions returned to his Mediter-ranean.

If the idea of an immediate descent upon Italy was opposed by the old King at Versailles, the Austrians must at least be driven from Barcelona. The new Emperor Charles left Spain early in September 1711 to make certain of his election in Ger-many. He showered upon the luckless Catalans promises of an early return. But the Habsburg game was up in Spain. Even now, the brilliant St. John, in the name of the Tories, was negotiating with the French, on the basis of Philip V keeping his throne; and before many years were out, a British fleet would be co-operating with his forces to subdue our former allies in Barcelona.

Some foreboding of their plight now inspired the Catalans to a fierce resistance, which not even Vendôme was able to overcome. Harassed by irregulars and lack of munitions, he was able to effect little before he was obliged to disperse his army into winter quarters.

The peace conference at Utrecht was about to open, and a

new French envoy, the Marquis de Bonac, arrived in Madrid to discuss the disposal of the Spanish Netherlands (now Belgium). They might go to the Emperor, or perhaps to that needy adventurer, the Bavarian Elector. In any event they would not remain Spanish. But the Spanish sovereigns insisted upon retaining a small piece of Belgian soil; for the sake of it they were prepared to wreck the conference. The truth was, Madame des Ursins, not content with the title of Highness lately given her, had set her heart upon acquiring the very substance of royalty; and had selected for her future dominion the pleasant little town of Laroche, in Belgian Luxembourg. When she had secured it, her intention was to exchange it with Louis XIV against a principality to be erected for her lifetime out of a strip of territory on the Loire. Thus would her royal ambitions be gratified, and the frontiers of France advanced. Never doubting the certainty of the old King's approval, she bought the property of Chanteloup, near Amboise, in the name of her reputed lover, d'Aubigny, and began to build there a princely seat. . . .

In the diary of his visit to Madrid, Bonac has left a picture of the Spanish monarchs, which is not without a gentle charm. He passed afternoons with the Queen and the little Prince of the Asturias, who would go through his military drill for the Ambassador and finish up with a fine minuet. Then the King would come in from shooting with a pack of dogs round his heels and a very melancholy face. The maggot he had got in Naples was eating deep; cares had dulled almost every impulse in him save his passion for the chase and for his exhausted young wife.

Vendôme and Alberoni were back in Madrid at the beginning of 1712, to concert plans for a new campaign. Alberoni was constantly in the sovereign's company, discussing the prospects of peace and the Queen's new pregnancy, cooking Lombardian dishes that recalled her tranquil childhood. But every-

LOUIS XV AS A BOY

PHILIP V OF SPAIN AS A YOUNG MAN

ARANJUEZ GARDENS

THE MANZANARES VALLEY OUTSIDE MADRID

thing seemed to conspire against a return to arms; there was no money; quarrels between Vendôme and Madame des Ursins paralyzed decision; in Utrecht at the peace conference Philip's exchanging Spain with his father-in-law, the Duke of Savoy, had been seriously mooted. Worst of all, Vendôme's gout flared up, attacking a hand.

Then suddenly during a few fateful days of March there occurred in France a series of events which were profoundly to affect Alberoni's subsequent career. The Bourgognes and their elder son, the little Duc de Bretagne, fell ill and died within a month of each other; the heir to France was now their second child, the Duc d'Anjou; it was said that he had only survived by being rescued from his doctors; and it was not imagined that this sickly baby would ever live to become Louis XV. Meanwhile the luckless Orléans was of course accused of these deaths that had brought him sensibly nearer to the throne.

In Spain money for the next campaign suddenly came to hand. Led by the French admiral Du Casse, the Spanish treasure fleet contrived to dodge the English cruisers, to ride through tempests off Martinique and the Canaries, and to bring into Corunna a very handsome sum. "Never was help more timely," cried the exultant Vendôme. Du Casse was given the Golden Fleece, an award that stung the little Saint-Simon into a wild indignation against "this son of a Bayonne pork-butcher." There was much to try Saint-Simon's temper these days, for Vendôme before he went off to resume the war was raised by the Spanish King to the rank of a prince of the blood. "The prince," wrote Alberoni to Parma, "may well become the chief personage of Europe. May God keep him for the good of our two monarchies, of which he is nowadays regarded as the sole support."

At the beginning of April the two friends set out from Madrid for eastern Spain. The Spaniards greeted Vendôme with raptures; the journey was more a royal progress than the return of a distinguished general to his campaign. "His Highness," Alberoni reported from near Valencia, "arrived here last Thursday. He was received like a Messiah. For three days on end there were fireworks and illuminations throughout the town. He has the gift of softening by his mere presence the most barbarous peoples and men of the evilest intention. No king was ever received with more acclamation."

Lack of equipment perforce retarded the opening of the campaign for several more weeks. "Making war in Spain," wrote Alberoni, "is a devil of a business." But they took advantage of these maddening delays to snatch a short holiday, first at Grao on the coast outside Valencia, then at Viñaros, a fishing village not far from the army's headquarters, and renowned for its excellent fish. The weather was superb — "the most beautiful sky I ever saw, where there is neither summer nor winter but an unending spring. For a month past they have been eating here strawberries of great delicacy, and exquisite green peas. If I had to choose a place to live in, it would be here."

Death instead of a wind came suddenly to ruffle those peerless days. The gout which in Madrid had wracked one of Vendôme's hands returned without warning and attacked his stomach; within a fortnight, under the eyes of a distraught and powerless Alberoni, the great man was dying.

"You'll be very surprised," Alberoni wrote to Parma on June 10th, "to learn of the Duc de Vendôme's death, without having received any news of his illness. So do men end; my tears prevent my telling you any more about it." He was prostrated by the calamity. There had been reverses and disappointments before, and he had always mastered them. But this last blow was more than one could survive, surely; to lose at a stroke protector, gay companion, the great captain who was to scourge the Germans out of Italy and institute a new age of freedom there.

"So end the great conceits of great men, as well as of small fry," he wrote, when the first transport of grief had subsided. "I've often told you that I had few illusions left about the world; this final catastrophe has removed the last of them. I am off to Madrid to cast myself at the feet of their Majesties. It will be a very painful occasion for me. God help me, that I don't fall ill."

But at Valencia his despair brought back an old fever; when he recovered, the discomforts of the journey in the swimming heat were unbearable. Madame des Ursins, however, prayed him to hurry, and he arrived at last in Madrid, exhausted and still feverish. The King and Queen, he found, were almost as inconsolable as he. They had decided that Vendôme for his services to Spain should be buried in the royal sepulchre at the Escorial. The dead prince's devoted servants had, however, already despatched the body to France, and Alberoni was consequently obliged to send couriers far and wide to recall it.

Of Vendôme's death Saint-Simon naturally has his own version. According to him, the monster had shamefully neglected the campaign, had retired to Viñaros, and lost himself there in abominable orgies; his death had been precipitated by these excesses, and his corpse had been robbed and abandoned by his servants. All Spain and France had rejoiced at the disappearance of the incompetent brute. Voltaire, on the other hand, an infinitely more trustworthy authority than Saint-Simon, wrote of the event: "the mood of discouragement widespread in France, and which I remember having witnessed, gave grounds for fearing that Spain, which he had preserved, would now be lost again through the death of the Duc de Vendôme." [12]

Alberoni's first thought apparently was to return to Parma; his Farnese masters decreed otherwise; they ordered him to stay in Madrid as an agent of somewhat vague denomination. Their accredited representative, Marquis Casali, had no great

[12] *Siècle de Louis XIV*.

love or ability for his office; and they must consequently have welcomed the assistance of somebody so well placed as Alberoni at the Spanish court. With truth did he write to his friends in Parma that no stranger had ever enjoyed more favour there than he. "This proud and arrogant sky I have found extremely courteous and kind towards me; though of course," he added as an afterthought, "the mere idea of dying in Madrid terrifies me." It was true enough, his boast. He was now bereft of his powerful patron, and penniless (for Parma was being as stingy as usual); yet this "vulgar buffoon of no merit," whom Saint-Simon castigates, enjoyed, at this coldest moment of his fortunes, the favour of the peerless young Queen, the friendship and assistance of such eminent grandees as the Dukes of Medina-Sidonia and Popoli, the Marquis of Mejorada, the powerful Cardinal del Giudice. The amiable Casali lodged him in the Parmesan mission, though half a dozen great gentlemen were proud to offer him rooms in their palaces. Somehow he scraped together enough money to buy himself a carriage and a pair of mules, so that he might not cut too despicable a figure.

Despite the protests of Germans and Dutch, the Tory Ministry in England had now concluded a settlement with France, and imposed it upon the Allies. During the last campaign in Flanders the English army, under the luckless Duke of Ormond, who had replaced Marlborough, acted in concert with the French rather than the Allies. It is lamentable that a peace so universally desired should have been attended with such shabbiness; but no qualms seem to have troubled the gaieties that attended the visit to Paris in July of Henry St. John,[13] to settle the final details of the treaty. The Secretary of State, recently raised to the peerage as Viscount Bolingbroke, was at the very height of his trajectory; no prescience of squandered promise, the unhappy future of half-hearted conspiracy and

[13] (1678–1751): one of the most brilliant intellects of the age.

exile, infected this fascinating young man, who charmed Paris with his looks, his wit, his diverting presents of Barbados Waters, and other outlandish liqueurs. Bolingbroke was no less seduced by France. For all his faults, he was the pattern of intelligent and voluptuous Englishman, exquisitely sensitive to the perfume of roasting coffee as it floats down some obscure Paris street, the rustle of a delicate dress, talk as light and finished as the Paris shoes or carriages. The French outdid themselves in his honour; his progress from the coast was of regal glory; at the play when he attended a performance of Corneille's *Cid*, the audience stood up to salute him; in Fontainebleau Park, the old King, who had lately taken to mumbling at prodigious speed, treated him to a harangue as flattering as it was unintelligible.

He encountered, one radiant day in Paris, a shabby, half-remembered figure — James Stanhope, whose release from his Spanish captivity the Tory administration had at last seen fit to secure. Bolingbroke offered to present him to the King, but the implacable Whig recoiled from the honour. He was induced, however, to come to a splendid party given by Noailles, against whom he had campaigned in Spain; and from afar to observe old Louis follow the royal hunt in his chaise, "with a bright retinue of ladies of the first quality, like Amazons on horseback." As Stanhope was guided in his worn coat through some glittering company, how could the petted St. John guess that this swarthy moth would soon rule at Whitehall in his place? Nor, when he found all the enchantment of France in the lustrous eyes of a runaway nun,[14] did he dream that one day, among the scented groves of La Source, he would yearn

[14] Madame de Tencin, later to be for a moment mistress of the Regent, and mother of the mathematician d'Alembert. Her liaison with Bolingbroke soon after she had thrown off the veil inspired the following lines:

"Bolingbroke, es-tu possédé?
Quel est ton désir chimérique
De t'amuser à chevaucher
La fille de St Dominique?"

for the stench of stale beer, strong tobacco and fog, the chatter of Whig and Tory.

His pleasures did not divert St. John from the business of his visit; he could pass from the debauch to the council table with intellect unimpaired, and there outwit the subtle French diplomats. During those halcyon days in France, he forced through his favourite scheme for eliminating the possibility of France and Spain uniting under one monarch, a danger that had lately been revived by the deaths in the French royal family. Philip V of Spain was now next in succession to the French throne after the sickly little Duc d'Anjou (the future Louis XV); and St. John insisted that he should give up all rights in France, if he would keep his present crown; Berry and Orléans must similarly renounce all claims to Spain.

One day in November 1712, before the assembled Parliament and a special British envoy, the Duke of Shrewsbury, Orléans and Berry acted as we required.[15] It was a solemn occasion, which did not fail suitably to impress young Berry. As he drove to the ceremony, however, his mood was some-

[15] The Duchess of Shrewsbury, the British Ambassadress, was able to affect a revolution in fashions such as had been beyond the power of Louis XIV. Until her arrival in Paris it was the fashion for ladies to wear their hair piled up in a sort of sugar-loaf some two feet high, that trembled and threatened to collapse with every movement of the head. The Duchess may have been a noisy ill-dressed Italian, but she brought to France the new English fashion of hair worn close to the head, the style of coiffure we associate with the pictures of Watteau and J. B. de Troy. "J'avoue," commented Louis XIV, "que je suis piqué quand je vois qu'avec toute mon autorité de roi en ce pays-ci, j'ai eu beau crier contre ses coiffures trop hautes, pas une personne n'a eu la moindre envie d'avoir la complaisance pour moi de les baisser. On voit arriver une inconnue, une guenille d'Angleterre avec une petite coiffure basse: tout d'un coup toutes les princesses vont d'une extrémité à l'autre." (Correspondence of "Madame," Duchesse d'Orléans.)

The new mode persisted until the reign of Louis XVI. In the middle of the eighteenth century Saint-Simon declared "reasonable men wait with impatience for some other mad foreign woman to liberate our ladies from those immense hoops and panniers which are unbearable both to themselves and to other people."

what spoiled by the levity of Orléans, who would chatter of kind beauties, and how in his youth he had climbed out of his father's palace to attend some orgy. But Orléans had little sense of fitness. . . .

Similarly, before the Cortes Philip V was to renounce his French rights. The British envoy for the Madrid ceremony, Lord Lexington, arrived in mid-October, in a very truculent temper, not brooking any nonsense. Philip resolved to break with Spanish etiquette, and receive him with the royal guards in full strength, halberdiers lining the steps, and a roll of drums for the envoy as he passed, as if he were a king. This unprecedented honour provoked angry words in the Despacho; yet Philip persisted in his intention. For all these attentions Lexington boggled at recognizing Philip as King of Spain; to do so, he declared, would exceed his instructions. Bolingbroke was in despair; this wretched point of etiquette, which should have been settled long since, now threatened to ruin the whole peace. "For God's sake, dear Matt," he enjoined Prior in Paris, "hide the Nakedness of thy country, and give the best turn thy fertile brain will furnish thee with to the Blunders of thy countrymen, who are not much better Politicians than the French are Poets."

Nevertheless, the eccentricities of Lexington's character remained to endanger good intelligence. Though in his youth he might have drunk confusion to King William, now, when he saw an Irish Jacobite representative of the Pretender about the court, his grenadier face would turn black, and the veins on his great neck almost burst from their fleshy anchorage, till the fascinated Spanish feared a calamity. Nor would Lexington stomach any contradiction; one word of disagreement, even on the weather, and he would be carried off by such a dark rage as seemed to portend murder.

But a few weeks in Madrid, and the monster was strangely tamed; he took a fine house, negotiated with Madame des Ursins a commercial treaty that by its favour to Spain was to put the House of Commons into a tumult; at his copious table, a garland of toasts seemed to unite the futures of England, France and Spain.

It is not unlikely that Alberoni was responsible for this transformation. His crony, the Duke of Popoli, had appointed him to Lexington's side for the visit. Recommended by Stanhope, he quickly captured the friendship of the new envoy, and was with him at all his feasts. If the abbé fell ill, Lexington would spend half the day by his bedside, talking of the coming peace, and Anglo-Spanish collaboration.

Peace was near at hand now. It was not a settlement much to Alberoni's taste, but at least its imminence brought about a withdrawal of the odious Germans from the Parmesan. "C'est par la vôtre du 23me du passé," wrote the exultant abbé to Parma, "que j'apprends que les Prussiens s'en vont à tous les diables. Dieu fasse qu'il arrive le temps que toute cette maudite race puisse s'en aller dans leur maudit pays."

In April 1713, the abbé's talents were officially recognized by the Duke of Parma. He appointed him Parmesan representative in place of the unhappy Casali. The promotion excited criticism both at Parma and Madrid; it was unprecedented for a post of such importance to be given to a person of obscure birth; the secretary of the departing minister declared that he could not serve a plebeian. The difficulty Alberoni did not entirely overcome by appointing the stubborn creature secretary of the Legation, not of the minister.

The reasons that prompted the Farnesi to give talent its due are still far from clear. It is possible that they already dreamed of placing a princess of their line on the Spanish throne, and considered that Alberoni through his intimacy with Philip V could serve their designs better than some unknown Parmesan noble. The health of poor Maria Louisa was already turning thoughts towards the possibility of a successor for her. The delivery of the Infant Don Ferdinand in the previous year had pulled her vastly down, but she was allowed no escape from her consort's insatiable embraces. Her courage could not master these pregnancies that succeeded one another with but the merest respite; as the summer of 1713 wore on, she found it increasingly painful to rise from her bed; nor could she stand for long. As her charming young face grew pinched, and dwarfed by her swollen glands, the melancholy of the King rose in a proportionate measure; but he never passed a night out of her bed.

Not only his Queen's health worried Philip; agonies of doubt for long racked him, when it came to ratifying the peace. He was closeted for hours with his confessor, enquiring of his conscience whether he could consent to England's retaining Gibraltar and Minorca; he kept the statesmen of Europe fuming, because for long he would sign nothing till Madame des Ursins's princely ambitions were satisfied. At last, however, he was obliged to give way and she, out of shame, left the sober d'Aubigny to cut what figure he could in the vast and splendid palace of Chanteloup that she was never to inhabit.[16]

Alberoni welcomed the peace with a divided heart. For it had given Naples and many places in North Italy to the Emperor. Such a peace, Alberoni declared, could not last; more and more his thoughts turned to the liberation of his country from the German yoke. "The kings of the Romans," wrote the Angevin Robert of Naples long before, "have been wont to be chosen from the German people, which holds rather to the savagery of barbarians than to the faith of Christ . . . since then they have nought in common with the Italians, we must

[16] Chanteloup half a century later knew fame as the seat of the Duc de Choiseul, Louis XIV's great minister. He built the great pagoda there, a more elegant affair than Sir William Chambers's similar construction at Kew.

Choiseul's pagoda still soared above the lovely grounds of Chanteloup in the spring of 1940.

needs watch that their German savagery does not turn the sweetness of Italy into bitterness."

For the moment, however, there was no course open but to wait, and gain in the meantime, by judicious presents, the favour of the great. For the Duchess of Havré of the great house of Cröy, whose husband led the Belgian faction at court, Alberoni obtained Mantua flowers and Venice masks. For Madame des Ursins sausages and cases of Parmesan wine; indeed nowadays she drank no other. The old Duke of Giovinazzo reminded Alberoni that in bygone times the members of the State Council were always given presents of various Italian delicacies. In a town like Madrid, where butter arrived half rancid in sausage skins, and fish was rarely seen, Alberoni's Italian dishes were a godsend; when the Queen tasted some of his macaroni which he sent one day to Madame des Ursins, she talked of it warmly for three days after, although it had been impossible to find in Madrid cheese of the proper fineness.

The autumn brought little but worries; Alberoni, his secretary, and most of his servants fell ill, so that the Legation was like a hospital; a consignment of sausages packed next to some Carnival dresses that the abbé had ordered in Venice for the palace ladies, was reported to have turned bad; if the dresses were involved in the catastrophe there would be consternation at court.

The Queen's health waxed and waned. Just before Christmas, she appeared at a party given by Princess des Ursins, and played games as if there were nothing amiss with her; soon after, however, there was a relapse, and she repaired to the villa of the Duke of Medina-Celi, in the country, and could take nothing but human milk. The new French Ambassador, Brancas, when she received him, was, however, astonished by her gaiety and sparkling appearance. Alas! her gaiety was the mere fruit of courage, her colour the work of rouge. By the middle of January 1714, her case was desperate; Helvetius, the most eminent doctor of his day, dashed down from Paris in an attempt to save her.[17] But it was too late. On February 14th she met her death with composure and piety, amid the lamentations of her subjects. An autopsy revealed a highly ulcerous condition of the entrails and lungs, together with stone. The King was for a time distracted; the death did not however long interrupt his sports. He was shooting the day of his Queen's funeral; for a time he watched the sombre procession wend its way toward the Escorial; then he turned his pale attention back to the chase. "Ces princes," commented Saint-Simon, "sont-ils faits comme les humains?"

[17] He seems to have taken on the case with great reluctance, believing it hopeless, and injurious therefore to his reputation. But Louis XIV insisted.

❊ VI ❊

THE COUP D'ÉTAT

Although Madame des Ursins's office at court ended theoretically with the Queen's death, she had taken all dispositions to preserve her power. In January 1714, a month before the end, she packed the Despacho with her partisans; and now she kept the widowed King in rural seclusion, picking for his only companions — the King's "recreadores," they came to be called — a few gentlemen devoted to her interest. At the same time, as governess to the young Infants, she contrived always to be at Philip's side, even playing chess with him a few hours after Maria Louisa's death. At the Medina-Celi Palace her own apartments were linked with Philip's by a wooden corridor, hastily erected on a Sunday, to the scandal of the public.

These doings excited curiosity in Madrid and Paris. That the King must quickly remarry was an open secret; only with difficulty had he been induced to leave his poor consort's bed on the last night of her life; a few weeks of widowhood, and his continence had excited violent headaches and sweatings, even causing fears for his sanity. Nor could the simple remedy of a mistress be invoked; Philip's conscience was still as strong as his lusts; an attempt of the Duc de Noailles and the Marquis d'Aguilar two years before to lure him into other arms than the Queen's had led to nothing more than a snub; Philip remained a man who could not do without a woman in his bed, but who would allow into it no woman that was not his wife.

In these circumstances, the imperious, secretive conduct of Madame des Ursins gave rise to reports that she designed to marry the King herself. Though she might be over seventy, and the King but thirty-two, yet so shrewd an observer as Père Robinet, Philip's Jesuit confessor, took these rumours seriously enough to tax him with them. . . .

They seem to have possessed little substance. The day following Maria Louisa's death, the King instructed Madame des Ursins to pass in review such princesses as might be worthy of filling the empty place in his bed; and it is probable that the camerera mayor then resolved, as the wise course, to find a pliant girl for him, whom she herself would control.

The event did not find Alberoni unprepared. There was a princess of Parma, Elisabeth Farnese, niece and stepdaughter to the Duke, who had married her mother, the widow of his elder brother. This Elisabeth was twenty-two, a very suitable age, and Alberoni already in January had expounded his plan to the Duke. The abbé moved without crudity or hurry; those qualities he left to the Bavarian Minister, who before Maria Louisa had grown cold was buzzing about Madame des Ursins with particulars of the Elector's daughter: or to the Savoyard representative, who plagued the King's doctor with assurances that if one princess from Turin had been worn out by the King, there was always a couple more, either of whom could be shipped to Spain at very short notice.

Such methods, it was obvious, could lead nowhere; undue eagerness would only irritate Madame des Ursins; she must be made to feel that she herself had thought of Elisabeth Farnese, without any outside prompting. So the abbé bided his time. But one day he and the camerera mayor found themselves watching Maria Louisa's funeral from the same palace window. The talk turned to the need for the King to remarry, and Madame des Ursins mentioned various young princesses. In every one of them Alberoni was able to find some fault. There was the Portuguese girl; too self-willed; Mademoiselle de Clermont, the Duc de Bourbon's sister; that meant a revival of

French influence in Spain. No; it was essential that Philip's new consort be endowed with a docile quiet temper, so that there could be no risk of her meddling in affairs of State, or, Alberoni hinted, of challenging the venerable authority of Madame des Ursins. His views were warmly applauded; but where was such a paragon to be found? Had he any ideas?

He paused, then casually let slip the name of Elisabeth Farnese: a good Lombard girl, he said, stuffed with butter and Parmesan cheese, brought up in the depths of the country, where she had heard of nothing save sewing, lace-making and the like. A girl as docile as you could wish: a girl who would not dare form her conduct except on the advice of an experienced person — of Madame des Ursins in short.

That was enough for the moment. During the next week or so he found opportunities to slip the idea of a Parmesan marriage into the heads of the King's immediate entourage — the Marquis de Mejorada, the Princess of Santo Buono, the confessor, Père Robinet. All three of them Alberoni had won by delicious Lombardian soups, and unforgettable risotti.

In Holy Week Madame des Ursins herself returned to the charge. Was Alberoni among those, she asked him, who wished to find a wife for the King? He protested he would never be guilty of such folly, and the Princess seemed pleased. She again began to run through the list of marriageable girls. They lingered on the name of the Bavarian princess; she was the principal danger to the abbé's cause; at least so he suspected; he did not like the way the Bavarian envoy, "a most solemn Tyrolese and as sly as the devil," hung about Madame des Ursins.

But she assured Alberoni that she could stomach neither the man, nor his employers; and hinted that the dashing of her hopes for a principality in the Low Countries must be somewhat attributed to the Bavarian Elector. What cause then had she to like his daughter, who in any case was vilely ugly? Not only that, added Alberoni, but so deformed as to provoke doubts for her fertility. . . . There was a pause. Then Madame des Ursins asked for a portrait of Elisabeth Farnese; she was delighted to learn the following day that it had already been ordered.

At this point the abbé's designs were favoured by fortune. A squabble developed between Brancas, the French Ambassador, and the Cardinal del Giudice, the Grand Inquisitor, who on the recommendation of Louis XIV had recently been appointed Prime Minister of Spain; the two of them went off to Versailles to pursue their feud in front of the old King. Alberoni was thus left alone with Philip, Madame des Ursins, and the handful of grandees at the isolated court, almost all of them his close friends.

The King moved in the last week of May to the austere seclusion of the Pardo Palace, a few leagues to the north-west of Madrid. Almost alone of the foreign envoys, Alberoni was in constant attendance, on the best of terms with everybody, sharing in Philip's pleasure when the little Prince of the Asturias shot his first rabbit, or wore his first proud pair of breeches. The abbé was however plagued by the Parmesan administration, who chose this of all critical moments to criticize the rate of his expenditure; still worse, the portraits of Elisabeth Farnese took an age to arrive; while the sausages, the cheeses, the wine, the hundred other Italian kickshaws that were half his armoury, suddenly ran low, or reached Madrid in a rancid or battered state. Notwithstanding, Philip V one day was graciously pleased to compliment Alberoni upon his table. The King was developing a certain affection for the Parmesan abbé. When the minor Italian states were forced tremblingly to recognize the Emperor's pretensions to the Spanish throne, all their missions were expelled from Madrid, with the exception of the Parmesan, which was preserved solely through the favour that Alberoni enjoyed. For this service the Duke of Parma rewarded him with the title of count.

In their political views, Philip V and Alberoni found themselves at one. The final peace settlement, that robbed the Spanish Crown of its entire Italian possessions and established the Emperor in Naples, and Victor-Amadeus in Sicily with the title of King, offended Philip in his honour, and Alberoni in his precocious nationalism; both men now began to dream more definitely than ever before of using the powers of Spain to expel from Italy the odious Germans. It must be realized that Spain's long association with Italy gave her in Italian affairs a position far less exotic than that of Savoy, a state that was at that time regarded as half French; and since neither Venice, eternally vexed by the Turks, nor priest-ridden Tuscany, nor the supine Papacy could give life to Italian aspirations, upon the Spanish monarchy now devolved the longings of many thoughtful Italians.

Hopes of liberation ran high in their hearts and in Alberoni's that summer, for England herself appeared to be turning against the Emperor. The supine and avaricious behaviour of the Empire in the late war had for a moment cured Englishmen of their disastrous passion for Vienna; and Bolingbroke was negotiating for an alliance of Great Britain, France, Spain and Savoy against the Germanic body. But Alberoni did not realize that Bolingbroke saw at least a century farther than did the rest of England. When in August Queen Anne died, and the Tories were ruined by their inept flirtations with the Jacobite cause, the triumphant Whigs, for want of any better, were to return, as we shall see, to a pro-Austrian policy, with consequences that plague us to this day.

But all that was lost in the future. Alberoni's subtle eloquence was meanwhile having its effect. The gravity of the King's vapours waxed daily; the question of his remarriage would no longer brook delay. In a series of urgent conversations with the Parmesan envoy, Madame des Ursins at last let herself be persuaded of Elisabeth's docility: [1] and on June 10th chose her for future Queen of Spain. Louis XIV was scarcely enamoured of the marriage; he would have preferred a Portuguese princess for his grandson; still, Elisabeth was heiress to Parma, and could lay a good claim to the inheritance of the sterile Medicis; the French King gave his consent, therefore, with no particular ill grace.

Soon after the betrothal, Madame des Ursins hatched doubts upon the perfect submission that she could expect from the new Queen; and she is credited, apocryphally perhaps, with endeavours at the eleventh hour to stop the marriage. For a moment she certainly nursed designs of retiring from the Spanish court, but she was dissuaded by urgent injunctions from Versailles, where she was once more in favour. At the same time Count Albergotti, Louis's representative at the marriage by proxy that took place at Parma in September, was instructed to urge upon the young Princess complete obedience to Madame des Ursins, whom she should regard as her benefactress and sole mentor. Albergotti professed himself enchanted with Elisabeth, who listened with flattering attention to his message. The marriage was celebrated in Parma Cathedral beneath Correggio's "Hash of Frogs," on September 16, 1714; fireworks, fantastic fountains, masques and all the paraphernalia proper to the occasion enriched the handsome streets of Parma; the Pope sent the usual golden rose.

[1] According to a largely apocryphal account in B.M. Addit 28, 787, Alberoni encouraged Madame des Ursins to think that Elisabeth Farnese could hardly write, and was compelled to dictate everything. The Princess was delighted, believing that this would limit Elisabeth's powers of interference in State affairs. He also caused a particularly ugly portrait of Elisabeth to be painted on one of his snuff-boxes; when Madame des Ursins saw it, she was convinced that the girl would never obtain a dangerous hold upon the King's affections. She instructed Alberoni against his will to substitute for it a portrait much more flattering to catch the King's fancy, overcoming Alberoni's feigned scruples with the promise of a bishopric.

These were trying days for Alberoni; all the preparations for the new Queen's arrival were on his shoulders; then there was Madame des Ursins to be kept in a smooth humour; and constant attendance demanded of him by the impatient King. Alberoni had recently been accorded the fatiguing honour of entry into the royal presence, even at times of purgings. When the jealous Madame des Ursins was out of earshot, Philip would ply him all day with questions about Elisabeth. The abbé had not of course seen her for eleven years, but he was able to answer that if her complexion had been somewhat marred by a savage attack of smallpox the previous summer, she yet possessed the finest shape imaginable. The King was almost distraught with pleasure and anticipation. Even when a portrait arrived with the face damaged by the heavy-fingered customs, Philip continued to profess delight, and clamour for the early arrival of his bride.

She was to come by galley from Sestri Levante; a feverish and exhausted Alberoni hurried to meet her at Alicante. Not till the end of a tiresome journey did he learn that sea-sickness had driven her into Genoa; she had then resolved to continue by land.

As he returned to Madrid along the new road which had been specially built for Elisabeth's coming, Alberoni appears to have made one of the great decisions of his career. The history of his relations with Madame des Ursins is an obscure one. In his time, he had, it will be remembered, helped to keep the peace between her and Vendôme. Since that day he had spared no effort, no gift of Italian delicacies, none of his skill in the kitchen, to please her. She in turn had manifested every sign of friendship.

Yet amid all these civilities, he was moving toward open war with her. During her first years in Spain, she had infused some life into the decrepit administration. But now she was grown old, deaf to new ideas, no longer capable of adapting

French principles of centralization to the regional eccentricities of Spain. In fact she had come to impede the efficient administration of the country. The reduction of the last Carlist stronghold of Barcelona, an operation then in progress, had revealed serious weaknesses in the Spanish army which could not, Alberoni believed, be cured so long as she ruled jealously at Madrid.

The earliest reference to the design for ruining her occurs in a letter written by the abbé from Madrid on August 6th to Rocca. "I have told you," he wrote, "that I have always considered that this tremendous stroke [would be] of the very greatest advantage if we knew how to play our cards. . . . If the Heroine [2] has confidence she will not be badly served, I can assure you; but it will be necessary to conduct the whole matter with the greatest dexterity." As he told his devoted faction at court and his friends in Parma, the King needed somebody to open his eyes.

Meanwhile Elisabeth showed no impatience to match her husband's. After an agreeable round of sight-seeing in Genoa, she pursued her leisurely way along the Riviera, rising late, flirting with the handsome chaplain of her Italian suite, lingering over her formidable meals. She possessed indeed a ferocious appetite, which amazed the Prince of Monaco when she stayed with him. Although she complained of the lack of garlic in his salads, she took with gusto to his French cooking and to his champagne. Dining with the Archbishop of Arles, she ate and drank so heavily that she was sick in the garden after dinner.

When she was not at table, her time was given to music, on which she doted, and to the dark eyes of Maggiali, the chaplain. In those days of leisurely journeying, many a princess on her way to marriage turned Iseult, and dallied on the road. There was, for instance, the recent precedent of the late King of Spain's first bride, the charming daughter of Monsieur and "Minette." The parts of the officer conducting her to the

[2] i.e. Elisabeth Farnese.

Spanish frontier had caused her to delay her progress, until the affair became an international scandal. Now the flirtation with Maggiali caused Alberoni a torment of apprehension. When we consider, however, the grey incarceration that faced her in Spain, can Elisabeth be blamed for her desire to prolong this gay journey?

On November 29th, she reached Pau. Her mother's sister, Anna Maria of Neuburg, the Dowager Queen of Spain,[3] came from Bayonne to meet her. During several days the two queens gave themselves up to gaieties, for which the dowager could only pay by pawning her jewels; then with a present of a fine calèche, and a diamond necklace that she could ill afford, she sped her niece on her way.

At Pamplona on December 11th Elisabeth said farewell to Maggiali and her Parmesan suite. There were triumphal arches by the score; artillery boomed, church bells rang, torch-lit processions conducted her to the old palace. In the square before her window there were comedies played to amuse her, ballets of dancers in the guise of birds or serpents; as the winter's night came on, it was repelled by bonfires and great setpieces which seemed to fire the brittle snow.

Alberoni had left Madrid to meet her late in November, taking with him "two bottles of quinine and complete resignation as regards everything that may happen." He reached Pamplona some days before Elisabeth; and now in the swaying light of the illuminations, he flung himself at her royal feet. He was "honoured with expressions of the greatest generosity and kindness." She appears to have taken to him from the first, and given him her confidence. As her concourse crept southward across the dead and moaning plateaux, among the bull-fights and the shivering addresses of loyalty, Alberoni opened his heart to her, painted the black calamity that lay ahead if she did not act with speed and vigour.

[3] She had been banished there in 1707 for her pro-Habsburg sympathies.

Sensing danger, Madame des Ursins had already flared into hostility. The governors of the various French provinces through which the regal concourse had passed were instructed to give her an account of the petty thefts committed by Elisabeth's Italian retinue; she filled Madrid with clamours against the Princess's ugliness, commonness, her general defects. To Madame de Maintenon she expressed the darkest forebodings.[4] The slow progress of the bride's journey particularly exasperated her; she bombarded Alberoni and Elisabeth with complaints, most of which went unanswered.

In a torment of impatience, Philip waited with the little Prince of the Asturias, at Guadalajara, on the Burgos road. The furious Madame des Ursins went on to meet the Queen at Jadraque. It was Elisabeth's intention to sleep there on December 23rd, and join the King at Guadalajara on Christmas Eve.

Riding ahead of Elisabeth, Alberoni reached Jadraque early on the afternoon of the appointed day. Hardly had he entered Madame des Ursins's room than a tornado of reproaches assailed him on the slowness of the Queen's journey, her decision to meet the King at Guadalajara on the morrow; it was insensate conduct; apart from the need to be properly dressed and not to appear in ridiculous clothes on so solemn an occasion, she ought not to chase about the country after a husband, like any common girl. . . . "She said to me that the qualities of this queen were very different from what I had represented; her every action was ridiculous"; her peasant taste in food — "I'm told," screamed the Princess, "she eats nothing but garlic and hard-boiled eggs" — betrayed the frivolity of her character, and the poverty of her talent.

---

[4] Madame des Ursins to Madame de Maintenon (November 30, 1714). "Je tremble, Madame, pour Sa Majesté Catholique qu'il ne trouve pas dans sa femme une figure aimable: de quelque manière qu'elle soit, il est trop saint et trop honnête homme pour ne pas bien vivre avec elle: mais il n'en souffrira pas moins intérieurement, et ce prince n'a pas besoin d'éprouver sa vertu dans une choix qui lui fera venir des vapeurs mélancholiques. . . ."

Alberoni heard her without emotion; then he secretly instructed two officers of the Guard, friends of his, to wait outside the Queen's door, lest she might need them at any time.

Towards eight o'clock that evening Elisabeth arrived. Sweeping a curtsy to the snowy crowd, she mounted to her apartment. On the stairs she met Madame des Ursins, in full low court dress, who in her injured pride would not go all the way downstairs to meet the Queen. Ignoring the discourtesy, Elisabeth embraced her, and took her into the royal bedroom. To this day we do not know precisely what then happened. It seems, however, that the door was hardly shut before the old woman had twisted Elisabeth about, and "God, Madam," she cried, "but you're devilish badly made, and as for your clothes!" The waiting officers then heard voices raised, and the Queen suddenly shouting: "Arrest this mad woman!"

Without so much as time to change her dress, the astonished camarera mayor was bundled into a waiting coach; accompanied only by a maid and one footman, she was despatched through the freezing night, under a strong guard, toward the French frontier. As her carriage staggered through Castile, "Venite Gaudeamus" came to her on the snowflakes, out of every church door. But there was only the black sky and the skirmishing whiteness for her, a cold so intense, it took off one of the coachman's hands, and nothing but hard-boiled eggs to eat. Her jibe against the Queen had come back upon her.

The following morning when Philip heard what had happened, he was moved by his confessor to mitigate the terrible sentence. He despatched by two of her relatives a message to Madame des Ursins to stay her journey, and await further instructions. But Elisabeth came to Guadalajara on Christmas morning through the heavy snow. They were forthwith married again by the Patriarch of the Indies (in the splendid Plateresque Infantado palace that was destroyed by the Italians in 1936); then they went to bed, rising only for midnight Mass.

In those few fantastic hours, with the snow scratching and whispering like a ghost against the panes, Madame des Ursins dwindled into a person of no consequence. That evening a fresh message was sent ordering her to proceed on her way out of Spain. She arrived exhausted at St. Jean de Luz in the middle of January 1715, having uttered not a complaint nor dropped a tear throughout her terrible journey.

At Bayonne she vainly tried to secure lodgings. The Dowager Queen of Spain, mindful of old injuries, refused to see her. She was reduced to eating at a Jewish restaurant in the noisiest and most crowded part of the town. At last she found for herself a small house by the sea. To Madame de Maintenon she wrote, "I await the King's pleasure at St. Jean de Luz, in a little house on the verge of the ocean, which I see sometimes raging, at others calm. . . . So it is with courts."

Alberoni was not unnaturally exultant. "Our great Queen," he wrote to the Parmesan minister in Paris, "has been a very Judith and has effected a revolution that has already raised her on to a pinnacle. She is busy with what remains to be done and from the sensible steps which she is taking she should not have much difficulty in bringing her wishes to fruition. As far as I am concerned she tells me roundly that she is well pleased with my humble services. . . ."

Through the heavy Christmas weather, the Spanish sovereigns made their way into Madrid. The King soon threw off the habits and associations of nearly fourteen years; he would say to his Queen, "We could never be as happy as this if she were still with us." Well might Alberoni have written when Philip knew no more of Elisabeth than her portrait, "She is already the mistress of his heart. Imagine what it will be after she's been two nights between the sheets!" Those two nights had made her mistress of Spain, and through her the son of a Parmesan gardener was now master of it.

❀ VII ❀

ALBERONI GAINS SUPREME POWER
AND MAKES FRIENDS WITH ENGLAND

A<small>T FIRST</small> it seemed as if nothing very extraordinary had occurred. Cardinal del Giudice, who had been in Madame des Ursins's bad books lately, and who for the last year had adorned the querulous assembly of exiles round the Dowager Queen at Bayonne, now returned to power, backed by the favour of Louis XIV. The Cardinal had quarrelled with the camarera mayor over the taxation of church property; and immediately on his return to Spain, it was exempted from all imposts; Philip dismissed Orry, the French official who had tried to put some order into the finances; the Cardinal's nephew, the Prince of Cellamare, was appointed to the Paris Embassy.

The Cardinal had but two ideas — peace at all costs, and the final ruin of Madame des Ursins. In February 1715 he crowned the pacificatory work of Louis XIV by making peace with Portugal; and a few months later, he enjoyed the satisfaction of seeing the former camarera mayor hurry out of France.

It was the failing health of the old King that sent her into voluntary exile. If he had never entirely pardoned her absurd intrigues for a principality, at least she was safe in France while he reigned; indeed, she was even able to secure some sort of pension from him. But as he sank, she grew terrified of what the new reign might hold in store for her. There was talk of Orléans becoming Regent. Whatever happened he was bound to increase in importance. Fear of the vengeance he might then take caused her in the summer of 1715 to slip out of Paris and flee first to the sunny boredom of Genoa, then into domination of the threadbare Stuart court at Rome. Her senile décolletages and her sharp tongue distinguished refugee society there until her death in great opulence and resignation seven years later. . . .

In Spain the Cardinal's internal administration was informed by a spirit of reaction alone. Macanaz, the only Spaniard with a grasp of financial technique, a man who had laboured unceasingly to reform the fiscal system, was exiled to Bayonne. The King's confessor, Père Robinet, was removed for having spoken his mind. The arrogant provinces were soon out of control. Worst of all, the French Embassy once more interfered in almost every branch of the administration.

Alberoni had not put Elisabeth Farnese on the Spanish throne merely to witness the kingdom's decline. But as usual when nursing a great design he worked out of sight, in the distinguished obscurity of the sovereign's apartments. Almost from the first day Elisabeth had accorded him the right of secret entry to her presence even when she was at meals; indeed it was at her table that he perfected the means of making himself supreme.

He noticed how in the first weeks she lost her Homeric appetite. "What makes me frightened," he wrote on December 31st, "is that she won't eat or that what little she does eat is pretty poor stuff. I have the honour of seeing her at lunch and dinner and the King is always at me to get her to eat a bit more." A few days later he appeals for the regular despatch from Parma of Italian wines. "H.M. not being able to accustom herself to these perfidious vintages, she won't eat because she has nothing to drink. . . . With indignation I watch H.M. drink an infamous white wine from Nice which certainly cannot be good for her health." A decent wine and food that pleased her must immediately be provided, or Elisabeth would never possess the vigour to people Europe with princes as he prayed she would.

The only things in those early days which she ate with real pleasure were the woodcock which her consort shot for her. "She's unswerving," the abbé reported in February, "in her taste for woodcock: she always eats one in the morning and another in the evening, and sometimes she leaves nothing but the drumsticks. They are for the most part, one might say almost always, killed by the King, and on the days (which rarely occur) when he doesn't kill any, he returns melancholy and discontented. This poor lady, you see, is reduced to living by her husband's gun."

But life with Philip V was not merely a dish of woodcock. Elisabeth was compelled to humour his every whim; she who on the journey from Italy had never got up before midday must now perforce be awake with the sun, to go shooting. She quickly became a respectable shot; she had not been many weeks in Spain before the Court News was proudly announcing: —

"On Thursday last the Queen in gentleman's attire went out shooting, and killed two stags and a boar, and shot from horseback at a rabbit running, leaving it stone dead, to the admiration of the King and bystanders on seeing H.M.'s extraordinary agility and skill."

As time went on, she became almost a better shot than her husband, though she retained a bad habit of firing too soon. She derived no doubt great pleasure from the chase, though it was sometimes a strain, walking for half the day and never being able to allow herself the luxury of one cross word. "She is even," declared Alberoni in admiration, "more subtle and more cunning than the occasion demands. . . ."

It was a continued mystery to him how this hoydenish girl from the easy simplicities of Parma could deploy and yet disguise such arts, so profound a knowledge of mankind. She contrived to make Philip see her as a simple, obedient child. "The King," Alberoni reported to Parma, "with his habitual graciousness tells me her character is an open one and that he saw to the very depths of it from the first. With my customary malice I replied that I wouldn't dare say as much."

But it was essential that this extraordinary young creature eat well, particularly since she had become pregnant within a few weeks of her arrival. Woodcock after all would never be a staple dependable food. It was Alberoni who solved the problem. He had received a few cases of sausages from Italy; one day he had the idea of cooking some for the Queen. She fell upon them with gusto. The next day out shooting he again regaled with his sausages, and afterwards was able to report "she had eaten competently."

In a few weeks Italian wines and dishes completely revived her appetite. Indeed, she now drank with such a will, it was necessary to pour a little water into the decanter when she wasn't looking, "for her health's sake." Having settled the question of her food and drink, the abbé was then called upon to order almost every other detail of her life, obtain Italian comedians for her, puppies, guns, and horses. "I repeated to her that I was no longer the Minister of Parma but her nurse; and she mockingly replied that I was of an age to serve her as midwife if need be. A brutal compliment!"

Only one quality in her still troubled him; when for hours on end he poured into her entranced ear his whole store of political experience and observation, she would cry out her admiration, vow that if it lay with her, he would be Pope in a week. Yet despite all his husbandry, a taste for politics grew in her but slowly. "I recognize," he admitted woefully, "to my great grief that it bores her to talk of business." Her attentions were entirely concentrated upon fighting off her Spanish boredom. To divert her he was compelled to give costly fêtes with supplies of oysters that did not run out for three days, and important fireworks. When all else failed, Elisabeth would organize battles of the courtiers, which began softly enough with the mere throwing of confetti, but ended in frantic horseplay, furbelows in ruins, wigs pulled out by the handful. These distractions were not, of course, to Alberoni's taste. But he was cunning; he made himself umpire, and stayed clear of the battle.[1] . . . Compared with such tumults, the bringing of Italian comedians from Parma was a labour of love. Elisabeth could summon up little taste for the Spanish theatre, where you would see spirits ascend from the infernal regions upon nothing more mechanical than a garden ladder. . . .

With time, however, and under Alberoni's delicate impulsion, the young Queen grew conscious of the politics that engirt her. In June 1715 the abbé could report with some satisfaction: "I'm succeeding better every day in accustoming H.M. to harness and to hard work at State affairs. I try to bring them in the form of mincemeat, in order to spare her all possible fatigue."

As in the days of Maria Louisa, the Despacho took to holding its sittings in the Queen's apartments. At first she did no more than sit near with her knitting, silently. Then at Alberoni's instigation, the King began to show her reports from the envoys abroad; she would occasionally make a suggestion, one that Alberoni had slipped into her mind; the suggestion would be adopted successfully; so the excitement of the game, a taste for glory grew. Before long the despatches were coming direct to her, often without del Giudice seeing them; and Alberoni would dictate the decisions to be made upon them. Methuen, the British Minister, was soon reporting to London that the Parmesan envoy was a man to cultivate if you wanted to negotiate with any hope of success; and the French Ambas-

[1] During his visit to Italy in 1701, Philip V, when not shooting sparrows out of his bedroom window, had distracted his boredom by games which involved his dwarfs throwing plates at him, butting him in the stomach and spitting in his face. On his return to Madrid little Queen Maria Louisa organized regular tourneys when at the head of fifty ladies she would charge the King supported by his dwarfs. These diversions were dubbed familiarly the "jeux du sérail" (Louville, Memoirs).

sador was formally instructed to deal with Alberoni, in preference to the Cardinal or any of his creatures.

The rise of this new star was not, however, entirely to the taste of Versailles; Cardinal del Giudice was after all the old King's favourite, the supine machine by which the French Embassy was to rule Spain. Now the whole delicate system was being disturbed by the Queen and her upstart. "If the Abbé Alberoni," cried the exasperated French Minister for Foreign Affairs in February 1715, "gets involved in trouble, many people will be all the happier." Instead, the power of the pestilential creature continued to grow: until old Louis XIV was compelled to decree that if it came to a pinch, it was the poor Cardinal who must be sacrificed, for the sake of French policy.

Tardy efforts were made to buy Alberoni's favour with a pension. He pocketed the money because he needed it — Farnese parsimony left him little cash to spare for oyster parties and fireworks; his eternal battles over "frais de représentation" would wring the heart of any modern diplomat — but he made it clear that he regarded this new pension as a mere resumption of his old one,[2] which had not been paid for some six years. Consequently, he hinted, he did not consider that he had undertaken with it any fresh obligations toward France. . . .

Alberoni might snap his fingers at the French Embassy, knowing how ardently the Court of Versailles would welcome his ruin. Yet in those early days he exerted himself to improve relations with France. He induced the sulking Elisabeth to write to Madame de Maintenon, a feat which not even Philip V had achieved; and through his agency again, the long captivity was ended of Orléans's two unfortunate agents who for five years had languished in Segovia jail.[3] This act of clemency bred warm protestations of goodwill between uncle and nephew. To Alberoni, Orléans wrote in highly flattering terms.

The reconciliation was little more than nominal; the Court

[2] See p. 46.   [3] See p. 86.

of Madrid continued to nurse against the Palais-Royal every sort of suspicion. After all, Louis XIV was fast declining; in London they were betting that he would not last till September; might not Orléans then endeavour to make himself Regent for the little Louis XV, and thus rob Philip V of what he conceived to be his rights?

Ever since the death of the Bourgognes, and of their eldest child, the infant Duc de Bretagne, that indolent and amiable libertine, Orléans, had withdrawn more and more into the shameful obscurity of his debauches, shunned by the whole court for a poisoner. Every calamity that afflicted the royal family, even the death of Berry, Philip's surviving brother, in 1714 from a riding accident, was attributed to Orléans's monstrous arts. There was no denying, however, that Philip's renunciation of his French rights and Berry's death had made Orléans second heir to the French throne, and had endowed him with the best title in law to the future Regency.

In the summer of 1714 the old King had made a will; for a year the secret of it tantalized the French court to the verge of hysteria. The corridors of Versailles, the saloons and coffee-houses buzzed with speculation. Who would be Regent? Orléans? But the King did not hide his hostility to him. The Duc de Maine? A bastard, but by a royal decree he had been made eligible for the succession. Philip V? It was said that the Cardinal del Giudice during his visit to Versailles in the summer of 1714 had pressed strongly for the renunciation to be set aside. Nevertheless, during the following winter, there grew a general sentiment for Orléans, which was discreetly fostered over the dinner-table at the Palais-Royal.

Nor did the matter leave Philip V supine in his Spanish sloth. Rightly had the French Ambassador reported that in Philip's view his renunciation was only in favour of his brother, Berry, and that he would not stand aside to make the hated Orléans King of France. Philip had only executed the renunciation to

BANQUET AT THE SPANISH EMBASSY IN PARIS
c. 1707

LOUIS XIV, THE "GRAND DAUPHIN," THE DUC DE BOURGOGNE
AND THE FUTURE LOUIS XV, WITH HIS GOVERNESS
by Largillière

please the pragmatical English, who could not understand that the rights of an "enfant de France" sprang from God, and were inalienable by men. It was a matter touching Philip's honour and his conscience, the only things besides the marriage-bed or a flushed woodcock that could rouse him for long from his dark lethargy, put lustre into the vacant eye.

Accordingly, before he left for the Paris Embassy, Cellamare was instructed to work for the formation in France of a party favourable to the assumption of the future Regency by Philip. It was a policy little favoured by Alberoni. In martyred Italy could be won quite enough glory to satisfy the tenderest honour, without upsetting solemn covenants, and bringing the bloodthirsty English to bark about the heels of Spain. To his schemes the goodwill of France, on the other hand, could bring incalculable force. Hence the reconciliation with Orléans, effected against Philip's dearest inclinations. It was a clear manifestation of Alberoni's growing power.

The last days of Louis XIV, for all the mischief he had wrought, were invested with an Aeschylean sorrow that wrung compassion even from his enemies. His age had ended with the war; Versailles was abandoned by the new youth of France; they follied in Paris, after a fashion that roused torments of indignation in Madame de Maintenon. "The men," she wrote, "are worse than the women. . . . They like their wives to take snuff, to drink and gamble, and go naked." They left about the King a vacuum, that neither his bastards nor the black hood of his pedagogic wife could ever fill. He sat there like a forgotten statue, shooting with a light arquebus from his painted calèche, brooding upon lost battles and dead posterity, hiding his pain when he learnt from the Dutch newspapers of the odious bets in London.

Then a sickness of his legs put even calèche and arquebus out of reach. He lay in bed, passing in review the sparkling suits that he would wear when he got up again. The legs hurt abominably, and his wife gave him no peace, urging upon him the claim to his throne with which he had endowed his bastard Maine. She had no need to; Maine, with his delicate attentions, in his face a look of the splendid Montespan, was all that remained of former glory; the old King doted upon him, had done his best for him in the will that would soon be opened. But remembering how his father's testament had been set aside, Louis had few illusions about his own.

There came a heat wave at the end of August, and gangrene set in. He could still hear the fifes and hautboys down in the courtyard, the violins that sighed behind the curtains; but as the music crept away, and the courtiers began to buzz about Orléans, the King knew that it was the end. He still clung to life, however, with an uncontrollable tenacity, so that he complained, almost in the words of his cousin, England, long ago, how it was vastly difficult to die.

Somebody gave him an elixir and he began suddenly to eat; turning from Orléans, the courtiers crowded once more about the great bed, despite the nauseous smell that the gangrene gave out. Though he was moved, Orléans could not withhold a pleasantry. "If my uncle," he cried, "eats another meal there'll be nobody left to pay court to me."

Then all at once the King sank back. The little Dauphin, the future Louis XV, was brought in; from his dying great-grandfather he received advice that in after years he was to keep constantly before his waking eyes and was almost as constantly to ignore.[4] "My child," said the old man, "you are going to be a great King; don't imitate me in the passion that I had for building and for war."

To Orléans Louis cryptically whispered: "You will find nothing in my will with which you will have any reason to be dissatisfied. . . . The arrangements I have made I consider to

---

[4] The old King's exhortation to him was inscribed on a tablet, and so placed it was almost the first thing that met his eye when he woke of a morning.

be the wisest and fairest for the good of the Kingdom, but as one can't foresee everything, if there is anything to be changed or improved, appropriate steps will be taken. You are about," he added majestically, "to behold one King in the grave and another in the cradle. Always keep before you the memory of the one and the interests of the other."

He ordered Orléans when the little Dauphin had become King to send the boy to Vincennes, where the air was good, while Versailles was being spring-cleaned; one of his last actions was to issue instructions for the refurnishing of the Vincennes palace that had been abandoned since Mazarin's day. On the brink of death he showed for others a consideration of which he had been rarely capable while in health. He asked the court to begin the preparation of their mourning, "and not to await his death before doing so; thus the workmen will have time to do their work with less strain." At the very end in the mirror above the mantelpiece he happened to catch sight of two valets seated at the foot of his bed, crying. "Why are you crying," he called out, "did you think I was immortal? I never thought so and considering my age you ought to be prepared to lose me." Then on September 1st, amid the jubilations of his fickle subjects, Louis XIV died.

A week before, Orléans had taken the precaution of suspending all posts to Madrid. When news of the King's illness reached him, Philip V talked of marching to Paris at the head of the troops he had concentrated along the Pyrenees. Then he learnt that his grandfather had rallied, and the matter seemed less urgent. He continued to talk of the march to Paris at the appropriate moment; and the new English envoy, young George Bubb, began to pack his trunks, being resolved to accompany the King. But while Philip talked, during that week when Madrid was cut off from Paris, Orléans with unexampled energy had made himself master of France. The crisis had caught the Spanish Embassy off their guard, and the swift progress of events left Cellamare powerless. The will of Louis XIV, it is true, was found to accord Orléans no more than the Presidency of a Regency Council that was packed with his enemies; while the care of the little King and the command of the Royal Guards (which carried with it control of Paris) were entrusted to Maine.

On the morrow of the old King's death, the Parlement was convened to consider the will. There were high words between Orléans and Maine; nor was the situation simplified by the behaviour of the dukes, and of Saint-Simon in particular. This, of all moments, was the one they chose to protest against the pretension of the President of Parlement to address the nobility with his hat on. When the assembly at last was free to despatch the business of the nation, Orléans and Maine almost flew at each other's throats; they were induced to continue their noisy squabble in a side-room. . . .

Suddenly Maine's nerve seemed to go; when the sitting was resumed after lunch, Orléans's triumph was evidently complete. He wrested control of the Guards from Maine, and cajoled Parlement into entrusting him with almost absolute powers of Regency over France. By the time the news reached Madrid, Orléans was indisputable master of the country.

This turn of events suited Alberoni admirably; it dissipated the danger of a rash adventure into France, and left him free to attack del Giudice, who no longer had the French King behind him. His innate conservatism could never be harmonious with Alberoni's reforming zeal, or plans for Italian liberation.

The two men had once been friends; but Alberoni's rise after the coming of Elisabeth Farnese inevitably flung them into conflict. Now Alberoni's power was much increased by the long stay he had made with the royal family at Aranjuez during the spring.

The court had left for the country after Easter 1715, so soon as the beperiwigged and bleeding effigies of Our Lord had vanished from the Madrilleno streets. After the dry clamour of the capital, the rocks that already sizzled in the early heat, Aranjuez robbed the coming summer of its terrors. Though one might be forced to move all one's household effects down there, even, as Alberoni complained, to the chamber-pot. Bright in the spray of waterfalls, bathed by two rivers, the valley of Aranjuez explodes its verdure in the midst of the dry Castilian plain. The palace, when Elisabeth paid this first visit, was a neglected affair very different from the graceful edifice, with its porcelain saloon like ever flowering pergolas, that now bestrides the Tagus. But she took to the site from the first. "Her Majesty," wrote Alberoni on arrival there, "has found this place particularly to her taste because it resembles certain spots in the vicinity of the Po. . . . Quantities of trees and an abundance of water. . . . Already Her Majesty has been out shooting three times after hares and rabbits and has killed her share of them." The hares Alberoni cooked for her in the Placentian fashion — one of the triumphs of Italian cookery; he fed her on gooseberries and Anolini alla Parmigiana.[5] "Eating such things," Alberoni reported, "it seems to her, she says, as if she were back in the good country." For a moment she must have felt — what with the delicious familiar dishes, and the unexpected trees whose shadows coursed round the antelope flanks of her palace, that she had never embarked upon that terrible galley, never crept along the coast past Monaco and Nice, never flirted with the persistent chaplain, who now bombarded her with love letters and demands for some appointment in Madrid.[6]

[5] A sort of small ravioli which is the traditional Easter fare at Parma. It is stuffed with Parmesan cheese, egg, a pinch of nutmeg, onion and very appropriately some sauce Espagnole.

[6] For some time after her arrival in Spain, she continued her flirtation with Maggiali by letter. Alberoni was able to intercept some of the correspondence. It caused him no little anxiety. When the Queen went so far as to show him a letter that she had written to Maggiali discouraging the idea of his coming to Spain, the abbé still remained apprehensive. "This

At Aranjuez Alberoni's distinction was publicly affirmed. "There are only three dinner-tables," he wrote to Parma, "those of the Cardinal, the Master of the Horse, and myself; for the crowds of people that come here a dozen tables would not be out of place." At Alberoni's board you found the best food, the most diverting conversation, the easiest path to royal favour. Yet for all his success, his life was no sinecure. He was racked with headaches and indigestion, but kept, nevertheless, in unflagging attendance upon the sovereigns, whether they were shooting the swallows that skimmed the water or went off for a day's organized battue in the hills between Aranjuez and Toledo. Then it was a matter of intolerable silent waiting in a crowded butt, and a few moments' fusillade for the royal family alone. Alberoni must ensure that the Queen's picnic food was to her taste, and that she ate heartily, to support the pregnancy lately declared. He would be on his feet all day, eating nothing till he had dragged himself back to the darkening palace. . . .

As the summer wore on, hostility towards him rose. "The jealousy," he wrote, "which the Queen's favours provoke is inevitable." He was careful, however, not to imitate the imperious behaviour which had been the ruin of Madame des Ursins. But the Queen had now such faith in him, she even invited the French Ambassador, the Duc de Saint-Aignan, to transact all his business with her dear abbé.

Saint-Aignan was hardly the man to appreciate Alberoni's virtues; the son of that Saint-Aignan who had acted as confidant in Louis XIV's first love affair: the brother of the Duc de Beauvilliers, poor Bourgogne's austere tutor, the new Ambassador

---

ought not," he wrote to the Duke of Parma on March 24th, 1715, "to lull us to sleep and make us believe that a great flame is extinct which with the least fresh fuel might kindle a gigantic blaze, all the more that I know Her Majesty to be tenacious in her affections and extremely wily, capable of profiting by a good opportunity to gull her husband, of whom she is absolute mistress, without his entertaining the slightest suspicion."

132

was obsessed by his own genealogy, and by the world of fashion. Success with women (of the highest birth, naturally), the orders and the colour of the coat he would wear at some dinner party, occupied his thoughts almost to the exclusion of vulgar politics; and his reports were so charged with details of the balls he gave, even the easy-going Regent sometimes turned his sarcasm upon the youth. Yet he did not bother to remove him from Madrid, where he displayed a consummate lack of tact.

He had come to Spain confident that he could revive the Golden Age of French domination. Never for a moment did he pause to admit the possibility of that low-born Parmesan priest resisting his bribes and his blandishments. Only by bitter experiment was he brought gradually to realize the abbé's disinclination to deal with him except upon a ground of equality, or to stomach the least interference from France.

In the autumn of 1715 Alberoni brought off his first great stroke of foreign policy. To men of vision, the most dramatic event of recent history had been the rise of England from a sort of Balkan dependence upon France, to the rank of first Power in Europe. The prodigies which she had wrought under Marlborough had made her respected and fashionable throughout Europe. To the distress of the reactionary Saint-Simon, the Regent was for ever praising English institutions, which Montesquieu and the young Voltaire were soon to misinterpret to an eager public. Elderly statesmen, obsessed by the memory of Louis XIV in his heyday, might still turn their gaze reverently towards France; but the new generation, to which Alberoni belonged, for all his fifty years and middle-aged corpulence, fervently believed that no country could contrive much in the world unless with English support.

Strangely enough, however, England in the year 1715 was almost friendless. Bolingbroke's manœuvres at Utrecht had alienated our old allies, for the sake of an entente with France. Now George I was flirting with Vienna again; yet the Jacobite rising, and its early success, hardly encouraged negotiation with the harassed Hanoverian régime; while the issue was still uncertain, only the faithful Dutch were ready to come out openly on George's side. Even his cousin, the Regent, was covertly abetting the Jacobites; while French influence at Madrid had procured for the Pretender a Spanish subsidy.

Alberoni, however, had scant faith in the Jacobite cause; and he resolved to bid for George I's friendship, at the very moment when that monarch most needed foreign support. The abbé was well aware that the British fleet could make or mar his ultimate Italian projects.

Lexington's commercial treaty in practice had given scant satisfaction. A twenty-four per cent *ad valorem* duty throughout the Spanish Empire, and a hundred pettifogging regulations curbed our trade; the local authorities often seized English ships without redress; these grievances became the excuse for widespread smuggling and privateering by the English, which perpetually exasperated the Spanish Government.

For months now, our envoy, Paul Methuen, had been lost in a fruitless wrangle with the Madrid Government. The settling of our trade with the Spanish world was the principal object of his mission, the balm for which the pride of Whiggery, injured at Utrecht, steadily clamoured. "Whereas," ran Methuen's instructions, "the preservation of the commerce between the Kingdoms of Great Britain and Spain was one of the chief motives which induced our two Royal predecessors to enter into the late long expensive war, and one of the principal benefits expected by our people from the conclusion of a peace after such a glorious and uninterrupted course of successes . . . you are to use your utmost application and endeavour . . . to obtain . . . a full confirmation of all the privileges and concessions . . . to the British merchants. . . ."

But the Spanish Government proved woefully unobliging; they would promise moon and stars, and yet withhold from

Methuen the merest gleam of satisfaction. He was driven mad too by the British merchants who bombarded him with irrelevant complaints, and "continue to overstock all the markets with goods they cannot sell." Soon after his arrival in Madrid, he grew desperate, reporting to Stanhope (who was a great man nowadays, a Secretary of State, high in the favour of George I): "I can see no remedy but war, and you are the best judges at home whether that be practicable or no."

Methuen was an experienced diplomat; he knew something about commercial treaties; as a young man, had he not had a hand in negotiating the famous agreement with Portugal, which was to lay up a fine heritage of gout for English posterity? But in this strange world of Madrid, where they gave credence to the wildest libels against the British Government put about by Irish adventurers, Methuen felt lost and helpless. He fretted himself almost into a decline, till at length he asked to be recalled, crying out dramatically to the Secretary of State: "I am reduced to so miserable a condition, that everybody thinks I shall not live to see your answer."

He was, however, relieved in the early summer of 1715, still hale enough to become himself Secretary of State not long after. At his suggestion he was succeeded at Madrid by a young man of twenty-four, George Bubb, who, if his father was a barber, as some said, or perhaps an Irish chemist, enjoyed the prospect of inheriting from his mother's family a handsome fortune, and a pretty packet of Parliamentary seats in Dorset. Bubb, known to posterity by the name of Doddington, which he later assumed, is remembered largely for his place-hunting in the reign of George II, the ostentation of his house in Pall Mall. His bedposts were crowned with peacocks' feathers, the hangings and carpets were cut out of his rich old coats, with the pockets still left in them, his mantelpieces were considered by connoisseurs to be overcrowded with icicles; an old-fashioned wig, and the flock of poetasters who preyed upon his

aging vanity, drew titters upon him wherever he went. . . .
Such was Bubb in decadence; but in 1715 he was a figure
neither extravagant nor ridiculous — merely a young Englishman slightly dazed by the position into which he had been
pitchforked, and burning to shine where the brilliance of a
Methuen had been dulled.

The prospect of success must have seemed slight enough during his first summer in Madrid. But unbeknown to him, he
possessed a powerful ally at court. Months ago, at the time
of Methuen's arrival, the Duke of Parma had urged upon his
envoy in Madrid the need for close relations with the British
Legation. Alberoni, eagerly embracing this view, had deplored
the Spaniards' handling of Methuen. "Our ministers," he reported, "have treated Methuen as if they wanted a breach;
their manners might at least have been more suave and agreeable, even if they thought it in the King's interest not to come
to an arrangement." Nor did he share the general pro-Jacobite
feeling which was fostered by the Irish refugees, and appeals
from Paris. Almost with his last letter Louis XIV had urged
Philip V to recognize the Pretender; and more than £40,000
had been wheedled out of him for the Stuart cause. But Alberoni continued to maintain that all the Stuart plans would
end in smoke. If Philip V did not take care, he declared, for
his share in the Jacobite venture he would be attacked by
England, with calamitous results. But as he wrote, Louis XIV
was dying, and leaving him free to change the policy of Spain.

The link between Alberoni and the British envoy was the
new Dutch Minister, Baron Ripperda, who came of a distinguished Catholic family in Gröningen. Few sorts of Catholi-
cism exist more stern than that to be found in South Holland.
Ripperda had not, however, allowed excessive religious scruples to hamper his ambitions. To aid his advancement, he had
first abjured the faith of his ancestors; now in Spain, he courted

popularity by dangling before the devout court the possibility of his reconversion.

Methuen had been charmed by his easy manners and specious tongue; "a very honest gentleman," he had called him, "heartily zealous for the service of his country." No judgement could have been much wider of the mark than this. History was to show up Ripperda as a venal rogue. From the moment of his coming to Spain, he meditated the abandonment of Dutch service for that fantastic, picaresque career, which was one day to perch him on the summit of power, then show him the inside of a prison, and at last bring him dishonourable and gluttonous felicity as a convert to Islam, among the Moors.

But in 1715, Ripperda was a diplomat of charm, who used his wife's riches decently to entertain his friends, and who urged the need for a close association of Spain with Holland and England. Upon this point he and Alberoni saw eye to eye; and it was by Ripperda's intermediary that the first message of goodwill reached Bubb. The Dutchman appeared, very mysterious, at the British Legation, late one September evening. A certain High Personage at the Palace, he said, desired urgently to talk to Bubb; this Personage had charged him to say that the Spanish King desired to live in perfect amity with the King of Great Britain, "and do all things reasonable to continue a good intelligence between His Britannick Majesty and himself. . . ."

Negotiation was conducted with extreme speed and secrecy. The Spanish monarchs were affability itself; Bubb was enchanted. "I have found the gentleman," he reported exultant, "who alone is absolute here. He has gained an entire ascendant over the Queen, and by that means over the King, who is not a lover of business and suffers himself to be led by Her Majesty. I ought to add I see no party forming capable of opposing him."

Alberoni wasted no time. By late October, the bewildered British Government had accepted his proposed Heads of Agreement. In the light of modern knowledge, Alberoni's motives in granting a treaty so advantageous become perfectly clear. He sought to gain British goodwill against the day of liberating Italy from the German yoke; he saw, too, that he could never turn the Spanish colonies to proper account until the British contraband trade with them was controlled. But these considerations were hardly appreciated at the time, outside Alberoni's cabinet, and so the sudden generosity of Spain towards a régime by no means firmly seated in England, seemed to many observers both incomprehensible and sinister. Suspicions were not allayed by the behaviour of Ripperda, who persuaded Bubb that Alberoni cared only for money, and would need some £13,000 for making a good treaty.

The acceptance of "douceurs" by statesmen during important negotiations was no uncommon practice in those days; the great Marlborough himself does not seem to have boggled at the thought of pocketing French gold, had certain peace negotiations after Ramillies been successful. But in Alberoni's case, the idea originated with Ripperda, and the substance of the bribe stuck to his swindling fingers. Alberoni had no knowledge of the matter, and was genuinely astonished when the British envoy hinted to him that he was now the pensioner of England. Coming to realize the force of the insinuation, he was furious and indignant, and summoned his old friend Stanhope to deny the charge. Stanhope became at last aware of the truth.

But at the time the accusation was handy enough for Alberoni's enemies. When news of the pending treaty leaked out, Cardinal del Giudice, furious at having been kept so long in the dark, hired bullies to cry "traitor" before the Parmesan Legation; in November he made a violent scene to the King. Philip was embarrassed, but could give the Cardinal little satisfaction; Elisabeth had declared that she would back her dear abbé through thick and thin. Del Giudice's power, Bubb reported, was in a general decline, and Alberoni was beginning publicly to sit on the various administrative councils. But the Cardinal still had power to obstruct, even if he could not prevent. "Whatever we settled with the King in the morning," Bubb reported, "the Cardinal and his party undid at night." But at last the Parmesan favourite contrived to push all opposition aside, and the treaty was at last ready for signature, with a Latin translation attached, "the worst piece of Latin," sighed Bubb, "which ever appeared since the monks' time."

The treaty was signed on December 14, 1715, in circumstances no less curious than its beginnings. The sulking Cardinal would not put his hand to it; Alberoni had no official status; full powers were therefore made out for the Marquis of Bedmar, a distinguished grandee, who though President of the Council of War, spent most of his time in bed. "In the evening," reported Bubb, "we met at that gentleman's house (who keeps his bed and I fancy never heard anything of the matter till dinner-time) and there, after the reading the Instruments, they were signed."

The treaty caused delight in London. George I, opening Parliament in the first days of 1716, declared that British trade with Spain "will stand settled for the future on a foot more advantageous and certain than it ever did in the most flourishing time of any of my predecessors." Particularly were the British Cabinet charmed with Alberoni; Stanhope wrote intimating that the abbé's present distinction was but the normal reward for distinguished talents, and one which his friends had long prophesied for him. Bubb declared roundly: "Alberoni has behaved himself very obligingly and heartily in the affair." In return the abbé was profuse in courtesies to the English statesman; and while for tactical reasons he maintained a trickle of subsidies to the Jacobites until he was sure of the treaty, he then behaved with scrupulous loyalty, refusing for instance to allow the Pretender into Spain, when he applied for asylum in the following spring.

Elsewhere the treaty caused consternation and annoyance. The Emperor, for instance, who had never recognized Philip V, and who still hankered after his Spanish kingdom, was particularly bitter at what he regarded as this new treachery of the English, his traditional allies. The Regent affected to believe that it meant the securing of British support for Spanish intrigues against his own somewhat precarious position in France. "So then," he cried out bitterly to our envoy in Paris, Lord Stair, "you are friends with Spain; however, I can tell you that Spain has done things for the Pretender which I would not do, and I could give you proofs of it." [7]

Alberoni was now in a measure triumphant; but one thing was still needed to confirm his authority — the Queen's successful delivery of her first child. By her death, even the still birth of her baby, his position might be seriously prejudiced. "So soon as the Queen is brought abed," Bubb reported just before Christmas, "I believe we shall have great changes here. Monsieur Alberoni promises to put able and honest men in the Employments. . . . Everything however must stand still till we see whether H.M. will live, for upon that all depends; she will lye in next month."

Alberoni was well aware of his danger; he devoted as much attention to Elisabeth's pregnancy as he might have done to some complication of foreign policy, guarding her health, studying her whims in every particular. "The Queen, thank God," he would write, "supports her pregnancy very well; but her lack of appetite continues, and she is reduced to eating the plain dishes of our country, which I have the honour to serve her — three courses at lunch, and two in the evening. Otherwise I can assure you she would fast. . . ." He ordered

[7] Stanhope's letter to Bubb of February 17, 1716 (N.S.) (R.O.).

for her from Italy more of the wine she loved, truffles in oil, gooseberries and marzolini — those excellent little spring cheeses from the Tuscan countryside. The Queen doted on marzolini; many of them arrived spoilt, though Alberoni had rushed them through the Alicante customs; Elisabeth ate them with spirit however, to the stupefaction of onlookers.

She was safely delivered in January 1716, of the Infant Don Carlos, one day to be Charles III of Spain. Alberoni could hardly conceal his exultation. "If things go on this way, we shall have princes to people the world. . . . The prince is as fat as if he were three months old. . . ." The delivery had been easy enough; just two or three "Ahi, ahais"; that was all.

There were fireworks and illuminations, and a state visit of thanks to the shrine of Atocha, with the Virgin's Mistress of the Robes decking her out in a fine new dress for the occasion, and loading her with all her glittering necklaces; the crowds were jubilant, but in no heart can there have reigned such jubilation as in Alberoni's. His heroine had not failed him; she had not died, nor was she barren; she was a good healthy Lombard girl, as he had always said. He was quite secure now. It is not by mere accident that the real beginnings of his administration and of his great reforms date from the birth of Don Carlos.

Elisabeth's appetite after this first delivery became ferocious. "The Queen," Alberoni would say, "has the appetite of a labourer." Gradually she came to eat only what was prepared for her in Alberoni's kitchen — generally with his own hands — ravioli, fegato alla Veneziana, aromatic polpettoni, those delicious forcemeat balls, roasted with herbs, which to this day are done to perfection in Alberoni's native Emilia.

The King might on the other hand be content to wolf boiled chicken at every meal; but his Italian delicacy was the person of his consort; and his appetite for it constant and voracious. By means of these two sorts of gluttony Alberoni established and confirmed his power. A constant supply of foodstuffs from Italy was essential to Elisabeth's contentment. But it was not easy to ensure their regular arrival; when truffles or sausages or wine ran out, she was soon reduced to such a hungry impatience, there was nothing she would not do to please her dear abbé and gain his goodwill, so that he would work miracles for her; if he wanted her to force some proposal of his upon her reluctant consort, she would even lock her bedroom door or set in motion the complicated system of springs that sent her bed shooting away from Philip's, and leave him fretting in solitude. It was rare for him to resist her long after the morning.

By these means, as well as by the affection and confidence with which Alberoni inspired the Spanish sovereigns, did he consolidate his power. But great though it was to grow, it never became absolute; however much he might impose his will upon Elisabeth and Philip, he always remained the servant of Parma; and though he might argue with the Duke, and seek at times to restrain him, Alberoni in the long run would bow to his master's will. This obedience was to lead him into courses that he himself deplored and dreaded; it was unjustly to saddle him with the reputation of a reckless and bellicose adventurer, when he was the last man to seek war except with a certainty of victory.

Early in 1716, the negotiations with England were resumed. The chief concern of these new hagglings was the Asiento — the monopoly of supplying slave labour to the Spanish colonies. Most of the indigenous population, particularly round the gold and silver mines of Peru and Bolivia, had been used up; for years now the Viceroys had been compelled to fall back upon black labour got forcibly from the West African coast. There was an immense waste of human life involved in the process; hardly one in three Negroes survived the cruel journey via Jamaica, Porto Bello, Panama, Callao, down the west coast of South America to Arica, and then up through the mountains to

Potosí; those wretches who did were soon worn out by the mines. The supply of this black labour in the vast quantities needed was a valuable concession, particularly since it carried with it the right to send two ships yearly to the great fairs of Vera Cruz in Mexico, and Porto Bello, where gold and precious stones were said to be rolled about the quays like common merchandise. In other words the Asiento held the key to the incalculable trade of the Americas.

Until Philip's accession, the right had been held by the Genoese, who established factories at Curaçao, Jamaica, and in Brazil. The transfer of the monopoly into French hands had been one of the main causes for the English entry into the late war; and when the Whig merchants cried: "No peace without Spain," Bolingbroke had calmed them by obtaining in principle the right for thirty years yearly to import into the Spanish colonies 4,800 Negroes, or 144,000 in all; by a new principle slaves for Potosí were shipped to Buenos Aires and sent over a comparatively healthy road to the mines. The English also obtained the right to establish a factory in the Argentine.

But Bolingbroke's treaty cried out for revision; the sections of it which dealt with the sending of trading ships to the Americas caused nothing but vexation, and, as we have seen, a habit of general lawlessness. Stanhope was quick to profit by Alberoni's benevolence to press for a revision of the offending articles. "This stumbling-block once removed," he wrote to him late in 1715, "I see nothing to affect the union between the two powers, which we in England think absolutely necessary for the tranquillity of all Europe. I wish with all my heart that you may have the honour to strengthen this union more and more, by your advice and good offices."

At that moment, the British Government seems seriously to have contemplated the gratifying of Alberoni's dearest wish — a close political association with Spain. There were rumours that Alberoni would drive the French out of the Spanish colonies. The sulking Court of Vienna believed that the Spanish treasure fleet would in future be escorted by British cruisers. Certainly Spain seemed the obvious ally for England at this time; French assistance to the Pretender had revived the traditional Gallo-phobia of the English; while Hoffmann, the Imperial representative, was obliged ruefully to inform Vienna that the Austrians were now little less unpopular in Great Britain than they had been in Bolingbroke's heyday.

Bubb pressed strongly for the political alliance. Under Alberoni's impulse, he reported, Spain was quickly reviving; soon she would have become a valuable friend, and a dangerous foe. The Emperor's ambitions in Italy were well known; had he not admitted to the British Government his designs upon Sicily? The subjection of that island would inordinately increase the Imperial power, and serve our interests little. Why not instead a close association with Spain, which would secure a Spanish guarantee of the Hanoverian succession, a predominant share for us of the New World trade, and would "most effectively disunite" the two Bourbon crowns?

Philip's capricious health, it was well known, inspired Elisabeth with dread of an early widowhood, of that poverty and oblivion which was the usual lot of a queen dowager in Spain. Two stepsons barred for her children the way to the Spanish throne; but she possessed after all good claims to the reversions of Parma, Piacenza and Tuscany; she seems consequently to have conceived the plan, soon after her arrival in Spain, of carving out of Italy heritages for her children whither she could one day retire in comfort. The scheme should be furthered, Bubb proposed, in return for her goodwill. "The absolute control over Spain," he told Stanhope, "will belong to the highest bidder for the Queen's son. That is the grand and only maxim, which has never changed since I have been here."

The conclusion of the Asiento Treaty caused further re-sentiment in France. Were the maritime powers, indignantly asked the French Ambassador in Madrid, to be allowed to ruin French trade? The Regent was consumed by a concern still more violent. Alberoni's overtures to England, he feared, were aimed at his own rights and position in France; the intimacy of the Spanish Ambassador with the clique of elderly marshals who wished to bring Philip V back to France did little to allay the Regent's suspicions. To Saint-Simon he might profess small hunger for the French throne; but then, it was not easy for him to open his mind to Saint-Simon. It was difficult for Orléans to open his mind to anyone; even to his mistresses and roués he was as close as an oyster; and Saint-Simon was separated from him by the barred doors behind which the nightly orgies bloomed. . . .

At all events, the Regent's policy was now to belie his declared indifference to his claims. He suggested a tripartite reaffirmation, by Spain, France, and Great Britain, of the Utrecht Treaty; obviously his main concern was with those clauses which made him heir to Louis XV.

The proposal was received coolly enough at Madrid; Alberoni, as much as any man at the court, wished to live in amity with France; but he was growing exasperated by Saint-Aignan's clumsy attempts to bribe him, and to interfere in the government of Spain. In vain did Huxelles, President of the Foreign Affairs Council, enjoin prudence on the young man. "Times are changed in every way," he wrote in February 1716, "we must be extremely careful to avoid giving any grounds for suspecting that France wishes to govern Spain." But Saint-Aignan would not listen.

Small wonder, therefore, if Spain rejected the French proposal, and with affected simplicity enquired what provisions of the treaty needed confirmation. The Regent hardly knew what next to do. Saint-Aignan's despatches bemused him with their conflicting rumours: Alberoni was sold to England — to

Portugal — to Austria — some people even believed him sold to France — with every courier from Madrid, the abbé's paymasters changed. But one fact seemed to emerge from Saint-Aignan's incoherencies — Alberoni was a purchasable commodity; of that the Ambassador was convinced. Yet when the Regent suggested another attempt to buy the monster, Saint-Aignan hopelessly objected: "France is not rich enough to satisfy his ambitions, nor capable of competing with the English on this score. . . ."

Meanwhile, between England and Spain all went merrily enough. George I and Philip V exchanged flattering messages. For Elisabeth, who found the Spanish horses too mettlesome, a string of hunters arrived from England; and when a new pregnancy prevented her immediately trying their manners, Alberoni and Bubb paraded them below her windows at Aranjuez. Bubb generally stayed with Alberoni at Aranjuez, which, said the latter enigmatically, gave you a chance to perceive the difference between Englishmen and Italians. It is difficult to imagine the abbé in England; its climate and cooking would probably have terrified him; but he had developed a genuine affection for the young Englishman, and Bubb returned it. He was lost, too, in admiration of the Queen. "Without her," he reported, "we would never have done anything here, and when she desists from supporting our interests, we may take our leave of Spain. I am fully persuaded that she is hearty for them now, and a sworn enemy to France, and I believe His Majesty may keep her so as long as he pleases. . . ."

THE REVIVAL AND REFORM OF SPAIN

Nᴏᴛ, ʜᴏᴡᴇᴠᴇʀ, by audacious diplomacy alone did Alberoni seek to make Spain great. Powerful alliances were, of course, essential, but they would turn into so much smoke unless Spain herself were strong.

We have already noted the country's misery at the beginning of the eighteenth century. With the accession of Philip V, the monarchy, it is true, had been infused with a fresh measure of vitality, so that in 1715, for instance, it was able to meet the cost of reducing the Balearic Isles out of revenue alone, and without any French subsidy. But, on the whole, years of war had accelerated the decline of the country. Communications by land, for instance, seemed to be breaking down entirely — it had taken the court eighteen days to reach Burgos in 1706, normally a journey of three to four days. The important port of Vigo lacked communications with the interior; corn from the Beauce in France could be sold in Cadiz for half the price of corn from Palencia, little more than a hundred miles away.

Throughout the kingdom, agriculture languished. The observant Abbé de Veyrac vigorously lamented the waste of soil. "Spain," Alberoni would cry, "is a country lying fallow. For twenty miles round Madrid, there's not a country-house, nor a tree, nor fruit to be seen. . . . That's the condition of a nation that once governed the richest countries in Europe, and now only thinks of living like niggers."

The Castilian or Aragonese farmer merely scratched the soil; what incentive had he to do otherwise, when nothing belonged to him? In Estremadura, good farming land was choked by weeds; and in La Mancha the farmers trembled beneath the tyranny of the Mesta, a powerful combine of live-stock owners. The Mesta herds, four million head, were driven up on to the hills in summer, and back down into the shelter of the valleys with the first frosts; by immemorial privilege, this avalanche of lowing, bleating flesh might sweep straight through gardens, pastures, grainfields, eating down to the bare earth what it did not trample into dust.

Andalusia, excellent land too, was equally desolate; only among the orange-groves of Murcia and Valencia was pros-perity to be seen. And if a peasant did make a bit of money, it was taken away from him by the tax-farmers. They swarmed everywhere, calling out the police at the merest sign of opposi-tion. Every commodity of life was taxed, meat, wine, vinegar, oil, candles, barley, fish, sugar, even the snow and ice that in the eighteenth century took the place of the refrigerator. The taxes varied from province to province, and the bemused lay-man was inevitably a victim of extortion. Then there was the Alcabala, fourteen per cent clapped on to every sale in the country; it worked on a compound system, so that an article passing through several hands would often pay taxes that far exceeded its value. A skinny chicken, or the dried salt cod that was Friday's meal in Madrid, sold for their weight in gold.

With all this savage taxation, the exchequer was never full; it was estimated that not one-tenth of the money bled from the people reached the Government. What the tax-farmers did not filch was a miserable enough sum. Then there were the tithes that swelled the bursting coffers of the Church. The great shrine of Santiago de Compostella, for instance, enjoyed, apart from the tribute of pilgrims, the fruits of a tithe upon all grain sold in the north of Spain. Such wealth made possible the re-facing of almost the whole vast Gothic bulk of the cathedral, and the construction of a new west front, of great elegance, in Baroque Churriguerresque, the work of Fernando Casas y Novoa.

It is a conception of considerable dexterity, in which all the ornament of Spanish Baroque, shells and palms, icicles and lanterns in pyrotechnic flight, pay graceful respect to the Gothic fabric. But what consolation can this have been to the Navarrese peasant, for instance? When he paid so much the more for his loaf, what did he care that the Torre del Reloj seems to fly sparkling through the bright sky? When could he afford the pilgrimage to Compostella?

The revenues of Toledo Archbishopric were immense; but they would not be spent upon the repair of the city waterworks, designed long ago by an ingenious Italian; nor upon the dredging of the Tagus to render it navigable once more. Rather were they lavished upon a new splendour for the cathedral already splendid, the "Transparente" of Narciso Tomé, perhaps the most eloquent symbol in the world of that mysticism which we associate with the Counter-Reformation. Not the sort of work which Alberoni would have felt free to approve, for he grudged every penny not devoted to the political greatness of Spain. Yet, in its hovering between the dream and reality, in its audacious improvisations, it is so typical of Alberoni's Spain that a description of it seems hardly inappropriate.

Toledo Cathedral is for the most part bathed in a grey Gothic darkness as soft as fur. Through this caressing penumbra you walk, past the half-seen storeyed richness of the High Altar, into the dark ambulatory behind. Suddenly you are almost dazed by a blaze of fierce sunlight. The Gothic vaulting seems to have burst open to reveal Our Lord sitting in radiance among bright clouds. At noon the beam of light coming through the "Transparente" has the conic violence of a searchlight, so that you can hardly see the Virgin and heavenly host rising skyward. By supreme virtuosity in his blending of architecture, painting, and sculpture to mask the mechanics of his design, Tomé has contrived more perhaps than any other artist of the baroque to achieve an effect of levitation. "This," you say to yourself, "this is what a miracle must be like; this is a foretaste of Judgement Day." As you watch the seraphims and prophets mount out of sight into that radiance, beneath a cupola that itself seems to fly, you can hardly believe the "Transparente" to be a work of the world and age that produced Sir Isaac Newton. . . . It was dedicated to an accompaniment of banquets, fireworks and bullfights. No doubt the wine flowed so abundantly, the absence of fresh water was not remarked. . . .

An energetic monarch might easily, one would suppose, have curbed this corruption and impractical extravagance. But in fact until Alberoni's day, the system of government in Spain kept the King in such a state of impotence, it would have needed a man far less lethargic than Philip V to impose his will upon the nation. The empire was ruled, or rather misruled, as we have seen, by a series of councils made up for the most part of hoary grandees. In these councils the good democratic principle of the consultative committee was carried to a point of ridiculous indecision. Personifying a sort of aristocratic republican tradition, the councils enjoyed powers that were quasi-royal, challenging and often surpassing the authority of the Crown itself. With the Council of State for instance lay the power of making war and peace, of contracting royal marriages and sanctioning foreign alliances; through their palsied hands were supposed to pass the reports of all Spanish representatives abroad. The Council of Castile was concerned with internal administration and could nullify any royal decree affecting the Spanish Kingdom; without the countersignature of the Council of the Indies the King was powerless in his dominions overseas; the Council of War enjoyed a despotic control over the armed forces; this control was largely devoted to ensuring that no officer of talent should ever reach a position of outstanding eminence.

Intelligent French visitors, used to the sublimation of royal authority, were scandalized. The Spaniards, they cried, wanted a mere likeness of a king, "un roi en peinture" under whose august cover they would be free to exercise their turbulent wills. Not that it would have mattered much if the councils had possessed any youth or vigour. Instead they were the honourable asylums of elderly gentlemen determined that the distinguished sunset of their days should not be disturbed by urgent business or original ideas. The pay was handsome, the perquisites immense, they enjoyed a half-royal prestige. Why should they bother about reforms, when at any moment the maggots might be getting to work upon the reforming of their own old bodies?

Then there was the corruption which Alberoni believed to exist in the royal household itself, the debasement of the coinage, and the almost total disappearance of skilled crafts from Spain. In Madrid for instance, he reported to Parma, one could not find a decent upholsterer, nor a reliable clock repairer. Spain was without industries, and the trade of the Americas, since Spain had little to export thither, went to enrich heretic smugglers, or the 200,000 odd foreign merchants who thrived in Spain itself.

Such in brief were the main difficulties under which the Spanish Empire laboured when Alberoni came to power. His assumption of authority enough to introduce reforms was but gradual. He began as we have seen by ensuring that the despatches from Spanish diplomatic representatives abroad should come directly through him to the Queen, instead of passing through the Council of State — what was called the substitution of the "via reservada" for the "via del Estado." Thereafter, he moved with extreme caution, at least until the birth of Elisabeth's first son had set his power on a solid foundation. The

Queen might clamour for open war against Cardinal del Giu-dice; Alberoni moved forward at his considered pace, saying that the matter must not be rushed, lest the Cardinal be turned into a martyr, a St. Thomas of Canterbury. All this time he was quietly preparing the ground for his later reforms, obtain-ing from Parma details of how the finances and royal house-hold of that well-managed duchy were administered: examin-ing the possibility of acquiring from Holland, from the English South Sea Company, and Hamburg, ships to revive the Spanish merchant fleet; and entering into earnest conclave with the interested merchants upon ways of improving the American trade.

At Guadalajara he set up a linen factory, with skilled Dutch labour, which was to become the pride of Spanish industry; English dyers inaugurated the manufacture of cloth at Valde-moros; 400 nuns were taught lace-making, and soon were ri-valling the products of Belgium. The Havana tobacco industry passed under royal control, and was transformed into an im-portant source of revenue; rich deposits of quicksilver, which had long lain neglected in the Andalusian soil at the foot of the Sierra Morena, were vigorously exploited to the Crown's profit; the ancient sail-making industry of Biscay was given a new vitality; and colonies of the most resourceful Parmesan farmers were introduced to turn green again the empty white-ness round Madrid, and to tempt Spaniards back to the soil by their example. In the northern hills, abandoned iron foundries glowed once more.

The merest detail of Spanish life was not too small for Al-beroni's care. In the Escorial he set up a paper mill, and an excellent printing press, to turn out for the clergy the religious books they had hitherto been obliged to buy in Antwerp. Did the fashionable world need crystal chandeliers? A factory for making them at once sprang into being, so that no longer was it necessary to purchase them from abroad by the export of good Spanish gold. For years past the official archives of the Kingdom had remained in chronic confusion; now Alberoni concentrated current papers in the Uzeda palace at Madrid; past archives were carefully stored at Simancas, to become a treasury for scholars of the future. The late Queen had established in Madrid a charity to care for ill prostitutes. The charity had been maladministered, and Alberoni found the poor women living in nauseous conditions — fifteen of them were so rotten with disease, "they were capable of infecting the whole of Spain." Alberoni caused their furniture and clothes to be burnt, their maladies to be treated and sickly bodies to be washed. Dressed in new clean clothes they attended a special service given for them at the shrine of Our Lady of Atocha; then they were moved to fresh quarters in the Monterey palace. The charity was rechristened by Alberoni "The Royal College of Protection," was handsomely endowed, and became one of the healthiest institutions of Madrid.

His first great administrative reform was the recasting of the household troops. On his arrival in Spain, Philip V had created regiments of household troops, largely recruited of Belgians and Irishmen. They had however served little purpose; Vendôme, when he clapped eyes on them, would have none of them — and that at a time when he was forming an army out of the scrapings of the countryside. Without danger to the royal family, Alberoni now decided, the guards might be reduced by half their official strength. There was immediately an uproar at court. The Duc d'Havré, colonel of the Walloon regiment, and his principal officers, protested violently; Bedmar, President of the Council of War, sided with them; even Alberoni's ally, the Duke of Popoli, in his capacity as governor of the little Prince of the Asturias, declared he could no longer be responsible for the safety of his sovereigns. "In that case," cried Philip with rare resolution, "I'll look after myself." Saint-Aignan, too, was full of remonstrations, and seems to have hinted without too much delicacy that the measure con-clusively proved Alberoni to be sold to some foreign power. An even temper was not among the abbé's pre-eminent qualities. His lack of it seems to have become particularly noticeable on this occasion. "Alberoni first of all replied," reported Saint-Aignan ruefully in due course, "that all the rumours about his understanding with the Emperor were nonsense, the result of the kind of suspicion which France was in the habit of display-ing on all occasions these days. . . . Then he told me that the King of Spain had no need of people who came to give him advice, and that in consequence he could get on very well with-out the advice even of France. As far as I was concerned, once I had completed what I believed to be my duty, by making the communication which I had just made, he advised me to keep clear of the matter. He added by the way that he failed to see why the King of Spain need bother about the opinions of the French Government, and that he couldn't understand why people would not allow Philip V the same freedom as he allowed others."

To all this fuss came a supreme, ridiculous climax. When Alberoni proceeded with his scheme for reducing the regi-ments, he found himself foiled; for they were already at half strength. "The King," he wrote to Cellamare at the Spanish Embassy in Paris, "has ordered that each regiment be reduced by 900 men, and when we came to do it, we didn't find a single man above that strength, which meant that 1,800 men were being paid who didn't exist, and the money was going into the pockets of the colonel and his officers. . . ."

Once the truth was out, Alberoni was merciless. Havré was dismissed; then his wife, a niece of Madame des Ursins, began to cabal against the reforms; the couple were promptly ban-ished back to Belgium; other recalcitrant officers were clapped into jail. The wives, of course, were full of calumny; apart from all his other crimes, Alberoni was now accused of starving the King's children by his first marriage, to curry favour with Elisabeth. Such examples of malice and stupidity would fill him with momentary despair. "I wonder," he confessed in April 1716, "whether I'll ever succeed in establishing a system of order and good government here. Everyone fights against it, and even if it's ever established, I wonder if they won't destroy it by sheer ineptitude. . . . Only a madman would think of reforming the world. The clever man is he who leaves it exactly as he found it. . . ."

Meanwhile the final issue between the nominal Prime Minister and the real one could no longer be delayed. From Paris Cellamare did all he could to reconcile his uncle with the abbé. The English, on the other hand, were heart and soul for Alberoni; during the June days when he was at Aranjuez, Bubb constantly exhorted his host to put himself publicly at the head of affairs. Alberoni counselled patience; a few weeks later the unfortunate Cardinal was forced to resign his office of Grand Inquisitor; he still clung for a time to his seat on the Council of State, until an order arrived forbidding him even that share in public affairs. "The Cardinal," Bubb reported exultant in August, "is entirely out of everything, and is retired to Villa Viciosa . . . in expectation of the return of his Courier from Rome with the Bull of his Dismission from his Employ of Inquisitor-General. So that there is nobody at present for the Publick Ministers to treat with. . . ." The Cardinal lingered on in Spain for some months, intriguing against Alberoni, and spreading the wildest calumnies. Finally at the beginning of 1717 he had become such a nuisance, he was ordered unceremoniously out of Spain, without even a chance to take leave of the King. He went off to Rome, from whence he maintained his war against Alberoni, with a vigour he had never lavished upon his administration.

Alberoni was now publicly accepted as first minister; he immediately set about the greatest of his reforms, which he had long meditated – the hamstringing of the Councils. The first one to suffer was the Council of State. The Presidency of it, with its semi-royal dignities, was abolished, although out of deference to the great age of Frigillano, the then holder of the office, his salary was still paid to him. Otherwise the Council that once had dictated the foreign and defence policy of Spain was reduced to confirming the decisions of Alberoni and his ministers.

The Council of Castile was next attacked. Salaries were reduced by one-third, all the comfortable perquisites, commissions on loans, free houses, lavish expense sheets, were abolished; every act of the body was henceforward scrutinized, and its members were made to understand that their main duty was submission to the royal will. The powers of the Council of War were reduced to the handling of judicial questions affecting the armed forces; while from the Council of the Indies five dotards were dismissed, and the Presidency conferred upon Admiral del Paëz, a man whom Alberoni could trust, and who burned to revive the maritime glories of Spain.

Alberoni now distributed the administration of the empire among various Secretaries of State, men of energy and "clean hands" as he put it. Grimaldo was given Foreign Affairs, the Marquis Castelar was sent to the War Department, and his brother Don José Patiño became Intendant of the Marine.

The financial system was overhauled with a view to the casting of a proper yearly budget. The chaos which his investigation revealed appalled Alberoni. "What confusion," he would cry to Parma, "in what a disorder I found this monarchy!" It was a labyrinth where even he got lost. True, he was able to put some system into the national tax-collecting machinery, to get rid of useless departments and officials. But when he came to the provincial revenues, dismay seized him. "Oh! Those taxes paid by the provinces," he cried, "all of

them levied on a provisional basis; not one of them in all prob-
ability can be called legal, and they employ a multitude of tax-
gatherers; above all that cursed 'millones' tax, which is enough
to destroy Spain before long; what harm they do to the people
and the King! The monarch doesn't receive half the proceeds
of them." But when the abbé wished to begin the reform by
cancelling the contracts to the tax-farmers, he met with his
one failure; he found himself beating vainly against the crazy
granite walls of the King's scruples.

As a buttress against lean years Alberoni instituted government stores, to provide the people in hard times with food at
reasonable prices; he tackled the appalling complication of the
coinage, a monetary anarchy to which the closest parallel was
lately to be seen in republican China. There were new silver
reales, and old ones rated at half the standard value: Andalusian
reales, and Catalan reales, and Castilian reales, each one of
which lost half its value when it wandered outside its own
province; there were piastres and pieces of eight, and piastres
from Peru or Mexico, which again were different. The milled
edge used in England since the Restoration had not yet reached
Spain; and there was universal clipping. When new coins were
minted, they soon left the country, in the paws of foreign merchants, who refused to be paid in money less bright and crisp.

But Alberoni struck a new piece of two reales, to be current
throughout the empire, and so well made, it could be neither
clipped nor counterfeited easily. To this day it is of course
wise in some parts of Spain, notably in Valencia, to bite the
change passed to you at bullfight or cinema; but Alberoni did
perhaps more than any man to give the country a good stable
coinage.

Then there were the law-courts. They opened at capricious
hours and rarely sat long enough to despatch current business.
If a magistrate felt particularly exhausted by the previous eve-

ning's pleasures, as like as not his court would not open at all that day. Alberoni changed all that. He decreed daily courts, and fixed inexorably their hours.

In this last matter he came to grips with the fundamental ill of Spain, the sloth that pervaded all classes but the very humblest. American riches fell like manna out of heaven; foreign labourers reaped the harvest; foreign troops fought for Spain; foreign generals led the native Spanish armies; in administrative sinecures the Spanish middle- and upper-classes dozed and gamed and thought about their honour. A British naval officer who had visited Spain during the late war wrote from behind the bastion of his robust prejudices, but perhaps with some truth: "Spain in general is a large garden of Butterflies, or rather a Hive of Old Drones, where neither wit nor industry is encouraged. A Spaniard is a sort of Amphibious Animal that is neither Fool nor Knave, but both; that has more Pride than Merit, that has more Impudence than a dozen of Watermen, more Conceit than six Country Squires . . . if he gets but a snuff box, a toothpicker . . . a spado at his side, an old cloak, and a Trencher-crowned hat, he fancies himself as great as the Prince of Condé. . . ." Alberoni for his part was driven almost mad by most of his collaborators. "It is death to have to deal with these ministers," he complained, "who, some from malice, some from ignorance, and others from laziness, will not work. Believe me, the one secretariat at Parma does more in a day than these four do in a week, and each one is composed of nine members, and that is no exaggeration." To Bubb he lamented that "neither he nor the Queen has one single person upon whom they can rely in Spain." This was not entirely true; in the Patiño brothers and del Paëz he found devoted assistants to execute the details of his greatest achievement, the maritime revival of Spain.

He had by now persuaded the Spanish sovereigns that upon the sea lay Spain's best chance of recovering her lost power.

Not that the army was neglected; indeed, a ragged, ill-armed mob had been metamorphosed into a smart force of 50,000 soldiers, clothed in new uniforms from Spanish looms, and equipped with arms from new Spanish factories. But it was essentially an expeditionary corps, a handsome complement to the great fleet that Alberoni was beginning to conjure up with little help from foreign shipyards. Almost all the raw materials for the enterprise he found within the Spanish dominions. No need for him to seek:

> ". . . the tallest pine
> Hewn on Norwegian hills to be the mast
> Of some great Ammiral. . . ."

Rather were the masts for the fleet felled on Spanish hills, and found in no way wanting. Keels were plated with Cuban copper. The very ropes, tar, and pitch, all were Spanish. At a time when war in the Baltic was disturbing our regular supplies of naval stores from the Gulf of Finland, Alberoni was giving a lesson in economic autarchy.

By the spring of 1717 a respectable fleet was in commission, with at least one first-rater, the *Principe de las Asturias*, built in record time. Cadiz and Ferrol, well-equipped bases now, hummed with activity. At a cost of 100,000 doubloons a great naval station was created at Barcelona. At the beginning of the work, Spaniards mocked Alberoni for a visionary, but in the end their jibes turned into fulsome praise. Alberoni was unmoved; he had a phrase for such encomia: "sporca adulazione" — "dirty adulation."

A new Indies fleet came into being, and sailed henceforward not at the convenience of some great lady who might be a passenger, but on a definite and published date. In 1717 a convoy of no less than ten large vessels sailed for the Indies, carrying cargoes that should, Alberoni calculated, bring in to the exchequer a profit of some seventy per cent. The Chamber of

Commerce for the Indies Trade — Casa de Contratación de las Indias — despite the fury of the Sevillanos, was removed from their city, which had been so undeservedly enriched by it, and established at Cadiz, its logical home. Cruisers were despatched to the West Indies to fight the smugglers, a struggle in which the British and Dutch Governments were invited to play their part. The Indies trade, the abbé believed, was the key to the Spanish problem; organize that trade properly, and Spain would be great again. "Believe me," he wrote to Parma, "unless some unforeseen accident occurs to upset the measures we've taken, in three years you'll see the trade brought to a point of perfection, and this King in consequence the happiest in Europe."

For all his success, Alberoni's existence at this time must have been well-nigh unbearable. Indeed, a high Spanish officer who had been a prisoner of the Moors always declared that he would sooner face slavery in Meknes again than change places with the abbé. His main worry was Philip's ambitions in France. He had never approved them, and every report from Paris which suggested an early death for Louis XV racked him with worry. He did not dare hope that the child might live.

The Duke of Parma might bluntly tell his niece not to encourage her husband in his pretensions to the French throne, lest by trying to better her condition she spoil it. Alberoni could not speak with similar freedom. He must give no weapon into the hands of his enemies, who inflated Philip's dreams of a triumphant return to his fatherland, to the green woods and the hunts which had enchanted his youth; and who seduced Elisabeth with prospects of French liberty and elegance, and the perils of Spanish widowhood dissipated for ever. To these illusions Alberoni was forced sometimes to give a sop. If he did not, his enemies would take advantage of him. So, without blowing hot, he would occasionally give Philip the pleasure of hearing that the French people yearned for him to come home, or that such and such a French officer had sworn undying loyalty to his cause.

The situation, already difficult, was of course complicated by the malice and hysteria of Saint-Aignan. He made one more futile effort to seek reconciliation with the abbé, hinting that France would be ready to pay well for his friendship. The reaction was immediate, and unsatisfactory. "In order," the Ambassador reported, "to put an end once and for all to such useless attempts, he again asked me to leave him in peace, since what I had to say could have not the slightest interest for him; he intended in future to have as little to do with me as possible." He told Saint-Aignan, Alberoni recounted to Cellamare, that "in future he may talk to me of rain and of good weather, but never of anything interesting."

Then there were worries enough nearer home. From the moment when Alberoni had begun to make Spain count again for something in the world, the Duke of Parma clamoured for help. He trembled under the Imperial menace; Charles VI had lately drifted into war with the Turks, and might at any moment use the affair as a pretext to invade Italy. Let a Spanish squadron immediately be sent, therefore, to forestall the danger. But Alberoni held that it would be folly for Spain to strike before she had regained her full strength. "It is my aim," he wrote in May 1716, "that the King should remain at peace with everyone, in order one day he may be in a position to make war on those who may not wish to be his friends." There was no telling when the crisis would come; in any event, Alberoni hardly hoped to be granted all the time he needed to make Spain great again; and he had no wish to see the brief moment of quiet unnecessarily curtailed by the impetuosity of his friends. "For Heaven's sake," he implored the Duke of Parma, "let Your Highness take every care to give the Ger-

mans no cause to pick a quarrel. All my plans are as yet undi-
gested." [1] Gloomily the Duke replied that the liberties of Italy
were in their death throes.

Then there was the strain of acting as nurse, confidant, secretary, cook, father, and impresario to the Queen. In the midst
of great affairs the abbé must keep a sharp eye upon her teeth
and at the first sign of discoloration procure a special tooth
powder from Italy for her. The despatch of delicacies from
Parma was often muddled. In April 1716 when his mind was
full of reforming the Indies trade and the currency, of negotiations with England and suspicions of Austria, Alberoni was
obliged to write sharply to Parma: "Her Majesty wants little
sausages such as are sold in the public shops at Piacenza, provided of course they're fresh and made this year; whereas the
big sausages received so far are old and hard as wood." The
Queen seems never to have received precisely the type of little
Placentian sausage for which she yearned. Years later, on the
very eve of his downfall, when he was at war with England
and France, was improvising a hundred different schemes to
save Spain, Alberoni yet found time to remonstrate with Parma
on the quality of sausages sent for the Queen. "I've never been
able to get them to send those ordinary sausages such as are
made by the purveyor Mazzari and his associates, particularly
the little raw ones that have a bit of fat mixed with them, and
the others that haven't, but which have got garlic in them.
Let me tell you that those which they did send were turned
down not only by the Queen, but even by my stable boys.
They're made of such horrible and such ancient meat, no human being exists who could get his teeth into them."

[1] He never ceased to urge a policy of *festina lente*. "We mustn't," he
wrote to Parma on July 29, 1716, "arouse hatreds and quarrels, but must
quietly and prudently get ourselves into a position where we can act at the
opportune and essential moment, so as to interest and unite all the Great
Powers in support of Italy's cause and rights." This of course gives the clue
to his intended policy, which the stupid obstinacy of his patrons contrived
to frustrate.

Then there was the troublesome question of truffles and of cheese. The Queen plagued her abbé about truffles, upon which she doted, and for cheese, which she considered essential to her meals. In February 1717, amid all the bustle of the Indies fleet setting off, he snatched a moment to lament the absence of promised truffles. Even when he heard that the truffles were on the way, a few days later, his irritation hardly lifted. "The Queen," he wrote, "has learnt of the despatch of wine and truffles, and with disgust has noticed that there is no mention of cheese. Those who have the honour to see her at table have observed that no dish goes without cheese."

There were too the incessant bothers stirred up by the Italian Comedians. In this silver age of the Commedia dell'Arte, at the moment when in Paris the Regent was lifting the ban upon it that the jealous Madame de Maintenon had once imposed,[2] when Antoine Watteau was peopling the yew hedges of his fancy with lamenting or ribald Harlequins, it was perhaps natural for an exiled Italian princess to yearn after the glittering Harlequinades, the stratagems of Pulcinello, the braggadocio of the Captain and the preposterous fancies of the Doctor.

It is difficult for us to appreciate the importance, the triumphant appeal of the Italian Comedians in Alberoni's day. We must imagine an entertainment with traditions which went back at least to Etruscan times, and yet which built upon that traditional foundation a structure brilliantly and preposterously improvised at almost every performance. The metaphysics of a Disney cartoon, the humours of the Marx Brothers, the slickness of a Maugham comedy and the improvisations of a New York diseur would if combined give an effect roughly approximating to the performance of good Italian comedians.

They were at this time to be found playing in almost every Continental town of importance, creating in their leisure that

[2] The Italian Comedians were banished from Paris in 1697, for satirizing Madame de Maintenon in a piece entitled "La fausse Prude."

disreputable Italian underworld where a Casanova could feel perfectly at home. Quarrelling, thieving, pimping, they perpetually tormented established authority; and the comedians whom Alberoni fetched from Parma for his Queen were truly in the tradition of their trade. Like Elisabeth herself, they refused to come by sea; costing a fortune in travelling expenses they wended a slow and unseemly way along the Riviera. And when they reached Madrid, it seemed as if the abbé's troubles had only begun. He was distracted by their perpetual squabbles. "The two chief comedians," he reported wearily to Parma in February 1716, "will I suppose end by cutting each other's throats. . . . If only there were others to amuse Her Majesty, I'd send both of them packing."

He put up with the rascals for a time, but a year later their behaviour became too scandalous to be borne. Harlequin married, and then proceeded to barter out the person of his wife, which, as Alberoni said, caused some dissension in the company. The Harlequin was dismissed, and in his place arrived another one, a good character and accomplished in his trade, who had been employed in the household of the Queen's uncle, Prince Antonio Farnese.

But the crowning vexation was Laura Pescatori, the Queen's old nurse, a cunning avaricious Lombardian peasant who came from Parma for the birth of Elisabeth's first baby. Alberoni put her up in his house when she first arrived, and did his best to be agreeable. The Queen, after all, doted on Laura. "She expects this woman," the abbé reported, "as though she were the Messiah." The mere prospect of seeing her beloved nurse again made Elisabeth neglect the puppies and birds which once had been her darlings.

The Pescatori's strident wit and tongue amused Alberoni for a time. Then he came gradually to see her as a mere intriguing harpy, an expense, and a fatal influence on the Queen. Elisabeth's privy purse was so small, she could permit herself few extravagances; only by stern economy and Alberoni's skill had she lately contrived to pay for some elegant carriages which she had ordered from Paris. Now the intolerable Pescatori fleeced the Queen incessantly, extorting chests of cypress wood, the finest linen, silver candlesticks, Heaven knew what else. She took bribes from all comers, and when she could get nothing out of Alberoni, to torment him she would sit wailing in some anteroom of the palace, brandishing her bare feet before the passing courtiers, and crying that she was not given money enough to buy a pair of slippers.

She brought with her a daughter whose grand airs enraged Alberoni; and she fetched her husband from Parma. This creature — his only virtue seems to have lain in a certain talent for painting fans — insisted upon travelling in greater state than did the Queen herself. In nine months the precious pair had wheedled or snatched more than £1,000 out of the Queen's privy purse, let alone what they got from the King.

Laura intrigued against Alberoni from her earliest days in Spain, working to upset his reforms, leaguing herself with his enemies, acting as go-between in a revived correspondence of Elisabeth with the handsome Maggiali. She even attempted to rival the abbé's triumphs in the kitchen, and it must have been a poor consolation to him that in her efforts she spoiled enough Italian sausages and gooseberries to regale not only the Queen for some time to come, but "six convents of friars" as well. He tried to keep his temper, but it was a hard trial. "The rascally woman," he wrote to the Duke in June 1716, pouring out his cup of woe, "abuses the Queen's good nature and treats her with such superiority and contempt, it kills me. . . . I find myself in a palace that has become a Babylon. I swear to Your Highness that she gives me more trouble and more work than all the affairs of the Crown put together. . . ."

But what in Laura Pescatori's conduct particularly enraged him were her efforts to seduce her mistress from public business. The clique of his enemies now imagined they could best destroy Alberoni by killing in the Queen her incipient urge towards political power. The King, they calculated, would fall back into their hands once Elisabeth was enticed away from affairs of State. With the Pescatori's help, therefore, they offered Elisabeth every form of frivolous distraction.

Alberoni scolded her soundly. Was she going to allow herself to be reduced to inaction by intriguers who flattered her? Where would her fame and honour be, when, dwindled to the mere role of a woman, she no longer enjoyed esteem in the world, nor the consideration of her subjects, when she had reposed her trust in those courtiers who yearned to govern in her place, and to distract her from business? The Queen listened to him. There was even talk of the Pescatori being sent away. But nothing came of it.

✿ IX ✿

THE GROWTH OF OPPOSITION

Whatever intrigues swirled round his plump person at court, Alberoni was now one of the great personages of Europe, the object of respect and fear. The Queen was his pupil, England his friend; under his touch, the moribund body of Spain was suddenly infused with new life; his growing fleet menaced the Emperor and seemed to promise liberation to Italy. Indeed, an intelligent observer in the year 1716 might safely have wagered that Alberoni and Stanhope, with the Regent of France as their yawning associate, would henceforward give the law to Europe. But in making that wager he would have overlooked the obstructive power of ancient prejudices, mankind's instinctive distrust of new men and untried principles.

The concept of an Anglo-Spanish alliance to rule the world was audacious. Had it been realized, the history of the British Empire and of the New World might have been altered; one overwhelming combination of power might have dominated the Atlantic seaboard of Europe, and the Americas from Cape Horn to Hudson Bay.

But the merchants of London and the Cabinet of George I, whatever Bubb might report, could not rid themselves of the belief that Spain was a dying state. Many British traders resented Alberoni's attempts to regularize their trade with the Spanish colonies. The instinct to singe the King of Spain's beard died hard, and the ordinary English ship trading to the Spanish Indies would turn freebooter or smuggler at little provocation. The Papist error of the ships they took or of the authorities they outwitted seemed to sanctify their behaviour.

The Cabinet, it is true, were at first well inclined towards Spain and appear, as we have seen, at one time to have contemplated a close political alliance. But with the collapse of the Jacobite rebellion, and the solid establishment of Hanoverian power in England, the traditional inclination of the Whigs and of their German King carried them back towards the Empire. Political parties in the England of that date divided almost as sharply on foreign policy as we have seen them do, to our cost, in the England of the last decade. The Tories under Queen Anne had favoured Spain and Sicily; well then, the Whigs under King George must do the contrary. "No sep'rate leagues with Sicily or Spain": in the doggerel of "Britannia Rediviva," a poem on the Hanoverian accession, the Whig instinct was interpreted and proclaimed.

The Emperor, then, was the proper ally for George I and his Whigs, against the power of France, which still obsessed us. The Whigs did not realize that the menace of France had been dissipated upon the field of Blenheim. For us danger was building a new abode across the Rhine. With that vision which generally proves fatal to the careers of British statesmen, Bolingbroke seems to have perceived the growing threat of the Germanic world: hence his efforts to conclude the league with France, Spain, and the Italian princes against the Empire. But Bolingbroke was gone now, and the Whigs yearned for the old association with Vienna.

The German influence of George's court heightened this inclination. The new King's stolid existence was passed among the mistresses and councillors he had fetched from Hanover, Frau Kielmannsegge, whose "two acres of cheek spread with crimson, an ocean of neck that overflowed," terrified the young Horace Walpole; Fräulein von Schulenberg, lean and aging; the sly Bernstorff, and the predatory small fry. To them rather than to the supercilious English did he turn for comfort and advice; and their advice was always given to the "Elector of Hanover" rather than to the King of England. The King did not attempt to conceal his dislike of life in England. If he had been sent packing, no doubt he would have sighed as much with relief as with regret.

His heart was in Hanover, and particularly at Herrenhausen. In that piece of dishonest poppycock, the *Four Georges*, Thackeray set before his American audiences a horrifying picture of the fat, jolly ogre in his "enormous, hideous, gilded, monstrous marble palace"; outside the world of labyrinths and cascades, beyond the park walls, "the landscape is awful — wretched wastes, beggarly and plundered; half-burned cottages and trembling peasants gathering piteous harvests; gangs of such tramping along with bayonets behind them, and corporals with canes and cats-of-nine-tails to flog them to barracks. . . . But round all that royal splendour lies a nation enslaved and ruined . . . it is the price of a miserable province that the king ties in diamonds round his mistress's white throat . . . and Versailles is only larger and not worse than Herrenhausen. . . ." And so forth, for many pages.

A cocksure Victorian, in the noblest and most enlightened of all ages, catering for a public that knew little history beyond a list of presidents, kings, and sea-fights, could of course write with confidence like this; and he could shut out from Onslow Square all thought of the children at the looms — whom a visiting clergyman likened to flitting butterflies — and the crowded fetid cellars where incest frolicked with disease. The genteel audiences of Boston and Philadelphia were no doubt edified by this revelation of evil in the decadent Europe from which their grandfathers had cut free. They were taught to avert their eyes from their factories where the immigrants from the Old World slaved till they were worn out (it was cheaper to starve them till they died, and then get fresh blood, than to pay a living wage).

For all Thackeray's ranting, the Electorate of Hanover in George I's day was not an unhappy sort of place; it even enjoyed a mild degree of prosperity. And George himself, however savagely he might treat his wife and son, was no monster, but a heavy sort of rustic patriarch. To see the peaches ripening on the garden walls at Herrenhausen, and his Electorate thrive was the summit of his ambition; and he was determined that it should benefit from his recent elevation to the British throne.

For several years the northern states of Europe had been squabbling over the Swedish Empire, recumbent since the defeat of Charles XII at Poltawa in 1709. Where good German territory went begging, George I wanted his share. With the connivance of Stanhope, his Secretary of State, he concentrated a strong squadron of the British fleet in the Baltic against Sweden, a state with which we were technically at peace. This violation of his constitutional promises [1] was covered by the pretence of lending protection to our traders coming with naval stores from the Gulf of Finland; and its reward was the Duchies of Bremen and Verden, which gave Hanover a precious outlet to the North Sea.

A desire to be confirmed by the Emperor in the possession of these territories, and his traditions as a German prince, irresistibly impelled George I towards an Austrian alliance. A pact with Alberoni would in the long run have meant conflict with the Empire, a course unthinkable for George I. Rather would he face trouble with Spain, however polite his messages to Philip V.

It was reasonably certain that there would be trouble if England let the Emperor have his head. It was tiresome enough

[1] He had promised not to use the resources of his British Kingdom in the interests of Hanover.

that he should still call himself "Charles III of Spain and the Indies," bestow the Golden Fleece, employ a Council for Spanish Affairs, stocked with vengeful Catalans and dominated by a Neapolitan donkey-driver. Lately he had begun to play the new Barbarossa, into the bargain claiming all Italy as his heritage. Above all, he yearned for Sicily, without which he considered the possession of Naples to be an empty pleasure.

Sicily had of course been allotted to Victor-Amadeus at the peace, with the title of King. A favourite of the Tories, Victor-Amadeus had enjoyed the protection of the British fleet so long as Queen Anne reigned. But George I had withdrawn it — perhaps because Victor-Amadeus possessed an infinitely better right to the British throne than he did — and the hold of the wily prince upon the island was nowadays precarious. Nor was his administration beloved there. Long the cherished dominion of Spain, the Sicilians now saw themselves a mere province of a remote and poverty-stricken duchy. Lately, too, Victor-Amadeus had become embroiled with the local clergy in a ridiculous squabble over a consignment of peas, which his revenue officers had seized from the Bishop of Agrigentum's gardener. The affair had raised the whole vexed question of ecclesiastical immunities, and had caused the expulsion of the Sicilian priesthood. They now thronged Rome in their thousands, starving, agitating, imploring aid from every quarter, particularly the Austrian.

For the Emperor Charles VI it seemed a Heaven-sent opportunity. In the negotiations which now began with England, he demanded the aid of the British fleet for his Sicilian design. By the Utrecht settlement, Sicily, if it passed out of Savoyard hands, must revert to Spain; but this detail was conveniently forgotten; and the Anglo-Austrian treaty of June 5, 1716 implied British support for the Austrian designs upon Sicily, however much Stanhope might explain away the instrument as purely defensive.

171

Alberoni was furious. He slowed up the Asiento negotiations and talked of frightening King George with the "scarecrow who lives at Avignon" — in other words, the Pretender. Stanhope at first tried to calm him. Were it not for the German ministers of George I, he assured him, the English would go much further toward a solid alliance with Spain. But he changed his tune when the negotiations with the Austrians were complete. "I believe that they" (the Spanish court), he wrote to Bubb, "can hardly think that . . . the King would be so ill advised as to contract any arrangement which could possibly lead him to quarrel with a nation whose friendship and commerce hath ever been esteemed the most beneficial to England." Once more was proclaimed that fatal partiality for the German world, and for Vienna in particular, to which Englishmen, alas! have always been subject. Bubb had always pretended that the rumours of an Anglo-Austrian rapprochement were wicked inventions to spoil our good relations with Spain. When the truth became known, Philip V was violent in his reproaches to Alberoni. "Where are your English now," he cried, "whose friendship and support you've so much advertised . . . ?" "England," added Alberoni in his turn, "has made an alliance with our deadly foe, who has refused to recognize Philip as King of Spain, who has covered him with insults, and whose vast power in Italy will engulf all the minor states in a common ruin."

Yet he continued with the Asiento negotiations, hoping at least to win the friendship of the English mercantile world. "I have always thought," he declared with some resignation, "that the community of interests between the Emperor and the King of England would keep them in accord, but . . . my aim has always been to win over the nation and consequently the Parliament, as one doesn't know what will happen."

"The Asiento has been concluded," wrote the abbé on June 6, 1716, "and in consequence a perfect intelligence has been established with England, without the Germans being able to confound it." England could not make Alberoni too great, declared the triumphant Bubb, for his greatness would imply wider influence in Spain than England had ever possessed.

The Duc d'Orléans, though he had got the Regency of France, was none too happy. How could one rest at ease upon a power so little absolute and solid? Everybody in the kingdom had been set upon a new form of government on the English model. It was inconceivable, wrote Lord Stair from the British Embassy, how much all there detested their condition, how passionately they longed to copy the English system. Unfortunately, there was no very clear idea of how that system worked; and so the nobility upon whose support the Regent depended — the lawyers, the only other organized political body in France, were at loggerheads with him from the first — fell back upon an idea that had been fashionable years before in the circle of the Duc de Bourgogne — government by predominantly aristocratic committees instead of by middle-class Secretaries of State.

A multiplicity of councils was consequently set up — a General Council of Regency, over which Orléans himself presided and on which Saint-Simon sat, to his exquisite pleasure; Councils of War, of Marine, of Foreign Affairs, Finance, Conscience — there seemed no end to them. As the Parisians put it:

"Français, ne craignez pas d'évènements sinistres,
Notre sage Régent a su tout prévenir,
Il a soixante et dix ministres."

For most people the new system seemed to have a commendably English air. One man, Cellamare, the Spanish Ambassador, remained unimpressed; he saw that the Regent was introducing into France the very administrative chaos which Alberoni had driven out of Spain. The councils had a Spanish cut, not an English one. "The French," he cried, "have dressed their government up in the Spanish fashion; but the golilla will become them as little as the cravat became us when we first took to it."

Indeed, the Regent was as much the prisoner of councils as ever any Spanish monarch had been; nor were the members of them particularly loyal to him. Few Frenchmen accepted the renunciations which had made him legal heir to the little Louis XV. Even the faithful Saint-Simon admitted to his master that should matters ever come to a head, his conscience would force him to regard Philip V of Spain as the rightful king of France.

Orléans's popularity was not improved by the tales of poisons which still hung over his genial head. His wife was normally indolent of habit; she lived remote from politics, on a white and gold chaise-longue, with a bottle of claret beside her, dozing away the days in the lovely boudoir that Oppernord had designed — boudoirs with skating monkeys, Chinese sages, and shellwork were replacing the draughty splendours of the old-fashioned salon. But the prospect of tormenting her husband was enough to end her delicious lethargy; and she now pretended that her life was in danger from him, because she sympathized with her brother, the Duc du Maine. She even sought a counter-poison from Maine, to protect her from the Regent.

The charge of poisoner was again brought home to him when he visited the little King. After drinking the cup of chocolate which was his lunch, Orléans would pass an hour or so with the boy. That little monster with the angel's face, upon whom Frenchmen had fixed their fondest hopes, would for a time leave off torturing his birds, tearing the furbelows of his ladies, or beating the courtiers about the face with his vicious small cane. For he was always charmed by the inimitable mixture of gaiety, respect, and affection with which his first subject treated him.

The Regent for his part delighted to amuse the boy; there was never anyone less suited to the part of wicked uncle than this disillusioned, over-intelligent epicure, whose main desire was to live in peace with his mistresses and his darling daughter "Joufflotte," the widowed young Duchesse de Berry, to enjoy his noble collection of pictures, to dabble in cooking, drawing, and fortune-telling, to be wrapped in noise, and fancy himself the reincarnation of Henri IV, his great-grandfather. But the old Maréchal de Villeroy and Madame de Ventadour-Lévis, who looked after the young King, belonged to the "old court" party, regarding Philip V as the rightful heir, and Orléans as a murderer. When, with infinite respect, the Regent offered his young sovereign a bowl of soup, Villeroy would find a pretext to knock it on to the floor. . . .

Something must be done to check the "old court" party. It was hand in glove with the Spanish court, drew its inspiration, in fact, from there. Now Alberoni was supreme at Madrid; therefore, argued the Regent, Alberoni was at the bottom of the mischief and must be got rid of.

At that very time Alberoni was writing to the Duke of Parma: "We must abandon long views like the succession to the throne of France and take advantage of this sacrifice to induce the best-disposed powers to give Spain some compensation." In short, between his views and the Regent's lay so narrow a gap, it should have been no matter to bridge it. But the Regent did not know how little the abbé was his enemy; and he now sought to ruin him, by means of the Parmesan Minister in Paris, a certain Marquis Hannibal Scotti.

The Duke of Parma let himself be persuaded by the Regent that Alberoni had lost sight of Italian liberation in his intrigues to take Philip V back to France; and Scotti — a tall thick man, Saint-Simon calls him, whose thickness showed in everything he said or did — was despatched to Madrid on a special mission, ostensibly to congratulate the Queen on the birth of her first child, really to ruin Alberoni with her, and if possible to supplant him.

Scotti arrived in April 1716; Saint-Aignan was confident that the detestable abbé was doomed: "his removal will not encounter more than feeble opposition from the Queen, when the insinuations reach her from the Parmesan court." But Scotti was easily outmanœuvred. Alberoni affected to believe that he had come to seek an appointment in the Spanish service. "Pray be convinced," wrote Alberoni, tongue in cheek, "of my desire to be of service to the Marquis Hannibal. . . . But . . . I have had less difficulty in reaching an agreement with England than in helping the said gentleman. . . . The Queen has a horror of soliciting the King, though of what lies in her own gift she would give away everything, down to her chemise. . . ."

Never did Scotti have a chance to speak in private to the Queen. At last he gave up the fight and went off to Parma with vengeance in his heart. "Marquis Hannibal," gravely reported Alberoni, "leaves this court in glory and triumph. . . . I flatter myself that he will remain convinced of my goodwill. . . ."

But the episode left a cloud of suspicion between the abbé and his master in Parma. A new secretary arrived, to spy on him. Then, the Duke was for ever warning him not to exasperate the French. Alberoni was unimpressed. "I know the French," he wrote to Cellamare in Paris; "the people who now invoke God's wrath upon me would invite me to supper tomorrow if I were in Paris. . . ."

The Regent now meditated another attempt to ruin the abbé. He conceived himself driven to it by the rising truculence of his enemies and the growing difficulties of his régime. He had hoped to bring France a new era of happiness; instead, after six months, life was getting harder; bankruptcies, unemployment were on the increase. At one of the masked balls, which were all the rage, the Regent fell in with a pretty girl dressed

in rags. "Qui êtes-vous, ma belle?" "La dame du royaume!"
came the reply as the mask vanished in the crowd. In the streets
the urchins sang:

> "Mais revenons à notre bal,
> Où jusqu'à l'excès on pousse l'insolence;
> Le Régent danse bien, de bon air, en cadence,
> A dit certain quidam; mais, parbleu, la Régence
> Danse fort mal!"

God-fearing Frenchmen — and there were many — shud-
dered at the rumours of the goings-on behind the locked doors
of the Palais-Royal. Even "Madame," though she adored her
son, would pause in her letter-writing, or her passionate ad-
vocacy of sauerkraut, to curb her apprehension. "Whenever it
thunders over Paris," she cried, "I expect to see fire pour down
from heaven, as it fell on Sodom and Gomorrah."

Then there were the antics of pretty "Joufflotte," the apple
of the Regent's quick, short-sighted eye. His passion for her
was said to exceed paternal bounds; certainly she acted a leading part in the strange ritual of his orgies; and her every whim
was gratified. She had her own regiment of guards — the standard of their physique was set particularly high; and she drove
through Paris with kettle-drums beating: two privileges that
belonged to the King alone. While the veterans raged at this
presumption, she would be off to Vincennes woods, to join in
round dances with the peasant girls and shepherdesses, inciting
them to sing erotic songs, and when their repertory failed, out-
doing them in bawdiness. As aunt of the little King, she claimed
precedence before all other ladies of the kingdom. It was hard
enough at the best of times for the dowagers of the last reign
to accord her that distinction; and harder still when they heard
of her at some riotous party surrendering to a nobody's caresses
those parts of her appetizing young person which should by

rights have been reserved for the pleasure of a crowned head —
and that only after a good marriage contract and a profitable
treaty of alliance. As the satirists put it:

> "La Messaline de Berry,
> L'œil en feu, l'air plein d'arrogance,
> Dit, en faisant charivari,
> Qu'elle est la première de France.
> Elle prend, ma foi, tout le train
> D'être la première putain."

Throughout the kingdom the tide of disapproval rose. The
conservatives persisted in crying that if the little King were to
die, they wanted as his successor not Philippe d'Orléans but
Philip from over the Pyrenees. Carrying from the couturière
some dress that seemed to float off its wearer like a cloud, a
cloud "à manches en pagodes, couleur de merde d'oie" perhaps,
the little seamstresses would sing:

> "Si Louis XV on enterrait,
> Philippe en France regnerait.
> Lan la derirette.
> Non pas le Philippe d'ici.
> Lan la deriri!"

Something must be done, and that quickly, to check the
growing sentiment for the King of Spain. Noailles and Saint-
Simon persuaded the Regent that efforts must be continued to
discredit Alberoni; once that was done, Spain would come to
heel. No trick was too small for their attention; the French
Embassy in Madrid organized sabotage in his linen factory,
tried to tempt away his artisans, fomented trouble in the dockyards; they even offered to sell him ships which they knew to
be unfit.

All this was but a preparation for another direct attack.
Noailles and Saint-Simon egged on the Regent to adopt a tech-

nique which has ever been the resort of French governments in extremities — that of pursuing simultaneously two separate and contradictory policies, one of them entirely unbeknown to the Foreign Minister of France. In this case the Regent in a mood of aberration was induced to send secretly to Madrid the Marquis de Louville. He was, it will be remembered, the closest companion of Philip V during the first years in Spain and had been dismissed, it was said, because he dared to advise the King to take a mistress while in Italy. He was now dug out of the country, where he was writing his memoirs, and invited to go to Madrid, ostensibly for some commercial negotiations, really to draw upon the capital of Philip's old affection, to regain paramount influence with him. He was to ally himself at first with Alberoni, to destroy the rest of the Italian clique. When Alberoni was isolated, Louville was to annihilate him also.

A frivolous mission, frivolously conceived. The archives of the Quai d'Orsay secrete the confidential code for Louville's secret correspondence with the Regent, unbeknown to old Huxelles, the President of the Foreign Affairs Council. It is a document that breathes the very spirit of the Regency, as the historical novelettes conceive it. Louville is to convey his impressions of the Spanish political scene by writing that "he has such a lust upon him since he arrived in Madrid, he is almost jumping out of his skin," or that he has found a pretty mistress with an amiable character, or has not come unscathed out of the battle of love. A copy of the code exists in the Regent's own hand; it must have been composed by him in person, perhaps during one of the famous suppers. The whole strange panorama of that age is set before us, the exotic trees of the Palais-Royal, Harlequins posturing in the depths of every mirror, with a plumed Indian head to crown it, tables that sway like Virtue upon their yielding legs: a servant seeking a place, who advertises in the newspapers not his industry, sobriety, and readiness to rise early, but an "interesting phisionomy."

The inordinate cravats whip the foam off the champagne; the fumes of "vin de Chypre" and iced Tokay thin out; and the brick-red Regent rises like a short-sighted amiable Triton from off a billow of fortune-tellers and naked breasts to eat carps' roes "en coulis d'écrévisses" — a dish of some delicacy and complication which he himself has devised with the help of his silver "batterie de cuisine."

Out of this extravagant order Louville came into the stern sunlight of Madrid, one July day in 1716, when nothing moved save the growing clamours in the King's poor head or a guitar idly struck in a dark doorway; where the finest coach stopped dead at the sound of the "Ave Maria" and its passengers knelt in the common dust. It was a far cry to Paris, flirtations and gossip in the dusk of the Tuileries Gardens, Joufflotte bullying the pensive Watteau to decorate her new Château de la Muette, in the Bois, with erotic fancies in the Chinese taste. . . . No less far a cry to the Spain Louville had known, the Spain that was almost a willing colony of France. Nevertheless, as he set down at the French Embassy, Louville nursed the fondest hopes of success. He only needed five minutes' audience with the King.

He had come by an unfrequented road through the Pays de Foix. But he had not, as he believed, slipped into Madrid unnoticed. "He's an insolent fellow," Alberoni had already reported, "who once governed the King despotically. The Duc d'Orléans and the Duc de Noailles imagine that he'll regain the King's confidence and serve as an instrument for attaining their ends. And those ends are well known; all the tricks of that prince are designed to assure him the throne of France. . . . It's the object of all his plans; to realize them, he'd make an alliance with the Turk. . . ."

Louville had not been many hours in Madrid when he received a command from Grimaldo, Secretary of State, to quit Spain forthwith and not to approach the palace. Louville pleaded the urgency of his mission, of the letters he brought; his nervous condition, he complained, made it impossible for him to travel. From the hot baths in which he lay interminably, a stream of remonstrance was poured upon the Spanish court. Alberoni came to see him in his bath, deplored the obduracy of Their Catholic Majesties. Alas! there was no changing it. . . . Exasperated and sweating, Louville would wait in some side street where the King was to pass. But Philip rode by with a granite eye.

It needed a formal protest to the Regent to effect Louville's recall. He left behind the famous code for Saint-Aignan to use and continued from Paris to make war upon the abbé. Louville was no fool. He now furnished Saint-Aignan with elaborate plans for rallying against Alberoni the jealous grandees, Father d'Aubenton, Philip's confessor, and if possible Laura Pescatori.

Saint-Aignan was full of hope; he soon reported the gaining of the secretary to the Indies Council and of the Duke of In-fantado, who had been sulking in his lovely palace at Guada-lajara ever since Alberoni came to power; there were hopes, too, of Grimaldo; despite the benignity with which he folded his short arms upon his tubby little belly, he was a furnace of jealousy and ambition.

The young Ambassador did not stay above stairs; the Queen's Flemish dresser and Bubb's valet promised to keep their eyes open. But the stroke that caused him peculiar pride was his success in making mischief between Alberoni and Father d'Aubenton. Anonymous letters, tittle-tattle, promises for the future, all were used upon the nervous old priest. Not much was effected; there was to be no real rift between the two clerics for another three years. But the ingenious Ambas-sador reported posthaste to Louville that it had already come to high words; for the architect of such a triumph, he hinted nothing less than the Golden Fleece would be a proper re-ward.

Louville was unmoved. "Ask for the Fleece, by all means," he agreed with some cruelty, "if you're bent on doing so. The Regent won't object, but, remember, he'll only laugh at you. The whole idea's childish, let me tell you; it reeks of the milk which is still your principal nourishment." Years later the poor Saint-Aignan was still pestering the Spanish Government for the precious, unattainable Fleece. . . .

Alberoni was as indifferent to these manœuvres as to the blandishments of the pro-Spanish party in Paris. Instead he was watching, with interest as yet untouched by apprehension, the ever increasing complexity of French policy. By now the threads of intrigue crossed and double-crossed until the Regent himself could no longer unravel them. His most secret agents were even intriguing against each other. But with it all he was isolated in Europe. He had failed in Spain, deserted Sweden in her troubles; when he asked the Emperor for a guarantee of Orléanist rights to the French Crown, he was met with outrageous demands for Alsace. In his predicament he suddenly began to cast eyes upon England and the Dutch.

His first approach to the British Government was coldly met. Terms were advanced, particularly on the point of expelling the Pretender from French soil, which even the easygoing Orléans considered derogatory to his honour. Undiscouraged, but not yet daring to brave the old anti-English marshals, he now had resort to the kind of romantic subterranean shift, which in the imagination of a Ouida is inseparable from the negotiation of a good treaty.

The instigator of this new attempt to upset the traditional alinement of the Powers was the Abbé Dubois,[2] a priest, like Alberoni, of obscure origin and remarkable ability. Destined to be Alberoni's bitterest enemy, like him he was to rise to the purple and know inordinate power. Like him he incurred

[2] Guillaume Dubois, born, Brives, 1656; died, Versailles, 1723.

Saint-Simon's hatred and was savagely caricatured — "a thin little man . . . with a blond wig and a ferret's face. . . . All the vices disputed with each other in him for mastery, making a continuous rumpus. . . ." Alberoni saw him as an "artisan of fantasies"; the lampoonists reviled him as the gross companion of the Regent's orgies and the rival of her father for Joufflotte's favours.

Dubois had certainly scant notion of priestly continence. (But, to do him justice, he was no officiating priest; he did not know how to say Mass.) He swore habitually in so long-winded a fashion, a pert secretary once suggested he should employ someone expressly to say his profanities and thus save precious time. To achieve his ends he would stomach any humiliation, or clown extravagantly; he possessed the rare combination of an agile mind and a body no less agile; much of his success in the Regent's circle came from his skill in climbing round the barest room, never putting a foot to the parquet, but creeping like a fly along some frond of woodwork, and delicately springing from thence on to a console table, by way of one of those new china-cabinets which were all the rage. . . . He was appallingly unmethodical and generally thought to be venal.

On the other hand, he had enjoyed the friendship of Fénelon; as tutor to the young Orléans, he had given his charge an education in brilliant contrast to the worldly-wise ignorance of a Louis XIV. After following his young master in his campaigns, he had fallen of recent years into the black books of "Madame"; during the first days of the Regency she issued from the stinking menagerie that was her boudoir a veto on his employment. But after a few months his persuasive tongue got the ban set aside. Orléans might despise Dubois, but he was reduced by him to such helpless laughter, he could refuse him nothing; and so, when a vacancy occurred in the Council of Conscience, Dubois slipped into it. As his last defences went down: "Un peu de droiture, abbé," Orléans had entreated, "je t'en prie!"

When the first negotiations with France came to nothing, Dubois saw his chance. He had known Stanhope for years; once they had been companions in gallantry, and then enemies in Spain. Dubois had lately revived his correspondence with Stanhope. Now he induced the Regent in July 1716 to send him secretly to The Hague, there to intercept the British Secretary of State on his way to Hanover with King George.

It was typical of Dubois that he should elect to travel in the guise of a wealthy connoisseur, interested in an important Poussin and the forthcoming sale of William III's library at Leiden. The Poussin was duly acquired, and Stanhope intercepted. At night in the privacy of Stanhope's lodgings the two men sparred over points of history, of a vintage, or of a mistress commonly enjoyed. The conversations lasted a space of time out of all proportion to their apparent triviality; yet at the end of them the course of European history had been changed.

Thrusting a present of champagne upon the English statesman, Dubois hurried back to Paris, triumph filling his labyrinthine heart. He found the Regent put out by Louville's failure at Madrid; the prince was all the more anxious therefore to secure what support he could from England, and he sent Dubois off to Hanover in the first days of August 1716.

There was negotiated the first Entente Cordiale. Stanhope and his Hanoverian colleagues were not at first particularly anxious for it, but in the midst of the conversations an event occurred which made them change their tune. Peter the Great suddenly made it up with Charles XII of Sweden and advanced into Mecklenburg, where he threatened important Hanoverian interests; indeed, the very Electorate itself. At once the proffered friendship of France assumed immense

LA REINA D'ESPAÑA.
Doña Isabel Farnesio Princessa de Parma nacio a 25 de Octu
bre de 1692 y caso con D.ª Phelipe Quinto Rey de España ã
16 de Setiembre de 1714.

ELISABETH FARNESE RETURNED FROM THE CHASE

CARDINAL ALBERONI
by Trevisani

value. "The King now wishes," wrote Stanhope to London in some apprehension, "and so doth your humble servant very heartily, that we had secured France. . . . I was, you know, very averse at first to this treaty, but I think truly as things now stand we ought not to lose a minute in finishing it." At all costs the spectre of a Franco-Russian alliance must be conjured away.

The agreement into which Dubois was now rushed, "en robe de chambre et bonnet de nuit," as he complained, provided for mutual guarantees of the Hanoverian and Orléanist successions; and the Pretender was to be sent out of France. It was hardly to the liking of Stanhope's colleagues at home, and there was a minor Cabinet crisis before signature was finally secured in February 1717. By the adhesion of Holland it was turned into a Triple Alliance.

It was no more popular in France than in England; the veterans fumed, Saint-Simon wrote indignant memoranda; in the fashionable cafés — Chez Procope, Chez la Veuve Laurent — the normal ritual of chess and bawdry was disturbed by rumours of the sums which the English had paid Dubois.

In reality it was he who had tried to buy Stanhope; the advantages of the alliance of the Orléans family were enormous; the Regent and his mother are reputed to have kissed the parchment of it with tears of pleasure, while Dubois was rewarded with a fat abbey and a place on the Foreign Affairs Council. Nevertheless, for George I there had also been solid gains; no longer need he fear a Franco-Russian alliance; when the Czar visited Paris in the following year, his overtures were fobbed off with a present of tapestries and musk-scented candles. . . .

It was perhaps Alberoni's greatest blunder not to appreciate the true import of this association. George I, by his ties with the Emperor and the Regent, through fear of the pro-Spanish party, were drifting inevitably towards a conflict with him; the contagion of an alliance, the fertility of communicated terrors, accelerated the trend.

The Protestant predominance in the new Triple Alliance caused heartburnings in Rome. The Vatican now put forward a fantastic scheme for a Catholic counter-alliance, of the Empire, Savoy-Piedmont, and Spain, to establish the Pretender in Great Britain and Philip V in France. Alberoni had little time to waste on such plans; he was no more than civil to Victor-Amadeus's envoy who came to Madrid to discuss the matter, for he had scant desire to become involved with that crafty prince, "who was in the habit of pulling his chestnuts out of the fire with a cat's-paw"; and though from deference to the Vatican he showed a disposition to treat with Vienna, he ensured the still birth of the negotiations by demanding the preliminary surrender of the Emperor's entire Italian possessions.

All the same, it was clear that the Emperor and the King of Spain could not, without danger to the peace of Europe, continue their schoolgirlish quarrels, each one refusing to recognize the other. The idea of ending the bickerings between Vienna and Madrid had already been in Stanhope's mind when he was negotiating with Dubois in Hanover. "If we close with France," he had written to his sore-tried colleague Townshend, "I think I have a plan for Spain which will not displease you."

The plan turned, as might have been expected, upon getting Sicily for the Emperor. Early in 1716, in a rare unguarded moment, Victor-Amadeus had betrayed his concern at the Emperor's refusal to recognize him as King of Sicily; and he had hinted that to secure good relations with Vienna he might be prepared to exchange Sicily against the infinitely less valuable island of Sardinia, at that time an Imperial possession. He had subsequently disclaimed the idea, but Stanhope had never forgotten it, and it now became the basis of his plan. He proposed that the Emperor should abandon all claims to Spain and guarantee the established successions in England and

France, receiving in return Sicily, Tuscany, Parma, and Piacenza (the latter three as Imperial fiefs), with guarantees of his Italian and Belgian territories. On the extinction of the Farnesi in the male line, Elisabeth's son, Don Carlos, was to be installed in Parma and Piacenza, with the Imperial investiture.

Alberoni did not at the time give the plan much attention. He was deeply involved in negotiating with the Vatican a concordat which was to end for the moment the autonomous ambitions of the Spanish Church; his object was to ensure the goodwill of the Holy See for his Italian projects. The question thereupon arose of rewarding Alberoni's pains with a cardinal's hat — not an unusual distinction for an eminent cleric who was Prime Minister of a leading Catholic state. Unfortunately Alberoni and the Holy Father had long been at loggerheads, and the quarrel had recently been heightened by the failure of the Spanish court to send aid to the Emperor in his newly opened war against the Turks. Clement XI had induced Philip V to promise the despatch of a Spanish squadron to the Levant; the sailing of the ships was unaccountably delayed, no doubt because of the rumours about Sicily. But Alberoni's enemies in Rome — Cardinal del Giudice had recently arrived, breathing vengeance — accused him of blackmailing the Papacy, until he was raised to the purple.

There was a deadlock over the hat. The Spanish monarchs were exasperated for they had been demanding it for months. "The Queen," reported Alberoni to Parma in February 1717, "is irritated and indignant at the scant attention which the Pope has paid to her appeal, written entirely in her own hand, in such strong and unanswerable terms, H.M. won't be able to use stronger ones to God when she asks permission of Him to enter paradise."

But it became necessary to forbid the entry into Spain of the Papal Nuncio before the Pope would agree. At last, in a special consistory on July 12, 1717, the College of Cardinals with general approval raised Alberoni to the purple. There was but one dissentient voice — that of Cardinal del Giudice, implacable to the last; and even he, who was expected to denounce the new creation with passion, could do no more than mumble "promotionem Julii Alberoni approbare non possum."

The reverend princes of the Church may have wondered at the ascent of their new colleague, a rise no less dazzling than the sun in Rome that July day. Did they but know it, the trajectory was flattening out; a few days earlier Alberoni had been forced on to a course which was bound to end in the foundering of his schemes. He had wanted three years to restore Spain to health and power. "Three years," he cried again and again to Parma, imploring moderation of the Duke, "three years; it's not an eternity. Provided no unforeseen accident occurs to upset our plans."

It had occurred.

ALBERONI'S HAND IS FORCED

For years the affairs of Spain at the Vatican had been in the charge of a certain Don José Molines, a tiresome octogenarian, whose senility and extravagant behaviour had won him some renown in his own country. There is perhaps no clearer sign of decadence in a great state than the respect given to stupidity when dignified by age. Had Molines been born in England a century ago, his loyal ineptitude might have gained the honour of a public statue, or the naming after him of a dusty street in Aldershot. In eighteenth-century Spain he was promoted to the dignity of Grand Inquisitor, in place of del Giudice. Alberoni had opposed the idea, pointing out that Molines could no longer walk, could hardly write, while his ancient voice had dwindled away into a quavering whisper. But Alberoni had been overruled; the dodderer was recalled from Rome to his new dignity, and on his way home afforded the Emperor just that opportunity for making trouble which he had long been seeking.

We have seen how travellers shrank from the sea-voyage to Spain in the lice-ridden galleys. At eighty-four Molines would not hear of it. Despite the need for prudence and the growing truculence of the Austrians, he elected to put confidence in a safe-conduct issued by the Imperial representative and crossed Imperial territory on his way home. There he was arrested for no valid reason, by Prince Löwenstein, the Austrian Governor of the Milanese, and committed to prison under the vengeful care of a Spanish refugee. He languished there for some years and then died, too late, however, to save the peace of Europe.

The news of the outrage, which reached Madrid on June 7, 1717, moved the Spanish sovereigns to fury. Nor did the Duke of Parma calm his bellicose stepdaughter. Philip V spoiled for vengeance. Would such an insult, he asked Alberoni, be tolerated? The abbé refused to lose his head. It must be tolerated, he answered; Spain was not ready for war. "It's a barbarous outrage," he wrote to his excited master in Parma, "but it was mad of that wretched Molines to cross the Milanese. He's one of those people who's passed with this nation for an oracle, while it seems to me that throughout his embassy he's manifested nothing but extravagance and eccentricity."

The abbé was almost alone in his prudence; Popoli, for instance, plumped for reprisals, suggesting an immediate descent upon Sardinia, Sicily, or Naples. Alberoni brought him back to sense. "Are we going to give people the idea," he wrote to him on June 12, "that a handful of Italians, out of an insane passion for their country, have pushed these young and innocent sovereigns to the very brink of ruin, and Spain to her total destruction?" Popoli quickly recanted; but Philip found out the cause of his change of heart and now felt a double resentment against Alberoni. He would seek venegeance, he loudly declared, whatever the view of his first minister.

It has been fashionable to paint Alberoni as a bloody warmonger who leaped at this pretext for hostilities. He waited only, they say, for his hat before flinging his armaments against an Austrian possession. His correspondence proves, however, that he fought for a month against the idea of war. Spain, he cried again and again, was not ready. But his masters would not believe him; they pointed to the splendid new battleships, the glittering regiments, the goodwill of England. Alberoni still argued against attacking the Emperor, particularly when he was involved in a Turkish war. One incidentally in which Philip had promised him aid. "As for the idea which you suggest," the abbé wrote to his Duke, ". . . it will mean the abandonment of the Levant enterprise. That would make a deplorable impression throughout the world. . . ."

But at this critical moment the flimsy if ingenious machine went wrong, by which Alberoni had hitherto controlled Spain. He might, amid all his worries, order a fresh consignment of raw sausages from Parma, "for the cooked ones nauseate Her Majesty"; he might call for the supply of truffles, to be continued when the weather turned cool; "they are the only things which in her present lack of appetite she doesn't abhor." He even wrote for fans — "those little wooden sticks and prints on them that come from France." But these attentions no longer made Elisabeth his slave. Why she rebelled against his gentle, wise authority we do not know; perhaps it was because her uncle in Parma on this occasion would not second Alberoni's advice. However it happened, he suddenly found himself no longer master of the power which he had revived.

At last, on July 9, 1717, three days before he became a Cardinal, he gave in. "I've nothing to add," he wrote wearily to the Duke of Parma, "to my previous letters; I will obey the orders of Your Serene Highness." In cipher he informed his master that the squadron which had been destined for the Turkish war would leave in a few days' time to reduce Sardinia. But he prophesied that it would afford the Emperor a pretext to make peace with the Turks and to concentrate his forces in Italy. Nor were his forebodings ill-founded; Prince Eugene at that moment was bringing to a climax at Belgrade the most brilliant campaign of his career; with British mediation, peace between the Empire and the Sublime Porte was soon to be concluded, leaving Charles VI with his hands all too free.

It was clear enough what calamities were likely to flow from a policy of war; now, too late, the Duke of Parma was invaded by apprehension; and he implored from Alberoni some sort of certificate, absolving him from any part in the affair. In due course he received a documentary alibi which he could show the Pope, or the raw-tempered Germans. "We are more than certain," the Cardinal obligingly wrote to him, "that by the change of resolve made by His Majesty to use against the Archduke [i.e., the Emperor], the force originally destined for the Levant will have surprised Your Serene Highness, who is no less anxious than the Holy See to solicit the intervention of Spain against the Turks." This testimonial worked pretty well.

The attack upon Sardinia drew agitated cries from the Emperor; the Pope was induced to disapprove the expedition, undertaken at a time when all good Catholic states should have united against the infidel; while Bubb was instructed to remind Alberoni of England's obligations towards Austria. The Cardinal quickly replied that "he had no part in this enterprise but the execution."

It was characteristic of the man that this enterprise, of which he so bitterly disapproved, should have been superbly executed. The conquest of Sardinia was effected with mechanical precision, by an expeditionary force of 8,000 foot and 600 horse, equipped in profusion with the most fashionable accoutrements of war. Except in the Cagliari citadel, there was little resistance; the Sardinians welcomed the return of Spanish rule. By the early autumn, the whole island had been reduced. His success gave the Cardinal scant pleasure. Sardinia might become a useful stepping-stone towards Italy, but he was by no means certain that it had been worth the expense and the interruption in his work of reform.[1]

[1] "This sudden expedition has completely surprised me, and . . . has upset the measures which . . . I believed to be necessary in the interests of the sovereigns, among which the first was to establish the maxim of the necessity for preserving peace for at least six years, to build up a good navy and secure trade, two points which I believe to be fundamental in order to restore to strength this poor, languishing and prostrate monarchy." (Al-

The Cardinal did not cease to deplore the impetuosity of his patrons; but there could, he saw, be no drawing back now; there must rather be an advance. Victor-Amadeus of Savoy, he knew, would be ready enough to exchange his Kingdom of Sicily against Sardinia — with a crown attached to it, of course. Sicily, Sardinia, Spain, England — what did it matter where he reigned, so long as he reigned as king? Besides, Sardinia lay close to his ancestral Piedmont, while Sicily was remote, difficult to hold in times of trouble.

In Florence the last male Medici lay mountainous in his huge bed, assisting the delivery of puppies on his hard-used coverlet, or making there in shameless fashion the fortune of the well-shaped young sinners who caught his fancy. When he and his childless sister were dead, Elisabeth could advance a better claim than most to his inheritance.

In these circumstances Alberoni now formulated a plan for an Italian settlement. Naples and Sicily were to be secured outright for Spain; Victor-Amadeus would become King of Sardinia; the Parmesan and Tuscan successions would go to the issue of Elisabeth; Venice and the Holy See would receive territorial bonuses, and all the states of Italy would be united into a league to expel the Germans and "re-Italianize" the Peninsula. It was a concept too revolutionary perhaps for its time; but it was perhaps a more practical one than Stanhope's, and it came near enough to success.

It met with approval in France; the Regent's ministers openly declared that never had there been such an opportunity to drive the Germans out of Italy, and were urging Victor-Amadeus to form a close union with Spain. Indeed, the cat's-cradle of French policy was now complicated by a new strand. In September 1717, when Dubois was away in London, discussing Stanhope's plan (which was now known as

beroni to Cellamare, July 13, 1717: Archives du Ministre des Affaires Étrangères).

the Quadruple Alliance), the Regent suddenly veered again towards the idea of a reconciliation with Philip V and of an Italian League under Franco-Spanish patronage. As an essential condition Philip would of course be required to guarantee the Orléanist rights to the French throne.

The midwife of this plan was that extravagant figure Peterborough, whom we last glimpsed as he querulously sauntered homeward from his Spanish command.[2] Ever since then he had nursed a lively hatred of the Emperor and of all Germans. He yearned, too, for his former authority, even the petty importance he had known in Bolingbroke's heyday, when he had flitted about Europe as a special envoy, breaking all records for speed of travel. He had fallen into limbo with the accession of George I; from the lovely obscurity of Twickenham, the arms of a pretty actress, and the sparkling company of his neighbour Pope, for a time he absented himself but rarely. Occasionally he was to be seen walking up St. James's Street, wearing the Garter and top-boots, with a goose under his arm that he had bought for dinner; then he would disappear once more into his verdant pleasures. Yet this retirement was too much for his restless spirit; there was a devil in him, said his friends, which would not allow him to keep still.

In the last days of Queen Anne he had been to Parma, discussing with the Duke the eternal possibility of an Italian League to drive the Germans out. This darling project he had never abandoned; now Giovanni-Angelo Gazzola, the new Governor of Parma, who while Parmesan Minister in London had become a close friend of Peterborough's, invited him to come out to Italy and discuss the plan once more with the Duke.

Peterborough immediately set off for Paris. Although the British Government might deny him any official status, he was received at Calais with military honours and found his schemes

[2] See page 87.

warmly applauded at the Palais-Royal. Orléans in particular was caught by them and fervently proclaimed his desire for good relations with Philip V.

The attitude of Victor-Amadeus, when Peterborough passed through Turin, was no less favourable; at Parma all went smoothly, and the Duke immediately recommended the plan to Alberoni. "The move of the Duc d'Orléans," cautiously commented the latter, "is as unexpected as it is daring, but it might prove useful. . . . Let's hope the Regent's speaking the truth!" He resolved to give him the benefit of the doubt. "I feel real joy," he wrote to him in due course, "on learning from the person we know that Your Royal Highness has taken the right road to secure your present and future interests. . . ." He opened immediate discussions at Turin, suggesting a concerted attack upon Naples for the following year. Soon Alberoni was able to report to the Regent that Victor-Amadeus would declare against the Emperor, once he was assured of Franco-Spanish support.

Knock-about comedy suddenly intruded into the midst of these great designs. Driven out of France by British pressure, the Pretender had for the moment fixed his needy court among the dazzling colonnades and the white bullocks of Urbino, that little town forgotten among the Apennines, which evokes the unearthly world of Piero della Francesca. Amid this white beauty, James Stuart whiled away his throne-less days, sauntering over the warm rocks, or listening to the concerts that the cultured Duke of Mar would arrange for him. It was incredible that any harm could be meant to that personable, melancholy young man, lost in the lovely desert of the Apennines. But for some reason, ever since the guard had saluted him at Calais, Peterborough was credited with a design to murder the poor prince; and the Jacobites implored the Pope to arrest Peterborough, as soon as he set foot on Papal territory. One day a post-chaise arrived at Bologna containing a foreign lady, with a leathery complexion and forceful bearing. Italy was not yet acquainted with the English spinster from the Shires; the demeanour of this brick-red Amazon consequently aroused suspicion, which was not allayed by the gleam of the Garter ribbon and badge, through a slit in her skirt.

It was, of course, Peterborough; the reason for his absurd disguise is obscure; but, in the true spirit of his age, he had been unable to separate himself from his Garter ribbon. He was incontinently clapped into prison.

The news first caused laughter in London, then resentment at this outrage to the dignity of the House of Lords. Various grievances against the Vatican were recalled, and particularly the Pope's uncivil habit of praying for a Stuart restoration. A warning was conveyed to Rome that unless Peterborough were speedily released and prayers for the Pretender forbidden, the British fleet would proceed to Civita Vecchia.

On an entreaty from Peterborough's cell,[3] the Regent also intervened; at last the Pope released his embarrassing prisoner, who, however, refused to leave prison until arrangements had been made to conduct him back to Bologna with almost regal honours. For years after, he would take his friends over every tedious detail of the episode, which had, he swore, cost him £10,000.

To his delight, he found that matters had not stood still while he was in prison. "Never," he reported to the Regent, "has a treaty been begun upon such a solid basis." But at that moment an illness of Philip V supervened to upset all hopes.

Excesses in the chase, in the bed, at the table, had finally prostrated him. "Neither the King nor the Queen," declared the exasperated Alberoni, "will listen to their most devoted

3 "There must be something strange about my star, for here I am, deprived of my liberty at the very moment when I am working to free from slavery those who threw me into prison . . ." (Peterborough to the Regent, September 17, 1717; Archives du Ministre des Affaires Étrangères).

servants when they counsel moderation." That was in September. A few weeks later the King had a nervous collapse. "On October 4," Alberoni reported, "he was seized with such a black melancholy, we thought he would expire from one moment to the next. The appeals of his confessor, his doctor, and myself had no effect. He believed, and still believes today, that out riding he had contracted sunstroke in that part of his head where he thinks there's something wrong. To all our arguments he would answer that it was sad not to be believed, but that his early death would prove him right." The wretched monarch seemed indeed to be fading away, while one looked at him; the doctor advised Alberoni to be ready for anything.

The shooting season was now at its height. Every year a grand battue took place towards this time at San Lorenzo, near the Escorial. The mountainsides and the lovely forests of the Guadarramas would be beaten for miles round, and during a noisy half-hour wolves, wild boar, hares, foxes, and badgers would be driven in packs past the royal butt. Philip was naturally the central figure at these drives; nobody could shoot till he had finished; and he had four loaders and twenty guns with him.

This year he was in no state to withstand the rigours of the day, but he would not hear of staying away; the result was complete collapse. He insisted on making a will, "for love of the Queen, who had reduced him to this condition." Indeed, it now became most necessary to provide for the future; nobody could say how long the King's reason would survive; already, in his sleep, he would be seized with convulsions, lacerate his face with his own fingernails, and then wake screaming "Murder!" through the blood. Sword in hand, he would rush upon the wavering dusty heroes who peopled the arras.

His will entrusted the Regency to the Queen during the minority of the Prince of the Asturias. The effect of the news upon Orléans was disastrous; if Philip were to die or go mad, the danger of his claims in France would vanish; no longer would there be any purpose in treating with Spain. Far from that, there might be a good chance of dominating her, during the minority of a King who was, after all, Orléans's step-grand-nephew.

Suddenly Saint-Aignan's shabby little intrigues among the servants' halls of Madrid became of the first importance to the Regent. "At all costs," he told them, "we must exclude the Queen from the Regency and the Government. The Queen will understand that it would be neither suitable nor reason-able for her to interfere in the administration of a kingdom belonging to a Prince whose stepmother she is." The intrigues were resumed with disgruntled grandees, the ambitious Duke of Veragua and the Count of Aguilar in particular. Plans were hatched for the seizing of power at Madrid; while thirty French battalions, with fifty squadrons of horse, were ad-vanced to the Pyrenees, "ready to enter Spain at the slightest request of the Spaniards, and in such numbers as may suit them."

But even in duplicity the Regent was inconstant. He con-tinued his discussions at Madrid, sending thither the Marquis Monti, an old crony of Alberoni's; and the idea of a Franco-Spanish alliance was once more mooted. The Regent's vacil-lating temper was congenital, and accentuated perhaps by his almost perpetual befuddlement (one night lately he had al-most lost an eye in a drunken tumble down stairs). Besides, he wanted to be left in peace with his pleasures; and the easiest course was to let each one of his advisers have his head — par-ticularly in foreign affairs, the intricacies of which he rightly found both boring and bewildering. His fine intelligence could appreciate the quality of a pair of breasts or of a draw-ing; but it did not bother to grasp the beauties of, for instance, the balance-of-power system; with this concept, to which for more than two centuries they were to remain fatally constant, the English were wildly in love. Stair would spend hours trying to explain it to the bored mercurial prince. "I think," he would report triumphantly, "I have convinced the Regent that it is in the interest of Britain that the Emperor should be a match, or near a match, for France." But later he would add regretfully: "Regularly the next day or two days after every one of our conversations I have been told by the Abbé Dubois that H.R.H. has changed his opinion. . . ."

It is hardly to be wondered at, therefore, if the Regent overlooked for a moment his negotiations in London, and Stanhope's plan for a European settlement. William Stanhope, cousin to the Secretary of State, had replaced Bubb at Madrid; he had begun his mission auspiciously, recommending the plan to Alberoni, with a bribe of some £40,000. The Cardinal annihilated the new envoy with a display of Homeric rage.

After this setback, matters in London must wait on the arrival of the Imperial representative. Dubois, with little to do, was almost drowned in a boisterous flood of English civilities. He dined with the King at Hampton Court, drank with His Majesty and Speaker Onslow a toast to the Regent in Cyprus wine ninety years old, which Onslow's brother had brought home from Constantinople; he attended a debate of the Commons — "a favour which was that day refused to several British peers" — and banquets in his honour of many hundred covers. Somehow he found himself at Guildford Races, and almost saddled with a house at Newmarket; nobody bothered to reflect that this elderly French abbé might not be particularly interested in horse-racing.

The most exhausting of the Palais-Royal orgies were child's play beside this. Within a fortnight Dubois was laid up in his Duke Street lodgings, with gout on the knee, rheumatism in the thigh, and a wildly disordered stomach. Somehow he repaired himself, made a way into the smart world by methods that recall Alberoni — presents of French delicacies; Pont-l'Evêque and Brie arrived by every mail, and truffles, when of course it grew cool enough for them to travel; two dozen pots of orange-blossom marmalade were judiciously distributed.

In his new suit of expensive velvet, with powder spilt on the shoulders to take off its look of vulgar newness, he sidled through the London drawing-rooms, a gift of brocades under his arm, or an ingenious doll which showed off the latest fashions of Paris.

For the Regent's daughters he bought fine English watches, and hairpin boxes for old "Madame"; she rewarded him by putting her paws upon some excellent Tokay, which Dubois had sent back from London for his own use. . . .

At last the conference opened, at Hampton Court, in November. In the midst of it Dubois, to his despair, learnt that his master was once more inclining towards Spain. There is no reason to doubt the sincerity of Dubois's belief that such a policy would end in tears for his master. But certainly his loyalties coincided conveniently with his personal interests. The champions of a Spanish alliance were swells, who knew more of Spain than he did and spurned him for his common ways; whereas his English connections were an asset of which few Frenchmen could boast. In the succeeding generation English friendships, a knowledge of English ways and literature, a park or garden laid out with enchanting English wildness, were the accoutrements of elegance in France. But in 1717 England for most Frenchmen was almost as unknown as Russia, a land where they cut off their kings' heads between mouthfuls of half-raw beef, eaten in a fog, and evolved their magical constitution from the saddle, as they chased the fox, quarrelling over the varying forms of heresy they affected.

In short, if France marched with England, Dubois would be indispensable; if with Spain, he might well whistle for power. The prospect was grey as the London streets. "Your Royal

Highness," he protested to Paris, "is tricked too often . . .
Monseigneur will shed tears of blood if he loses this unique
chance of making himself independent, and of saving the kingdom. To aspire to be the liberator of Italy would be an ill-
placed distinction. You'll lose your allies, and if the question
of the French succession comes up during the war, you'll find
yourself without resources either internal or external. . . .
Get ready a suppliant tone, for you'll have to sue Cardinal
Alberoni for peace."

Not that he put much faith in the power of his appeal. Out
of twenty Frenchmen, eighteen, he admitted, would prefer
war to Stanhope's plan. Nor was England wholeheartedly
against Alberoni; he was said to be flirting with the opposition; Robert Walpole frequently mentioned him in his toasts.

Alberoni, meanwhile, was addressing to the Regent appeals
no less impassioned than Dubois's; it was a tug of war for the
Regent's will, with the champions of Spain pulling the harder;
there were even rumours of a French incursion into the Austrian Netherlands. The agitated Dubois rushed back to Paris.

A fortnight's argument, and the Regent was his once more.
"I'm afraid," Alberoni commented, "that there's little to hope
from the negotiations, on account of the Duc d'Orléans's notion about the King's health being precarious." Indeed, Philip
was still in a sorry way. "The King's person," lamented the
Cardinal, "gives me more trouble than do his interests. . . ."

In short, the King's illness had finally tipped the scales
against a French alliance with Spain. Early in December the
Regent proclaimed his readiness to negotiate a treaty with the
Emperor, on terms which did not disregard the interests of
Philip V. He was not happy, however, about Stanhope's plan,
which envisaged the recovery of Sardinia from Spain, by
force. "I'm quite clear," he wrote to Dubois, "that my own
interests would not be affected by such an injustice. But I'm
Regent of France, and I ought to behave in such a manner

that I can't be accused of having thought only of myself." The Emperor seemed to delight in rendering odious a position already difficult. "After all," cried the exasperated Regent, "it would be more to my advantage not to make an alliance with the Emperor than to ruin myself in the eyes of the great mass of the French nation, without whom I shan't have the kingdom, despite all the treaties concluded with foreign Powers."

Through this whirlpool Alberoni swam unruffled. He was, he knew, a match for the Emperor; and he did not believe that either France or England, whatever they said, would come to blows with him. Secure in his miscalculations, he turned his ire upon the internal scene. Spain might be a country of fantastic promise; but sometimes the stupidity, corruption, and inefficiency almost drove him mad. His model agricultural colony at Aranjuez,[4] for instance, had been ruined by the local Governor's cruelty. When the court was away, the brute bullied those excellent Parmesan husbandmen till they struck and demanded their passage home. Alberoni was beside himself. "This is an evil race," he wrote furiously to Parma, "and I protest that were it not for all the gratitude I owe the Queen, I'd have abandoned the lot of them to their evil genius. They don't want to do good themselves, nor will they let anyone else do it."

Then Elisabeth worried him to death over San Ildefonso, or La Granja — the Grange — the dairy farm of a convent hidden in the pine-clad Guadarramas not far from Segovia, upon which Philip and Elisabeth had come by chance one day when hunting. Struck by the wild, verdant beauty of the place, they bought it and began to build there a hunting palace.

It was a strange enough site to fire the imagination of a baroque monarch; but Elisabeth in particular had a passion for La Granja. Her dear Cardinal would sometimes cry out in exasperation that she cared less to cut a great figure in Europe than

4 See page 152.

to be Countess of San Ildefonso; for her works there she was always purloining the price of a battleship or of an important battery.

But the result was a feat of enchantment supreme in that fantastic age. Lovely though it is, with its rosy brickwork and the dazzling white of its trophies, the palace, by Ardemans and the great Juvara, has a dozen cousins scattered through Piedmont and down the valley of the Main. But the peculiar glory of San Ildefonso is the fountains, fed from a tank some 3,000 feet above. The groves and vistas are thronged with sculpture by Charlier; and on certain favoured days, from among the nymphs and graces, from the nostrils of Hippolytus' engulfed chariot-team the water shoots almost 200 feet into the flashing air. Mattresses of lesser jets break the prismatic fall of these high plumes; and frogs, the former enemies of Latona, spew out a vault of airy spray, which, as it drifts away, carries an overpowering scent of chestnut, lime, and sweetbrier. The fleeting perfection of these fountains haunts the memory long after one has climbed the pass that leads back to Madrid. Such virtuosity, one feels, can never be repeated. It belongs to the lonely world of the perfect firework, or of the high C which Mozart once heard fluttering through Modena opera-house.

Europe in the winter of 1718 displayed all those symptoms which our luckless generation would have recognized as the presages of war. From all sides came protestations of a desire to keep the peace and much talk of sovereign rights. And all the while nations armed, and tempers grew frayed, and a fever of intrigue infected Europe. Alberoni and the Regent alone seemed to keep their heads. The latter was determined to secure decent terms for his Bourbon relative in Spain, an offer from the English to return Gibraltar, and a private guarantee to Elisabeth of the Spanish Regency in the event of Philip's death. It was all very well for the arrogant Stair to boast that they would soon force the King of Spain to reason; Dubois and his cronies might declare that in dealing with Spain you must have Gibraltar in one hand and a thunderbolt in the other. But the Regent was acutely aware that in every hamlet of France there lived veterans who had spent years of discomfort and danger to win the Spanish throne for Philip V. How would they regard a war against him now, with their late enemy as France's ally? All together Orléans was far from happy.

But in these days he was utterly in the hands of Dubois. There is perhaps something symbolic in the manner of his appearance about this time at one of the masked balls in the Opéra. He loved these balls; the mingling of classes, the infusion of chance even into lust, pleased his whimsical temper. But one evening anonymity went too far, even for him. To preserve his master's disguise, Dubois, it had been arranged, was occasionally to kick him; he fell so smartly to his duty, the poor Regent let go a cry: "Vous me déguisez trop, abbé, vous me déguisez trop! . . ."

The situation in Italy was daily increasing in complication, largely through the duplicities of Victor-Amadeus. He was in an agony of fear lest Sicily should be taken from him by one side or the other, without proper compensation. Desperately he struggled to make a deal on the side, with the Emperor one minute, with Alberoni the next. At Vienna he bargained for the reversion of Tuscany, and the hand of the Emperor's daughter for his son — which might have given the Empire to the house of Savoy; to Alberoni he offered alliance against a promise not only of Sardinia, but of the Milanese too.

All these manœuvres were of little avail. Victor-Amadeus's bargaining came to nothing. The truth was, the old rascal nowadays deceived nobody; he was losing his grip; his wiles could no longer prevail against the will of the Great

Powers. The Savoyard representative in Paris might hero-
ically declare that "his master would not let himself be led
like a lamb to the sacrifice. He's a generous lion, whose claws
you could file down before he would give in." Fine words,
but nobody listened; the fate of Sicily would be settled with
hardly a glance towards its agitated owner.

All this while the Duke of Parma had been gradually recovering his dangerous courage. After the descent upon Sardinia, when the Emperor threatened him with august anger,
he had become a jelly of fear, proclaiming his innocence to
the Pope, to the Regent, to anyone who would listen, and
brandishing the famous certificate that Alberoni had given
him. With a return of courage, he began to pester the Cardinal for an expedition against Naples.

Certainly the Germans needed humbling. Now that the
British Cabinet was harnessed to their chariot, the pretensions of the Vienna court had grown monstrous; in the recent negotiations had not the Emperor demanded Mexico
as the price of abandoning a hopeless claim to the Spanish
throne? "The character of the Germans," Alberoni declared,
"is to be insolent and unbearable when things are going well
for them; they would do well to reflect that Fortune by her
very nature is capricious, and that there's nothing fixed under
the moon." He was convinced, too, that the existing order
in Italy must soon be upset. "She suffers," he would say,
"from ills against which mere palliatives are inadequate; specific remedies are needed, iron and fire. . . ." Thus far he
was at one with his Duke; but circumstances at that moment
dictated caution. Spain, as he put it, could not go alone to the
ball, when the Emperor might enjoy the help of the British
fleet.

Suddenly, at the end of March 1718, came revived hope of
a peaceful settlement. A special envoy from the Regent, the
Marquis de Nancré, brought to Madrid the pill of the Quad-

ruple Alliance, thickly coated with Gibraltar sugar. One of the Regent's cronies, whom Saint-Simon describes as the most civilized and corrupted of men, the charming Nancré soon broke through Alberoni's anger and gained his esteem. Before long the two men were united in a common attitude, and Dubois was accusing Nancré of treachery when he reported that the Cardinal sincerely wanted peace.

But it was true enough. ". . . To bow to necessity seems to me the only course we can take, accepting any compromise which the mediators propose. But Their Majesties, encouraged by our vast preparations, by the favourable temper of the people, and by the loyal addresses which have come from every quarter, would consider it an act of cowardice and weakness to abandon an enterprise which has already been so much talked about; so that my opinions don't meet with the least approval." So Alberoni informed Parma. He and Nancré were able to make some progress towards a compromise while the Queen was occupied with one of her countless deliveries; hardly was she about again, when their fragile construction was overturned. "During the last two days," Nancré reported to Paris on April 27, "everything we recognized as tending towards the success of the affair has been upset, and that solely by the whim of the Queen, who won't hear any word but war. To such a point that for the last two or three days the Cardinal has not been speaking to the Queen; if matters had depended upon that minister, my journey would not have been fruitless. . . ."

But now Philip V formally rejected Stanhope's terms. "Out of deference to my grandfather the King," he declared, "and in the interests of European peace, I acquiesced in the Utrecht treaties, which were dictated to me by a handful of private individuals. I have no desire to submit a second time to their dictation, since God has put me in a position of independence, where I need no longer bow under the yoke of my enemies, to the shame, scandalization, and utter indignation of my subjects."

If he did not approve Philip's action, at least Alberoni sympathized with his mood. The British Cabinet, he told William Stanhope, were a pack of rogues sold to Vienna. "All the chancelleries of Europe have lost their heads," he wrote to his friend Bubb in London; "national welfare is abandoned to the whims of a few individuals, who without rhyme or reason, and perhaps for their own personal ends, cut up and pare states and kingdoms as if they were Dutch cheeses. . . ."

Yet with James Stanhope he maintained a friendly correspondence that half convinced the British Cabinet of his continued wish for peace, while even when delivering to Nancré Philip's rejection of the Quadruple Alliance, he attempted a last compromise. His master, he hinted, might be induced to accept the odious terms, were he permitted to keep Sardinia. The Regent found it an excellent way out of the impasse, "provided," old Huxelles added, "H.M. the King of Great Britain gives his consent, for which I do not dare to hope. . . ."

Alberoni and his dazzling rise still excited the envy of Europe; the public continued to imagine him as the happiest of mortals. But occasionally, round some turning of the tedious labyrinth that was international politics in 1718, we catch a glimpse of the nightmare his life had now become. Probably under the Pescatori's influence, the Queen was in open conflict with him, though she still expected him to fritter away his precious time in arranging the supply from Italy of her wines and foodstuffs, or of a prodigious astronomical clock which had been bought in Venice for the King's amusement. Philip had lately become a sombre wreck again; deaf to warnings against indulgence, he continued to eat an inordinate quantity of boiled chicken, and dully to perform such feats behind the bed-hangings that a fiery posset became a necessity of his breakfast — a concoction of wine, milk, sugar, cinnamon, cloves, and raw egg-yolks. There was little sense to be got out of him these days.

Nor was the Cardinal's health any too good. The proud digestion was ruined, and the fabulous vitality sapped, so that he rarely went out nowadays except to the royal apartments, and only drank water, "having nausea and aversion" for wine "and feeling sick at the mere sight of it on the table." He was plagued, too, by his tiresome relatives, and particularly a nephew who was supposed to be studying for the priesthood. But the Jesuits let the boy do just as he pleased, know uncanonical pleasures, and choose his own studies. He had picked, if you please, on the violin; and what possible good, the irate Cardinal asked, was scraping a fiddle going to do him in his cure of souls?

Elisabeth continued her clamour for war. Alberoni could not indefinitely play for time. He waited until the end of May 1718; it then became clear that his proposal to retain Sardinia would never be accepted by the Powers. Only two alternatives remained — tame submission or war. "The decisions of this court are already made; to all appearances they are opposed by those Powers who under disastrous influences desire the aggrandisement of a prince they ought for every sort of reason to fear and to humble. Nevertheless, when dealing with big issues you . . . cannot do anything with a pair of callipers in your hand; you must leave something to chance. The armament will sail from Barcelona with land and sea forces in such strength as has never before been known in history. Nobody has yet thought of transporting by sea a force of 33,000 effectives, 100 siege pieces, 25 field guns, 40 mortars, 100,000 cannon-balls, 1,000 tons of powder, 30,000 bombs, with grenades in proportion. . . . Spain, well administered, is a monster of unknown possibilities . . . a good war is needed that will continue till the last German is driven out. . . ." [5]

[5] Alberoni to Count Rocca, June 6, 1718.

Sicily was the object of the expedition; it was a possible springboard for attacks on the mainland, and besides, the British fleet was under no obligation to defend it. On June 17, 1718 Alberoni's armada, conjured from nothing in three short years, weighed out of Barcelona, under sealed orders, only to be opened off Sardinia. "Comprising 600 sail, it takes up six leagues of sea. May the blessings of God go with it!"

❊ XI ❊

EUROPE AGAINST ALBERONI

S OME days before this sailing for Sicily, a British squadron of twenty battleships under the command of Sir George Byng stood out from Spithead. It was bound for the Mediterranean; its official purpose was to exact tardy reparation for Peterborough's arrest. But not even Peterborough, in awe though he might be of his own importance, could well have believed this story. During the leisurely refit of the ships it had become common gossip that they were to do the Emperor's business in Italy.

Monteleone, the Spanish Ambassador in London, was no fool; early in the year he had pressed Stanhope to say that the squadron would not be used against Spain. From the Englishman's harsh and embarrassed manner Monteleone framed his own opinion, began to work upon his friends in the City, and Members of Parliament who were interested in the Spanish trade; surely the merchants of the Exchange would not let it be jeopardized in order that King George might increase the Elector of Hanover's power and curry favour with the Emperor?

But paradoxically George I by his very insecurity could wield in England such a power as his more solidly enthroned successor never knew. By their savage persecution of the outgoing Government, the Whigs had lost all hope of Jacobite clemency should there ever come a change of régime. They were in fact tied fast to the King's personal interests and must risk everything for them. The system of the Quadruple Al-

liance, they believed, would shore up the King's position; for
its sake they were prepared even to fly in the plump face of
the City.

Stanhope himself does not seem to have believed that it
would ever come to a rupture with Spain. In May 1718 the
growing tension brought East India shares tumbling down;
the South Sea Company sent a deputation to the Secretary
of State, protesting against the despatch of Byng's squadron,
and enquiring whether it was safe for the company's annual
ship, with £80,000 worth of cargo, to sail for the Spanish
colonies. Philip V had already rejected the Quadruple Alliance. Yet Stanhope advised the company to let the ship go;
he had every hope that Spain would swallow the terms in the
end; if there were trouble, he said, as like as not the British
squadron would be on Spain's side.

The worthy merchants would probably have gone away
less happily had they known the tenor of the secret instructions even then in preparation for Byng. The growth of Alberoni's fleet had been watched with apprehension by the
British Government. "The growing power of Spain by sea,"
His Majesty's Minister at Genoa had written in August 1717,
"is what should require our attention at present. You see what
a fleet they have been able to fit out this year, and all accounts
agree that the next year they will have fifty sail of men-of-
war. . . . If they meet with any considerable success in their
present projects, I don't see how the maritime powers can
stand neuter. . . ." Their Lordships at the Admiralty were
reminded of how in Charles II's time the English had un-
wisely allowed the French fleet to grow into a menace; they
were determined not to imitate this costly mistake.

While Byng therefore was officially instructed to use his
mediation in the Mediterranean and to defend the Emperor's
territory from attack, he was secretly encouraged, it seems
clear, to be much more aggressive. The Imperial Ambassador

was informed that "Byng would do his duty, or otherwise would have to pay for it with his head, as besides his instructions he had been given verbal orders; and that he was to go straight to work and not be afraid of doing too much."

"Should you be directed," Craggs wrote to the Admiral in supplementary instructions on July 25, "to attack the Spanish fleet, you should waste no time on single ships, but try, with the first blow to destroy their entire fleet."

Thus did the ruthless self-assured Englishmen of the eighteenth century face even the possibility of a threat; no fobbing off with promises of parity uttered by an irresponsible prime minister. . . .

The Quadruple Alliance was now due to be signed between France and England; but at the last moment the Regent's qualms returned. His manner with Stair, rarely cordial, chilled noticeably.

Dubois in London grew desperate. "I have just been with the Abbé Dubois," Stanhope informed Stair in June, "who has shown other letters from France which strengthen the suspicions above-mentioned that the torrent of opposition to this plan is so great in France that it is much to be feared that the Regent may be drawn aside and brought into measures with the Kings of Spain and Sardinia."

At Dubois's suggestion, Stanhope was sent off to Paris in the hope of bringing the Regent back to reason; there was a question of Stanhope's going on to Madrid, "for if I am empowered to speak in H.M.'s name, seconded by his fleet, and have leave to produce the instrument signed by the Regent, it is judged here that notwithstanding all Cardinal Alberoni's rodomontades, he will reflect more seriously, and come into more prudent and pacific measures than those he purposes at present. . . ."

To his surprise, Stanhope was greeted at the Palais-Royal with "much good sense and seeming frankness and sincerity"; the Regent had suffered yet another unaccountable change of heart. A sumptuous party at Saint-Cloud marked the happy end of the negotiations; nothing remained but to sign.

Yet suddenly a new obstacle sprang up; not a minister of France would put his name to the infamous document. At Stanhope's suggestion, the matter was referred to the Council of Regency; "speaking divinely," Orléans carried the day. Only Maine dared to raise a faltering protest against this project which almost all Frenchmen detested; even old Huxelles was browbeaten into submission by fear of losing his post (in any case he would not keep it long). As the squibs put it:

> "Huxelles dit: 'Cette paix,
> Cette Quadruple Alliance
> Est la peste de la France.
> Je m'y souscrirai jamais.
> Contre ces projets iniques
> Je fus toujours indigné.'
> Après ces mots héroïques,
> Le maréchal a signé."

Stanhope then requested passports for Madrid. The move puzzled Alberoni. Philip V, he told the British Legation, could not allow the First Minister of England to come to Spain if the two countries were in a state of war; he assumed that while a compromise was still in the wind, the British fleet would suspend all action. In this understanding he granted the passports; but suspicions lingered on. "It's a queer request," was his comment to Nancré, "at a time when the two fleets may well be fighting in the Mediterranean. It's as if he wished to make the King of Spain play Punchinello, to whom they bow and scrape while pulling long noses at him and beating him with sticks."

This was precisely the role to which the British Cabinet had condemned Philip V. Not that they necessarily meant him ill. They wanted to do the right thing by him; but the right thing did not include permission for him to own a strong fleet. Nor did they apparently stop to reflect that warlike action against Alberoni's ships, if undertaken while Stanhope was in Spain, might lay them open to a charge of treachery.

The truth was, they believed that whatever happened, Spain would in the end accept their terms; and they despatched Stanhope to Madrid with far less apprehension for his success than for his safety. Alberoni, they feared, might clap him into a fortress, but would never reject these last overtures. "I reckon," wrote Sunderland to Stair on July 25, "that Lord Stanhope may be in Madrid by this time, where I can't but think he will have success; for though the Cardinal has a good warm projecting head of his own, yet one can hardly imagine him mad enough to stand out against the whole world. . . ."

The Spanish forces had landed near Palermo on July 1. The raw Savoyard garrisons were no match for the invaders, aided as they were by the local population. Only the orders of the Spanish King, the Sicilians said, had made them accept Victor-Amadeus as their sovereign. Philip V had now decided to take back the island; it was for them to obey him.

Palermo fell easily enough. The inhabitants of Catania rose against the Savoyards; soon the Savoyard Viceroy was pinned into the hills round Syracuse.

The Duke of Parma now urged Alberoni to throw the army across the Strait of Messina against southern Italy. But the Cardinal would not do so while Spain fought alone. He sought only to take Sicily and hold it as a pawn for future negotiations. For the time being, there could be no extension of operations. "Nothing to be done," declared the Cardinal, "without the League of the North at which I've been working for the last eight months, moving heaven and earth, but these people were born in a cold and changeable climate."

The Spanish landing in Sicily caused consternation throughout Europe. The news reached Cadogan, as he was dining with Stair at the Paris Embassy; he was so agitated by it, he quaffed down the contents of his snuff-box instead of his wine. It had its effect, too, upon the mood in which Stanhope found the Spanish court. At first all was fair words. The Cardinal greeted his old friend with effusion; he was charmed by Stanhope's praises of his reforms; the Englishman's proposal for a three months' truce seemed to win his assent.

Laughter for once warmed the Escorial; Philip V showed rare affability. With puppy squeals the little Infants sprang out upon the Cardinal from dark corners, to rummage in his pockets after sweets and comfits.

Yet when it came to real negotiation, there was little progress. News of successes in Sicily arrived inopportunely and stiffened the obstinacy of the Spanish monarchs. Indeed, Elisabeth was unyielding from the first, for the terms brought her no advantage. "We would have done better," Nancré said with truth, "to have thought of the Queen rather than of the Infants."

Soon Stanhope grew restless. Heaven alone knew what might be happening in the purple waters off Sicily; he had no wish to be held captive in Spain for a second time. Betraying to the Cardinal, therefore, his anxiety lest an encounter had taken place between the British and Spanish fleets, Stanhope behind a screen of compliments withdrew from Spain. "The Cardinal," he wrote from the sanctuary of Bayonne, "shed tears when I parted with him, has promised to write to me, and to let slip no occasion that may offer of adjusting matters. Upon the whole, I am of opinion that before next spring, *fata viam invenient* of adjusting this business amicably; notwithstanding the ill success I have had, I am far from repenting my having made this journey."

The ink upon this letter was hardly dry before Stanhope was writing another, to Admiral Sir George Byng: "If you find a favourable moment to attack the Spanish fleet, I'm persuaded that you will not let the chance slip. The two great objects which in my opinion you should have in view are if possible to destroy their fleet, and to gain a foothold in Sicily, to permit the landing of an army. . . ." This was on September 2, 1718. Stanhope could have spared himself the trouble; on the eve of his arrival in Madrid to treat with Alberoni, the British navy had done its work.

So soon as Byng with his score of battleships had reached Cape St. Vincent, he sent word to Alberoni of his arrival in Spanish waters, offered his mediation, and announced his orders to oppose with all the power at his command any attack upon the Emperor's dominions in Italy, or upon Sicily, "which must be with a design to invade the Kingdom of Naples." Stung by this high-handed tone, Alberoni replied that the King of Spain "would run all hazards" before he called off the expedition; "the Spaniards were not to be frighted"; and if Byng should think fit to attack them, Alberoni added, "he should be in no pain for the Success."

It has long been the fashion for historians to take this incident for proof of the Cardinal's truculent and obstinate temper. It must be remembered, however, that friendly messages were then passing between him and James Stanhope, who turned up in Madrid one month later. Meanwhile the British squadron had vanished into the blue Mediterranean wastes — vanished with a completeness hard to envisage in this public age.

The Austrian Viceroy of Naples was fretting in some apprehension of a Spanish attack when on August 1 the British squadron appeared in the bay, a flock of white-winged saviours. The boats that came out to it brought not only provi-

PHILIPPE D'ORLÉANS, REGENT OF FRANCE
by Coysevox

LA DUCHESSE DU MAINE

sions and sightseers but also Jacobite agents, to fan the dislike which the lower deck already felt for the enterprise. Byng's captains, however, were solidly anti-Jacobite and shared the Admiralty's jealousy of the new Spanish fleet; against their inflexible will no agitator's tricks could prevail.

When Byng learnt how the Spaniards had already reduced almost all Sicily save the hills, he quickly set sail, steering south. Arrived off Sicily, he sent a flag of truce to the Spanish commander, alleging that the seizure of the island by His Catholic Majesty "gives grounds for thinking that he projects an invasion of the Kingdom of Naples," and proposing a two months' cessation of hostilities. But the Spaniard declared that he had no power to treat. Byng's reaction was to lead his squadron two days later to one of the most senseless, or at least inglorious, victories of our naval history.

Standing into Messina on August 10, he came in sight of the Spanish fleet, which bore away from him down the eastern coast of Sicily. There can be no doubt that the Spanish admiral did his level best to avoid trouble; through the breathless summer's night the galleys laboured to tow their "heaviest sailors"; but the splendid British squadron gained steadily on them and without any declaration of war forced battle the following morning, off Cape Passero.

The engagement developed in circumstances of some confusion; it has even been said that the first shot was fired from a Spanish ship. There can be no doubt, however, that Byng, by dogging the Spaniards with his superior force, made a conflict inevitable.

There was no proper Spanish line of battle, and single combats became the rule. The *Grafton* engaged Alberoni's darling, the *Principe de las Asturias;* the *San Carlo* fell upon the *Kent;* the *Oxford* was soon involved in a running fight with the *Santa Rosa*, a 64-gunner, and forced her to strike her flag.

It was from the first an action so unequal that in the opinion of many naval authorities it cannot rank as a true battle.[1] The Spanish force, outnumbered and outgunned at best, had been weakened by the despatch of important units to Malta and elsewhere. Moreover, if Alberoni in three years had been able to build a fleet that excited the jealousy of the English, there had been no time to train and "shake down" the crews. The Biscayan fishermen and Irish adventurers of which they were largely composed fought bravely enough; but they lacked the cohesion and steadiness of the seasoned English matelots.

By nightfall the action was over. Less than half the Spanish fleet had escaped destruction or capture; their admiral, Castañeta, was a prisoner. Not even the galleys and lighter ships which scattered towards the shelter of the coast succeeded in eluding disaster; they were chased by Captain Walton with eight warships. His report of the operation is the only detail of the action we generally remember. "Sir," wrote Walton to Byng, "we have taken and destroyed all the Spanish ships and vessels that were on the coast, the number as per margin. . . ."

The first lieutenant of the *Superb*, who led a boarding-party on to the Spanish flagship *San Felipe*, lost an arm, but got the Spanish admiral's pennants and flags in exchange. He took them back to his native Lowestoft, where for years they were used to deck the town at weddings.

The victory aroused little enthusiasm in London. In the taverns they might bawl this doggerel:

"There were fourteen sail of men-o'-war
We made captive that day.
Seven sail we sank and burned, boys;
But the rest, they ran away.
Three Flag Ships we took that day,
But the Fourth that same night,
Full of dread and faint-hearted,
Spread their sails and took flight."

[1] See Admiral A. T. Mahan's *Influence of Sea Power upon History*.

But as Craggs, the Secretary of State, put it to Stair in Paris: ". . . it is wonderful how much some people who have the greatest interest in the affair are dejected with it." And no wonder; this was one of the few occasions when England has richly deserved the epithet of "perfidious." What can have possessed Stanhope, normally an honourable man, to act with such duplicity, to negotiate with Spain while secretly encouraging Byng to attack the Spanish fleet? Not even his most distinguished and devoted biographer, Mr. Basil Williams,[2] can explain the shabby mystery. As Alberoni put it in a letter of October 10, 1718 to the Spanish Ambassador in London:

"Men were universally surprised at the arrival of the First Minister of Great Britain at the court of the Catholic King, there to make proposals of peace and of suspension of arms, at the same time that the naval force of the potentate who should have been mediator, was performing the actions of an open Rupture. . . . 'Tis nowhere to be found in history, nor is it compatible with good faith, neither have the most barbarous people yet learned the maxim of sending a minister from one court to another with the character of a mediator, there to treat of peace, and of executing at the same time the utmost rigours of war."

The nearest modern parallel to Stanhope's behaviour is perhaps the Japanese envoy Kurusu's negotiating with the State Department at Washington at the moment of the attack on Pearl Harbor. But Kurusu may not have known what the militarists planned; Stanhope, on the other hand, was the supreme authority.

Suitably rewarded by the Emperor, Byng and his squadron remained in Italian waters for the rest of the year, ferrying Austrian troops to Sicily. Victor-Amadeus now resigned himself to accepting the terms of the Quadruple Alliance. The

[2] *Stanhope: A Study in Eighteenth-Century War and Diplomacy.* By A. F. B. Williams (1932).

Austrians took over from him the struggle against the Spaniards in Sicily; they were not at first very successful in it.

When the news of the disaster reached Madrid, some ten days after Stanhope's prudent disappearance off the Spanish scene, Alberoni's bearing was stoical in the extreme. To Parma alone did he betray his grief for the efforts wasted and vain ambitions. "The infamy of the English could not be blacker . . . the work and strivings of years rendered vain in the space of a moment. . . ." But above all he blamed his imprudent officers who had failed to conquer Sicily with proper speed. The trouble was "non habemus hominem"; there lay the tragedy. Alberoni was essentially the organizer, the inspirer of great enterprises; but there was no Vendôme at his side to carry them to triumph on the field.

"We must adore the judgement of God and abide by it," he cried in a mood of temporary resignation. It had never been his habit to whine, and he would not do so now. Instead he put on a calm that awed the ministers of Great Britain and France; Nancré, indeed, when he saw him, broke down and wept.

From the first news of the engagement, the British and French Governments adopted a very virtuous air. They were indignant when the remnants of the Spanish fleet came home and burnt what British merchant shipping still lay in Spanish ports, and at the issue of letters of marque to Spanish privateers. As Stair rather incoherently put it: ". . . the tender regard the king has expressed for the Catholic king and his interests (which has appeared as well since the engagement of the two fleets as before) has produced no other effect than the king of Spain's making war upon the king and his subjects, and seizing their goods and effects, in violation of the solemn faith of treaties. The king will be obliged to defend himself in such a manner as will quickly convince the Cardinal that he is in a condition to do himself and his subjects justice. . . ."

For the Regent it was impossible to speak so harshly against

the grandson of Louis XIV. He resorted to a stratagem, therefore, which was to be generally adopted in the ensuing measures against Spain; he employed the fiction that the real
enemy was not Philip V, nor the Spanish people, but the
wicked Cardinal, who had misled them — a highly convenient
expedient, devised apparently by Dubois. "The defeat,"
Orléans proclaimed, "of the fleet of Spain, or rather of Cardinal Alberoni, must have opened the eyes of the blindest and
most prejudiced Spaniards. Before them I need no other justification. . . ."

In reality, of course, the unhappy Cardinal was now the
main element for peace at the Spanish court. Spain, he was
convinced, must bow to force and accept the hateful terms
of the Quadruple Alliance. At first he had nursed hopes of
building up his fleet again, of giving his enemies something to
think about in the coming spring. But reflection showed him
that he was done, that at Cape Passero he had been struck a
blow from which there was no recovery. His best troops
were now bottled up in Sicily, fighting well, but continuously pressed back by a superior weight of Austrians.[3] The
Czar still wavered between England and Spain; Charles XII
of Sweden, while promising to invade Scotland, had insisted
upon first prosecuting a tedious campaign in Norway. Worst
of all, the very Italy that Alberoni burned to free turned at
this moment against him. Venice, the Pope, the Grand Duke
of Tuscany, and Victor-Amadeus, all hurried to lick the
Viennese boot. "O homines ad servitutem paratos," cried
Alberoni in the despairing words of Tiberius. He was caught
in a mood of discouragement, blacker than any that Garibaldi
was to know a century and a half later. But Garibaldi was
lucky enough to interpret rather than outstrip the dreams of
his age.

[3] As late as June 27, 1719 they were to win a brilliant victory over the
Austrians at Franca Villa.

With the lovely autumn days Philip and Elisabeth went off shooting, as if they had never set Europe by the ears. The Cardinal did not accompany them, but spent his time closeted with Nancré and d'Aubenton, trying to devise some way of breaching the regal obstinacy. There was little time to lose. Spain had been given until the end of October to adhere to the Quadruple Alliance; and then, if she still refused, there must be war.

Till the middle of the month Philip was inaccessible at La Granja; then on October 17 Nancré, the Cardinal, and the confessor had a chance of wrestling with his obstinacy at the Escorial. The conditions of the Quadruple Alliance included a firm offer of Gibraltar,[4] and the fullest guarantees of the Regency for Elisabeth should Philip die or become incapable while the Prince of the Asturias was still a minor. It was a difficult interview, for Alberoni no longer enjoyed that close alliance with Elisabeth which alone had given him his ascendancy over the King. "Let's make no mistake about it," the shrewd Nancré told the Regent, "the Cardinal is no longer able to sway the King as he wishes."

Nevertheless, after hours of argument, the three of them seemed to make some headway. At one moment, indeed, it appeared certain that peace would yet be preserved. But all these final hopes were dashed next morning. The negotiators of the Quadruple Alliance were providing heritages for Elisabeth's children; they had done nothing to dissipate the fears that haunted her of a poverty-stricken seclusion as Queen Dowager of Spain. It was upon the rock of this omission that all hopes of compromise foundered.

In a brief audience before he rushed off to shoot, Philip on the morrow betrayed an utter change of heart. He exploded into a blaze of abuse against the Regent and the terms. It was a declaration of war, and there was nothing left for Nancré

4 Later this offer was to be half disavowed by the British Government.

but to pack his trunks. During the final audience he noticed upon Elisabeth's face a smile which, he afterwards said, he would have described as malicious were it not disrespectful to use such terms of royalty. As the confessor discreetly put it: "The night brought evil counsels; the alcove this time had triumphed over the prie-dieu."

Open hostilities between an isolated Spain on the one hand and England, France, the Empire, and Savoy-Piedmont [5] on the other were now inevitable. The taciturn William Stanhope took his leave of the Cardinal with many expressions of regret and esteem, which hardly presaged his return in the following year as agent and supervisor of destruction. Nancré shed many tears before he left for Paris. From there, till his death a few months later, he worked ceaselessly with Alberoni, seeking to avert hostilities long after war had been formally declared.

Now that there seemed no chance of turning back, Alberoni flung off the melancholy exhaustion that had sat all these last months on his shoulders like a carrion crow. "Let me," he cried, "have time, patience, good health, and a few more years of life." He laid down new keels; plans for the Swedish invasion of Scotland were pressed forward; through his Scotch doctor, Erskine, Peter the Great was encouraged to attack the Hanoverian who barred his path into Germany; and the Hungarian Kagotczy was incited to harass the Emperor from Transylvania. In Berlin Alberoni's agent played upon the King of Prussia's dislike of his father-in-law, the King of England. At last the Stuart Pretender now found himself becoming a distinguished pawn of Spain.

Moreover, now that he had nothing more to hope from the Regent, Alberoni decided to vex him at home, using the Spanish party in France, of which he had always disapproved, and in particular the Duchesse du Maine.

We have already had occasion to mention Anne-Louise-

[5] Victor-Amadeus joined the Quadruple Alliance in November 1718.

Bénédicte de Charolais, Duchesse du Maine.[6] The sister of Vendôme's wife, she was the grand-daughter of the great Condé — "Monsieur-le-Prince-le-Héros"; her father, who earned no title better than "Monsieur-le-Prince tout court," [7] was eccentric to the point of epilepsy; from time to time he would imagine himself metamorphosed into a white rabbit or a dog and terrify his family by his silent barking; or he would refuse to eat, saying that he was already dead. On the mother's side there was Gonzaga blood, which was perhaps the cause of Louise-Bénédicte's minute stature. "Madame" called her "la poupée royale"; and indeed there was something at once doll-like and royal about the tiny graceful body, the brightly painted face, the flaxen hair and bright blue eyes, the haughty ambition which would suddenly and incongruously fill them and betray itself even in the fluttering gestures of the childish hands.

Too intelligent to be a princess, she was yet unable to forget her descent from the great Condé. Her wits were sharpened — or perhaps oversharpened — by early association with La Bruyère, her eldest brother's tutor. It was La Bruyère who fostered in her that latent, precious elegance which distinguished her court at Sceaux and which would cause her to retard a political conspiracy while she polished the prose of some manifesto.

Her megalomania was inflamed by her marriage in 1692, before her sixteenth birthday, to the Duc du Maine, the darling bastard of Louis XIV, out of Madame de Montespan. For all his withered leg, which, even courtiers were obliged to admit, gave him "une marche fort incommode," and a natural timidity hidden behind a biting tongue, the young man was a great catch. Madame de Maintenon adored him as if he were her own son; she encouraged the King to push Maine forward in every conceivable way. After the death of the Duc and Du-

[6] See page 53.   [7] See page 72.

chesse de Bourgogne she no longer bothered to conceal her ambition that Maine should become King of France.

He had been proposed for the Academy at the age of seven to fill the vacancy left by Corneille's death; a few years later he was made Governor of Languedoc, colonel-general of the Swiss Guards, and general of the galleys; that pathetic spinster the "Grande Mademoiselle" was bullied by her cousin, the King, into making over most of her vast fortune to the youth.

The plundered old maid might sneer at "ce beau couple d'un boiteux et d'une manchotte"; but that could not dim the brilliance of the marriage, or of the bride's dress, encrusted with sea-shells and emblems of the winds, in allusion to the bridegroom's naval distinctions. The town of Lyon composed for the occasion the song "Nous étions dix filles dans un pré," which keeps alive in French nurseries to this day the memory of turbulent tragicomic Madame du Maine; children are lulled to sleep by rhymes written to honour a woman who was rarely able to make her sleepless nights pass quick enough. . . . [8]

[8] "Nous étions dix filles dans un pré [bis]
    Y avait Line
    Y avait Chine
    Y avait Claudine et Martine
    Ah! Ah! Catherinette et Catherinon
    Y avait la belle Suzon,
    La duchesse de Montbazon,
    Y avait Madeleine,
    Y avait la du Maine.

    L'fils du roi vint à passer [bis]
    Salua Line,
    Salua Chine,
    .   .   .   .   .
    Embrassa la du Maine.

    A toutes il fit un cadeau [bis]
    .   .   .   .   .
    Diamants à la du Maine.

    Et puis il les fit coucher [bis]
    Paille à Line,
    Paille à Chine
    .   .   .   .   .
    Paille à Madeleine,
    Beau lit à la du Maine."

Soon bored with her husband and with the tedious ritual of the court, she ran away, back to the society of La Bruyère and the wits. Reconciled again to marriage, reducing her husband to a sort of discreet servitude, she rarely appeared at Versailles; instead she created about her an oasis of grace and gaiety, to which, as we have already seen,[9] the younger courtiers escaped with thankfulness.

Sceaux was the site of this oasis. Symbolically enough, this fine demesne lay on the road towards Spain, a few miles outside Paris. Louis XIV had parted from his grandson there, it will be recalled,[10] when the boy set out for his new kingdom. But Sceaux was a place better suited to lovers' meetings than to kings' farewells. The château had been built for the great Colbert himself, thirty years before, by Claude Perrault; Lebrun had decorated it, and Lenôtre had planned the fabulous gardens. Perrault's château has been pulled down long since; but the noble groups by Coysevox at the gates, the canal, the terraces, and the Temple of Aurora, with Lebrun's decorations still surviving in the dome, give some idea of what a palace of enchantment was Sceaux in its heyday.

In Colbert's era the parties had been enriched by elaborate spectacles, by masques and fireworks and Italian comedies, or operas by Lulli to texts of Racine. This tradition Louise-Bénédicte maintained, though in the changed form of a new age. Where thirty years before a gentleman paid a poet to write his masques, as he might pay his tailor to cut a suit, nowadays he composed the masque himself, or one of his guests would try his hand at it. If he happened to be a rising young genius like Monsieur Arouet de Voltaire, so much the better; but in no circumstances was he a paid servant: only a cherished guest singing for his supper. Similarly, where a Colbert for his diversions hired a pack of actors who as like as not made off with the silver, Madame du Maine acted herself. Old fogies might raise their eyebrows at the spectacle of the great Condé's grand-daughter playing *Les Femmes savantes* to a chosen public; but the newspapers declared that no talent to equal hers had trod the boards since Molière's day. Whatever else might happen to her, Louise-Bénédicte would never lose her passion for the theatre; it affected and dictated every reaction of her tumultuous little character. "She will continue," declared Voltaire, "to love the theatre until her last breath, and when she is sinking, I advise you to administer to her some play instead of the Extreme Unction. We die as we have lived. . . ."

In her age the frontier between the stage and ordinary earth, between the dream and reality, was slender enough even for people with imaginations less lively than Louise-Bénédicte's. At Sceaux the smallest detail of life was a masquerade, and rhymed at that. Millamant's hair, it will be recalled, knew no law unless her curl-papers were made from love-letters in verse. But without rhymes the whole absurd, charming machinery of this court at Sceaux would have stopped. Ear-ache, a gift of salad-bowls, an invitation to dinner, all were the subject for verses, and removed from the rut of ordinary existence, as befitted a life predestined, so Louise-Bénédicte believed, to know the dizziest distinction. Even when she was pregnant and feared that during her nine months' penance she must do herself the violence of forswearing champagne, her secret inclinations would be justified, thus:

> "Laissez-là ce triste régime,
> Princesse, suivez le maxime
> Que Bacchus dicte à ses enfants:
> Buvez du vin! L'enfant auguste
> Qui respire en vos chastes flancs
> En sera cent fois plus robuste!"

During the first years at Sceaux she concerned herself but little with politics; she was happy enough with her lovers —

the ingenious poet Malézieu, the Duc de Nevers, the dazzling Cardinal de Polignac; and with her little court, Rose Delaunay, eccentric old Madame de la Ferté, the Abbé Genest, whose preposterous nose was a godsend to lampooners and had indeed helped to establish this poor midwife's son in the smart world. Then there was her "Ordre de la Mouche à Miel," of which she was tutelary goddess; it was composed of the ingenious gentlemen who liked to frequent Sceaux.

It was, indeed, the temple of all that was witty and elegant in the last years of Louis XIV; the entertainments known as the "Grandes Nuits de Sceaux," ancestors at once of the modern mimed ballet and of the *revue intime*, attracted those who were lucky enough not to bore Louise-Bénédicte, and who could slip out of Versailles without being challenged by a regal frown.

Bumping over vile country roads, past the Longjumeau pastures which Louise-Bénédicte had recently sold at great profit to the butchers of Paris, you came suddenly into the cropped and scented order of her demesne. There you found your hostess, ever so slightly drunk, seated in an arbour of sea-shells, waited on by her officers of the guard, who were disguised as satyrs. There would be a visit from the Prince of Samarkand, or a ballet of ninepins, and a chorus of nymphs and satyrs singing:

> "Si vous m'êtes propices,
> Beaux yeux remplis d'attraits,
> Dans des flots de délices
> Je me plonge à jamais.
> Et vogue la galère.
>
> Les graces vous ont faite
> Pour plaire et pour charmer.
> Pour boire à ma Laurette,
> J'avalerais la mer.
> Et vogue la galère!"

Towards the peacock dawn the diversion would end in extravagant praises of Sceaux's diminutive, tipsy, but still sleepless mistress. She was, they said, a Boileau, a Racine, the most eminently gifted princess in the world. What harm could there be in these hyperboles so long as one never strayed out of that half-dreamed world which is said to have inspired the "Embarquement pour Cythère"? They exercised, however, a disastrous influence upon the boiling mind of Louise-Bénédicte when most of Louis XIV's legitimate posterity were dead, and when her own shrinking lazy husband had been declared capable of succeeding to the French throne, for all his being born on the wrong side of the blanket. She hauled him out on balconies in Paris to throw largesse to the cheering crowds who didn't recognize him, when peace was concluded in 1713; and in the following years politics became with her a passion as imperious as the theatre. Not that the old love was neglected; intrigues were interrupted for rehearsals, ambition was dressed in the trappings of a romantic novelette.

That first fatal meeting of the Regency Council,[11] when Maine was worsted in his half-hearted bid for power, drove her to beat him and to loathe the Regent. Two years later her treacherous, one-eyed nephew, the Duc de Bourbon, succeeded in engineering a reversal of the edict which had made Maine eligible for the succession. This last blow robbed Louise-Bénédicte of her remaining scant stock of caution. Hatred of Orléans became her obsession. Under the eaves of Sceaux she had arranged for herself a luxurious eyrie — a sort of penthouse of the time — adorned with objects not unworthy of the view to be enjoyed from the windows. Mounting to it by her lift, which was a bergère moving on a system of ropes and pulleys, she would brood there for hours upon her wrongs, the need for destroying Orléans, and for getting the Regency into her own hands.

11 p. 130.

Characteristically, her first attack upon the Palais-Royal was poetic. To supplement the lampoons, many of which she apparently wrote or inspired, she commissioned a hack writer, La Grange Chancel, to compose a full-length satire on the Regency. Published under the title of *Les Philippiques*, it enjoyed an immense success; even the indulgent Regent was amused by certain lines:

"Dans ces saturnales augustes
Mettez au rang de vos égaux
Et vos gardes les plus robustes
Et vos esclaves les plus beaux.
Que la faveur, ni la puissance
La fortune, ni la naissance
N'y puissent remporter le prix,
Mais que sur tout autre préside
Quiconque a la vigeur d'Alcide
Ou le visage de Pâris!"

But he was not so well pleased when a little further on he came across the old accusation of poisoner and an invitation to assassinate him. God, declared the satirist:

". . . mit le fer dans la terre
Pour en frapper l'usurpateur."

But poetry was not enough, even for Madame du Maine. She resolved to canvass Alberoni. Her first attempt was made through a preposterous Belgian adventurer, the Baron de Walef, who all too easily gained her confidence. Vague spy for the Pretender, art dealer, agent provocateur, Walef was one of those smooth rogues who seem made to exploit ambitious disappointed women. He promised to leave for Madrid immediately and enlist the help of the wonderful Cardinal. He disappeared, was supposed to be on the road to Spain; suddenly he was back again, protesting he had no money for the

journey, and offering to sell Louise-Bénédicte his collection of
Chinese porcelain. She seems to have given him some funds,
and he vanished again, only to reappear at Turin this time;
then he was heard of in Rome, very friendly and communi-
cative with, of all people, the Imperial representative. He
reached Madrid at last, in April 1718, where William Stanhope immediately recognized him from campaigning days;
apparently Walef had hardly distinguished himself in Flanders.
Alberoni paid little attention to him; at the time the Cardinal
still had his aversion from meddling in French internal politics.

But when all hope vanished of an understanding with the
Regent, renewed overtures from Sceaux were no longer rejected out of hand. This time Louise-Bénédicte approached
the Spanish Ambassador, Cellamare. Few diplomats possessed
temperaments less conspiratorial than this elderly sceptic who
enjoyed good food, pretty women, and receiving his friends
at his fine embassy in the Place des Victoires. Neither he nor
the Cardinal appears to have placed much faith in the plotters
of Sceaux; but it might be worth while hearing what Madame
du Maine had to say. And so we find Cellamare proceeding
through the small hours of a late spring morning in 1718 to the
Arsenal, where Louise-Bénédicte lived when she came to
Paris. It must have diverted the jaded Ambassador to observe
how rigorously were maintained the conventions proper to
this secret occasion; he was required to put on a black cloak
and an enormous black hat, and to hide himself in the depths
of one of the Maine coaches, which had been painted a discreet
grey. The Comte de Laval, a ruined nobleman high in the
councils of Sceaux, was on the box.

There were other interviews; nothing very heinous came of
them; nothing to compare with Saint-Aignan's plottings in
Spain. Plans were discussed for convening the States-General,
to depose Orléans and bestow the Regency upon Philip V,

who was in turn to delegate it to Maine. Sympathizers were canvassed; a few of the old marshals gave a cautious blessing, and some young hotheads, the philandering Duc de Richelieu among them, pledged their support to the last extremity. Draft manifestoes were composed, to be addressed by Philip V to the young King, to the States-General, to the French people themselves. There was even a vague proposal to kidnap the Regent some evening as he returned tipsily across the Bois from supper with his shameless daughter at La Muette. But that came to nothing.

Instead the summer was frittered away in polishing the manifestoes, for not a comma must be out of place in prose that was issued from Sceaux. Meanwhile the Regent was preparing to humble Louise-Bénédicte.

Now that the old King was dead, the Parlements were beginning to raise their impudent heads. Recruited from the magistracy, they exercised functions not unlike those of the Judicial Committee of the British Privy Council in these days. But the publication of the famous Cardinal de Retz's memoirs reminded them how the Parisian Parlement seventy years before had fought Mazarin on equal terms; across the Channel they saw a body with a similar name giving the law to half mankind. No longer, they resolved, would they remain mere machines for registering royal edicts.

The Breton Parlement, encouraged by Cellamare and Louise-Bénédicte, first raised the flag of recalcitrance, refusing to approve certain taxation imposed by a tactless Governor. The Parisian Parlement violently opposed the devalorization of the currency; encouraged by the Regent's pliancy, they then set themselves up as the censors of the whole Government in open defiance of the Palais-Royal. The Regent acted quickly. He called a "Lit de Justice" at the Tuileries and by a show of force overawed the populace of Paris, which was inclined to sympathize with the magistrates. Nevertheless it was

a difficult moment for the tried voluptuary; more was at stake
than the mere authority of a pack of self-important lawyers;
it was the final attempt of his enemies to curb the Regent's
power and to turn France towards Spain rather than England.

On the eve of the "Lit de Justice," when he was still uncertain of his ability to carry off the situation, the Regent was
offered the decisive support of the one-eyed Duc de Bourbon;
he was asked in return to deprive Maine of the King's education, in favour of this grasping new ally. He agreed, and was
able to win the day.

It was the end of Louise-Bénédicte's hopes. She could do
nothing but wreck the apartment at the Tuileries which went
with her husband's office and would now belong to her hateful
nephew. It was the end, too, of the pro-Spanish party. Villeroy
might try to excite the masses with tales of poisoned biscuits
found in the little King's room. But the Regent was now supreme. Dubois and the English influence were also triumphant.
The Councils, which never worked well, had been for some
time moribund; now, to Saint-Simon's infinite regret, they
were suppressed, and France returned to a system of Secretaries of State. At Stanhope's suggestion, foreign affairs were
henceforward entrusted to Dubois. Thus did the Parisians
comment on the appointment:

> "Je ne trouve pas étonnant
> Que l'on fasse un ministre
> Et même un prélat important
> D'un maquereau, d'un cuistre;
> Rien ne me surprend en cela.
> Eh! Ne sait-on pas comme
> De son cheval Caligula
> Fit un consul de Rome?"

Dubois could afford to let the public laugh; he and Stanhope
were now free to declare war upon Spain, or rather upon Al-

beroni; it was a matter, he said, of doing that turbulent Minister all possible harm.

Not that the French people yet saw eye to eye with Dubois. Mindful of how much French property there was in Spain, they by no means burnt for war. But, as Saint-Simon put it, Dubois had learnt in England the art of unmasking a conspiracy, to frighten public opinion into docility.

He had got wind of the Sceaux conspiracy as early as July, when he was in London. For the neat inditing of the manifestoes the conspirators had employed a certain Buvat, copyist in the Bibliothèque Royale; to safeguard himself, Buvat had methodically transmitted to Dubois's office details of every document from Sceaux that passed through his hands. This did not of course give Dubois proof enough to strike; but on the night of December 2, 1718 fortune was kind; in one of the most distinguished brothels of Paris, the tasteful establishment of La Fillon, a young secretary of the Spanish Embassy blurted out the news that a courier of particular importance was leaving for Madrid on the morrow.

Revolutionary epoch though it was, the Regency had not abandoned that respectable tradition which makes every brothel-keeper into a police agent; within a few hours Dubois had learned La Fillon's news. A detachment of cavalry pursued the Spanish courier, the young Abbé Porto-Carrero, out of Paris, and caught up with him at Poictiers. The anxiety which he betrayed for the fate of his diplomatic bag confirmed the suspicions of the police; the bag was opened; inside were found the famous manifestoes, and lists of persons favourable to the King of Spain's cause.

On December 9 Cellamare was arrested, for all his diplomatic immunity, and his office was searched in his presence by Dubois and Leblanc, the Acting Minister for War. To the end the so-called "Conspiration de Cellamare" preserved its quality of drawing-room farce. During the search Leblanc was about to open a certain strong-box. "That's not in your province, Monsieur Leblanc," Cellamare cried; "nothing there but letters from women; leave that to the abbé who's been a *maquereau* all his life!"

Kept for two months in custody at Blois, Cellamare was then put across the Spanish frontier. To the end he stoutly maintained that his conspiracy had no substance. Shown a letter from Alberoni instructing him to "fire his mines," he answered that they were mines without powder. . . .

Some nincompoop, to amuse her, told Louise-Bénédicte of the arrest, while she was gambling in Paris. She laughed, but with a cold heart ran off to Sceaux. Then, after unbearable days of waiting, she could not resist coming back to Paris. She was arrested there on December 29; her husband, who loudly proclaimed his innocence in the affair, was apprehended the same day at Sceaux. All the other conspirators — Polignac, Laval, Rose Delaunay, and the rest — were clapped into the Bastille.

With gentle malice the Regent decreed that Louise-Bénédicte should go into detention at Dijon, under the supervision of her terrible nephew, the Duc de Bourbon, in his capacity as Governor of Burgundy. "Finding herself," the Regent pointed out with some irony, "under the direct control of Monsieur le Duc, she will understand that no hope of flight exists for her, nor any other resource whatsoever."

She was bundled out of Paris in a hired carriage — supreme humiliation for a Condé! At Fontainebleau, however, the Archbishop of Sens lent her his equipage for the rest of the journey. Other mitigations of her fall soon followed; special furniture and ladies-in-waiting came from Paris.

After a year she was moved to Chalon-sur-Saône under a slightly relaxed discipline. And an unwonted philosophy crept upon Louise-Bénédicte. Her great-aunt, the lovely Madame de Longueville, once marooned amid rustic tediums and reminded of the pack of hounds that awaited her pleasure, had cried: "I don't care for innocent pleasures!" Louise-Bénédicte from her makeshift prison, or from the light calèche which her mother had sent her, uncomplaining watched the hours slide by as sluggishly as the refuse of the Burgundian vineyards on the yellow river. Her closest friend was a little donkey that cropped the grass in the prison moat. With graceful irony Voltaire sang of this friendship:

> "Dans ces murs malheureux votre voix enchantée
> Ne put charmer qu'un âne et les échos.
> On vous prendrait pour un Orphée,
> Mais vous n'avez point su, trop malheureuse fée,
> Adoucir tous les animaux!"

Louise-Bénédicte was released a year later, after making a confession in which she took upon herself the blame for the whole absurd business. In unseemly contrast was the behaviour of her husband, who, after protesting his innocence, divided his time between tears and fantastic pieties.

Neither the Regent nor his mother took the conspiracy very seriously. The manifestoes, said "Madame," were too violent in tone to harm her son. But then, she added, assuming them to be Alberoni's work, how could a gardener's boy be familiar with the language of crowned heads? (It was lucky that Louise-Bénédicte never heard of this comment!) But the episode in general served Dubois's purpose. It caused consternation enough in France to justify a declaration of war against Spain (January 9, 1719).

To the last moment Saint-Aignan lingered on in Madrid, intriguing, though his boxes were packed and everybody knew a rupture to be imminent. Finally Alberoni lost patience and forcibly ejected him from Madrid. "I sent that mountebank packing," he explained, "when his extravagances had amused Madrid enough and had served as supplement to the Carnival."

Saint-Aignan's exit from Spain and from history was as undig-
nified as had been his behaviour. Hearing of Cellamare's arrest,
as he neared the French frontier, the Ambassador took fright
and crossed the wintery Pyrenees in disguise, on a mule. His
unfortunate wife, though pregnant, had perforce to go with
him; his valet and her maid proceeded in his coach to Pamplona, playing master and mistress.

It had been an easier matter for the British Government to
declare war on Spain. Public opinion was whipped up with
loyal addresses from the City and tales of Spanish perfidy; in
his newly founded *Whitehall Evening Post* Defoe declared
that "Great Britain cannot acquiesce in letting Spain possess
Sicily, without giving up her trade to Turkey and the Gulph
of Venice . . . To Zant for currants, to Gallipoli for oyl, to
Messina and Naples for silk, and in a word . . . the whole
commerce of the Mediterranean"; the naval strength of Spain
must not be allowed "to grow to such an immoderate and monstrous pitch." Then, with rare inconsistency, he says in the
next breath that Spain's defiance of the Allies is "nothing but
a State lunacy, an infatuation beyond what was ever seen before (the holding out of Jerusalem against the Romans ex-
cepted)."

Nevertheless the Government were forced to spend a good
deal of money and favours to secure a vote for war. In the
Lords, Cowper raised his distinguished voice to denounce the
proposal; Robert Walpole in the Commons described Passero
as a crime against the laws of nations. The motion for hostilities
was carried, however, and a formal declaration of war was
made on December 28, 1718. Stanhope assured the Lords that
"he durst answer beforehand that upon the strictest examina-
tion it would be found that H.M. and his ministers had done
nothing against the faith of Treaties or the honour and interest of the nation. . . ."

THE "STATE LUNACY"

Good God, My Lord," wrote Bolingbroke from La Source in December 1718, "what have we seen in this age? The Princes of the North, the Jacobites in Britain, the faction of the old court in this country, the Pope and some of the princes of Italy underhand, and the great Turk himself till he was beat out of these measures, acting in concert together, and Alberoni at the head of the League."

To the casual observer, indeed, the Cardinal appeared to have made up the loss of his navy and his best troops and to be heading a combination of powers capable of throwing the Quadruple Alliance into confusion. He had, for instance, at last united the Czar and the Swedish King in hatred of George I; it seemed only a matter of time before Hanover and Scotland would be invaded; and he was fomenting the discontent of Brittany. The Dutch had contrived to keep out of the quarrel; if by diversions Alberoni could paralyze French and British action, he might yet be a match for the Empire.

But as Bolingbroke was writing, another blow fell upon the Cardinal. Charles XII of Sweden on December 11, 1718 was killed at the siege of Frederickshald, a town in Norway obscure even by Norwegian standards. Whether an enemy's or a traitor's bullet did for him is immaterial; whichever way it was, in falling he knocked the bottom out of Alberoni's plans. So vanished in a moment of futility that half-demoniacal, half-heroic figure, with his high cropped head, his cold madness, his hatred of all the arabesques of pleasure that gave the contour to his age.

In Whitehall, Craggs, that bellicose Minister, might well ask: "Will it be possible for this red-hot cardinal to resist so many blows and to support himself during such a precarious life as the King of Spain's, much more after his death?" Alberoni was feeling anything but red-hot. "It's the King," he complained to Nancré, with some melancholy, "who believes it would be prejudicial to his honour to accept the project. . . . He'll allow the four corners of Europe to be set ablaze unless some expedient can be found . . . to convince him that his honour is taken care of. It's for H.R.H. [i.e., the Regent] to provide me with one, and then he'll see how I'll act."

But no expedient could be found to throw down the maddening obstinacy of Philip V. Seemingly unaware of the crisis they had provoked in Europe, he and his consort pursued their placid sensuous existence, shooting, and diverted by their Italian comedians, or by the Atlas clock, which had at last arrived — "an innocent life, unique perhaps among the European courts," says Alberoni loyally, and goes on to ask for more and ever more sausages, truffles, wine, "it being eight days that Her Majesty has lacked wine and has been obliged to drink Canary, which never fails to heat her blood."

Since Philip like a dog by an unwanted bone mounted guard over his precious honour, all hope of compromise languished, and Alberoni was forced to prosecute the war. The Pretender was invited to Madrid at last. He set out from Italy at the beginning of February 1719. It was not a moment too early; funds were running low — the pension paid by the British Government to his mother, Queen Mary of Modena, had died with her in the previous May; besides, Stanhope, who had got wind of the Jacobite plots cooking in Spain, was now pressing the Pope to arrest the young man.

The departure was ingeniously contrived; a carriage apparently bearing Prince James went north out of Papal territory, with Mar and Perth in it; it was punctually apprehended in the

Imperial dominions, and the Whigs in London were exultant — exultant, that is, till they learned how they had been tricked. Meanwhile the real Pretender had quietly slipped off for Spain from the Papal harbour of Nettuno.

On that disagreeable journey the Prince could hardly tell from what he suffered most, the English cruisers that came so soon upon his trail, or the tempests that turned him into a twitching ghost. He had never been a good sailor; on this occasion unusually severe weather so prostrated him, he was obliged to put into the Île d'Or, off Hyères. Even then his torments were not ended. The inn was sordid, the company numerous, insistent, and unsavoury. It was Carnival time, and poor Prince James, for all his aching stomach and the still unsteady floor, was forced into dancing with the innkeeper's slatternly wife.

He reached Madrid at last and was suitably housed in the Palace of Buen Retiro. His chief general, the Duke of Ormond, who had fled from England after Queen Anne's death, preceded the Prince to Spain by several months, crossing the frontier in a valet's disguise toward the end of 1718. After endless delays an expedition which he and Alberoni organized sailed from Cadiz (beginning of March 1719). It was composed of ships which had escaped destruction at Passero, and 5,000 troops; the destination was the west of England, which was supposed to be ripe for revolt.

Forewarned, the home fleet under Lord Berkeley waited for the Spanish squadron off the entrance to the Channel; but the days went by, and no enemy appeared. "I believe," wrote Berkeley to Stair on April 10, ". . . their being sailed is perfectly true, but if with so little provisions as they say, they must certainly be perished in the sea. Indeed, I am very apt to believe . . . that we shall have a very dismal account of them whenever we hear of them, for they can have met with nothing but contrary winds and very bad weather."

That was putting it mildly. The day after the Pretender's arrival at Madrid, the little fleet was shattered and dispersed by a violent storm off Finisterre; The Tory clergy of Bristol were left vainly waiting to sing their "Te Deums" in honour of a Jacobite landing.

The other part of Alberoni's Jacobite venture, that on Scotland, fared no better. The day after Ormond's expedition sailed for the west of England, two Spanish frigates, with 300 troops and a quantity of arms, headed towards Scotland, under the resolute Lord Marischal. His younger brother Keith, who was later to become a field-marshal and a hero in the Prussian service, had already slipped off to Paris in the inevitable valet's disguise, to raise the Scotch lords resident there. The gallant Keith was all too successful; the gentlemen he brought with him to Scotland, to join the Spanish force already landed there, paralyzed action with their ridiculous squabbles. The Highlanders came in all too slowly. When the Government troops under General Wightman attacked them in the Pass of Glenshiel early in June, the Jacobite-Spanish force was routed. Little remains to commemorate the action save for an occasional long Spanish sword still hanging in some castle armoury, or the ghost of a Captain Downes, killed in the fight, who is said to walk the glen on certain evenings.[1]

During the night following the encounter, the Highlanders slipped back to their homes, and the Scotch lords escaped in disguise. On the morrow the unfortunate Spaniards surren-

---

[1] An English naval officer wrote the following verses on the action:

"Not famous for one martial deed,
But that they ran away at speed,
And nimbly skipped from rock to mountain
And of their heels made most account on.

The hardy Marshal, I protest
He ran as fast as did the best.
Lord Seaforth, that great man of Mars,
Was glad, like Mars, to shew his arse."

dered. For a time there was thought of parading them through the country, to whip up popular feeling for the war; but upon the ladies of Edinburgh, where they were first brought, the Spanish prisoners with their fine manners and flashing eyes produced an effect so contrary, it was thought best to ship them home straightway from Leith.

Still Alberoni did not lose his philosophy. "Human schemes," he declared, "unaided by Providence, are of little or no use. Of the plans I devised, had but one of them been successful, it would have been enough to upset the enemy's designs. God has contraried all of them; there is nothing to be done but to adore His judgements and to submit with complete resignation to His divine will. . . ."

At last the Duke of Parma agreed with him and urged that Spain should sue for peace through the mediation of Holland. "Your Highness's reasoning," said Alberoni, "could not be more sound and sensible . . . but the King and Queen will not be persuaded. . . . They believe that when they are in the presence of the French army, the whole of it will pass over to their service."

The French army in question had, of course, already invaded northern Spain. "You've got to see it all to believe it!" wrote Alberoni. French troops had actually taken the field against their own King's uncle, a Bourbon prince; and, supreme infamy of all, when the other marshals had declined this invidious command, the Duke of Berwick, half-brother to the Pretender, victor of Almanza, recipient of countless Spanish honours, father of a Spanish Duke, was not ashamed to assume it. Where duty was concerned, he said, he had no human feelings, and he cheerfully became the instrument of a cause directly hostile to his own Stuart blood.

One of England's main purposes in entering this unhappy war was to complete the paralysis of Spain's renascent navy — an object profoundly unsympathetic to most Frenchmen; but not so to Dubois. He had become little more than the agent of the British Government; his subservience to Stanhope's commands provoked bitter comment:

"Anglois, tenez-vous en repos.
On vous donne l'abbé Dubois.
Mieux que vous il fait vos affaires."

It was Dubois who particularly enjoined Marshal Berwick to destroy the northern Spanish dockyards; and Berwick carried out his instructions with spirit. He crossed the unprotected frontier on April 21 and immediately marched on Los Pasajes, one of Alberoni's principal dockyards. "Well, My Lord," the Duke wrote briskly to Stair a few days later, "on the slipways we found six large battleships not yet ready to be launched, and which they're destroying at the moment. A prodigious quantity of masts and timber was also found. They say there was enough there to build twenty warships. I am shipping it to Bayonne. . . . I've no doubt, My Lord, that you will be pleased to learn this news. . . ."

This French invasion at last roused the Spanish monarchs from their respectable lethargy. Philip turned overnight from rustic hypochondriac into defender of his people. Accompanied by his consort, he announced, he was proceeding forthwith to the front, to put himself at the head of his army. To Alberoni these antics seemed idiotic. There was no army, properly speaking; it was locked up in Sicily; and the raw levies in the north could not possibly hold the French. But his advice counted for little these days; Philip and Elisabeth were set upon making their heroic gesture; and since he did not dare let them out of his sight, the Cardinal went wearily with them.

For the young sovereigns it was at first a dramatic and by no means disagreeable change of existence. For the campaign the Queen had ordered from one of the best tailors in hostile Paris a smart blue and silver habit, "à l'amazone"; with a courtesy typical of the age, fighting was suspended while the precious parcel was passed under a flag of truce from the French to the Spanish patrols. Dressed in her new get-up, and mounted on an English hunter with pistols at her saddle-bow, Elisabeth delighted to pass in review the sorry army.

For Alberoni life had a more sombre complexion: bad lodgings, little to eat till he had seen to the Queen's precious meals, incessant headaches, couriers to and fro the whole time. There were worries without end: the thought of his warships, his forests of timber and vats of tar, all lost or crackling into the neutral sky; despite friendly words, the French in the New World had seized from Spain the rich Bay of Pensacola; the Austrians were trying to bully the Pope into taking Alberoni's hat away from him; they had already induced the Holy Father to refuse him the bull of appointment as Archbishop of Seville, to which his sovereigns had recently raised him. Then they would persist in sending from Parma red wine for the Queen, when, as everyone knew, she habitually drank white. . . . The Cardinal, in short, felt all of his fifty-five years; campaigning no longer delighted him. "When," he cried in real anguish, "when shall I be able to get out of this maze? If God but gave me the means of making peace, it would be soon done. No, this sort of existence can't go on!"

Suddenly at Pamplona, one day in June, his melancholy reserve was shattered. Berwick's army before Fuenterrabía was suffering a steady drain of desertions; Philip V had formed a special regiment in the Spanish army, the "Royal de France," to enrol those men who scrupled to fight against Louis XIV's grandson. The rate of these desertions now encouraged Philip to think that his mere appearance before Berwick's force would be enough to win over the larger part of it. He therefore proposed to march on Fuenterrabía with but a handful of companions.

The Cardinal was moved to the last extremity of exasperation. He was prepared, he cried, to pass for the animator of the war, the disturber of European peace, to be the object of universal hatred, but this harebrained scheme he would never countenance. If anything went wrong, as it almost certainly would, "the world, which already laid everything at my door, would say that my extravagances could not finish otherwise, that there was nothing else to be expected of a maniac."

This outburst had no other effect but to increase the rancour against the Cardinal, which was now rapidly growing in the hearts of his master and mistress. The royal party, for all Alberoni's attempts to lose the way, advanced to within a few miles of the French lines; only Berwick's determination to avoid all unnecessary embarrassments kept them from falling into the hands of a French patrol. At the same time every effort was made to capture Alberoni; but the officer who aspired to betray him was denounced in time.

San Sebastián fell in mid-August; under the cold impulsion of William Stanhope, who was now attached to Berwick's staff as British representative, the French destroyed all dockyards down the Atlantic coast. Late in September a small British force under Lord Cobham landed at Vigo; when they had become accustomed to the Spanish wine, they spread destruction and panic into the surrounding countryside. The Basques and Catalans were promised Anglo-French guarantees of their liberties if they would but rise against Alberoni.

The Regent's policy, interpreted by Dubois, was everywhere triumphant. Soon Philip V would be compelled to affirm the rights of the Orléans family in France; and the manipulations of that ingenious Scotchman Law were rapidly turning France into the wealthiest country in the world, so that Paris was filled with the suddenly enriched, bespattering their carriages with gold leaf and perching upon golden chamberpots. It seemed, indeed, as if the Regent had at last conjured up that prosperity which he had so long and passionately desired for the French. He was successful in everything he touched. But suddenly his triumph turned to ashes; his beloved Joufflotte died.

She had lately been dominated by a venal rogue called Riom. He commanded her life down to its merest detail: the colour of a ribbon, or the way she was to wear her hair at some party. He would take pleasure in countermanding his orders when she was fully dressed; and she, his adoring slave, in floods of tears would hurry to obey his new fancy, though it meant dressing all over again. She had even insisted upon marrying the creature, a step to which her indulgent father had only consented if it were kept a secret; he had apparently believed that time and proximity would cure her of this unfitting passion.

But, for all his spotty face, Riom was endowed with attributes against which puny reason could hardly prevail. Joufflotte's masochistic obsession for him grew to fantastic heights. Egged on by Madame de Mouchy, her lady in waiting, who shared with her the vigorous attentions of dear "Riri," she sought in March 1719 to make public her marriage; it seemed that she was pregnant. For once, however, her father put his foot down; "Riri" was packed off to campaign in Spain, and behind the closed doors of the Luxembourg Joufflotte gave birth to a child who had the discretion immediately to die. So little had the public heard of Riom, the question of the baby's paternity caused some mystification; the lampooners leaped to the obvious conclusion:

> "Que notre Régent et sa fille
> Commettent mainte peccadille,
> C'est un fait qui semble constant.
> Mais que par lui elle soit mère,
> Se peut-il que d'un même enfant
> Il soit le père et le grand-père?"

Too soon after her difficult confinement Joufflotte gave a dinner of reconciliation for her exasperated father. At this sumptuous affair, which took place on the terrace at Meudon, she caught a chill, from which she never recovered. The errors of her doctors were magnified by her enormous, furtive appetite. Dwindled to a ghost, she was moved to La Muette; there, amid Watteau's new decorations she died, on July 20, 1719, her twenty-fourth birthday. The Regent was reduced to such a state of despair that the spectacle of the wretched Madame de Mouchy stealing everything, even the tapestries, under his nose aroused no flicker of annoyance. On the other side of the Bois his grief was new material for a lampoon:

> "Est-ce du trépas de Berry
> Que ta perfide âme s'oppresse?
> Je vois que ton regard pâlit,
> Est-ce du trépas de Berry?
> La pleures-tu comme mari,
> Comme ta fille ou ta maîtresse?"

To the distracted Orléans it must have seemed but an instant since that moment of perfect triumph in the previous autumn when, to celebrate the victory over the Parlement and the bastards, the one-eyed Duc de Bourbon had given a party at Chantilly, a miracle of a party, with musicians, harlequins, pyramids of fruit and pâtés down every scented alley of the gardens. There had been a pleasant flutter of excitement when one of Bourbon's tigers had escaped from his menagerie; and a still greater buzz when the guest of honour, poor Joufflotte, had appeared in the new fashion which Dubois had obligingly brought back from London — panniers or hoops that often made the skirts twelve feet round, and which exaggerated the beauty of the small neat heads. There were panniers "en coupole," "en gondole," "en pagode," "en ballon," or "considérations" that made their wearers seem to be sweeping perpetual curtsies. "J'ai des bannes, des cerceaux, des volants, des matelas piqués," says Harlequin turned dressmaker, "j'en ai des solides pour les prudes, des pliants pour les galantes, et des mixtes pour les personnes de tiers état. . . ."

For five days, to honour Joufflotte, the woods had glowed with torches, fireworks had prolonged the lakes into infinity; it had been the apotheosis of that strange epoch which was to carry Europe from the heroic age of Louis XIV into the familiar one of Madame du Deffand. Now Joufflotte's death had, as it were, broken up the party; and the other great figures of her era — her father, Alberoni, Stanhope, Dubois — were soon to follow her into the grave or to the oblivion of misfortune. . . .

Though his enemies did not know it, Alberoni's power at the Spanish court was fast slipping away. The sovereigns had returned from the front; musket was exchanged for sporting-gun, and Alberoni was left with an apparently free hand to save Spain as best he might from the consequences of her sovereign's folly.

But in the secrecy of Elisabeth's dressing-room, and in the ducal palace at Parma, an intrigue to ruin him was steadily hatching. The hero of it was Peterborough, who had never ceased to work for a reconciliation of the Regent with Philip V. For months he had been bombarding the Farnesi with advice; now, in June 1719, he appeared in Paris to urge his views upon the Regent. While there he seems to have been won over to the idea which Dubois had made fashionable, that Alberoni was the supreme obstacle to peace.

It accorded with opinions that had been gradually forming in his own mind. "The Cardinal embarrasses everybody," he had told his friends already in April; "he's a sort of Don Quixote." Now from Paris his tone became even more hostile: "the Cardinal, for an Italian minister, is too fond of playing the man of honour. A minister who keeps on talking of honour,

"LA GRANDE MADEMOISELLE"
by Mignard

CHARLES XII OF SWEDEN

without giving proofs of it, is very like a woman who always has the word virtue on her lips, and love in her eyes."

It was in some measure, no doubt, Peterborough's intrigues that in July brought to the Spanish headquarters, then in Pamplona, the heavy familiar figure of the Marquis Scotti. To Alberoni his manner was friendly; but this time he somehow contrived to see the Queen alone, and he hinted to her that the dismissal of her Minister might be the easiest way out of her embarrassments. No shadow of a scruple seems to have tugged at Elisabeth's heart; if there was nothing else to be done, she agreed, they must send Alberoni packing. But Philip would not hear of the idea. It was not loyalty that inspired him, but fear lest an imposed dismissal of his Minister might damage his own precious dignity. This dignity was now the sole obstacle to peace. "It only remains," remarked the French representative in London, "to save decorums. . . ."

At last, however, the Spanish sovereigns agreed to stomach a compromise, and Scotti went off at the end of July to seek Dutch mediation. He carried away with him solid evidence of how the Cardinal's star was waning — on his return he was to take over care of the Queen's table. The last and most powerful weapon was slipping out of Alberoni's tired fingers.

For all that, he could still contrive to harry his enemies, or at least hope to do so; there was again some prospect of assistance from the Russian Czar, who had fallen out anew with George I, and played with the project of invading Scotland; there was talk of the Czarevitch marrying a Spanish infanta. At the same time the Cardinal opened negotiations once again with the Breton malcontents.

Their sullen resentment, first manifest in the recalcitrance of their Parlement, had lately turned into open revolt. A Breton agent, Mélac-Hervieux, called upon Alberoni at the Spanish headquarters before Fuenterrabía, in June; and the Cardinal agreed to furnish four battalions, under Ormond,

with arms and money, against a Breton undertaking to put 12,000 foot and 4,000 horse into the field.

Had Spanish help ever reached Brittany in strength, had the rebels been content to wage a guerrilla campaign, the Regency might have been seriously harassed. But once again Alberoni's loss of sea-power proved fatal. Most of his transports were blockaded in the port of Coruña, while the rebels' operations were betrayed and mismanaged. The retired army officers who led them insisted upon fighting a proper field campaign; guerrilla tactics, which alone might have succeeded, were to them something strange and dishonourable. The outcome was disastrous; the insurgents were quickly outmatched and dispersed. Most of the leaders escaped to Spain; four of them, however, were caught, and executed at Nantes in the following year.[2]

Scotti, meanwhile, had reached Paris and was demanding a passport for Holland. At first the Regent seems to have favoured the idea of Dutch mediation. But Stanhope had lately become inspired with implacable hatred for Alberoni; if the conception of Alberoni as a satanic figure was Dubois's invention, the English Minister now out-heroded Herod. Given three years, he was wont to say, and Alberoni would turn Europe upside down. And so he proclaimed that the Cardinal must be destroyed before there could be any talk of peace. "His unbounded ambition has been the sole cause of the war. . . . If he is compelled to accept peace he will only yield to necessity. . . . When he is reduced, let us not suffer him to recover. . . . Let us hold forth this example to Europe as a means of intimidating every turbulent minister who breaks

[2] "En Bretagne on a été obligé d'employer la sévérité; 4 personnes ont été décapitées: l'une d'elles qui devait s'embarquer pour l'Espagne ne voulut pas partir. On lui demanda la cause de son refus. Il répondit qu'on lui avait prédit qu'il mourrait *de la mer*. Au moment de l'exécution il demanda au bourreau comment il s'appela. Celui-ci répondit: Je m'appelle La Mer. Ah! s'écria la gentilhomme, je suis mort!" (Correspondence of "Madame," Duchesse d'Orléans.)

the most solemn treaties and attacks the persons of princes in the most scandalous manner. . . ."

The Cardinal's disgrace now became for the Allies the essential condition of peace. Scotti's passport for Holland was refused; it was then a simple matter to persuade him to abandon his mission and betray the man who had once humiliated him. Before his cunning ox-eyes Dubois dangled the fabulous possibility of his succeeding to the Cardinal's place and gave him a handsome bribe; then, with Parma's approval, he sent him back to Madrid.

Under the assumed name of Antonio Gavassi, Peterborough in the meantime had proceeded to Italy. In the hills between Novi and Genoa he met the Parmesan representative, his old friend Gazzola. Although the British Government were still at some pains to disavow him, Peterborough now accomplished Alberoni's final disgrace. As a result of these theatrical negotiations the Duke of Parma agreed to contrive the Cardinal's dismissal, provided that the Regent strengthened his hand by a declaration on the necessity for the step. In return for this service, the breaking of a man who had served the Farnese house for a generation and had raised it to unexampled heights, Gazzola was instructed to press for Parma or Piacenza to be chosen as the site of the European conference which must inevitably be convened to settle the future of Europe. The amenities of the two cities were warmly canvassed in the midst of these shabby conversations.

The Cardinal, vaguely conscious of all these intrigues, tried to keep Scotti out of Spain. The man, he said, had accomplished nothing in Paris; he would do no better at Madrid; he had best go back to Parma. The persistent creature turned up, for all that, still full of apparent amity. But Alberoni was taking no chances. He seems already to have been contemplating retirement from a position that brought him nothing but disappointment; yet he would go in his own time, not as a result of some furtive plot. He therefore used all his powers once more to prevent Scotti from enjoying any private conversation with the Queen. For a time he was successful, but at last, in mid-November, Scotti found a way through the Cardinal's defences. "It's all arranged now," he wrote triumphantly to the Duke of Parma; "whether the Cardinal likes it or not, I won't leave Spain except on Your Highness's orders. When I wish to talk to Their Majesties, it will be they who will summon me, so as to elude the Cardinal's watch. . . . I'll tell you one day how I did it; the Cardinal will never find out. . . ."

The truth was, Scotti had bribed Laura Pescatori, "a decent woman," he called her, adding disingenuously: "she lets herself be swayed by the basest motives." She took advantage of a moment when the King was at confession to slip into the Queen's hand, as she was putting her stockings on, a secret letter from the Duke of Parma announcing the unanimous decision of the Allies to accept no settlement so long as the Cardinal remained in power. At the same time the plotters won over old Father d'Aubenton with stories of the Cardinal intending to entrust the King's conscience into other hands. . . .

On November 28, 1719 Alberoni received an urgent appeal from Parma to humiliate himself before Europe; the implied alternative was resignation. Scorning both courses, he made one last effort to end the war honourably. By the intermediary of a French officer in the Polish service, who happened to be on his way to England, he despatched a private letter to Stanhope, offering to accept the Quadruple Alliance, with certain reservations, and to extend England commercial advantages in Mexico. But by the time Alberoni's letter had reached London, it had lost all purpose.

On December 5, 1719, when the Spanish sovereigns had gone off shooting, thus avoiding unpleasant farewells, the half-expected blow fell. The King's private secretary brought Alberoni an order of immediate dismissal from all his Spanish offices. He was to leave Madrid within eight days and be out of the kingdom within three weeks. All requests for an audience were refused by the embarrassed sovereigns.

He accepted defeat in the grand manner. "It was the least sacrifice," he declared, "that one could make to give peace to Europe." He did not bother to conceal his knowledge of the sordid intrigue which had brought him down; and in his message to the Duke of Parma irony delicately flavoured submission: "In Italy, whither I'm bound, it will be easier for me to receive the respected orders of Your Highness. . . ."

EPILOGUE

THE GRANDEES flocked to his defeated door, with tokens of affection and regret. At court, abuse of the disgraced Cardinal might now be the surest way to favour; but for many he was still the magician who had made Spain feared once more.

Before he left Madrid, Alberoni struck one last blow. He addressed to Philip V a tart letter, placing the blame for the war where it was due. Then, when he had flung the King into a passion of anger and fear by it, he went his way, through the frozen expanses of Catalonia and Aragon, in weather that brought to mind the humbling of Madame des Ursins, almost exactly five years before.

Philip and Elisabeth, it seems, suspected him of carrying with him documents which might expose them for what they were before the whole of Europe. As a consequence Alberoni's party was repeatedly attacked on their journey by disguised police or Catalan "miqueletes" in efforts to seize his baggage. The Cardinal, under the inspiration of these ambushes, rose to his old stature. One sees for an instant again something of the passionate, reckless, bellicose young abbé in that ancient figure, beneath the great travelling hat of his rank, charging down the iron hills at the head of his servants and sending the marauders to scurry for cover across the bare plateaux outside Lérida.

The Catalans, who had chafed under his authority, sped him on his way with cries of "Go to the Devil." When he reached Perpignan, Alberoni could no longer curb his bitterness against the nation of which he had hoped so much; before the assembled crowds he thanked God to be in a Christian land once more. To the Chevalier de Marcieu, a brother-in-arms from the old campaigning days, who had come to escort and spy upon him, the Cardinal did not mince his words. The King of Spain, he declared, needed nothing in life but a prie-dieu and a woman's thighs; sometimes, reported the scandalized Marcieu to the Regent, sometimes the Cardinal would refer to his former patrons in terms too "strong to be applied to crowned heads." Indeed, he now allowed himself a moment of weakness; he offered to let the Regent know how best to abase the Spanish monarchy; and he promised to help Dubois in securing a hat.

The news of the Cardinal's fall was received at the Palais-Royal with joy. "Madame," who firmly believed that he had tried to encompass the murder of her son, burst into delighted tears. A courier went immediately to London, and a secretary of the French Embassy hurried round with the news to Stanhope, in the House of Lords. Embracing the Frenchman, Stanhope announced the tidings to an exultant Chamber. The undoing of a great man who had ardently wished to be a friend of England was hailed by the Peers as a victory; in the Commons the general felicity was only disturbed by Walpole, who spoilt everything with a sneer and continued in private to drink Alberoni's health.

Voltaire celebrated the event in graceful numbers. He had been, and would always remain, the Cardinal's warm admirer. But after his association with Sceaux, the boldness of his satire upon the Regent in *Œdipe* — a blow which Orléans had countered with a smile and a purse of money — the young writer found it best to march with the victorious host. The following lines were promptly addressed to Dubois:

"Alberon pour un temps nous éblouit la vue.
De ses vastes projets l'orgeuilleuse étendue
Occupait l'univers, saisi d'étonnement;
Ton génie et le sien disputaient la victoire.
Mais tu parus, et sa gloire
S'éclipsa dans un instant,
Telle au bord du firmament
Une comète affreuse éclate de lumière
Ses feux portent la crainte au céleste séjour,
Dans la nuit ils éblouissent,
Et soudain s'épanouissent
Aux premiers feux du jour."

While Voltaire thus obsequiously rhymed, the spent comet dropped slowly through Provence towards Italy, harried by the gaping crowds. At Antibes a State galley from Genoa awaited him, to take him into sanctuary. The hospitality of the Genoese Republic was not untimely, for further trouble was now brewing. Their Catholic Majesties and the Duke of Parma were wildly apprehensive of revelations by Alberoni, and they did everything in their power to gag him in time. The Pope was pressed to strip him of the purple. With a view to his early imprisonment, enquiries into his private behaviour were set on foot in Rome and Madrid. He was accused of not having said Mass for six years, of blaspheming, of not wearing long robes, even of fornication with his mustachioed old house-keeper.

His extradition from Genoese territory was demanded. But for once the Doge and Senate were not to be bullied; with spirit they resisted the threats and cajoleries of half Europe. Then suddenly the Cardinal eased their situation. Staying only to set forth in a curt memorandum the true qualities of the Spanish sovereigns, he contrived in the spring of 1720 to vanish as utterly as if he were a magician.

There was a price on his head; the agents of Spain, England, and Parma hunted for him across the vernal hills. But beyond a vague rumour of his having shown up for an instant near Lugano, the Alps seemed to have swallowed him. Indeed, as the months went by with no broadside from him, no entreaty, no sound of rage or despair to break his silence, royalty at Parma and Madrid began to breathe freely once more. The Cardinal must be dead; evidently the rigours of the mountains had been too much for him; with some satisfaction it was recalled that he had never spared his constitution. Queen Elisabeth could now with quiet heart enjoy the maturing delights of La Granja. To think that the Cardinal had dared to disapprove her expenditure on the fountains! Well, time had shown him to be nothing but a rogue. Time had killed him as a punishment for his presumption.

Then, in the spring of 1721, Pope Clement XI died. The College of Cardinals was at once placed in a pretty quandary. The election of a new pontiff is not valid unless every living member of the College is afforded an opportunity to attend. Alberoni was the bugbear of the Great Powers; his alleged misdeeds were even now under legal investigation. But his hat had never been taken from him, and his death had never been formally established. The matter was debated to and fro. At last it was resolved to issue a summons for Alberoni to attend the forthcoming conclave. It should be displayed outside the Alpine churches in that part of Genoese territory where he had last been seen for certain. It should be accompanied by an offer to suspend the proceedings against him until a new pope had been chosen, and to afford him a safe-conduct for his journey to Rome. If within a reasonable time the Cardinal had made no answer to this summons, the College would assume him dead.

The Spanish and British Ministers in Genoa were considerably riled by this measure. Did it not imply that the Cardinal was close at hand, when they had been at pains to satisfy their governments that he was nowhere on Genoese soil, if indeed in the world of the living? Their irritation was not allayed by the news that he had popped up almost as soon as the summons had been displayed, and was even now on his way to the conclave.

One fine evening in April 1721 he appeared at the gates of Rome. Crowds were waiting to gaze on this famous Eminence. He entered the city less as a respited fugitive than as a hero. His strong nerves, his distinguished affability, quickly caught the imagination of the Romans. The dramatic circumstances of his resurrection enchanted them. What other cardinal would have thought, they asked each other excitedly, of braving the spite of England and Spain to appear before the gates, superb on a white horse? Soon the lampoons were portraying him as the most influential figure in the conclave. Certainly his triumph was respectable. When he paid his ceremonial visits to his fellow princes in their cells, only del Giudice was able to resist his brilliance, the charm of his address. Except that his troubles were still unresolved, it was agreed that he was eminently "papabile."

An old friend, Cardinal Conti, was chosen, under the name of Innocent XIII. Though of somnolent habits, he was a Pope of courage; and when it became clear that the evidence laid before the Board of Enquiry could justify no other verdict but one of absolution for Alberoni, with full reinstatement, Innocent XIII was not to be intimidated by the bad humour of Madrid and Parma. Indeed, he protested violently against their attempts to interfere with the board's decision. Alberoni's honesty, chastity, and piety had been impugned; now it had been vindicated. Very well then, his innocence should be proclaimed, and a fig for high politics! In September 1723 there came a Papal declaration, triumphantly acquitting Alberoni on every score.

He was now free to do as he pleased — to struggle with the irrigation of his vineyard outside the Porta Pia, to look after his Roman parish, and receive his friends decently in a small palace. After a few years he patched matters up with the Spanish sovereigns; once or twice there was even a question of his returning to Madrid, to rescue the monarchy from the pass into which it was soon reduced by the incapacity of those who followed him. Certainly many patriotic Spaniards came ardently to desire his reinstatement. Macanaz, for instance, who had been exiled in 1715,[1] and had no particular reason to like him, declared one day to the Queen that "if the return of the Cardinal to this court were certain . . . I would give up to the last drop of my blood to see him here; for his mere presence would be enough to consternate our enemies." But the English would not hear of it; they almost broke blood-vessels when the idea was broached.

So Alberoni never went back into that maze where he had wandered with such torment. Instead he lingered on in Rome for some nine years, rising in the favour of successive Popes, and even obtaining a handsome number of votes in one conclave. At first he found himself face to face with his two late enemies, Madame des Ursins and Cardinal del Giudice. But after a few years they died off and were forgotten. He struck up a warm friendship with the Pretender and his unhappy wife, Princess Clementina Sobieska, and on the Pope's orders in 1727 he made repeated efforts to compose their quarrels. In 1730 he published a plan for a sort of European federation with a federal army and a permanent congress to arbitrate in international disputes. The scheme roused, of course, little interest; it was always Alberoni's misfortune to outstrip the concepts of his age.

He never lost his sore-tried admiration for England; many Englishmen who visited Rome became his friends — among

[1] See page 121.

them the third Duke of Beaufort. The Cardinal is supposed to have helped him form the large collection of antique marbles and Italian paintings which was brought back to Badminton towards 1730. Many of the marbles are now to be found in Wyatt's uneasy cloister at Wilton, but all trace is lost of a fountain which Alberoni presented to the Duke, the bringing of which to Gloucestershire seems to have cost a fortune. On the lovely walls of Badminton hang two contemporary portraits by Trevisani, of the Duke and his aged friend the Cardinal. They commemorate, no doubt, an agreeable association between the young English swell, fascinated by the Mediterranean world, and the septuagenarian peasant, who symbolized it in all its contradictions, his formidable temper, and his quiet dignity in misfortune, his unabated pleasure in brilliant company, and his taste, no less strong, for the peace of his villa at Castelromano.

There he occasionally entertained, it is true, a few intimate cronies, treating them to dishes that he cooked with unflagging mastery. His conversation was as spirited and fantastic as ever: dissertations on his adventures in Spain, his campaigns with Vendôme, or the current political situation — a bright torrent of ideas and wit poured out in a confusion of Italian, French, and Spanish, with here and there an apt tag from Tacitus, or a silver saucepan banged upon the kitchen table to point a remark.

For some time now the Cardinal had toyed with the project of founding a college to train young aspirants for the priesthood, to give them easily such an education as he had only won by luck and charm. In 1733 the Pope put into his hands the old hospital of San Lazaro outside Piacenza. Its name would suggest that it had originally been a lazaret; at this time it was a moribund sort of almshouse, which Alberoni immediately pulled down. In its place there soon began to rise the graceful façade of his college.

In 1735 Clement XII made him Legate of Ravenna, which involved the government of most of the Romagna. Long years had passed since he was last in Ravenna, the poor nobody who had the luck to amuse Bishop Barni. Beside those low-lying shores bridges were built, marshes drained; new roads linked the lovely dying cities. It was the sort of administration in which Alberoni excelled, and the citizens he ruled showed their admiration by erecting many a triumphal arch to commemorate in florid Latin the Cardinal's administration.

Then in 1739 he became involved in a squabble with the Republic of San Marino over the arrest there of a malefactor who could make some shadowy claim to ecclesiastical immunity. The drunken San Marinans in their sheepskin coats, with hats as big as umbrellas, were a constant worry to the Papal authorities, an enclave of banditry, smuggling, and lawlessness. The Cardinal now resolved to teach the San Marinans a sharp lesson.

When it would not come to heel, he proceeded to blockade the disreputable little state, and by a Papal bull assumed sovereignty over it. In October 1739 he rode up the long hill from Rimini to take possession in the name of His Holiness. No question now of a brave fleet setting sail across a summer's sea to conquer a rich island; only a tired old Cardinal jogging up a mountain road on a mule to reduce by his spirit and his terrible eye five slatternly villages no longer worthy of their freedom. . . .

They might laugh at him, dub him an old gambler who, having played for thousands at the high table, now staked pennies on a small one. He subdued San Marino all right, though there may have been a little unpleasantness, and certain of the republicans saw their houses sacked. The Cardinal, however, quickly crushed all resistance, without loss of life.

Yet into this petty affair now intruded that element of ill luck which always attended his conquests. On his return Alberoni, to his indignation, found at Rimini letters from the Vatican virtually disavowing his action. The truth was, the San Marinans had secretly invoked the sympathies of France and the Empire. The foreign relations of the Holy See were complicated enough as it was; the dying Clement XII took fright at this new imbroglio. "We want," he declared, "no dominion over this place, only protection." When Alberoni's Legation ended in the following year, a special Papal Commissioner was sent to San Marino; on his recommendation the republic was restored to its ancient liberties, which it continued to abuse.

The new Pope, Benedict XIV, forthwith appointed Alberoni to the all-important Legation of Bologna (1740). There he devoted his talents to reforms and the economic development of his charge. When in 1743 the War of the Austrian Succession brought his mission to an end, he returned to Piacenza and completed the institution of his college. This great seminary still thrives, largely upon the funds with which Alberoni endowed it out of his own modest fortune. This foundation and the name San Lazaro Alberoni are as good a memorial as any for him.

There he passed the last years of his life, in honour and contentment. He corresponded with the leading personages of Europe, and was at last recognized as one of the great figures of his age. Frederick the Great admired but misunderstood him, conceiving him as a sort of Satanic genius; "had he," he would say, "been given two worlds like ours to destroy, he would have asked for a third." Voltaire esteemed and comprehended him much better.[2]

He kept a modest but no doubt excellent table for his passing friends and distinguished travellers. In 1745 when the Spanish army captured Piacenza, we have what is almost the

---

[2] See his reference to Alberoni in his *History of Charles XII* and his subsequent correspondence with the Cardinal.

last view of him. The Spanish officers, who showed him a reverential respect, were entertained with an omelet cooked over a fire of wood which the old Cardinal himself gleaned from the burning and deserted town. A fitting exit from our vision. Seven years later he died, aged eighty-eight, secure in the knowledge that he had triumphed after all. His enemies by destroying him had not been able to deflect Spain from the course upon which Alberoni had set her; Naples and Sicily passed to the issue of Elisabeth Farnese, and until the end of the century the Germanic hold upon the Italian peninsula was gradually loosened. But for Alberoni, the history of the nineteenth-century risorgimento might have had a different and less happy ending.

As for Spain herself, Alberoni released in her a new vitality that was not finally expended until the misfortunes of Godoy's rule and of the Peninsular War. The last tragic century has not destroyed her; that vitality which for a time the Cardinal released is still latent in the Spanish character.

Most of the other players in Alberoni's tragicomedy died before him, or less happily than he. Stanhope, for instance, lived little more than a year after Alberoni's fall, which he had so largely contrived. His last months were plagued by the scandals of the South Sea Bubble. One day in February 1721 the wild young Duke of Wharton attacked him violently in the Lords, hinting that he was deliberately making bad blood between George I and the Prince of Wales. Stanhope was so carried away by temper that a blood-vessel broke in his head as he rose to answer; he died next day.

Dubois rose to be Archbishop of Cambrai, and even Cardinal. But an abscess in his bladder supervened to rob him of all pleasure in his hat, in his new wealth, or in the toadying speeches that welcomed him into the Academy. In the summer of 1723, after attending a review on horseback, he found himself in unbearable agony. Those fashionable specialists

Chirac and La Peyronie called for an immediate operation. As the lampooners explained to Paris:

"Monsieur de la Peyronie,
Visitant le Cardinal,
Dit: C'est à la vessie
Que Son Eminence a mal!"

The old ferret was lifted to an exaltation of pain where only the most fantastic of dreams still held reality. He would become Pope, and be greater than his patron; he would revive in his own favour the temporal powers of his Archbishopric, and make a sovereign state out of the Cambrésis.

Though exasperated by these fancies, Orléans expended infinite pains and gentleness on persuading the stammering but truculent old man to the operation. It was a failure; but Dubois clung tenaciously to life; he insisted upon receiving Extreme Unction in the ceremonious form reserved for Cardinals. Nobody quite knew what that was; a messenger was therefore sent to Paris to find out. The weather was thundery, and Orléans felt the old exasperation creep back; he could not resist making the sort of pleasantry he seemed to reserve for occasions of great tension. "J'espère," he murmured, "que ce temps-là fera partir mon drôle." It did; Dubois died before the messenger could return, on August 10, 1723, without the last rites in proper form. When they came to look at his papers, they found thousands of letters and despatches of which he had never bothered to break the seals.

Orléans took over the office of Prime Minister (the Regency had ceased on Louis XV's majority in February 1723). But he only survived his creature by four months; he was worn out by private griefs and public worries. His dream of a happy, prosperous France had been shattered long since, by the crash of Law's "system" in 1720. When the smoke cleared, it revealed a middle-class ruined and a nobility impoverished;

the majority of Frenchmen had been inspired with a distrust of banks and government, which nothing in their later history was to dissipate. The Regent's prestige had fallen apart, and with it his confidence. As the crowds outside his windows shouted: "Vive le Roi, et La Régence au diable!" he would cry out to Dubois: "Unhappy country, governed by a drunkard and a pimp!" (1721–2).

The death of "Madame" at the end of 1722 removed the last person to whom he could turn for sympathy and common sense. She remained terrible, honest, and kindly to the last, telling her doctors to go to the devil, because she knew she would not recover; and saying to a lady-in-waiting about to kiss her hand: "You can embrace me; I'm going to a country where everyone's equal!"

Her son dragged out another year, but he was visibly falling to pieces. His sight was now so bad, he was obliged to bow his great head to within a few inches of the paper and was always catching the pen in his wig; his neck almost burst from the cravat; his complexion was an angry purple. The doctors diagnosed an apoplectic condition; if, they said, he did not change his habits, he would die at a moment when he was least expecting to. "But that," he rejoined, "is precisely what I'd like to do. . . ."

His wish was granted in December 1723. He had a new mistress, Madame de Falaris, whom he seems to have treasured less for the white enchantment of her young person than for her talents as a story-teller. He liked to sit by the fire, occasionally stroking her wonderful blond hair, while she beguiled him with stories as marvellous as any of his mother's, and considerably less decorous. Thus he was passing the evening of December 2, and the Falaris was just warming to her story, when he fell forward on to the floor and never spoke again. He was only forty-nine. . . .

The squib-writers were kind to him in death. Obscurely

they recognized in him, for all his debauches, the qualities of a virtuous and enlightened ruler. Thus they sang of him:

"Ci-gît celui dont la Régence
Sut maintenir en paix la France.
Qui joignit à la dignité,
Un cœur sensible, la clémence,
La valeur et la volupté,
L'amour des arts et la gaieté.

En qui l'on vit d'intelligence,
L'homme d'Etat et le Héros:
Qui ne fut trompé qu'en finance,
Et qui ne déplut qu'aux dévots."

Cardinal Fleury, the King's old preceptor, to whom the government of France fell soon after, was able to assist Spain in the realization of many designs originally conceived by Alberoni. For him, indeed, Fleury cherished a vast admiration. "Your Eminence knows," he wrote to him in 1732, "that sovereigns easily forget good turns, particularly when they can't pay them back. But I know that you never had any other idea but to establish complete unity between the two crowns. But obstacles arose to upset things, and particularly another Minister whose character Your Eminence well knows."

As for Saint-Simon, that hurrying, indignant little busybody never got his heart's desire. He did, however, know real distinction for one moment, the climax of his self-important career. In 1721–2 was arranged a series of Franco-Spanish royal marriages. The Regent's fourth daughter, Mademoiselle de Montpensier, became the bride of the Prince of the Asturias; another one, Mademoiselle de Beaujolais, was betrothed to the Infant Don Carlos; the Infanta Anna-Maria-Victoria, then aged three, was brought to France as Louis XV's future Queen.

Saint-Simon solicited for himself the ceremonial Embassy to Spain in connexion with these marriages. Even from the first, his enjoyment, alas! was alloyed with pettifogging vexations. Dubois took pleasure in forcing the little Duke to lay out prodigious sums on his servants' liveries, would personally inspect each suit, declare as like as not that it did not carry enough gold lace, and send it back to the tailor. Even when the Embassy was at last ready, it was sent off without the usual autograph letters from the French royal family; and once across the frontier, Saint-Simon was haunted by the fear that Dubois might never allow him back into France.

The Spanish sovereigns received him cordially enough. In Philip V he found few traces of the youth he had known at Versailles. With the years the King had grown extravagantly taciturn; his face, all chin now, lit up only when he talked of some day's hunting in Fontainebleau Forest twenty years back. He wore constantly a shabby shooting-suit, of a kind of baize, relieved only by the Cordon Bleu and the Golden Fleece; as he walked, he continually tripped over his inturned toes.

For all her pock-marks, Elisabeth charmed the diarist with her figure and friendly gaiety. Never, he noticed, did she let the King out of her sight; and she was always flattering him, even asking the embarrassed Saint-Simon whether he did not think her husband the handsomest man he had ever seen? Then the poor, fond King would shamble off, his long face creased by a precious smile.

There were superb illuminations on the Plaza Mayor in honour of the marriages, and at the signing of the contracts stately ceremonies, and the nicest points of precedence to resolve. In the complexities of doffing and putting on one's hat during an audience Saint-Simon could luxuriate, for he was made a grandee. Then there was the fascinating nobility of Spain to study and catalogue, a paradise of genealogies which almost made him forget Dubois's teasing malice and the tricks which the permanent French Ambassador at Madrid played upon him. He was able to satisfy his curiosity over the daily life of the sovereigns; through a friendship struck up with their Irish doctor, he contrived to taste the famous posset with which Philip was awakened every morning at nine o'clock; he found it slightly greasy, but from the pinnacle of his chastity could pronounce it: "un restaurant singulièrement bon à réparer la nuit passée, et à préparer la prochaine. . . ."

At last Mademoiselle de Montpensier, the bride, arrived. According to her grandmother, "Madame," she was by no means bad-looking, but "the most disagreeable person I have ever seen. . . . I shed no tears when we said good-bye, no more did she." The young Princess behaved extravagantly from the first. She sulked when the Queen spoke to her, and refused to go to the court ball; she hated dancing; early to bed, she said, was her motto. She hated Saint-Simon, too; his well-turned speeches made her yawn. When she received him in farewell audience before his return to Paris, the valedictory compliments were met with three prodigious belches.

On the Regent's death, even Saint-Simon's hopes disappeared. Retiring to the country, he spent the next thirty years working upon the incomparable memoirs. It is significant of his hot little nature that this masterpiece, for all his editing of it, still pours forth like a lava stream, sublime, fantastic, turgid. Nor did it entirely use up the fires that burned within him. Once, on a visit to Paris in his old age, at the Duchesse de Mancini's, he took his wig off, to be comfortable, and set it on a chair beside him. The astonished company suddenly perceived that his shaven old pate was smoking. . . . He died in 1755, at the age of eighty, talking, to the last, "like the most interesting and agreeable of dictionaries."

For Louise-Bénédicte du Maine, after her release from prison, life gradually resumed a course vaguely familiar.

Loudly protesting that he never wished to see her again, Maine came back, hungry for her scoldings. Her old cronies, Malézieu, the Cardinal de Polignac, Rose Delaunay, appeared once more, perhaps a shade less sprightly since they knew the Bastille. The parties were resumed, discreetly non-political, more literary than ever.

In 1736 Maine died of cancer; his brother, the gallant Toulouse, followed him to the grave soon after. Maine's sons, Dombes and Eu, thought only of hunting; Penthièvre, Toulouse's heir, had time for his watches alone, and wore them as coat-buttons, all going at once, if his grandson, King Louis-Philippe, is to be believed. So ended the ambitions and the hopes of Madame de Maintenon.

The later years of Louise-Bénédicte, when only the blind Lamotte-Houdart could be found to love the ageing doll, would be tragic did we not know that a final burst of glory was reserved for her. Till it came, existence was a graceful monotony: Sceaux, Anet,[3] and the bathing at Dieppe. Occasionally Louis XV would pay her a visit, or the enthralling quarrel over precedence would be revived with her one-eyed nephew; there would come an insulting message from Chantilly, and the war would flare up anew, till it seemed like old times. But for the most part the days were empty enough; it is not perhaps strange that in her theatre at Sceaux the comedy *La Vie n'est qu'un songe* should have been the piece most often played.

Then in 1747, when she was seventy-one, Voltaire came back into her life, Voltaire, whom she had hardly seen since those far-off conspiratorial days, which left one no time to consider what the grave might be like. The great man turned up at Anet for ten days in August with Emilie du Châtelet. The visit was hardly a success; they exasperated their hostess by shutting themselves up for hours at a time to write; when

[3] It had come to her from her sister, Vendôme's widow.

they left, it seemed unlikely that Louise-Bénédicte would again clap eyes on either of them for a long time.

Yet in October Voltaire was her guest once more, at Sceaux this time, and — ineffable pleasure — without that interfering Emilie. He had gone with her to join the court at Fontaine-bleau. One night, standing by her card-table, he noticed a player who was grossly cheating; Madame du Châtelet lost heavily, and the great man, unable to bear it any longer, suddenly cried out that she was playing with rogues. He spoke in English, but was understood well enough. Horrified at his own temerity, he bolted from the Court. It became urgently necessary to hide till the episode was forgotten. But where? Then, as he bowled vaguely along the road towards Paris, he remembered Sceaux, the temple of his youth.

Received with delight, he was hidden in an attic on the garden side. The long hours when the great house was awake, and he did not dare stir, were perhaps the most glorious of his career; it was then he wrote the cream of his short stories — *Memnon, Babouc, Micromégas, Scarmentado, Zadig* — the distillation of all his virtues, the passion for justice, the hatred of cant, prose refined and polished till it shone like poetry.

At two o'clock in the morning, when the château was at last asleep, Voltaire would creep downstairs, with candle and nightcap, a *cahier* under his arm. In his old hostess's bedroom a delicious supper awaited him, and she bursting with an impatience that her innumerable shawls could hardly contain. He would eat, and then the *cahier* would be opened and he would begin to read. Those eternal phrases flashed through the room, bringing life back to it. . . . Then it was dawn, and old age once more; Louise-Bénédicte must snatch a few moments' sleep, to gain strength for the long ordeal of the dressing-table, the hours devoted to her make-up, which remained elaborate and high-coloured till the last. Voltaire crept back to his attic, lay for a while on the bed, then started pen flying over paper once more.

The death of Madame du Châtelet, not long after, flung him more than ever on to the resources of Sceaux. For three years it was a whirlpool of comedies, impromptus, flashing conceits. Then came the enticement to Potsdam. Voltaire continued, however, to shower Louise-Bénédicte with affectionate messages. "One longs," he wrote from Sans-Souci on New Year's Day 1751, "for your conversation here, so necessary to the maintenance of true politeness. . . ." Three years later, when he returned to the civilized world after the final quarrel with Frederick the Great, his old friend was dead, expiring in a welter of parties and theatricals. . . .

In January 1724, a few weeks after the Regent's death, Philip V of Spain astonished the world by abdicating in favour of the Prince of the Asturias, a youth of seventeen, who ascended the throne as Luis I. Philip had long been racked by doubts and scruples; he had, he believed, offended the Almighty by giving up his French rights; and old d'Aubenton was no longer in the confessional to calm his fears.

Elisabeth followed her husband quietly enough into sumptuous retirement at La Granja. But she did not renounce the substance of her power. Young King Luis, though he danced well, was a case of arrested development. He was happier robbing his own gardens by night, or breaking into the bedrooms of the ladies-in-waiting, than yawning in Cabinet Council. The nonentities who sat there with him gradually surrendered their powers to Elisabeth, and not many months were out before she was once more supreme in Spain.

Suddenly in August 1724, after a seven months' reign, the young King died of smallpox. The Infant Don Ferdinand, who might have been expected to succeed him, was pushed into the background, and Philip was bullied into resuming his throne.

The late King's widow, who had tried Saint-Simon so hard, proved little less vexatious to her parents-in-law. Her habit of running about the gardens in an unfastened dressing-gown, the curiosity she aroused in gardeners and sentries when thus undressed she scrambled up ladders to pick fruit off the warm walls, the enormous meals at improbable hours, long walks in the rain, with skirts gathered up to her thighs — all upset the decorous rhythm of the court. It was finally decided to send her home to France. There her eccentricity steadily increased. An English visitor, Lord Perceval, dining at Vincennes, gives us a view of her in 1726:

"She was fat, not seventeen, gluttonous, ate with both hands; the two men attendants carried her off swinging in their arms, like a fat spirit in Henry VIII; her feet did not touch the ground till she was landed in the third room, and then she fell a-boxing them; she never reads or works, seldom plays cards, and cuts her hair like an English schoolboy. . . ."

Elisabeth's second reign was on the whole a triumphant one. In 1736 her eldest son, Don Carlos, became King of Naples and Sicily. Ten years later his brother, Don Philip, was installed as Duke of Parma. And in time Philip V was cured of his itch to abdicate the Spanish throne. At first he still talked of it incessantly, so that Elisabeth did not dare let him get his fingers on anything more formal than a pencil. But the awful example of Victor-Amadeus at last cured him. For a mistress's sake that old Savoyard rascal abdicated in 1730. Years before, his harshness had driven his eldest son to suicide. The second, Charles Emmanuel, who now became King of Sardinia, was the instrument of his brother's revenge. On the pretext that the old man was plotting against him, he flung his father into prison, where he died shortly afterwards. The incident so profoundly impressed Philip V, it became possible to allow him a pen again.

But his mind continued in disorder; he hardly went to bed, and supped at three o'clock in the morning. Then he took suddenly to his despised couch, and for months on end refused to wash, shave, or change his clothes. He could only be regained to sanity by rumours of wars, and as a sort of psychopathic treatment a continuous military bustle was maintained about him. There were interludes of sanity, when he would spend the days quietly fishing in the pools of the Alhambra or talking with pride of his growing navy. Then the furious melancholy would come back, and there was no arguing with him.

But as the itch to abdicate had been cured in due course, so was the melancholia, and by means no less curious. Ferdinand, Prince of the Asturias, had married a Portuguese Princess who brought music into fashion at the Spanish court. No less a celebrity than Domenico Scarlatti settled there for a time to play for the King. Then, in 1737, Carlo Broschi, otherwise known as Farinelli, the most ravishing singer of the age, was summoned from abroad, to charm away Philip's boredom. He fell utterly under the dominion of that fabulous voice; only for the pleasure of hearing it again, he would reassemble his scattered wits, consent to wash, and submit quietly to the barber.

Sometimes the old madness would come on, for all that; ". . . the King," reported Sir Benjamin Keene in 1738, "himself imitates Farinelli, sometimes air after air, and sometimes after the music is over, and throws himself into such freaks and howlings that all possible means are taken to prevent people from being witness to his follies. He had one of these fits this week, which lasted from twelve till past two in the morning. They have talked of bathing him, but fear they shall not persuade him to try that remedy. . . ."

On July 9, 1746 Philip died of apoplexy, or — as d'Argenson

put it — "of chagrin and corpulence." Ferdinand VI, who succeeded him, his son and Elisabeth's stepson, applied many of Alberoni's ideas; he even made some essays in unemployment and famine relief. But while incapable of begetting an heir, he was afflicted with a priapism exceeding his father's; the satirists accused him of possessing his ugly but charming Portuguese consort even as she lay dying.

Her death completely deranged his reason. Already when he had learned of Damiens's attempt on Louis XV in 1757, his behaviour had been extravagant. "Stilletato di quà, pistolato di là: ed io in mezzo! Oimé!" With that, he had plunged beneath his wife's bed.

He did not long survive her. In 1759 his half-brother succeeded him — Charles, King of Naples and Sicily, the prince whose birth Alberoni had chronicled so exultantly forty-three years before. From Charles all subsequent Spanish Bourbons are descended, and those of Naples, too.

Thus Elisabeth's male posterity, far from languishing in a stepsons' limbo, got three thrones for themselves. The only prince for whom she could not provide was her youngest, Don Luis (1727–85); for him she aspired to Tuscany — but in vain. The young man was in any case something of a disappointment; he had little hunger for a crown; he did not even care much for the Cardinal's hat which had been clapped upon his baby head. The workshop where he made excellent watches, the bright splendours of the aviary at La Granja, the no less brilliant eyes of his mistresses were all the happiness he sought. At last, one day out hunting butterflies, he was netted by a pretty commoner. Resigning the hat, he declined into blissful marriage.

Elisabeth did not die till 1766, the year in which James Watt, on the far-off Clyde, was bringing in our Age of Steam. For some time now she had been unable to stand except with the aid of two attendants. But she still had energy enough to turn night into day, as Philip had taught her to do, and to flay her enemies in that voice which had once been melody itself. In those last years she must often have been brought to think of the plump, smiling friend who had made her Queen of Spain, and who even as Cardinal was not too proud to cook her dinner. He had made her Queen of Spain; and through his teaching she had become something more than a mere consort; she had left her mark on the world, on everything about her. Long years after she and Alberoni had been laid to earth, it was her personality that haunted Beckford when he visited the palace at Madrid. Despite the innumerable clocks that ticked there, time had stood still since the day of Elisabeth and Alberoni. There was no sound save this universal ticking, or the faint noise of old court servants who tiptoed beneath Tiepolo's new ceiling, across the shining floors, to scratch the heads of countless elderly, dozing parrots.

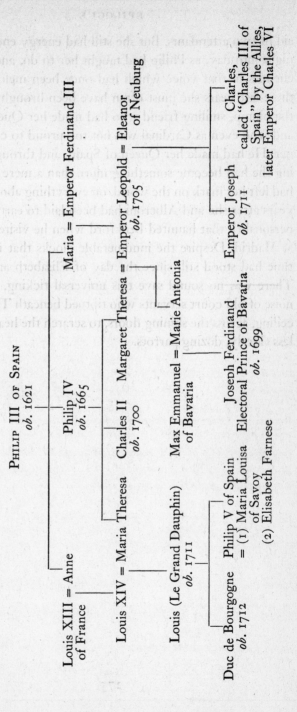

THE SPANISH SUCCESSION

BIBLIOGRAPHY

ADDISON, JOSEPH: *Remarks on Several Parts of Italy* (1701–3).

ALBERONI, CARDINAL GIULIO: *Scheme for Reducing the Turkish Empire* (1736).

——: *Testament politique* (1753).

ANQUETIL, L. P.: *Louis XIV, sa Cour et le Régent* (1789).

ARATA, A.: *Il Processo del Cardinale Alberoni* (1923).

ARMSTRONG, E.: *Elizabeth Farnese* (1892).

AUBERTIN, C.: *L'Esprit publique au XVIIIᵉ siècle* (1873).

AULNOY, COMTESSE D': *Voyage d'Espagne* (1682).

BACALLAR y SANA, V.: *Comentarios de la guerra de España* (1730).

BARAUDON, A.: *La Maison de Savoie et la Triple Alliance* (1896).

BAUDRILLAT, A.: *Philippe V et la Cour de France* (1889).

BAUDRILLAT, H.: *Histoire de luxe privé et publique* (1878).

BAYERN, PRINZ ALPHONSO VON: *Das Ende der Habsburger in Spanien* (1929).

BECKFORD, WILLIAM: *Travels in Italy, Portugal and Spain.*

BELANDO, N. DE J.: *Historia civil de España* (1740).

BERSANI, S.: *Storia del Cardinale Alberoni* (1861).

BIANCHI, G.: *Giulio Alberoni e il suo secolo* (1901).

BLIARD, P.: *Cardinal Dubois* (1901).

BONAFOUS, L. A. DE: *L'Âme des Bourbons* (1783).

BOURGEOIS, E.: *Lettres intimes d'Alberoni* (1893).

——: *Le Secret des Farnese* (1909).

Byng Papers, ed. B. Tunstall (1930).

CABANES, A.: *Une Allemande à la Cour de France, La Princesse Palatine* (1916).

CAPEFIGUE, J. B.: *La Duchesse de Bourgogne et la vieillesse de Louis XIV* (1867).

——: *La Comtesse de Parabère et le Palais Royal sous la Régence* (1863).

BIBLIOGRAPHY

CARLETON, CAPTAIN G.: *A True and Genuine History of the War against France and Spain* (1741).

CARUTTI, D.: *Storia della diplomatia della Corte di Savoia* (1875).

CASTAGNOLI, P.: *Il Cardinale Giulio Alberoni* (1929–31).

C.F.: *I Delitti della famiglia Borbone nelle due Sicilie* (1848).

CHANCEL, J. DE LA GRANGE: *Les Philippiques* (1720).

CHURCHILL, WINSTON: *Marlborough* (1933–8).

CIMBER, M. L.: *Archives curieuses de l'histoire de France* (1834–40).

COMBES, F.: *La Princesse des Ursins* (1858).

Correspondence of: Alberoni,
       Bubb Doddington,
       Lady Cowper,
       Mme de Maintenon,
       Earl of Stair,
       Earl Stanhope,
       Princesse des Ursins,
       Voltaire.

COURCY, MARQUIS DE: *L'Espagne après la Paix d'Utrecht* (1891).

COXE, W.: *Memoirs of the Kings of Spain and of the House of Bourbon* (1813).

DELFICO, M.: *Memorie storiche della Repubblica di San Marino* (1804).

DESDEVISES DU DEZERT, G.: *L'Espagne de l'ancien régime* (1897–1904).

——: *Richesse et civilisation espagnole au XVIIIe siècle* (1893).

DESNOIRESTERRES, G.: *Les Cours galantes* (1856).

DICKSON, W. K.: *The Jacobite Attempt of 1719* (1895).

DREI, G.: *Giulio Alberoni* (1932).

DUMONT, J.: *Histoire militaire du Prince Eugène et Marlborough* (1729–47).

DUSSIEUX, L. E.: *Généalogie de la maison de Bourbon* (1869).

EASY, A.: *Alberoni. A Vindication* (1720).

ERLANGER, P.: *Le Régent* (1938).

EVES, C. K.: *Matthew Prior, Poet and Diplomat* (1939).

FILTZ-MORITZ: *Lettres et mémoires sur l'Espagne* (1718).

FREIND, DR. J.: *An Account of the Earl of Peterborough's Conduct in Spain* (1707).

BIBLIOGRAPHY

GALLIER, H. DE: *Les Mœurs et la vie privée d'autrefois* (1911).

GAYOT DE PITAVAL, F.: *Bibliothèque des gens de la cour* (1722).

Gazettes and Journals: E. Barbier: *Régence and Louis XV*,

J. Buvat: *1697–1739*,

P. de Courcillon: *Marquis de Dangeau* (1684–1720),

M. Marais: *1715–37.*

GONCOURT, E. DE: *Portraits intimes du XVIII° siècle* (1857–8).

——: *La Femme au XVIII° siècle* (1862).

——: *L'Amour au XVIII° siècle* (1875).

HAVARD, H.: *Dictionnaire de l'ameublement et de la décoration* (1888–9).

HERVEZ, J.: *Les Sociétés d'amour du XVIII° siècle* (1906).

HOPKINSON, M. R.: *Anne of England* (1934).

JAGERSKIOLD, S.: *Sverige och Europa 1716–1718* (1937).

JOSZ, V.: *Fragonard. Mœurs du XVIII° siècle* (1901).

JULLIEN, A.: *Les Grandes Nuits de Sceaux* (1876).

KLOPP, O.: *Der Fall des Hauses Stuart und die Succession des Hauses Hannover* (1875–88).

LACRETELLE, J. C. D.: *Histoire de France pendant le XVIII° siècle* (1812).

LAMBERTY, G. DE: *Mémoires pour servir à l'histoire du XVIII° siècle* (1735–40).

LA PLACE, P. A. DE: *Pièces intéressantes pour servir à l'histoire* (1785).

LAVISSE, E.: *Histoire de France* (1920–2).

LECLERCQ, DOM H.: *Histoire de la Régence pendant la minorité de Louis XV* (1922).

LEGRELLE, A.: *La Diplomatie française et la succession d'Espagne* (1888–92).

LELOIR, M.: *Histoire de costume* (1934).

LEMONTEY, P. E.: *Histoire de la Régence et de la minorité de Louis XV* (1832).

LEROUGE, G. L.: *Jardins anglo-chinois* (1776–87).

MACANAZ, M. R. DE: *Disertación histórica que sirve de explicación a algunos lugares . . . en la historia . . . del Cardinal Alberoni* (1788).

279

MACAULAY, T. B.: *History of England.*

MAHAN, A. T.: *The Influence of Sea Power upon History, 1660–1785.*

MAHON, LORD STANHOPE: *History of England from the Peace of Utrecht to the Peace of Versailles* (1836).

MALAGOLA, C.: *Il Cardinale Alberoni e la Repubblica di San Marino* (1886).

MARICOURT, A., and BERTRANDFOSSE, H. DE: *Les Bourbons 1518–1830. Hérédités, pathologie, amours et grandeur* (1936).

MAUREL, A.: *La Duchesse du Maine* (1928).

Mémoires of: Marquis d'Argenson,
                Charles Pineau Duclos,
                Elisabeth Farnese,
                Marquis de Louville,
                Elisabeth Charlotte d'Orléans — La Palatine,
                Duc de Noailles,
                Chevalier de Piossens,
                Baron Pöllnitz,
                Count Phélypeaux de Maurepas,
                Baronne de Staal Delaunay,
                Baron Ripperda,
                Duc de Richelieu,
                Earl of Stair,
                Marquis de Saint-Philippe,
                Duc de Saint-Simon,
                Marquis de Torcy,
                Marquis Maréchal de Villars.

MICHAEL, W.: *The Beginnings of the Hanoverian Dynasty* (1936). Vols. I and II.

MIEGE, G.: *The Present State of Great Britain and Ireland* (ed. 1748).

MOORE, G.: *Lives of Cardinal Alberoni and the Duke of Ripperda* (1806).

MOUFFLE D'ANGEVILLE: *Vie Privée de Louis XV* (1781).

MUCCIOLI, A.: *Sulla occupazione della Repubblica Sammarinese* (1869).

NEMEITZ, J. C.: *Séjour de Paris* (1727).

Newspapers (contemporary): *Gazette de France,*
                                Mercure de France,

Mercure Galant,
Tatler,
Postboy,
Mercator,
Whitehall Evening Post.

NICOLARDOT, L.: *Les Cours et les salons du XVIIIe siècle* (1879).

NICOLI, F.: *Dissertation historique sur les Duchés de Parme et de Plaisance* (1722).

OPPENORD, G. M.: *Œuvres* (c. 1725).

PAPA, V.: *L'Alberoni e la sua dipartita dalla Spagna* (1876).

PARISET, C.: *Il Cardinale Giulio Alberoni* (1905).

PELET, J. J.: *Mémoires militaires relatives à la succession d'Espagne* (1835).

PEREY, L.: *Une Reine de douze ans. Marie Louise Gabrielle de Savoie* (1905).

PETRIE, SIR C.: *Bolingbroke* (1937).

PHILPIN DE PIEPAPE, L. M.: *La Duchesse du Maine* (1910).

PIACENZA: *Fondazione del nuovo collegio di San Lazaro dell' Emo* (1739).

POGGIALI, G. D.: *Memorie storiche di Piacenza* (1757–66).

PROFESSIONE, A.: *Giulio Alberoni agli assedi di Vercelli e Verrua* (1889).

——: *Giulio Alberoni dal 1708–1714* (1890).

——: *Il Ministero in Spagna e il processo del Cardinale Giulio Alberoni* (1897).

RIPAULT DESORMEAUX, J. L.: *Histoire de la maison de Bourbon* (1772–88).

ROTA, E.: *Il Problema politico d'Italia dopo Utrecht ed il piano antitedesco di Giulio Alberoni* (1934).

ROUSSET DE MISSY: *Histoire du Cardinal Alberoni* (1719).

——: *Histoire publique et secrète de la Cour de Madrid* (1719).

RUSSELL, EARL JOHN: *Memoirs of the Affairs of Europe from the Peace of Utrecht* (1824–9).

SEILHAC, COUNT V. DE: *L'Abbé Dubois* (1862).

SEVELINGES, C. L. DE: *Mémoires secrètes et correspondance inédite du Cardinal Dubois* (1815).

281

SEWARD, W.: *Anecdotes of Some Distinguished Persons* (1795).

SITWELL, S.: *Southern Baroque Art.*

SPAIN: *Relación de los progresos de exercito del Rey . . . en el campo de Villaviciosa* (1710).

SUTTON, R.: *The Lexington Papers* (1851).

SYVETON, G.: *Une Cour et un aventurier au XVIII* siècle: le Baron Ripperda* (1896).

——: *Louis XIV et Charles XII* (1900).

TAYLER, H.: *Jacobite Epilogue* (1941).

TINDAL, N.: *History of England: tr. Rapin Thoyras* (1725).

TOTH, C.: *Französisches Salonleben um Charles Pineau Duclos* (1918).

TREVELYAN, G. M.: *England under Queen Anne* (1930–4).

TURBERVILLE, A. S.: *English Men and Manners in the Eighteenth Century* (1926).

VATOUT, J.: *La Conspiration de Cellamare* (1832).

VAYRAC, J. DE: *État présent de l'Espagne* (1718).

VOLTAIRE, F. M. AROUET DE: *Siècle de Louis XIV.*

——: *Œuvres.*

WEBER, O.: *Die Quadrupel Allianz vom Jahre 1718* (1887).

——: *Der Friede von Utrecht* (1891).

WIEGLER, P.: *Glanz und Niedergang der Bourbonen* (1938).

WIESENER, L.: *Le Régent, Abbé Dubois et les Anglais* (1891–99).

WILLIAMS, A. F. B.: *Stanhope. A Study in Eighteenth-Century War and Diplomacy* (1932).

——: *The Whig Supremacy* (1939).

INDEX

i

76, 125, 126, 187; news, 122; shuns
d'Orléans, 126; moves to Aranjuez,
131; intrigues at, 167; Germanic in-
fluence in English, 168
Cowper, Lord, 237
Coysevox, 226
Craggs (Secretary of State), 212, 219,
239
Cranach, 23
Cremona, 39, 41, 44, 49
Culture, Anglo-Saxon, 30; Spanish,
31

Defeatism, 65
Deffand, Madame du, 248
Defoe, Daniel, quoted, 237
Delaunay, Rose, 228, 235, 269
Despacho, The, 103, 108, 124
Dieppe, 269
Diplomacy, French, 15; of Louis
XIV, 23, 24, 25; Alberoni's, 109,
110, 111, 113n, 147, 151, 238
Don Carlos, The Infant, 141, 266
Don Ferdinand, Infant, 105, 271
Dubois, Abbé (after Archbishop of
Cambrai) and Cardinal, 182–6, 193,
199, 200, 201, 204, 206, 212, 221, 233,
236, 243, 245, 247, 250, 251, 254, 255,
263, 264, 267
Dürer, 23

Ebro, The, 88
Emilia, 16 and n, 141
Empire, French plans for, 24; Spain's,
30, 150; Turkey's, 30; Austria's, 30,
168; Anglo-Saxon, 30; war with,
37; Swedish, 170; Alberoni and, 238
Enghien, Mademoiselle d', 72
England, alluded to, 3, 23; trade with
France, 27; post-war conditions in,
27; and Franco-Spanish monopolies, 38; Victor-Amadeus negoti-
ates with, 45; invades Spain, 51; the
Tories of, 55; with Savoy invades
Provence, 56; breaks down peace
negotiations, 70; tired of the war,
70; captures Cadiz and Gibraltar,

80; and the New World, 91; her
status in Europe, 133, 134; negotiations with Spain, 137; and Alberoni's Treaty, 138, 139; Austria unpopular in, 144; coinage of, 157,
and alliance with Spain, 167; foreign policy of, 167, 168; German
influence at Court of, 168, 172; ne-
gotiates alliance with Austria, 171,
172; coldness to the Regent of, 182;
Dubois and, 184; a Cabinet crisis
in, 185; rupture with Spain, 211,
212, 214; and the Spanish navy, 242;
Alberoni's friends in, 259
Entente Cordiale, The, 184
Escorial, The, 11, 43, 99, 152, 197, 215,
222
Eugene, Prince, 38, 39; defeated by
Vendôme, 46; his victory in Italy,
50; at Belgrad, 191
Eure valley, The, 53
Europe, the Thirty Years' war and,
23; fear of France in, 24; and the
British-Spanish Treaty, 139; Alberoni's influence in, 167; presages of
war in, 203; Spain's invasion of
Sicily and, 215; Alberoni's alleged
danger to, 250

Falaris, Madame de, 265
Famine, its effect on recruiting, 67
Farinelli, *see under* Broschi
Farnese, Alexander, 16
Farnese, Duchess Maria Maddalena,
20
Farnese, Prince Antonio, 164
Farnese, Queen Elisabeth, alluded to,
109, 110, 111, 139, 167, 202, 222; des
Ursins's approval of, 112, 113 and
n; betrothal and marriage of, 113,
118; attended by Alberoni, 114, 115,
116; conduct of, 115; flirtation with
Maggiali, 116, 131n; a progress of,
116; her meeting with des Ursins,
118; Alberoni's friendship with,
121; entertainments of, 122, 123,
124; at Aranjuez, 132; effect of fa-

PRINTER'S NOTE

This book was set on the Linotype in Janson, a recutting made direct from the type cast from matrices (now in possession of the Stempel foundry, Frankfurt am Main) made by Anton Janson some time between 1660 and 1687.

Of Janson's origin nothing is known. He may have been a relative of Justus Janson, a printer of Danish birth who practised in Leipzig from 1614 to 1635. Some time between 1657 and 1668 Anton Janson, a punch-cutter and type-founder, bought from the Leipzig printer Johann Erich Hahn the type-foundry which had formerly been a part of the printing house of M. Friedrich Lankisch. Janson's types were first shown in a specimen sheet issued at Leipzig about 1675. Janson's successor, and perhaps his son-in-law, Johann Karl Edling, issued a specimen sheet of Janson types in 1689. His heirs sold the Janson matrices in Holland to Wolffgang Dietrich Erhardt.

Composed, printed, and bound by The Plimpton Press, Norwood, Massachusetts. The typographic and binding designs are by W. A. Dwiggins.